FEMINIST
INTERPRETATIONS
OF
JOHN LOCKE

RE-READING THE CANON

NANCY TUANA, GENERAL EDITOR

This series consists of edited collections of essays, some original and some previously published, offering feminist reinterpretations of the writings of major figures in the Western philosophical tradition. Devoted to the work of a single philosopher, each volume contains essays covering the full range of the philosopher's thought and representing the diversity of approaches now being used by feminist critics.

Already published:

FEMINIST INTERPRETATIONS OF JOHN LOCKE

EDITED BY
NANCY J. HIRSCHMANN
AND
KIRSTIE M. McCLURE

THE PENNSYLVANIA STATE UNIVERSITY PRESS
UNIVERSITY PARK, PENNSYLVANIA

Mary Lyndon Shanley, "Marriage Contract and Social Contract in Seventeenth-Century English Political Thought," originally appeared in *Political Research Quarterly* 32.1 (March 1979): 79–91. Reprinted with permission of the University of Utah.

Teresa Brennan and Carole Pateman, "'Mere Auxiliaries of the Commonwealth': Women and the Origins of Liberalism," originally appeared in *Political Studies* 27.2 (1979): 183–200. Reprinted with permission of Blackwell Publishing.

Melissa Butler, "Early Liberal Roots of Feminism: John Locke and the Attack on Patriarchy," originally appeared in the *American Political Science Review* 72.1 (March 1978): 135–50. Reprinted with permission of Cambridge University Press.

Terrell Carver, "Gender and Narrative in Locke's *Two Treatises of Government*" is based on chapter 7 ("Locke: Overtly and Covertly Gendered Narratives of Political Society") in *Men and Political Theory* (Manchester University Press, 2004), 153–76. Copyright Terrell Carver.

Jeremy Waldron, "Locke, Adam, and Eve," is adapted from *God, Locke, and Equality: Christian Foundations in Locke's Political Thought* (Cambridge University Press, 2002). Reprinted with permission of Cambridge University Press.

Linda K. Zerilli, "Philosophy's Gaudy Dress: Fantasy and Rhetoric in the Lockean Social Contract," originally appeared in the *European Journal of Political Theory* 4.2 (2005): 146–63. Reprinted with permission of Sage Publications.

Library of Congress Cataloging-in-Publication Data

Feminist interpretations of John Locke / edited by
    Nancy J. Hirschmann and Kirstie M. McClure.
        p.   cm.—(Re-reading the canon)
Includes bibliographical references and index.
ISBN-13: 978-0-271-02952-8 (cloth : alk. paper)
ISBN-10: 0-271-02952-8 (cloth : alk. paper)
ISBN-13: 978-0-271-02953-5 (pbk. : alk. paper)
ISBN-10: 0-271-02953-6 (pbk. : alk. paper)
1. Locke, John, 1632–1704.
2. Feminist theory.
I. Hirschmann, Nancy J.
II. McClure, Kirstie Morna.

B1297.F46   2007
192—dc22
2006030178

Dedication

For Teresa Brennan and Susan Moller Okin, two founding mothers of feminist political thought, who died too young. They both demonstrated that feminism is, indeed, a large tent. We miss them dearly, but future generations of feminists will keep them alive for a long time to come.

Contents

Preface

Nancy Tuana

Take into your hands any history of philosophy text. You will find compiled therein the "classics" of modern philosophy. Since these texts are often designed for use in undergraduate classes, the editor is likely to offer an introduction in which the reader is informed that these selections represent the perennial questions of philosophy. The student is to assume that she or he is about to explore the timeless wisdom of the greatest minds of Western philosophy. No one calls attention to the fact that the philosophers are all men.

Though women are omitted from the canons of philosophy, these texts inscribe the nature of woman. Sometimes the philosopher speaks directly about woman, delineating her proper role, her abilities and inabilities, her desires. Other times the message is indirect—a passing remark hinting at women's emotionality, irrationality, unreliability.

This process of definition occurs in far more subtle ways when the central concepts of philosophy—reason and justice, those characteristics that are taken to define us as human—are associated with traits historically identified with masculinity. If the "man" of reason must learn to control or overcome traits identified as feminine—the body, the emotions, the passions—then the realm of rationality will be one reserved primarily for men,[1] with grudging entrance to those few women who are capable of transcending their femininity.

Feminist philosophers have begun to look critically at the canonized texts of philosophy and have concluded that the discourses of philosophy are not gender-neutral. Philosophical narratives do not offer a universal perspective, but rather privilege some experiences and beliefs over others. These experiences and beliefs permeate all philosophical theories whether they be aesthetic or epistemological, moral or metaphysical. Yet this fact has often been neglected by those studying the traditions of philosophy. Given the history of canon formation in Western philosophy, the perspective most likely to be privileged is that of upper-class white males. Thus, to be fully aware of the impact of gender biases, it is imperative that we reread the canon with attention to the ways in which philosophers' assumptions concerning gender are embedded within their theories.

This new series, *Re-Reading the Canon,* is designed to foster this process of reevaluation. Each volume will offer feminist analyses of the theories of a selected philosopher. Since feminist philosophy is not monolithic in method or content, the essays are also selected to illustrate the variety of perspectives within feminist criticism and highlight some of the controversies within feminist scholarship.

In this series, feminist lenses will be focused on the canonical texts of Western philosophy, both those authors who have been part of the traditional canon, and those philosophers whose writings have more recently gained attention within the philosophical community. A glance at the list of volumes in the series will reveal an immediate gender bias of the canon: Arendt, Aristotle, Beauvoir, Derrida, Descartes, Foucault, Hegel, Hume, Kant, Locke, Marx, Mill, Nietzsche, Plato, Rousseau, Wittgenstein, Wollstonecraft. There are all too few women included, and those few who do appear have been added only recently. In creating this series, it is not my intention to rectify the current canon of philosophical thought. What is and is not included within the canon during a particular historical period is a result of many factors. Although no canonization of texts will include all philosophers, no canonization of texts that excludes all but a few women can offer an accurate representation of the history of the discipline, as women have been philosophers since the ancient period.[2]

I share with many feminist philosophers and other philosophers writing from the margins of philosophy the concern that the current canonization of philosophy be transformed. Although I do not accept the position that the current canon has been formed exclusively by power relations, I do believe that this canon represents only a selective history of the tradition. I share the view of Michael Bérubé that "canons are at once the location, the index, and the record of the struggle for cultural representation; like any other hegemonic formation, they must be continually reproduced anew and are continually contested."[3]

The process of canon transformation will require the recovery of "lost" texts and a careful examination of the reasons such voices have been silenced. Along with the process of uncovering women's philosophical history, we must also begin to analyze the impact of gender ideologies upon the process of canonization. This process of recovery and examination must occur in conjunction with careful attention to the concept of a canon of authorized texts. Are we to dispense with the notion of a tradition of excellence embodied in a canon of authorized texts? Or, rather than abandon the whole idea of a canon, do we instead encourage a reconstruction of a canon of those texts that inform a common culture?

This series is designed to contribute to this process of canon transformation by offering a rereading of the current philosophical canon. Such a rereading shifts our attention to the ways in which woman and the role of the feminine are constructed within the texts of philosophy. A question we must keep in front of us during this process of rereading is whether a philosopher's socially inherited prejudices concerning woman's nature and role are independent of her or his larger philosophical framework. In asking this question attention must be paid to the ways in which the definitions of central philosophical concepts implicitly include or exclude gendered traits.

This type of reading strategy is not limited to the canon, but can be applied to all texts. It is my desire that this series reveal the importance of this type of critical reading. Paying attention to the workings of gender within the texts of philosophy will make visible the complexities of the inscription of gender ideologies.

Notes

1. More properly, it is a realm reserved for a group of privileged males, since the texts also inscribe race and class biases that thereby bar certain males from participation.

2. Mary Ellen Waithe's multivolume series, *A History of Women Philosophers* (Boston: M. Nijoff, 1987), attests to this presence of women.

3. Michael Bérubé, *Marginal Forces/Cultural Centers: Tolson, Pynchon, and the Politics of the Canon* (Ithaca: Cornell University Press, 1992), 4–5.

Introduction

Johnny, We Hardly Knew Ye

Nancy J. Hirschmann and Kirstie M. McClure

If the works which form the basis of our political and philosophical heritage are to continue to be relevant in a world in which the unequal position of women is being radically challenged, we must be able to recognize which of their assumptions and conclusions are inherently connected with the idea that the sexes are, and should be, fundamentally equal.

—Susan Okin, 1979

When Okin penned these words in *Women in Western Political Thought*, she was not referring specifically to Locke, but clearly she could have been. In the short but intense history of modern feminist thought, John Locke has come to figure prominently. Consideration of such canonical thinkers of the Western tradition is one of the two major strains that has informed feminist political theory and philosophy since the 1960s—Marxist feminism being the other—and feminist works such as Okin's, Jean Elshtains's *Public Man, Private Woman*, Lorenne Clark and Lynda Lange's *Sexism of Social and Political Theory*, and Zillah Eisenstein's *Radical Future of Liberal Feminism* opened the intellectual enterprise of political philosophy and theory to the explicit consideration of gender. Where, after all, were all the women in the history of political thought? These feminists not only challenged accepted readings of canonical texts by posing questions that had previously been unthought, they challenged the very disciplines of political theory and philosophy by calling into question the dominant paradigms of what was considered "acceptable" inquiry. Whether as a target or as a resource for feminist critique, Locke soon became an important touchstone for such analyses, and was the subject of some of the earliest articles published in the field of feminist political thought as well, three of which are reprinted here.

Locke's special prominence may be due to his linkage to historical liberalism, which, as Gordon Schochet argues in Chapter 4, provided a language of rights and individuality that early liberal feminists found attractive and important to their struggles for legitimacy within both the academy and political society more generally. This same language, of course, was regarded by early socialist feminists as a distinctly modern vehicle of patriarchal oppression, and this division among feminists is itself a key source of continuing engagement. But beyond the contemporary political dilemmas that inflect the field, Locke may hold a particular fascination for feminist political theorists and philosophers precisely because his stance on sexual equality is so ambiguous. Unlike Aristotle and Kant, who are seen as decidedly and perhaps unequivocally sexist, Locke seems to advocate both sexual equality and the subordination of women to men. This ambiguity has provided fertile ground for feminist analysis, debate, contention, and interpretation, and ensured the centrality of Locke's work to feminist efforts to reread the canon.

Locke's Ambiguity

Locke's ambiguity on gender functions on a number of levels and touches a number of issues central to feminist critiques, such as the question of human nature, the meaning of political concepts such as rights and freedom, and the structure and operation of his social contract, as well as the more obvious matter of whether authority in the family is patriarchal. For instance, it might be objected that Okin sells Locke short when she states categorically that in the Western canon of political theory, the human nature "described and discovered by philosophers such as Aristotle, Aquinas, Machiavelli, Locke, Rousseau, Hegel, and many others, is intended to refer to only male human nature," and suggests that they did not perceive "the rights and needs that they have considered humanness to entail . . . as applicable to the female half of the human race."[1] Others have argued that Locke may well have included women in his thoughts on a number of issues relating to the nature of men and women, such as reason, education, and even property. Melissa Butler, one of the first scholars to publish a feminist analysis of Locke, placed at the center of her argument the fact that he considered women entirely capable of reason and entitled to an education equal to that of their brothers. This is a contention that others since Butler have questioned, and even rejected, but the persistence of the debate suggests the degree to which Locke remains ambiguous on this question; and as a number of essays in the present volume suggest, such ambiguity has far-reaching implications for his political philosophy.

Okin is more on target with Locke when she comments that "the most important factor influencing the philosophers' conceptions of, and arguments about, women has been the view that each of them held concerning the family" (9). But whereas she is correct that Plato, Aristotle, and Rousseau, at least, deemed women's role in the family as unilaterally subordinate to men, and reduced that role to "their sexual, procreative, and child-rearing functions within it" (9), Locke's construction of women's place in the family is, once again, more ambiguous. On the one hand, as part of his refutation of Filmer, Locke explicitly acknowledges women as the equals of men in the family. As various contributors to the present volume note, Locke grants women rights of contract in marriage, including the right to negotiate the terms of such contracts in matters of childcare, custody, and divorce (though the welfare of children put certain limits on what could be negotiated in the latter two matters). He also acknowledges women's rights to medicinal alleviation of the pain of childbirth, despite biblical prophecy of pain and sorrow; some control of property and possibly rights of inheritance; and a shared authority, with men, over their children, who owe their mothers as well as their fathers equal respect and obedience. Though this may hardly be the model of contemporary egalitarian marriage (a standard the majority of contemporary marriages fail to achieve, it might be added),[2] it is certainly a relatively "enlightened" view of women's abilities and status compared to a number of Locke's contemporaries, as Schochet suggests (although, he also notes, Locke is admittedly less progressive than others among his contemporaries). It is this *relative* equality, however, not to mention Locke's place between those more and less progressive contemporaries, that gives rise to the charge of ambiguity and fuels continuing feminist debates over Locke.

On the other hand, as many contributors to this volume also note, Locke's works are also marked by passages that point in the opposite direction. He does grant men ultimate authority over common concerns in the family, and the final word in disputes, because they are "abler and stronger," and notes, almost reluctantly, "a foundation in nature" for women's subjection and inferiority to husbands in the family. Further, he intimates a lack of control over property and a denial of many rights of property and inheritance, and aside from a few gestures toward Elizabeth I, he nowhere suggests that women should be participants in politics, even as voters, much less as agents of state power.

These ambiguities make Locke a philosophically intriguing, intellectually engaging, and politically infuriating resource for "re-reading the canon." Hence feminist interpretations of Locke, certainly more than readings of most other canonical figures, diverge widely on the question of Locke's views on women, and therefore his accessibility and usefulness to contemporary feminists. Some scholars excoriate him, relatively straightforwardly, as just another patriarchal political theorist, while others view him, almost equally straightforwardly, as a liberal feminist. Between these two tendencies, however—both of which are represented, in varying degrees, in this book—lie a variety of newer re-readings that recognize the intellectual and theoretical power of ambiguity. Such perspectives are less invested in creating definitive answers and more inclined to deepening and complicating the questions that we ask, less likely to provide critical closure to perennial puzzles of Lockean and feminist scholarship and more likely to open those puzzles to new angles of vision, as well as, perhaps, confusion. Locke's ambiguity lends itself particularly well to such new kinds of reading and new ways of undertaking feminist analysis, even as Locke's work continues to be relevant to more conventionally framed modes of feminist interpretation and critique.

Rereading the Canon, Rereading Locke

The theme of "re-reading" that characterizes the volumes in this series is expressed here on a variety of levels and in a number of complementary ways. In the most obvious sense, Locke allows us to reread how "the canon" is defined. Specifically, Locke differs from a number of other canonical figures included in this series in that his contemporary currency is preeminently framed as that of a political theorist rather than a philosopher. As Joanne Wright notes in Chapter 7, Locke trained at Oxford as a physician—in large part because he had a certain degree of antipathy toward Aristotle, who was the major focus of philosophical study at Oxford in the seventeenth century. And as Locke's biographers note, it was this training as a physician that eventually led to the writings for which he is so famous. After saving the life of Lord Anthony Ashley Cooper, later the Earl of Shaftsbury, he became his personal physician. This position served as Locke's entrée into the world of politics and political theory, as Shaftsbury involved Locke in writing position papers and advising him on matters of political intrigue and the controversies of the day.[3]

This is not, of course, to downplay the significance of the Oxford philosophical curriculum for Locke's intellectual development, nor is it to disregard his teaching duties at that institution in the 1660s as Censor in Moral Philosophy. Certainly, anyone who reads Locke's *Essay Concerning Human Understanding* knows that Locke is a more than capable philosopher, and Linda Zerilli's chapter in particular demonstrates the philosophical dexterity that Locke exhibits both in his account of language and in his related theorization of "the subject." Similarly, Jeremy Waldron's chapter on Locke's views of Christianity demonstrates Locke's close attention to theology and his careful use of scriptural evidence in his critique of patriarchal authority. Locke's corpus of writings, however, extends beyond metaphysics and epistemology, and Carol Pech's (Chapter 9) and Nancy Hirschmann's (Chapter 5) considerations of his various economic writings attest to his interest in finance, economics, and public policy. But Locke's political writings are what make Locke stand out in the canon, and it is that literature to which feminists have most often attended. Early works in feminist political thought posited Locke as a key canonical figure for feminist analysis precisely because of the apparent contrast between the liberal politics of freedom and equality that informed his theory of the social contract and his seeming acquiescence in a conventional gender hierarchy. As a consequence, some of the earliest articles in feminist political theory, reprinted here, by Mary Lyndon Shanley (Chapter 1), Carole Pateman and Teresa Brennan (Chapter 2), and Melissa Butler (Chapter 3) took Locke as an appropriate focus for the project of bringing women into the canon of explicitly *political* theory.

Yet despite the fact that political theorists are more likely to attend to Locke than philosophers are, the approach we have taken in this volume to "re-reading" Locke is strongly interdisciplinary. We have included historical as well as philosophical approaches, approaches that draw on liberal, democratic, and postmodern theoretical frameworks, to pursue topics ranging from religion to midwifery to masculinity. Moreover, the questions raised by our contributors about Locke's various writings extend the boundaries of both the canon and feminist scholarship. For the kinds of questions that are traditionally asked in canonical study are dramatically expanded, shifted, and opened up to acknowledge that the philosophical, medical, economic, theological, financial, and public policy issues with which Locke concerned himself are intimately tied to the "mainstream" political questions that Locke asks in his most familiar texts. Locke is clearly, from a feminist perspective, intensely political even when he ostensibly seeks not to be.

Hence a second way in which the chapters in this book reread the canon is to engage Lockean texts that feminists and nonfeminists alike have too often neglected. Whereas the *Two Treatises of Government* are generally considered as Locke's single "canonical" text—the one taught in most survey classes in political theory and political philosophy—our contributors consider the less frequented texts to be no less important to defining Locke's status in the canon, and to rereading the meaning of his political thought. Thus Linda Zerilli engages Locke's *Essay Concerning Human Understanding,* Jeremy Waldron his letters on toleration and other religious writings, Joanne Wright his letters offering advice on pregnancy, Carol Pech his works on money, and Nancy Hirschmann his writings on the Poor Law. These and other essays recur as well to his early manuscripts on natural law, to his writings on education, and to his posthumously published *Of the Conduct of the Understanding.* This diversity of texts attests to the diversity of Locke's interests, concerns, and writings, as well as to the diversity of approaches and concerns pursued by our contributors, but the book as a whole operates within the context of, and with a sensitivity to, the intense involvement Locke had in political questions and issues.

A third way in which this collection rereads both Locke and the canon is much more literal. We open with reprints of three classic feminist analyses of Locke, followed by "responses" written by the original authors. These articles include Melissa Butler's "The Early Liberal Roots of Feminism" (arguably the first publication in feminist canonical analysis published in the *American Political Science Review*), Mary Lyndon Shanley's "Marriage Contract and Social Contract in Seventeenth Century English Political Thought," and Teresa Brennan and Carole Pateman's "'Mere Auxiliaries to the Commonwealth': Women and the Origins of Liberalism." Contemporaneous with the book-length works noted earlier, these three articles broke new ground in political science and political philosophy in the decades of the 1970s and 1980s, taking up key questions of where women fit into the history of political theory within the work of a political philosopher who devoted relatively little direct attention to women. In contrast to, say, Rousseau, or Mill, or even Plato, all of whom explicitly theorized about women, Locke's comments on women are oblique, made almost in passing. Yet these early articles demonstrated that gender could be readily excavated from Locke's writings, and that he had extremely important contributions to make on the matter. Shanley and Butler were fairly complimentary to Locke, maintaining that his arguments held great feminist promise, whereas Brennan and Pateman were much more critical of his patriarchalism and pessimistic about his views. But all three articles transformed feminist analysis of canonical thought and allowed us to look for gender where there was (as Locke said about consent to the social contract), "no Expressions of it at all."[4]

In a sense, these articles are themselves part of an emerging "canon" of feminist political theory and philosophy, a canon that is here itself reread. Specifically, these three articles are retrospectively engaged by their authors, as Shanley, Butler, and Brennan and Pateman have offered us contemporary rereadings of their own original arguments. In each of these pieces, the authors reflect on how their views have changed—or not—in light of the research and writing that they have done in the roughly thirty years since publishing their original articles. These rethinkings and revisitings provide scholars of Locke's thought, both feminist and otherwise, with a broad and robust perspective on the trajectory of feminist political thought over the past quarter century. But they also offer unique insights into how feminist writings on Locke have developed over the years with the discovery and appropriation of diverse methodological tools, intellectual frameworks, and scholarly approaches to the history of political thought.

Power, Equality, and Locke

These reprints and their contemporary "updates" set the stage for the rest of the book's reconsideration, reconstruction, and rereading of the

Lockean texts. Indeed, the three original articles are frequent touch-stones for many of the other chapters in this book, and they are thus "re-read" by the other contributors to feed further "re-readings" of Locke. The themes and questions raised by these various papers revolve around three broad topics: power, equality, and gender. The question of power, it should be said, extends considerably beyond the issue of whether Locke considered women to be equal to men or inferior, on which, as we have already noted, Locke is generally ambiguous. Rather, it pertains to the construction of Enlightenment categories of thought and to a range of political concepts that are central to contemporary politics but which gained their salience during the seventeenth century. In the history of political thought, of course, Locke is often associated with the concept of freedom. Regarded by many as the quintessential liberal contract theo-rist, his claims of natural freedom ground the idea—much more consis-tently and recognizably to modern sensibilities than his predecessor Hobbes—that governmental legitimacy can be founded only on individ-ual choice. The natural partner to freedom, viz. equality, is in Locke's work seen as a secondary value. Defined principally as an equality of right rather than of, say, wealth or strength, equality is somewhat derivative of freedom, which is taken as the prior value. Yet when considering Locke on gender, equality becomes a much more salient ideal, for when we focus on that concept, issues concerning power appear more prominently. In particular, feminists ask two questions: What is the limit of men's power over women? And how much power do women really have? The former question involves not merely the family, which is the most obvi-ous locus of men's power over women, as Brennan and Pateman, as well as Schochet, argue, but religion and doctrine, including scriptural inter-pretation, as Waldron suggests, economic policy, as Carol Pech and Hir-schmann both reveal, and the definition of identity and the construction of meaning, as Zerilli and Carver both discuss.

The latter question, of how much power women really have, is, of course, intimately tied to the former, of men's power over women, for women had power in the family, as Shanley and Butler both maintain, though the case for women's power in other realms is less clear. However, Schochet claims in this volume that although Locke "was not an egalitar-ian on any grounds, hardly least among them, sexual," Locke's theory nonetheless "considerably widened the category of the political person even though it retained the traditional restriction of that status to males." Schochet argues that Locke's real contribution to feminism lies in the transition he marks from the idea of status as naturalistically *given* to that of status as conventionally *created*. In this, Locke generated "the theoretical possibility of full political membership for women," even if he did not himself extend his arguments that far. In effect, although in practical terms "women were no more accorded civil status by . . . Locke than they were by Filmer," Locke's focus on contract and consent made possible the reconceptualization of women's political status as voluntary members of the polity, as agents who could both choose their political affiliations and express claims based in individual rights.

Along significantly parallel lines, but with a different starting point, Jeremy Waldron claims that Locke was an "equality radical." According to him, those who "read Locke as someone who pretended to believe in equality, but who was really in favor of massive *in*equality between classes and between the sexes" have little standing, because "there was no particular advantage to Locke" in such duplicity. Waldron thus asks "why Locke did not follow Samuel Pufendorf and his own friend James Tyrrell in making the exclusion of women explicit," and considers the feminist failure to recognize the strong egalitiarian implications of such indicators in Locke's theory as unjust to Locke. As Waldron notes, however, "it is one thing to articulate a premise; it's another thing to hold fast to it, in the detail of one's social and political thinking." And of course Locke, the strong opponent of slavery in chapter 5 of the *Second Treatise*, was a stockholder in the Royal African Trade Company, which was a major player in the emerging slave trade of the seventeenth and eighteenth centuries. Locke is a man of apparent contradictions. Those contradictions, as Schochet notes, may be more a function of silence than of words; but it remains possible that Locke's reticence on issues of both gender and race suggests not sympathy to egalitarian claims, but something else entirely.

In this context, Schochet as well as Hirschmann proffer rather more critical views. Albeit in different terms, both suggest that regardless of Locke's overt commitments, or lack thereof, to equality, the scope of his egalitarianism was severely constrained by the framework of his project. Previous critics such as Pateman and Brennan, of course, contended not that Locke was consciously duplicitous, but rather that his initial premises are often undermined and thwarted by the subsequent development of his argument. Certainly all texts hold meanings and contradictions that the writer did not intend, but on the issue of Lockean equality, it appears that the jury remains divided.

Rereading Gender, Rereading Feminism

The question of intent, however, is complicated by the notion that women's power, as Zerilli, Carver, and Pech particularly suggest, is to a significant extent derived from the subversive disruption that women's presence places on the masculine landscape. This disruption not only provides feminists with a powerful tool for rereading Locke, but may be linked to the aforementioned ambiguity Locke displays on gender. "The linguistic turn" is thought by some to have already become passé, but feminism requires us to acknowledge the importance of language, of the mental and social construction and representation of what we observe, in constructing the social categories of meaning and understanding. For gender is a key such category. Locke's emphasis on "the strictly conventional character of language," as Zerilli suggests, implies a placement of individuals, as gendered beings, in relation to things, and moreover, ensures that the relationship itself both forms and reflects the meaning of those things: "the psychological relation of language to world" indicates the duality of reflection and construction, and suggests that language both produces the meaning of what we observe and is fed and informed by that observation. Such a duality marks the ambiguity of gender in Locke's thought. It is one's placement within the symbolic gendered economy that affects one's understanding, use, and deployment of language, one's entrance into the symbolic economy of representation.

The notion Zerilli puts forth that, for Locke, "words take on the force of objects, they create sensations which give rise in the subject to Ideas whose connection to reality is in question" indeed might make Locke sound kin to Judith Butler. At the same time, it returns us to Waldron's question of intent: Did Locke recognize the disruptive power of gender? Did he try to repress it by granting women some measure of recognition, thus relieving systemic pressure on epistemology and language without seriously undermining patriarchal culture? Most likely not, on both accounts. But these latter questions reveal that the theme of power intersects with a second theme, namely the meaning of gender. Most essays in the Re-reading the Canon series, like feminist writings more generally, take "women" as a term that denotes a particular social category that coheres with body type, location and role in the institution of the family, and a primarily reproductive heterosexuality. Thus the conceptualization of gender offered by most analysts is the quintessentially modernist one of the formal roles that women and men have in the family; gender is conceived as a socially constructed social role, in contrast to sex, which is a matter of bodies and biology. This conception of gender, however, intersects with the meaning of women in feminist analysis to narrow the scope of relevant analysis and forestall certain kinds of questions and inquiries to the point where "gender" is, as Carver complains, "a synonym for women."[5]

Indeed, Carver carries his expansion of gender analysis further to address issues of masculinity. Carver suggests that there is both a "covert" and "overt" gender discourse at work in Locke, and that when Locke appears to be gender neutral, a covert gendering is nevertheless at work. Starting from the unusual image Locke offers of "nursing fathers" who nurture emerging civil society, Carver suggests that the narrative strategies that Locke deploys are covertly gendered, for instance in the case of property inheritance serving as a mode of tacit consent. It is this covert gendering that makes Locke's work appear so ambiguous on questions of gender, and which makes Locke so difficult to pin down on the question of women's roles, place, and power.

The theme of gender immediately connects to an additional theme, the meaning of feminism. This is not a theme overtly taken up in this book, but rather is a function of the essays we solicited and selected for the volume. We view the theme as implicit in the different approaches taken by the contributors. The two themes of gender and feminism, though distinct, are in this book considerably intertwined because questions of method so often converge on the meaning of gender. Accordingly, the preponderance of essays in most of the works in this series, including some in the present volume, consider primarily what the selected canonical figure has to say "about women" along various thematic vectors: whether women have or can use reason, whether they may hold property, women's relationship to citizenship and political participation, women's position in the family and the degree of power and control they have within the institution that predominates in their lives, and whether women have a different, perhaps even oppositional "voice" that stems from their position in the family and relation to reason, property, and the state. Some of the chapters in this book follow that normal formula, and this formula makes valuable contributions to deepening our understanding of the canonical works. But others do something quite different, and it is our intention that, in offering diverse feminist interpretations of Locke, we offer up challenges to how feminists might think about "rereading the canon." For instance, very few articles we have encountered in other volumes in this series take up the issue of masculinity, a theme that is of obvious and vital importance to feminism, as Terrell Carver, Carol Pech, and Linda Zerilli clearly illustrate with regard to Locke. Similarly, hardly any articles in this series, with the exception of the forthcoming volume on Marx, give explicit or more than passing reference to class, despite the proclaimed importance of "intersectionality" that contemporary feminists reiterate. If "gender" is a synonym for women, it might also be a synonym for "white and middle class." Yet class is central to Locke's construction of gender, as Hirschmann suggests. Whereas Schochet maintains that Lorenne Clark, and other early second-wave feminists, missed the point that Macpherson collapsed gender into class, Hirschmann seeks to rearticulate the relationship between the two. Though the idea of the "intersectionality" of gender, race, and class is a dominant theme in contemporary feminist theory, Hirschmann notes that when feminists focus their attention on the Western canon, "women" once again becomes a term devoid of race and class differences, and embodies the norms of the white upper and middle classes. Yet Locke attended to laboring-class women as well as men, particularly in his "Essay on the Poor Law," and this provides a different understanding of his take on gender. Femininity in this context is differentially structured by class.

But the security of masculinity as a symbolic order may be called into question as well, and this is a possibility pursued by both Carole Pech and Linda Zerilli. Pech's psychoanalytically informed examination of Locke's writings on the "clipping controversy"—which centered on the practice of shaving metal from the edges of silver coins—shows how money took on a more explicitly symbolic value as the weight of clipped coins fell increasingly short of their face denominations. The anxieties of masculinity Pech traces through this controversy suggest the centrality of gender not only to the distribution of property and wealth, but also to the very ascription of abstract value to money. Thus, Pech argues, even as the instability of value spawned by clipping threatened the masculine order, Locke's response was associated with a feminine semiotic of fluidity as well as a fetishistic fixation on natural value. Here, psychoanalytic categories reveal gender as more complicated and multilayered than conventional, sociologically framed feminist readings might assume; for we find that it was not only one's place in the economic order that was riddled by gender, but the symbolic dimension of the emergent monetary system as such. Drawing also on the rhetorical and symbolic aspects of language,

Zerilli directs critical attention to the narrative elements of Locke's work. She argues that the "gaudy dress" of rhetoric that Locke regards as superfluous to philosophy is essential to his own account of the freedom of political beginnings. Indeed, rather than a monument to reason, rationality, and the rational subject, Locke's story of the social contract is itself a matter of "passionate speech" that offers a "figure of the newly thinkable." That imaginative figure, Zerilli contends, is precisely what enables Locke's account of political founding as "the emergence of a 'we' that is not already given" by the historical record. Do these different approaches to the concept of "gender" actually shift the meaning of "feminism"? As Teresa de Lauretis, quoted by Pech, maintains, "the subject of feminism is not only distinct from Woman with the capital letter . . . but also distinct from women, the real historical beings and social subjects who are defined by the technology of gender." Instead, it is a "theoretical construct (a way of conceptualizing, of understanding, of accounting for certain *processes*, not women)." Many of the chapters in this book, including those apparently written about "women," would agree with this account, but it may be most fully illustrated by Zerilli's (Chapter 10), which in methodological terms seems to be quite distant from the standard feminist approach. Zerilli hardly even mentions the word "gender," much less "women"; is this the logical extension of poststructuralism that feminists have long feared, the disappearance of women from feminism— and, by implication, the disappearance of feminism? We think not.

Rereading Political Philosophy

The diverse themes that run through this book thus suggest multiple and multilayered constructions of the idea of "re-reading the canon," for they reread more than a particularly prominent figure in the modern canon. Beyond this, they reread as well the significance of the canon itself, and feminism's relationship to that canon. In so doing, they interrogate the meaning of gender and feminism, how feminist inquiry might be conducted, the range and kinds of questions that can be asked, and the modes of analysis that could be undertaken. As central as reading Locke is to every contributor to this volume, these essays offer their readers a wide range of methodological, philosophical, theoretical, and political issues that run well beyond the question of the authorial Locke.

Accordingly, our readers will be a diverse group as well. This is an additional way in which the present volume "re-reads the canon," by rereading what, and who, can do that rereading. We purposely set out to combine a range of scholars, some of whom are well-known contributors to feminist scholarship, others of whom, such as Waldron and Schochet, are prominent scholars of Locke. In so doing, our hope is to attract a wide variety of readers and raise a variety of questions along the feminist spectrum, in addition to questions of Lockean analysis. Compared to many other disciplines—history, sociology, and literary studies, for example—philosophy and political science are lagging when it comes to considerations of gender, the hiring of women in academic departments, and the granting to women of professional status and recognition. We believe that this disciplinary foot-dragging is unhealthy and unproductive, that it stifles creative intellectual endeavor. It is time that scholarly engagement with the question of gender was normalized by the profession, with "mainstream" scholars acknowledging and writing about gender dynamics rather than ghettoizing these inquiries in Women's Studies programs. With the recent rise of transgender theory and issues, with the steady growth of women's presence on university and college faculties, with the growth of women's studies courses across the curriculum, neither political science nor philosophy can afford to ignore the important changes taking place in the academy and in our scholarship.

Locke is a particularly appropriate figure through which to conduct such an effort, for the ambiguities and uncertainties that characterize Locke's treatment of gender resonate strongly with the unsettling of gender in today's academy. It is important that "mainstream" Lockean scholarship attend to questions of gender, for they are central to Locke's texts. As feminists are criticized for ignoring class, for neglecting various methodological issues, or for ahistoricism, so must scholars of Locke, of consent theories, and of the historical and theoretical roots of what is now called liberalism be criticized for neglecting the fundamental role that gender plays in Locke's understanding of politics, economics, religion, language, and epistemology. Whether concerned with a world well lost, or the world that is, or a world yet to be won, without attention to gender, readings of Locke necessarily diminish their own political and theoretical purchase. In rereading both the canon in general and Locke as one of its continuing figures, we advocate, both implicitly and explicitly, the rereading of our modern disciplines as well.

Notes

1. Susan Okin, *Women in Western Political Thought* (Princeton: Princeton University Press, 1979), 7; subsequent references in text.

2. Martha A. Fineman, *The Illusion of Equality: The Rhetoric and Reality of Divorce Reform* (Chicago: University of Chicago Press, 1991).

3. Richard Ashcraft, *Revolutionary Politics and Locke's "Two Treatises of Government"* (Princeton: Princeton University Press, 1986).

4. John Locke, *Two Treatises of Government*, ed. Peter Laslett (Cambridge: Cambridge University Press, 1988), 2.119.

5. Terrell Carver, *Gender Is Not a Synonym for Women* (Boulder, Colo.: Lynne Rienner, 1996).

1

Marriage Contract and Social Contract in Seventeenth-Century English Political Thought

Mary Lyndon Shanley

Seventeenth-Century English Liberal political theory asserted that human beings were free and equal in the state of nature. But in the every-day experience of most seventeenth-century Englishmen, the vast majority of social relationships took place between persons who believed themselves to be unequal. Indeed, well-born and lowly alike thought that hierarchy in human relationships was essential to the maintenance of social order: magistrate must rule over subject, minister over congregation, master over servant, parent over child, and husband over wife. Most persons regarded these hierarchies as integrally related; each was governed by God's command to "Honor thy father and thy mother." So important was status to social order that disruption in any one relationship could produce ill effects in all the others: the Puritan Divine Richard Baxter was convinced that "most of the mischiefs that now infest or seize upon mankind throughout the earth, consist in, or are caused by the disorders and ill-governedness of families."[1]

The ideas of status by ascription and of the similarity of all authority were not, however, immutable. Some seventeenth-century theorists advanced the proposition that the only legitimate basis for relationships of super- and sub-ordination was the free consent of the individual. While contractarian ideas first developed in analyses of the proper basis of authority, they gradually began to appear in discussions of other human associations as well.

One of the most striking instances of the extension of this conceptual revolution was the change which took place in the conceptualization of the marriage contract in the course of the seventeenth century. In 1640 virtually all writers still spoke of the "contractual" element in marriage as being simply the *consent* of each party to marry the other. Both man and woman consented to take on the rights and obligations of their respective stations. The man's role was that of head and governor, the woman's role that of obedient follower. To contract a marriage was to consent to a status which in its essence was hierarchical and unalterable. By 1690, however, John Locke suggested that if marriage were a "contractual" relationship, the terms of the contract as well as whether or not to enter into the relationship were negotiable. Nothing inherent in the contracting of marriage dictated woman's subordination to man. Women, like men, were free beings able to define their relationship to others by their own wills and consent. Moreover, the marriage contract did not need to be life-long or unchangeable.

Much of the change in thinking about the basis of the marriage relationship was provoked or inspired by the political debates of both the Civil War and the Restoration. The royalists thought they had found in the marriage contract a perfect analogue to any supposed contract between the king and his subjects, for marriage was a contract but was in its essence both hierarchical and irrevocable. Parliamentarian and republican writers were forced by these arguments to debate the royalist conception of marriage as well as of kingship. They gradually extended their individualistic premises into the depiction of domestic order. The parliamentarian discussions, however, were beset by various inconsistencies. It was John Locke, who, more clearly than his predecessors, saw the implications of contractarian ideas for marriage, and who solved several of the dilemmas which had beset earlier attempts to compare the marriage bond to the social contract.

These changes in the conceptualization of the marriage contract provide an excellent example of the role of analogy in political discourse. The course of the argument between royalists and parliamentarians illustrates the ways in which an analogue—initially introduced to support one argument—may itself become a focus of debate. If the analogue is a powerful one, both sides will attempt to control it and bend it to their respective purposes. In the process, the image itself may be altered or transformed. This is precisely what happened with the notion of the marriage contract in the course of the seventeenth-century political debates in England. The theoretical arguments which emerged from these debates over political sovereignty eventually—although very slowly—became the bases for Liberal arguments about female equality and marriage.[2]

The Civil War Years

The Royalist View of the Irrevocability of the Social and Marriage Contracts

Although the development of contractarian thought in England is usually associated with advocates of parliamentary or popular rights, by the early seventeenth century "contractarian principles had taken a firm hold of nearly all political thought."[3] Supporters of Charles I of course frequently relied upon patriarchal and divine right arguments to support their position. But they also used the notion of contract to argue that the people had ceded their rights to the original monarch in a contract of submission, and "had no right to do anything but endure [even] the tyranny of a lawfully constituted ruler."[4] Therefore when the parliamentarian Henry Parker claimed that since power had originally been conveyed from the people they could take it back, Sir John Spelman replied, "I should rather think if Regall power were originally conveyed from the people, they by conveying it over have divested themselves of it."[5] Sir Dudley Digges, joining the fray against Parker, argued that civil government was created by "a consent and mutual obligation . . . of [men] not using their natural power but only as the law shall require, that is, of not resisting that body in which the supreme power is placed." So it comes about that "in acquittal for our submission of our private strength, we are secured by the united power of all and the whole kingdom becomes our guard."[6] By 1640, part of the debate between royalists and parliamentarians was being conducted over the nature of English monarchy's ancient compact with the people, ratified by every ruler through the coronation oath.[7]

Because it admirably suited their purposes, royalists introduced, and initially profited more from, the analogy between social contract and marriage contract than did their opponents. The marriage contract was useful to royalists because it provided an example of a contract which established a relationship of irrevocable hierarchical authority between the parties. Supporters of Charles I pointed out that marriage was a relationship which both man and woman entered by their free consent, but in marriage God established the husband in a position of rule over his wife. Neither the spouses' own agreement nor a violation of God's ordinances concerning marital duties could alter that relationship or free husband and wife from their obligations. Similarly, men might originally have freely agreed to establish a monarchy, but once the agreement was struck, the sovereign's powers were as fixed as those of the husband.

Henry Ferne, for example, used the marriage contract to ridicule the notion that Parliament holds some sort of "reserved power" to judge the actions of the king. Such an idea was a pernicious and harmful doctrine, "a very seminary of jealousies and seditions. . . ." To give Parliament such powers was

> as if, in Matrimony (for the King is also *sponsus* Regni, and wedded to the kingdom by a ring at his Coronation) the parties should agree, on such and such neglect of duties, to part a sunder . . . ; what our Savior said of their light and unlawfull occasions of Divorse, *non suit ob initio*, it was not so from the beginning, may be said of such a reserved power of resistance, it was not so from the beginning.[8]

In the same way Dudley Digges considered absurd the parliamentarian contention that "there is a mutuall contract between King, and subjects, and if he break the covenant, He forfeites the benefits of this agreement, and He not performing the duty of a King, they are released from the duty of Subjects."[9] Digges marshaled evidence from both scripture and family conduct to show that the existence of an initial contract did not mean that the parties to the contract, even a party who was seriously abused, had the right to rescind the compact or withdraw from it.

> The Jewes could have made this plea, grounded in the nature of a Covenant, the breach of which (though instituted by God be-tweene King and People, Deut. 17.) was no dispensation for them to Rebell, as was evidenced formerly. . . . So there is a contract between Husband and Wife, the violation of which on the man's part doth not bereave him of his dominion over the woman. I confesse, a great obligation lyes upon Kings. . . . And if they abuse their power, God's punishment will be as high as their ingrati-tude.[10]

Political resistance was forbidden. The notion of justifiable rebellion was as ludicrous as the notion that a wife might be released from the subjection to her husband either by their mutual agreement or because of his abuse.

According to the royalists, thinking about marriage when thinking of political authority made it possible to see that consent once given can establish an unalterable relationship. Digges argued that no person living in the England of his day partook of the original freedom of the state of nature: "Else no contracts could be of force, because by the law of nature men were free. . . ." People lost that freedom through their civil compact "which it was in our power not to make, but having once made it, we have tyed our hands from using positive liberty."[11] Or, as Ferne explained it, "many things which are altogether in our disposing before we part with them, are not afterward in our power to recall. . . ."[12] Consent might have indicated initial freedom, but it did not guarantee continuing choice.

The usefulness of the marriage contract as an analogy for the social contract was not lost upon supporters of Charles I. They saw in it a means to demonstrate to those who prattled about "natural freedom" and of the "original compact" between king and people, that bonds created initially by free consent are not necessarily either alterable or revocable. The royalists' use of the marriage contract to support absolutist arguments posed a difficult challenge for republican theorists.

The Parliamentarian Response and the Dilemma of Divorce

As defenders of the absolute and inalienable authority of the king tended to argue that God had commanded wives to be subject to their husbands, that men were by nature superior to women, and that the marriage contract once made could not be broken, so advocates of parliamentary or popular checks on the king's prerogative tried to paint the marriage relationship as one in which the authority of husbands over wives could be limited or even broken. To answer the royalists' claims concerning kingly authority, the parliamentarians had to debate their conception of marriage as well.

The parameters of the parliamentarians' arguments concerning marriage were set by prevailing notions concerning marriage and divorce.[13] Under canon law, true marriage was held to be a sacrament. There could be no divorce in the sense of a real dissolution of marriage with the possibility of remarriage. Divorce was only *a mensa et thoro* (separation from bed and board), and even this only by the sentence of an ecclesiastical court. In pre-Reformation England, the grounds of judicial separation were limited, more restrictively than elsewhere, to adultery and cruelty.

Many Protestant reformers, from Luther on, favored granting divorces for adultery, with permission for the innocent party to remarry. The Ordinances of Wittenberg (1553) and of Geneva (1561) recognized both adultery and desertion as valid grounds for divorce. In England a proposed *Reformatio Legum Ecclesiasticarum* in 1552 reflected a similarly liberal point of view. Although Henry VIII died before he could force this act through Parliament, and the House of Commons defeated it under Edward VI, the reform principles apparently received considerable acceptance throughout the Elizabethan period. From the beginning of the seventeenth century, and especially under Archbishop Laud, however, a contrary trend prevailed. The *Constitutions and Canons Ecclesiasticall* published in 1604 urged closer adherence to the pre-Reformation practices, declaring that ecclesiastical courts should grant separations only with the utmost caution and only after the parties posted a bond that neither would remarry during the other's lifetime.[14] Jurisdiction over all separations remained with the ecclesiastical courts.

The Puritans resisted this trend backwards toward the canon law. In the early seventeenth century a split developed between those Puritans who admitted remarriage after divorce (divorce *a vinculo*) and those who only allowed divorce *a mensa et thoro*.[15] Even those who favored divorce *a vinculo*, however, narrowed Luther's list of grounds to encompass only adultery and desertion.[16] Despite the Puritan reform movement, during the first half of the seventeenth century the dominant opinion and practice among Puritan and Anglican alike was that divorce could only be granted for adultery, that such divorce was only *a mensa et thoro*, and that it did not dissolve the marriage bonds nor permit remarriage even of the innocent party.

It was in this context that the parliamentarian pamphleteers attempted to convert the analogy between marriage and compact between king and people to serve their purposes as effectively as it had the royalists in theirs. Two main strategies appeared in parliamentarian pamphlets. Parliamentarians agreed with royalists that the husband was superior to the wife in marriage. But some argued that despite the husband's superiority there were *inherent* restrictions on his power. Bolder writers enlarged on this and asserted that if a husband transgressed those limitations, his wife had the right to oppose him and in extremity to separate herself from him.

William Bridge argued the position of inherent limitations on husbandly power to refute the absolutist claims of Henry Ferne, supporter of Charles I. One of Ferne's arguments in *The Resolving of Conscience* had been that if there was an original covenant between king and people, then its terms (as evidenced by the Coronation Oath) made no provision for resistance by Parliament.[17] Bridge replied that "though there be no such words expressed . . . *ratio legis* being *lex*, in reason that must be implied," and relied on a comparison between marriage and government, two institutions equally ordained by God for man:

> there is a covenant stricken between a man & a woman at Marriage; when they marry one another it is not verbally expressed in their agreement, that if one commit Adultery, that party shall be divorced; and yet we know that that covenant of Marriage carries the force of such condition.[18]

Although Bridge did not explicitly contend that if God in establishing marriage provided the remedy of separation, so in creating government He must similarly have provided the remedy of resistance, that was the implication of his argument. Others might, and later did, draw upon the suggestion.

Henry Parker had much the same objective as Bridge—to argue for implicit restraints upon the power of the king—when he wrote of the relationship between marriage contract and social contract in *Jus populi*:

> In Matrimony there is something divine . . . but is this any ground to infer that there is no humane consent or concurrance in it? does the divine institution of marriage take away freedom of choice before, or conclude either party under an absolute formalization? . . . And if men, for whose sake women were created, shall not lay hold upon the divine right of wedlock, to the disadvantage of women; much less shall Princes who were created for the peoples sake, chalenge any thing from the sanctity of their offices, that may derogate from the people.[19]

The argument that scripture countenanced no absolute coercion by husbands was directly relevant to Parker's contention that comparing the power of a husband to that of a king showed that there must be limits to kingly authority.

Herbert Palmer and his co-authors of *Scripture and Reason Pleaded for Defensive Armes* carried Bridge's and Parker's argument about inherent limits to authority a step further. They reasoned that if husband or king transgressed the implicit limits of his respective office, *active resistance* in home or state was justified. Using the notion of self-preservation, Palmer introduced the concept of individual rights into the discussion of marital obligation:

> A Wife is tyed to her Husband by the Covenant of God, (so called *Prov.* 2.) and by the Ordinance of God more ancient, and no lesse strong then that of Politick Government. She cannot recall wholly her Husbands Authority over her . . . *Yet for her necessity, she may* by the Law of God and Conscience . . . *secure her Person from his violence by absence* (though that ordinarily be against the Law of Marriage, and the end of it.) or *any other meanes of necessary defence.*"[20]

Palmer and his associates argued that the right of self-preservation gave an abused spouse the right to separate, just as the right of self-preservation gave Parliament the right to raise an army under defensive arms.

John Milton, more clearly than other parliamentarians, saw what the political debates implied for the understanding of marriage. Milton, himself anxious for release from an unhappy marriage, used the fact that parliament was in arms to argue for divorce *a vinculo*. Where the political pamphlets had argued that the social contract was like the marriage contract, Milton *reversed* the terms of the analogy and argued that understanding the political bond can help one to understand the nature of marriage. His dedicatory letter "To the Parliament of England with the Assembly," prefaced to the second edition of the *Doctrine and Discipline of Divorce* (1644), was a brilliant appeal to a body which was in arms against the king:

> Advise yee well, supreme Senat, if charity be thus excluded and expulst, how yee will defend the untainted honour of your own actions and proceedings: He who marries, intends as little to conspire his own ruine, as he that swears Allegiance: and as a whole people is in proportion to an ill Government, so is one man to an ill marriage. If they against any authority, Covenant, or Statute, may by the soveraign edict of charity, save not only their lives, but honest liberties from unworthy bondage, as well may he against any private Covenant, which hee never enter'd to his mischief, redeem himself from unsupportable disturbances to honest peace, and just contentment. . . .[21]

Milton, with a boldness matched by none of his contemporaries and roundly condemned by most of them, used this notion of saving "honest liberties from unworthy bondage" to argue for divorce *a vinculo* for any incompatibility which made the marriage partners unable to be true companions and help-meets.[22]

Challenged by the royalists to show why resistance to authority was any more justifiable in politics than in marriage, the parliamentarian pamphleteers were pushed to consider what, if anything, could limit a husband's authority over his wife or authorize resistance to his power. The Civil War political debate therefore generated a secondary debate on the nature of the marriage bond. Apologists for resistance to Charles I were forced to take more liberal positions with regard to marriage and divorce than were generally acceptable.

Despite the efforts of men such as Bridge, Parker, and Palmer, the parliamentarians had difficulty turning the image of the marriage contract to their own use. Their assumptions about marriage did not accommodate their rapidly developing arguments about legitimate political authority. Parliamentarians like royalists believed that women were naturally inferior to men and were commanded by scripture to be subject to their husbands in marriage. While parliamentarians continued to accept the injunction "Wives, be subject to your husbands," many wished to argue that parliament shared authority with the king. Parker was almost alone in allowing a wife any resistance to a violent husband other than absence, but many argued that men might take up arms against the king. And although the parliamentarians eventually argued that if the terms of the political contract were abused and broken then the contract must be revocable, they had serious doubts about divorce *a vinculo*. Had the victory in the war between parliament and king gone to the party best able to turn the image of the marriage contract to the service of its position, Charles I would not have become a royal martyr.

The Later Stuarts

Natural and Contractual Hierarchy in Marriage

During the reign of Charles II when parliamentarians and royalists resumed their political debates, they continued to use marriage as an analogue for the proper relationship between king and parliament. The anti-royalist tracts during the Restoration, however, were more influenced by social contract reasoning than those of the Civil War years had been. This shift to social contract theory occurred when arguments from natural law began to replace those based upon scripture. Where scripture had been adequate to prove that God had intended subjects to be subordinate to the prince and wives to be subject to their husbands, it was now necessary to show that both kinds of authority were based upon free consent. In the political debate this meant that it was possible to argue for parliamentary limitations on royal prerogative. In the discussion of marriage, contract theory called into question the natural hierarchy of husband over wife which both parties in the Civil War debates had taken for granted.

The work of James Tyrrell reflected the new concerns of liberal theorists during the Restoration. Tyrrell, a life-long associate and correspondent of John Locke, was concerned to demonstrate that patriarchal justifications of royal authority were absurd.[23] Tyrrell argued that "a man without his own act or consent can never lawfully fall into the power of possession of another."[24] Since patriarchal theory asserted that the authority of the king in the state was like that of the father in a family, Tyrrell also attempted to show that male rule in the household was based upon consent. Where many Civil War pamphleteers had wondered whether the power that husbands naturally exercised over their wives could be revoked if it were abused, Tyrrell sought to justify the hierarchical relationship itself.

Tyrrell's work was indebted to the continental natural law theorists who insisted that consent—not nature or scriptural admonition alone— established the relationship of super- and sub-ordination in marriage. Grotius believed in the natural "superiority of [the male] sex,"[25] and argued that "the difference in sex" gives the husband authority over the wife even in the state of nature.[26] Pufendorf, however, was anxious to substitute the voluntary origin of women's secondary position in marriage for assumptions about her "natural" subjection.

> We presuppose at the outset that by nature all individuals have equal rights, and no one enjoys authority over another, unless it has been secured by an act of himself or the other. For although, as a general thing, the male surpasses the female in strength of body and mind, yet that superiority is of itself far from being capable of giving the former authority over the latter. Therefore, whatever right a man has over a woman, inasmuch as she is his equal, will have to be secured by her consent, or by a just war.[27]

Tyrrell's thought about the authority of husband over wife was beset by ambivalence. On the one hand, he argued that a wife's subjection to her husband had to be established by her own consent. Discussing parental authority, Tyrrell stated that

> the power of the Father does not commence barely from Generation, but is acquired from the Contract of Marriage; which (till I meet with some reason to the contrary) I see not why it might not be so agreed by the contract, that the Father should not dispose of the Children without the Mother's consent. . . .[28]

This implied that the marriage contract involved something more than the consent to marry and might contain stipulations about the terms of the relationship. Tyrrell made a serious effort to shift the ground of woman's subordination in marriage from scripture to nature and finally to her own consent.

On the other hand, Tyrrell also asserted that "the woman, as the weaker vessel, is to be subject to the Man, as the stronger, stouter, and commonly the wiser creature."[29] Such an argument from nature seriously undercut his contractarian impulses. Even when Tyrrell tried to bring these two points of view together by arguing that women themselves accepted their inferiority when they agreed to marry, he allowed a woman to subject herself to her husband so that she became "as a Slave."[30]

Tyrrell's efforts to ground familial as well as political authority in consent was not wholly successful. Despite his contractarian convictions, Tyrrell believed that God and nature dictated that men should rule their households. Further, while Tyrrell thought the political contract was revocable, he, like his Civil War predecessors, could not bring himself to sanction divorce. Tyrrell insisted that "Christ hath taken away the liberty of divorce," which even in Mosaic law existed only for adultery. Indeed, Tyrrell concluded that men should be allowed to chastize their wives without reproof or hindrance precisely because they do not have the recourse of divorcing them![31]

Tyrrell is typical of liberal thinkers who wrote between the Civil War pamphleteers and John Locke. His adoption of natural law reasoning allowed him to solve certain problems which had beset the former when they compared the marriage contract to the original pact between king and people, but his adherence to a patriarchal conception of marriage left it to Locke to carry the implications of the contractarian image of marriage to their logical conclusions.

John Locke's Resolution of the Republican Dilemma: Limited and Revocable Marriage Contracts

John Locke made great strides toward resolving the dilemma faced by those parliamentarians who attempted to argue with royalist theorists over the nature of the marriage contract. Locke did not make a sudden new departure from earlier thought about the family, but he took the premises of the natural freedom and equality of family members more seriously than had previous thinkers. In doing so, he strengthened the liberal arguments concerning the voluntary origin of all obligations.

Nonetheless, even as he solved certain conceptual dilemmas which permeated early liberal discussions of the relationship between marriage contract and social contract, Locke emphatically rejected the notion that familial and civil authority were analogous. Both Locke's individualism and his spurning of the family/state analogy were to affect future discussions of marriage and the family.

Anti-royalist use of the marriage contract/social contract analogy had floundered on the notions that even though men and women possessed the same rights in the state of nature, husbands were superior to wives in marriage; that it was impossible to make stipulations to alter that hierarchical relationship; and that the parties enjoyed no right of revocation of their marriage contract no matter how discomfiting it became. If theorists took this view of marriage contract to be analogous to the political contract, there could be no justification for the resistance to Charles I or for the Glorious Revolution.

Locke's first step in resolving these difficulties was to abandon unequivocally reasoning from scripture in favor of natural law theory. Locke did not deny that scripture might be a guide to God's will. He did not, however, rely on biblical writ to discover the proper bases of human relationships. This freed him from debates over the correct interpretation of contested biblical passages, and allowed him to consider afresh and more radically both the political and the marital bonds.

Locke began his reconsideration of marriage and the marriage contract indirectly, in the course of his analysis of patriarchal ideas concerning parents and children. Locke rejected the patriarchal premise that generation creates paternal rights which last until the father dies or surrenders them. Children are, of course, born dependent upon their parents. But temporary dependency is not the same thing as life-long subordination. Children cast off their subordination to their parents as they cast off their swaddling clothes: "Age and Reason as [children] grow up, loosen [the Bonds of Subjection to parents] till at length they drop quite off, and leave Man at his own free Disposal."[32] Indeed, children have no *duties* until they know the law of nature, and then their duty is to owe "honour, respect, gratitude and assistance" to their parents;[33] parents, on the other hand, have the duty to nurture and educate their children.[34]

Locke's consideration of parents' duties to care for the child led him to discuss the relationship between father and mother, husband and wife. Locke insisted that *both* parents are required by the Law of Nature to care for their children.[35] Attributing parental duties to mother and father

alike, of course, served Locke well in his argument against the patriarchalists,

> for it will but very ill serve the turn of those Men who contend so
> much for the Absolute Power and Authority of the *Fatherhood*, as
> they call it, that the *Mother* should have a share in it. And it
> would have but ill-supported the *Monarchy* they contend for,
> when by the very name it appeared that the Fundamental Author-
> ity from whence they would derive their Government of a single
> Person only, was not placed in one, but two persons jointly.[36]

It might appear that Locke's attribution of parental authority and responsibility to mothers was simply an expedient of the anti-patriarchal argument. After arguing that mothers share in parental authority he quickly
slipped back into using the common phrase "paternal" power rather than
"Parental" power,[37] or used the terms as if they were interchangeable.[38]
On balance, I think that this resulted from the force of customary usage.
Locke made his *theoretical* point self-consciously when he asserted that
"paternal" power should be termed "parental," and that "whatever obligation Nature and the right of Generation lays on Children, it must certainly bind them equally to both the concurrent Causes of it."[39]

To argue that the child is obligated to mother and father alike showed
only that a woman could exercise authority over her child; it did not say
anything of her relationship to her husband if the child were not involved. Locke based his analysis of the origin and nature of "conjugal
society" upon the contractarian model of the natural law theorists. Conjugal society is formed by "a voluntary Compact between Man and
Woman.[40] In contrast to others who argued that marriage was the result
of contract, meaning thereby consent to the pre-established duties of the
marital state, Locke extended the analogy of contract and suggested that
the parties themselves might not only agree to marry, but might set at
least some of the terms of their relationship.

Locke explicitly rejected the notion that marriage requires absolute
sovereignty in the husband: "the ends of Matrimony requiring no such
Power in the Husband, the Condition of *Conjugal* Society put it not
in him, it being not at all necessary to that State."[41] The only thing
which nature does dictate about the marriage contract, in its essence,
therefore "consist[s] chiefly in such Communion and Right in one anoth-
ers Bodies, as is necessary to its chief End, Procreation," along with "mu-

tual Support, and Assistance, and a Communion of Interest too, as necessary not only to unite their Care, and Affection, but also necessary to their common Off-spring, who have a Right to be nourished and maintained by them. . . ."[42]

It is the exigencies of the care of children, not any particular attribute of either sex, which set the only natural or *prima facie* terms to the marital relationship. Therefore, argued Locke, many of the conditions which now seem to be intrinsic to the married state, need not be so at all. Stipulations concerning any of these conditions might themselves be set by contract. "Community of Goods, and the Power over them, mutual Assistance, and Maintenance, and other things belonging to Conjugal Society, might be varied and regulated by that Contract, which unites Man and Woman in that Society, as far as may be consistent with Procreation and the bringing up of Children. . . ."[43] Locke carried the implications of his contractarian view of marriage to the point of arguing not only that the terms of the relationship could be set by contract, but also that once the ends of the contract are fulfilled, it might be terminated.

> It would give one reason to enquire, why this Compact, where Procreation and Education are secured, and Inheritance taken care for, may not be made determinable, either by consent, or at a certain time, or upon certain Conditions, as well as any other voluntary Compacts, there being no necessity in the nature of the thing, nor to the ends of it, that it should always be for Life.[44]

Beginning from the premises that the end of marriage is the procreation and nurture of children and that marriage is a contractual relationship, Locke concluded that husband and wife might set whatever terms they wished to their relationship so long as these were conducive to the care of their young.

Locke did not, however, completely abandon male supremicist notions with regard to marriage and the family. Marriage, he thought, could not be a completely egalitarian relationship because it took two—and two only—to make a marriage; if husband and wife disagreed on anything concerning the management of the family, their differences could not be decided by majority rule.

> But Husband and Wife, though they have but one common Concern, yet having different understandings, will unavoidably some-

times have different wills, too; it therefore being necessary, that the last Determination, i.e., the Rule, should be placed somewhere, it naturally falls to the Man's share, as the abler and the stronger.[45]

This sounds like parts of Grotius, Pufendorf, and Parker, not to mention Filmer and Digges.

There are, however, two qualifications to Locke's bow to male superiority. First, Locke immediately remarked of this grant of power that it reaches only "to the things of their common Interest and Property." Where husband and wife disagree about their domicile or the purchase of households goods, for example, the husband has the final say. Nonetheless, even in these cases he noted that such matters may be regulated by contract.[46]

Second, other parts of Locke's theory seriously qualified the idea of the husband's superiority over his wife. At the very outset of the *Second Treatise* Locke asserted that "men live together by no other Rules but those of Beasts, where the strongest carries it . . ." emphatically rejecting the proposition that strength gives any right to rule.[47] Locke's qualification of the sphere of husbandly power reflected his (perhaps unconscious) discomfort with assigning a "natural" dominance of one being over another when both were free and equal in the state of nature.[48] It was a position his own theory could not support.

Locke carried the notion of the contractual nature of marriage very close to its logical conclusions. If all beings were free and equal in the state of nature, then when they agreed to marry they were free to set whatever terms to their relationship they wished, as long as these were consonant with the procreation and care of children. Locke did not take his voluntarism to the point of saying that the purpose of the association also had to be set by contract (a popular assertion today),[49] but this was the only absolute limit he placed on the couple's freedom. In Locke's view, the marriage contract was revocable, and its terms were negotiable. Locke's new picture of marriage eliminated the embarrassments which earlier anti-royalist writers encountered when they tried to speak of the analogy between the social contract and the marriage contract.

Although Locke had finally made the marriage contract compatible with parliamentarian ends, he broke with earlier theorists and rejected the idea that the family was analogous to civil society, and that the justification of authority in one realm was the same as the justification of authority in the other.

> I think that it may not be amiss, to set down what I take to be Political Power. That the Power of a *Magistrate* over a Subject, may be distinguished from that of a *Father* over his Children, a *Master* over her Servant, a *Husband* over his Wife, and a Lord over his Slave. . . . it may help us to distinguish these Powers one from another, and show the difference betwixt a Ruler of a Commonwealth, a Father of a Family, and a Captain of a Gallery.[50]

This was part and parcel of Locke's liberal politics—the family was a private association which preceded civil society and into which the state should not intrude. Precisely because he did view it was distinct from the political association, perhaps, Locke was able to maintain that the husband should exercize rule as "the abler and the stronger," while he rejected any such argument with respect to political authority.

Despite his capitulation to patriarchal ideas about male superiority, Locke anticipated important reforms in marriage law and practice. Locke's notion that contract might regulate property rights and maintenance obligations in marriage was an astonishing notion, and not for the seventeenth century alone. Only with the passage of the British and American Married Women's Property Acts in the latter half of the nineteenth century did either English or American law allow that "Community of Goods, and the [husband's exclusive] power over them" was not a necessary part of the marital order.[51] The law has continued to hold down to the present day that mutual assistance and maintenance by the husband are essential to the marriage relationship.[52] Similarly, Locke's notion that marriage might end "by consent, or at a certain time, or upon certain Conditions" anticipated reforms of our own day: limited term marriage and "no fault" divorce. When opponents of patriarchal practices in later centuries attacked both the formal (mainly legal) and informal underpinnings of the patriarchal family, among their strongest tools were the individualistic premises which Locke incorporated into both his political theory and his depiction of marriage.

Conclusion

John Locke both solved the theoretical dilemmas of earlier parliamentarians who had attempted to incorporate the view of marriage as an hierarchical and irrevocable relationship into an emerging liberal political framework. Locke's deep voluntaristic convictions and his sensitivity to more affectionate and egalitarian human relationships also influenced the terms in which people subsequently discussed marital rights and duties.[53] In this sense the analysis of marriage in the *Two Treatises* both culminated fifty years of changing images of marriage in political discourse, and laid the groundwork for ensuing debates concerning the "contractual" nature of marriage.

Notes

The author wishes to thank Professors Lawrence Stone of Princeton University, Julian Franklin of Columbia University, and Gordon Schochet of Rutgers University for their generous help and comments at various stages of this project.

1. Richard Baxter, *A Christian Directory* (London, 1673), 514.

2. Later discussions which draw on arguments suggested in the seventeenth century debates are found, for example, in Mary Wollstonecraft, *A Vindication of the Rights of Women* (New York: Norton, 1967), and in Harriet Taylor Mill and John Stuart Mill, *Essays on Sex Equality*, ed. Alice Rossi (Chicago: University of Chicago Press, 1970).

3. J. W. Grough, *The Social Contract: A Critical Study of Its Development* (Oxford: The Clarendon Press, 1936), 78.

4. Ibid., p. 79.

5. Henry Parker, *Observations upon Some of His Majesties Late Answers and Expresses* [London, 1642], 18–19; John Spelman, *A View of the Printed Book* (Oxford, 1642), 9.

6. Sir Dudley Digges, *The Unlawfulness of Subjects Taking up Armes against their Soveraigne, in what Case Soever* . . . (n.p., 1643), 3–4.

7. The debates over the nature of the original contract between king and people are too extensive to go into this paper. See J. G. A. Pocock, *The Ancient Constitution and the Feudal Law: A Study of English Historical Thought in the 17th Century* (New York: Norton, 1967), for an excellent summary and analysis of the issues involved.

8. Henry Ferne, *Conscience Satisfied: That there is no warrant for the Armes now taken up by Subjects* . . . (Oxford, 1643), 12. In Ferne's eyes, indeed, the case against resistance was even stronger than that against divorce. While divorce was forbidden to Christians, it had been allowed under Mosaic law, but no similar biblical sanction was given for political resistance. Ibid., 70.

9. Digges, *The Unlawfulness* . . . , 112.

10. Ibid., 112–13, emphasis added.

11. Ibid., 121.

12. Henry Ferne, *The Resolving of Conscience upon this Question, Whether* . . . *Subjects may take Armes and resist?* . . . (Cambridge, 1643), 19.

13. This and the following two paragraphs draw upon George Howard, *History of Matrimonial Institutions*, 3 vols. (Chicago: University of Chicago Press, 1904), 2:60–75; L. Chilton Powell, *English Domestic Relations, 1487–1653* (New York: Columbia University Press, 1917), 1–100, esp. pp. 61–65; Ernest Sirluck, "Introduction," *Complete Prose Works of John Milton*, ed. Don M. Wolfe (New Haven: Yale University Press, 1953–74), 2:144–57 and 237.

14. Powell remarks that posting a bond against remarriage did not curb the abuse of remarriage after divorce *a mensa et thoro*. The bond functioned more as a penalty than an insurmountable

impediment; the party who remarried sacrificed the security he had posted. Powell, *English Domestic Relations*, p. 87 at note 1.

15. Ibid., p. 81.

16. William Whately, for example, in his book *A Bride-bush* (London, 1619), as quoted in Powell, *English Domestic Relations*, 68–69, wrote that: ". . . if it shall fall out, that either of the married persons shall forwardly and perversely withdraw themselves from this matrimoniall societie (which fault is termed desertion), the person thus offending, hath so farre violated the covenant of marriage, that . . . the bond of matrimony is dissolved, and the other party so truly and totally loosed from it, that (after an orderly proceeding with the Church and Magistrate in that behalf) it shall be no sinne for him or her to make a new contract with another person." The most definitive statement of the reforming Puritans was that of the Assembly of 1643, published in 1651: ". . . in the case of adultery after marriage, it is lawful for the innocent party to sue out a divorce, and after the divorce to marry another as if the offending party were dead. Nothing but adultery or such wilful desertion as can no way be remedied, by the Church or Civil Magistrate, is cause sufficient of dissolving the bond of marriage. . . ." *The Late Assembly of Divine Confession of Faith* (London, 1651), quoted in ibid., 88.

17. Ferne, *The Resolving of Conscience . . .* , 21.

18. William Bridge, *The Wounded Conscience Cured . . .* (London, 1642), 44.

An anonymous parliamentarian had introduced the notion of tacit agreement and limitation about a year earlier with the argument that "when the *Militia* of an Army is committed to the Generall, it is not with any expresse condition, that he shall not turn the mouths of his Cannons against his own Souldiers, for that is so naturally and necessarily implyed, that its needlesse to be expressed . . ." *A Question Answered: How Laws Are To Be Understood, and Obedience Yeelded*, quoted in Sirluck, "Introduction," *Complete Prose Works of John Milton*, 2:19.

19. Henry Parker, *Jus populi* (London, 1644), 4–5.

20. Herbert Palmer, *Scripture and Reason Pleaded for Defensive Armes* (London, 1643), 35–36. Emphasis added.

21. Milton, *Complete Prose Works of John Milton*, 2:229.

22. Powell, *English Domestic Relations*, 93, notes that the *Doctrine and Discipline* was considered "revolutionary." The Presbyterian clergy apparently attempted to get the work suspended. Sirluck, "Introduction," *Complete Prose Works of John Milton*, 2:140.

23. On Tyrrell's relationship to Locke see Peter Laslett, "Introduction," in John Locke, *Two Treatises of Government*, ed. Peter Laslett, rev. ed. (New York: Mentor Books, 1963), esp. 69–74.

24. James Tyrrell, *Patriarcha non Monarcha* (London, 1681), 64.

25. Hugo Grotius, *De Juri Belli ac Pacis Libri Tres* [*On the Law of War and Peace*] (1625), trans. Francis W. Kelsey (Oxford: Clarendon Press, 1925) Book II, ch. V. sec. i, p. 231.

26. Ibid., V, viii, 234.

27. Samuel Pufendorf, *De Jure Naturae et Gentium Libri Octo* [*On the Law of Nature and Nations*] (1673), trans. C. H. Oldfather and W. A. Oldfather (Oxford: The Clarendon Press, 1934), Book VI, ch. 1, sec. 9, p. 853 (hereinafter VI, ch. 1, o, 853).

28. Tyrrell, *Patriarcha non Monarcha*, 14–15.

29. Ibid., 14.

30. Ibid., 110. Similarly, while Tyrrell thinks that a married woman might retain the right to control those things which pertain to her as an *individual* (such as managing her inheritance and making contracts or taking vows), the husband must control those matters which pertain to her as a *wife* (such as domicile). A women, in effect, consents to abandon her individuality when she marries and becomes part of a unit which the husband controls.

The notion of female subordination in marriage was even clearer in Tyrrell's *Biblioteca politica* than in *Patriarcha non Monarcha*. In *Biblioteca politica* Tyrrell remarked that political power cannot be derived from paternal power because women and children were subject to the husband/father *before* the Fall. In contrast, political power entered human life only after the Fall, when "the state of Mankind was altered." When women consent to marry, they simply agree to abide by that order which God himself ordained, they do not create a new authority in their husbands unknown in Eden. James Tyrrell, *Biblioteca politica* (London, 1691/92), 11.

31. Tyrrell, *Patriarcha non Monarcha*, 111.

32. John Locke, *Two Treatises*, II, 55, p. 347.

33. Ibid., II, 66, p. 354.

34. "The *Power*, then, *that Parents have* over their Children, arises from that Duty which is incumbent on them, to take care of their Off-spring, during the imperfect state of Childhood." Ibid., II, 58, p. 348. Also, "The first part of then of *Paternal* power, or rather Duty . . . is Education. . . ." Ibid., II, 69, p. 356. Locke remarked in his notebook that "education not generation gives the obligation and the affection of children to their parents. John Locke, *The Educational Writings of John Locke*, ed. James L. Axtell (Cambridge: Cambridge University Press, 1968), 112 at note 4.

35. Locke, *Two Treatises*, II, 56, p. 347.

36. Ibid., II, 53, p. 346.

37. See, for example, ibid., II, 105, 107, 110, 112, 118.

38. See, for example, ibid., II, 69, 170, 173. See also Gordon Schochet, *Patriarchalism in Political Thought* (New York: Basic Books, 1975), p. 249.

39. Locke, *Two Treatises*, II, 52, p. 343; see also I, 55 and 61 and II, 86.

40. Ibid., II, 78, p. 362.

41. Ibid., II, 83, p. 365. This passage makes it clear that an earlier passage in the *Second Treatise* which states that God may "by manifest Declaration of his Will set one [being] above another, and confer on him by an evident and clear appointment an undoubted Right to Dominion and Sovereignty," does not refer to the rule of men over women. Ibid., II, 4, p. 309.

42. Ibid., II, 78, p. 362.

43. Ibid., II, 83, p. 365.

44. Locke, *Two Treatises*, II, 81, p. 364.

45. Ibid., II, 82, p. 364.

46. Ibid., II, 83, p. 365.

47. Locke does acknowledge that certain inequalities (such as one person being "abler" than another), may give "a just Precedency," but not a right to rule. Ibid., II, 54, p. 346. I am indebted to Dr. Nathan Tarcov of the University of Chicago for this observation.

48. Ibid., II, 1, p. 308. My sense that Locke was considerably less happy than his fellow contractarians with the assumption of male dominance in marriage is reinforced by his attitude toward women in *Some Thoughts Concerning Education*. Locke thought that girls might well receive much the same education as boys. In February 1685 he wrote to Mrs. Clarke in response to a letter from her apparently asking whether his strictures for Edward Jr. might also be applied to the education of young Elizabeth Clarke. Locke answered: "Since therefore I acknowledge no difference of sex in your mind relating . . . to truth, virtue, and obedience, I think well to have no thing altered in it from what is [writ for the son] . . . There is only one or two things whereof I think distinct consideration is to be had." Girls, says Locke, should exercise outdoors just as boys do, but should be shielded from the sun. They should wear wet shoes to condition themselves against colds (a pet theory of Locke's) just as boys do, but Locke is worried it "will be thought both an odd and new thing" and so will not insist on it. "This is all I can think of at present, wherein the treatment of your girls should be different from that I have proposed for the boys." Ibid., pp. 344–46.

49. The idea of "contract marriage," in which couples would themselves decide such matters as the goals of their relationship, what support and property provisions they desire both during the marriage and in the event of divorce, and when and under what conditions they will divorce is the latest manifestation of the continuing discussion of the extent of contract in mariage. See, among many others, L. Edmiston, "How to Write Your Own Marriage Contract," *Ms.* (Spring 1972): 66–72;

K. Fleishmann, "Marriage by Contract: Defining the Terms of the Relationship," *Family Law Quarterly* 8 (Spring 1974): 27–49; N. Sherensky and M. Mannes, "A Radical Guide to Wedlock," *Saturday Review* (July 29, 1972): 33; L. Weitzman. "Legal Regulation of Marriage: Tradition and Change," *California Law Review* 62 (July–September 1974): 1249–78.

50. Locke, *Two Treatises*, II, 2, p. 308.

51. The common law held that husband and wife were "one person" in the law. As a consequence, marriage resulted in the "civil death" of the women. A wife could contract neither with her husband nor with third parties; a husband took control of his wife's property; a wife could not sue or be sued without her husband joining her. The Married Women's Property Acts declared that women could buy, sell, and otherwise manage their own property. The Acts were therefore an important attack on the common law doctrine of spousal unity. See Leo Kanowitz, *Women and the Law: The Unfinished Revolution* (Albuquerque: University of New Mexico Press, 1969).

53. On the legal duties of husbands and wives, see Kanowitz, *Women and the Law*, 35–99.

53. I find evidence of Locke's more tender sensibilities both in the *Two Treatises* and, particularly, in *Some Thoughts Concerning Education*. For example, with regard to the relationship between parent and child, Locke advises Clarke, "as [your son] approaches more to a Man, admit him nearer your familiarity: So shall you have him your obedient Subject (as is fit) whilst he is a Child, and your affectionate Friend, when he is a Man." (sec. 40, p. 145). Children should come to regard their parents as "their best, their only sure Friends; and as such love and reverence them" (sec. 41, p. 145). And Locke also recognizes that nurtured by the parents' efforts as much as by the child's: "Many Fathers, though they proportion to their Sons liberal Allowances, yet they keep the knowledge of their Estates, and Concerns, from them with as much reservedness, as if they were guarding a secret of State from a Spy, or an Enemy. . . . And I cannot but often wonder to see Fathers, who love their Sons very well, yet so order the matter by a constant Stiffness . . . as if they were never to Enjoy or have any comfort from those they love best in the World . . . (96, p. 202). This aspect of Locke's work lends a new perspective to the dominant contemporary view of Locke as the apologist for the acquisitive ethic and material inequality of modern society. That view owes much to C. B. Macpherson, *The Political Theory of Possessive Individuallism: Hobbes to Locke* (Oxford: The Clarendon Press, 1962).

Afterword

Equality, Liberty, and Marriage Contracts

Mary Lyndon Shanley

The invitation to revisit "Marriage Contract and Social Contract in Seventeenth Century English Political Thought" after twenty-five years gave me a welcome opportunity to think about how my ideas have developed and changed in the intervening years. And while I still find basically sound my views on the use of analogy in the pamphlet wars of the English Civil War, I now find the idea of the contract as a model for the marriage relationship problematic. I will engage, not the interpretations of Locke that have appeared since I published "Marriage Contract and Social Contract," such as Kirstie McClure's excellent *Judging Rights*,[1] but instead (albeit sketchily) recent debates in feminist theory and jurisprudence about families and marriage.

I remember distinctly the moment at which the questions that led me to the research for this article entered my mind. I was reading the *Second Treatise* in preparation for an Introduction to Political Theory class when I was struck by Locke's contention that "tho' [there] are ties upon mankind which make the conjugal bonds . . . firm and lasting in man . . . yet it would give one reason to enquire, why this compact, where procreation and education are secured . . . may not be made determinable, either by consent, or at a certain time, or upon certain conditions, as well as any other voluntary compacts, there being no necessity in the nature of the thing, nor to the ends of it, that it should be for life." English law did not allow for civil divorce (except by Act of Parliament) until 1857, and then only for adultery, and the kind of "no fault" consensual divorce that Locke was envisioning appeared in England and the United States only in the mid-twentieth century, nearly three hundred years after Locke wrote. What was going on here? Where had Locke gotten this idea; did other writers of his time entertain the same notion; how seriously did he advance the idea of consensual divorce; to what extent did he think marriage was a contractual—and so a conventional and humanly constructed rather than a natural—relationship?

In "Marriage Contract and Social Contract" I argued that there was great radical potential in two aspects of Locke's view of marriage as a contract. One was the idea that women and men were the same in rational and moral capacity. The other was that (at least some of) the terms of marriage could be set by the marriage partners themselves, suggesting that marriage was the result of a contractual agreement. This, in turn, reinforced the idea that the marriage partners were to be regarded as equals, since contracts are agreements struck between equals.

Locke takes neither of these positions unambiguously in the *Second Treatise*. He follows his assertion that men and women are equals with the observation that while there is no way to make decisions by majority vote in a marriage, since it is necessary "that the last Determination, i.e., the Rule, should be placed somewhere, it naturally falls to the Man's share, as the abler and the stronger."[2] So much for equal rationality and moral authority (and so much for Locke's assertion that strength alone does not make right). Moreover, while Locke flew in the face of both ecclesiastical and civil law by asserting that the duration of marriage could be set by agreement, he regarded the procreation and rearing of children as the self-evident and "given" end or purpose of marriage. Thus some of the terms of marriage were given in nature, and some might be decided by the wills of the partners.

The tensions in Locke's thought were not simply the result of an idiosyncratic failure to carry his ideas through to their logical conclusion, or of an inability to break free of the assumption of his times. Rather, they also reflect qualities that have made it difficult for liberal theory to encompass family relationships and have divided feminists in our own day.

The first tension concerns how to carry out concretely liberalism's commitment to equality: Is the equality between women and men best conceptualized and reflected in policy by treating them similarly or differently? Should laws be framed in gender neutral terms (sameness) or in a way that takes into account sexual and reproductive capacities (difference)? With respect to marriage, should wives be treated differently than husbands, should mothers be treated differently than fathers? The second tension concerns how to realize liberalism's commitment to liberty: To what degree should marriage partners be able to set the terms to their own relationship? Or, to ask the same question the other way around, what, if any, legitimate interest does the state have in marriage? When I wrote "Marriage Contract and Social Contract," I simply noted these tensions and then optimistically assumed that once the sexism underlying the contradictions was exposed, progress would just be a matter of working out the details of the nonsexist part of the dilemma. But things are not so simple. Committed feminists are still debating the nature of human autonomy and freedom, of sexual equality, and of parental and spousal relationships. Interestingly, their disputes are rooted in the passages in the *Second Treatise* that grabbed my attention in the late 1970s.

Equality

At the heart of "Marriage Contract and Social Contract" was a deeply felt aspiration for and commitment to achieving spousal equality. Looking back, I suspect that the reason I paused on Locke's call for consensual divorce and his challenges to patriarchal authority in the family had as much to do with my personal experiences and stage of life as it did with my scholarly ability to identify an anachronism like consensual divorce when I saw one. My commitment to spousal equality reflected both the agenda of "Second Wave" feminism to dismantle sources of inequality between men and women, and my own situation as a recently married young woman hoping to forge a genuinely reciprocal, mutually respectful, marital relationship. I clearly thought I had found in the ideas of John Locke not only a persuasive rebuttal to royalist arguments for the supremacy of king over Parliament, but principles that might be used to ground women's equal citizenship and to reconstruct gender relations.

It was not inevitable or logically necessary that Locke consider the nature of the marriage contract in order to respond to Filmer. In rejecting Filmer's analogy that the king has the same authority over subjects that husbands have over wives, or fathers over children, Locke could have said, "Women are simply different than men, so we don't need to worry about the similarity or difference between marriage contract and social contract. Wives are to be subject to their husbands by nature, it is true, but a citizen is not a wife and is bound only by consent." By this line of reasoning, the social contract might have become a pact among men (and perhaps unmarried women) who were equals, while the marriage contract remained hierarchical. Gordon Schochet's *Patriarchalism and Political Thought* explores Locke's refutation of Filmer's ideas, while Teresa Brennan and Carole Pateman in "Mere Auxiliaries to the Commonwealth" (Chapter 2) explained how it was that a "free and equal female individual [was] always assumed to place herself under the authority of a free and equal male individual." By the sexual contract women became subordinate to their husbands. These male heads of household then entered the social contract, rendering women auxiliaries to rather than authors of the commonwealth.

The potential remained, however, to return to the notion of free and equal individuals—male and female—and to reexamine and restructure both marriage contract and social contract. In *Feminism, Marriage, and the Law in Victorian England*, I showed how nineteenth-century feminists in both England and the United States invoked classical liberal notions of individual freedom and equality to argue both for woman suffrage and for the end to the common law doctrine of coverture by which a married woman's legal personality was subsumed in that of her husband. Coverture denied married women the right to enter into contractual relationships. Nineteenth-century feminists argued forcefully that this denied them fundamental rights of self-possession. The right to *possess* property belonged to all individuals and was an essential component of the right not to *be* property. Marriage law grossly violated a married woman's rights to freedom and equality by taking away her independent legal personality when she married, subordinating her to her husband's will, and subjecting her to restrictions that did not apply to unmarried women or to any men. In feminists' hands, liberal political theory became a tool with which to dismantle the ideological and legal underpinnings of the subordination of married women and their exclusion from the activities of public life.[3]

Only by assuming that the principles of justice that should govern the public realm did not apply to family relations, feminists argued, could one rationalize the legal subordination of wives to their husbands. And only by assuming that being members of a family excluded women, but not men, from the public sphere, could one justify women's disfranchisement. Women's domestic and political subjection were interlocking and mutually reinforcing.

What are the possibilities for confronting and eliminating this domination? The question of what difference sexual difference, in particular women's childbearing capability, makes is one of the most intractable that feminists have faced. Mary Wollstonecraft thought that women should be the custodial parents of their children, because they bore and raised them. Carole Pateman insists in *The Sexual Contract* that "to take embodied identity seriously demands the abandonment of the masculine, unitary individual to open up space for two figures; one masculine, one feminine." Teresa Brennan wrote in the Afterword to Chapter 2 of this book of the "rights of the flesh" as well as of labor. Martha Fineman calls for different treatment for "Mothers" than for other adults and for custodial rights to rest exclusively with Mothers in her book *The Neutered Mother*.[4]

When I wrote "Marriage Contract and Social Contract," my ideal was more gender neutral, and that hasn't changed very much despite the fact that the insights of alternative viewpoints makes me constantly question my position. An example of my attempt to use similar rather than sex-differentiated rules for men and women was contained in my discussion in *Making Babies, Making Families* of whether unwed fathers should be accorded any parental rights immediately following the birth of their offspring. Arguing against *both* those who say biology creates parental rights ("my sperm, my baby") and against those who argue that until the child has received care for some period of time outside the womb the mother alone should be recognized as the custodial parent, I contended that the unwed father should be accorded some parental status if (and only if) he performs actions analogous to those of the pregnant woman.

Actions analogous to carrying a fetus might include providing physical, financial, and emotional support to the pregnant woman and publicly acknowledging his paternity and desire to care for the child. Consistent efforts to act responsibly toward the fetus and the mother might create the right to seek custody if the mother decides to relinquish the child for adoption. I argued that the provision of care is a large part of the grounding of parental rights, and that caregiving activity combined with biology in the case of unwed fathers, and with clear expressions of an intent to parent in the case of nonbiological lesbian co-mothers, could establish their parental claims from the moment of birth.[5]

I am much more skeptical today than I was when I wrote "Marriage Contract and Social Contract" of the liberatory power of unreconstructed liberalism. In fact, *unreconstructed* liberalism does not have such a potential. I am still a liberal, however, in the sense of endorsing equality and freedom as foundational values of political life and in believing that it should be possible to develop an understanding of the human individual that recognizes sexual difference without endorsing gender roles and inequalities. But how to get from a present in which sexual hierarchy predominates in familial and public institutions to a future in which such hierarchy does not exist is a real problem. On the one hand, if one treats people who are differentially situated by similar or "equal" rules, the result will be inequality. Lenore Weitzman in *The Divorce Revolution* and Martha Fineman in *The Illusion of Inequality* demonstrated that similar treatment of men and women in divorce creates injustices both with respect to financial resources and to child custody and visitation.[6] On the other hand, if one uses different rules for women and men, one reinscribes difference and runs the risk of perpetuating subordination.

I don't see any easy or quick resolution to the debate about sameness or difference as the foundation for equality for two reasons. First, people differ in their perceptions of the strength of the link between sex and gender, that is, between sex characteristics and social roles. Second, figuring out what in practice will produce greater lived equality between women and men requires what Aristotle called "practical wisdom" or knowledge of how things transpire in the world. Such knowledge is hard to come by, and unanticipated events and unintended consequences constantly force reconsideration of what one thought one knew. Locke was able to have sameness and difference, along with human equality and gender hierarchy, only by embedding a contradiction in the center of his depiction of both the marriage contract and the social contract: women and men were equals, and women were men's subordinates. Contemporary feminists cannot accept this contradiction; it is theoretically incoherent and practically an affront to equality. But the debate on how best to get beyond the contradiction continues.

Liberty

The second tension in Locke's theory was his assertion that a husband and wife could agree to end their marriage when their children were grown, but that providing for children until they reached the age of majority was a "given" that was not subject to the agreement of the marriage partners. Marriage, it appeared, was both a "natural" and a "contractual" relationship.

The assertion that the care and upbringing of children till they reach their majority is the purpose of marriage reflects in part the fact that in an age before reliable contraception any act of sexual intercourse might result in pregnancy. I'm not sure what Locke thought created parents' obligation to take care of and educate their offspring. Was it procreation itself—the fact of being one of the child's biological parents—or was it marriage? Under the common law it was marriage. A biological father was not responsible for his children born out of wedlock: a child of an unmarried woman was *filius nulli*, the child of no one. The child of a married woman, in contrast, was presumed to be the child of her husband, regardless of whether or not he was the biological father. Children born within marriage were thus protected from the stigma and practical consequences of bastardy. A man's legal relationship to a child's mother determined whom the law would regard as that child's parents.

Locke assumed that parents have a natural obligation to sustain and raise their children; indeed, Locke regarded parents as acting as stewards for God in sustaining and supporting their children. But are both parents obligated to their children? Clearly Locke thought that they were if they were married, and did not address the question of unmarried parents. It seems as if people who have a child together (or intend to have a child together) are obligated to marry, and raising their child(ren) imposes obligations that are not subject to contract or modifiable by the adults' wills. Other aspects of marriage, however, may be subject to contract, and the relationship itself may be dissolved at will once children are grown or (Locke's reasoning suggests) if there are no children.

In our own day, without reference to Locke, feminist legal theorist Martha Fineman has seized upon the tension between contractual and natural ordering of families that lies at the heart of Locke's discussion of marriage and carried both his view of natural obligations and his contractualism to their respective logical conclusions. Fineman argues that the legal construction of family relationships that begins with the relationship of man and woman and then proceeds to their relationship with children approaches the matter the wrong way around. Analysis and legal regulation of family life, she contends, should begin not with marriage—the horizontal relationship between man and woman—but rather with the vertical relationship between generations. The relationship between child and caregiver is one of inevitable dependency and cannot properly be thought of as contractual.[7]

Human intimacy and care are at the core of family life, and the primary caretaking unit is that of caregiver (whom Fineman calls the Mother, but insists can be either a man or a woman) and child. So important is caregiving to children's welfare and the well-being of the nation, that governmental and nongovernmental associations and programs must provide support to caregivers and children, sustaining those relationships which provide the necessary context for raising the next generation.

Fineman's proposal takes the Mother/child dyad, not the marital couple, as the foundational familial relationship. Once the Mother/child relationship is recognized and supported, if adults then want to join together in performing these functions, they can marry by contractual agreement. In Fineman's hands, Locke's question becomes, "Where the children are provided for, why have state-defined marriage at all?" If the purpose of marriage has been the care of children, and now children and their caregivers will be provided for by both remunerative labor and the state, then let the adult partners decide *all* aspects of their relationship for themselves. There are other proponents of contract marriage, but Fineman's brilliance was to recognize the moral and practical imperative of providing for children's well-being, and of making that a public rather than a private responsibility. With public provision for children's well-being, the way was open to make marriage a genuinely contractual relationship, not a state-defined status masquerading as one.

Does Fineman's proposal resolve the problem created by the fact that when Locke depicted the social contract, he imagined all those agreeing to it as unencumbered individuals (and therefore male), rather than imagining some of them as adults who were taking care of children? If the Mother/child relationship is noncontractual, and the marriage relationship is contractual, is it appropriate for the state to outline the duties of the custodial parent (the Mother), and leave the terms of the marriage contract to the partners themselves? Are contracts in lieu of marriage the logical conclusion for those who agree with Locke that the purposes of marriage are not given in nature?

Although I admire Fineman's attentiveness to caregiving and her insistence that children's needs should be met regardless of the marital status of their parents, I think contracts in lieu of marriage cannot do the work of reconstructing marriage on egalitarian and reciprocal grounds. The emancipatory potential of contract is limited because contract has limited ability to rewrite economic realities, cultural conditioning, and social pressure as forces shaping marriage and other relationships.

Contract implies a relationship between equals, but the social mechanism of contract places excessive rule-writing authority in the hands of the powerful. John Stuart Mill lambasted the notion that women could be said to choose freely to marry. First, the terms of the marriage contract were given, and could not be negotiated by individual couples. Second, if a woman did not marry, what else could she do to support herself? he asked. Few remunerative occupations were open to women in the nineteenth century; for them, marriage was a "Hobson's choice," "that or none." Marx similarly saw the way in which the notion of "freedom of contract" masked relationships of unequal power; employer and employee are scarcely in equal bargaining positions.

The individualism and emphasis on rational bargaining that are at the heart of contracts rest on misleading models of the person. Marriage partners are not only autonomous decision-makers; they are fundamentally social beings who will inevitably experience need, change, and dependency in the course of their lives. While the obligations of adult to child are absolute, because the child cannot fend for itself, it is a mistake to draw a bright line between childhood dependency and adult self-sufficiency, whether material or emotional.

Moreover, while contracts are useful devices for facilitating communication about each partner's expectations and aspirations, not all of what spouses may properly expect of each other can be stipulated in advance. Contracts create obligations by volition and agreement; they do not account well for the obligations that may arise from unforeseen circumstances, including illness or disability of an aging parent, a spouse, or a child.

What does it mean when liberals assert that people can only be bound by agreements of their own making, a question explored at length although with different examples by Nancy Hirschmann in *Rethinking Obligation*?[8] Does respect for liberty demand that people actually choose their courses of action, or is it sufficient that they agree to measures to which any rational person would consent (regardless of momentary inclination)? In particular, does respect for the liberty of marriage partners require that they actually set the terms of their association, or is it sufficient that the terms of marriage meet criteria of justice? As Fineman has developed the first position with respect to marriage, Susan Okin and Martha Nussbaum have taken the lead in applying Rawlsian principles to the understanding of what a just marriage law would entail.[9] The debate over contracts in lieu of marriage reminds me of Hannah Pitkin's essay "Obligation and Consent," in which she argues that people's obligation to obey the law does not stem from any actual act of consent (either tacit or explicit), but rather from the nature of the government that enacted the laws. The proper question, said Pitkin, is not "When did I consent?" but "Is this government of the sort to which a rational person would give consent?"[10] This leads in turn to the question of the characteristics of a legitimate government. With respect to marriage, one should ask, "Are the laws governing marriage those under which a person would agree to live regardless of whether the person is male or female?"

The tension in Locke's depiction of marriage as, on the one hand, a contractual agreement whose terms might be set by the partners themselves and, on the other hand, as a civil status whose terms were given by nature, surfaced only occasionally during the three centuries prior to the passage of no-fault divorce laws in the late 1960s. The divorce revolution, followed by the movement for women's legal equality, called into question not only particular marriage laws but also the entire rationale for state-defined marriage.

When I wrote "Marriage Contract and Social Contract," I thought that once the contradictions in Locke's thought were uncovered, the egalitarian aspects of his thought could be developed and the traditional assumptions about sex role differences and sexual hierarchy in marriage, now discredited, would be discarded. Law and social practice could be reconstituted, I thought, on the egalitarian premises that I regarded as more fundamental to Locke's theory. My subsequent work on marriage and family law made me realize that things are not so simple. Feminist theorists have not resolved the deep issues concerning the gendered individual, the status of the child, inevitable dependencies not only between children and adults but also among adults, and the relationship between contract and human freedom that are embedded in Locke's inconsistencies. Feminist thinkers whom I profoundly respect vigorously refute the view that the idea of the social contract can be salvaged. They reject my attempt to use the idea of the social contract as a hypothetical agreement among largely androgynous beings who are thoroughly acquainted with the dynamics of sex discrimination and the burdens of childrearing. Many contend that the only way to have marriage reflect the values of equality and freedom is to abolish state-defined marriage and have a regime of state protection of Mothers and their children and contracts in lieu of marriage.[11] Revisiting Locke shows us something of the genealogy of our present dilemmas and disagreements.

Notes

1. Kirstie McClure, *Judging Rights: Lockean Politics and the Limits of Consent* (Ithaca: Cornell University Press, 1996).

2. John Locke, *Two Treatises of Government*, ed. Peter Laslett, rev. ed. (New York: Mentor Books, 1963), 2.82.

3. Zillah Eisenstein, *The Radical Future of Liberal Feminism* (New York: Longman, 1981), analyzes the radical potential of the liberal ideas of equality and liberty.

4. Carole Pateman, *The Sexual Contract* (Stanford: Stanford University Press, 1988), 224; Martha Albertson Fineman, *The Neutered Mother, the Sexual Family, and Other Twentieth Century Tragedies* (New York: Routledge, 1995).

5. Mary Lyndon Shanley, *Making Babies, Making Families* (Boston: Beacon Press, 2001), chap. 2.

6. Lenore J. Weitzman, *The Divorce Revolution: The Unexpected Social and Economic Consequences for Women and Children in America* (New York: Free Press, 1985); Martha Albertson Fineman, *The Illusion of Equality: The Rhetoric and Reality of Divorce Reform* (Chicago: University of Chicago Press, 1991).

7. Fineman, *Neutered Mother*.

8. Nancy J. Hirschmann, *Rethinking Obligation* (Ithaca: Cornell University Press, 1992).

9. Susan Miller Okin, *Justice, Gender, and the Family* (New York: Basic Books, 1989); Martha C. Nussbaum, *Sex and Social Justice* (New York: Oxford University Press, 1999).

10. Hannah Pitkin, "Obligation and Consent: I," *American Political Science Review* 59, no. 4 (December 1965): 990–99.

11. Essays discussing these views are contained in Mary Lyndon Shanley, *Just Marriage*, ed. Deborah Chasman and Joshua Cohen (New York: Oxford University Press, 2004).

2

"Mere Auxiliaries to the Commonwealth": Women and the Origins of Liberalsim

Teresa Brennan and Carole Pateman

> ... the peculiar character of man's domination over woman in the modern family, and the necessity, as well as the manner, of establishing real social equality between the two, will be brought out into full relief only when both are completely equal before the law.
> —F. Engels, *The Origin of Family, Private Property and the State*.

Women, more specifically married women, constitute a permanent embarrassment and problem for liberal political theory. If this is not usually acknowledged, it is only because theorists rarely bother to consider whether their arguments have any relevance to women as well as men. Both the character and magnitude of the problem posed by married women, and the form of certain popular contemporary feminist arguments, can only be properly appreciated through an examination of the origins of liberal theory in the social contract theory of the seventeenth century. The arguments of Hobbes and Locke, which we shall discuss here, were developed as part of a conflict with patriarchal theorists. Yet, today, if women are taken into account in liberal theory, most writers retreat to patriarchal assumptions and assertions. The conflict between liberal and patriarchal theory is far from concluded: liberal theorists still have to confront, and answer, a very embarrassing question, namely, why it is that a free and equal female individual should always be assumed to place herself under the authority of a free and equal male individual.

The idea of individual freedom and equality, or the view that individuals are all "by nature" free and equal to each other, and its corollary that authority relationships are grounded in convention, have been bequeathed to liberal theory by the social contract theorists. The emergence of these ideas in the seventeenth century marked a decisive break with the traditional view that people were "naturally" bound together in an hierarchy of inequality and subordination. Traditionally, the family had also been seen as a model of, and symbol for, authority relationships throughout society. The belief that the family is the source of all authority relationships is basic to patriarchal theory, but the latter, as Schochet points out, emerged as a developed political theory at the same time as social contract theory.[1] Commentators on the political theory of the seventeenth century have recently begun to emphasize the importance of patriarchal ideas to all writers of the period, obscure as well as famous. For some, this provides another key to the reading of the classic texts; for Hinton, for example, "the least assailable side of [Hobbes's] argument" is his patriarchalism.[2] But such a claim can be made only by ignoring the fact that the contract theorists, and Hobbes in particular, denied the central tenets of patriarchal theory. Moreover, to emphasize patriarchal arguments does nothing to explain why it is that social contract theory and patriarchal theory emerged together and engaged in mutual criticism.

To find an explanation it is necessary to consider the integral relationship between political theories and specific forms of social life, a relationship that is also crucial to an understanding of the difficulties that married women pose for liberal theorists. Once the idea had gained ground that individuals were "naturally" free and equal, or were born free and equal to each other, the patriarchalists were forced to clarify and systematize their arguments in order to combat the spread of such a subversive conception. But why should the contract theorists have argued that individuals were born free and equal; why, in their theories, do such creatures inhabit the state of nature? Social contract theory was part and parcel of the emergence of the capitalist, market economy, and the liberal, constitutional state—of the emergence of liberal society. Individuals cannot be seen as freely entering contracts and making exchanges with each other in the market, and as able freely to pursue their interests, unless they have come to be conceived as free and equal to each other. Furthermore, unless they are seen in this fashion, they have no need voluntarily to agree to, or consent to, government or the exercise of authroity. To show that individuals were justified in consenting to government the contract theorists used the device of the state of nature. However, for individuals to be seen as free and equal "by nature," they must to some degree be seen in isolation from (or as separate from) other individuals, and in abstraction from their social relationships. Now, if individuals are conceived of in this abstract manner, their sex is irrelevant. Each abstract entity, taken singularly, is an "individual" with specified "natural" characteristics. But this means that the conception of "natural" individual freedom and equality is incompatible with patriarchal authority, whether that authority is exercised in the state or the family.

Or, at least, the two are incompatible all the time that females as well as males are seen as "individuals." *Logically,* there is no good reason why a liberal theorist should exclude females from this category; *in practice,* an in most liberal political theory, for three centuries the "free and equal individual" has been a male. Discussions of patriarchal arguments unfailingly concentrate on the relationship between the father and the male children. The mother remains a shadowy figure indeed, and her status is obscure. Of course, the relationship between father and son is central to the conflict between the contract theorists and their opponents; how can it realistically be said that sons are not born in subjection to their fathers? Furthermore, in the strict sense, "patriarchy" refers to rule by fathers. Sir Robert Filmer's *Patriarcha* is the best known statement of the patriarchal case. He argues that God gave Adam, the first father, absolute monarchical power by virtue of his procreative powers, and this power passed to his male heirs. All political authority is absolute and monarchical, and the power of kings is identical to that of fathers, and vice versa. However, fathers are, at one and the same time, husbands. Filmer also argued that God gave kingly power to Adam over Eve. Eve was made naturally fit for subordination, to be ruled by her husband.[3] This aspect of patriarchalism is generally ignored, although the status of wives and mothers within the family remains as an unsolved problem at the heart of liberal theory. Contemporary theorists conspicuously fail to address themselves to the question of how a husband's authority over a wife is to be justified without giving up some basic principles of liberal theory.

Discussions of social contract theory tend to gloss over the question of who exactly enters the contract and so consents to government. This is not surprising, for once the question is asked it exposes a profound ambiguity in the contract theorists' conception of the state of nature. If the state of nature is purely a logical fiction (useful in aiding us to understand the proper basis of obligation to government) then it is peopled by abstractly conceived, "naturally" free and equal individuals, all of whom can participate in the social contract. On the other hand, if the state of nature is conceived as a sociologically and anthropologically realistic condition, or as an historical reality, it will be seen as composed of families, and an explicit attack must then be maintained on all aspects of patriarchalism if fathers *and* mothers of families are to enter the social contract. Neither the social contract theorists—with the notable, if partial, exception of Hobbes—nor their successors, have been willing to take their criticism of patriarchal ideas to its logical conclusion. Explicitly or implicitly the "individuals" who enter the social contract are assumed to be fathers of families,[4] with all that this implies for the place of the sexes in civil society.

It might be objected that, in the seventeenth century, if not today, such an assumption was hardly unexpected. The authority of the father as head of the household was taken for granted by everyone, and the contract theorists were merely reflecting the convictions of their time when they supposed that fathers entered the social contract on behalf of their families. However, the conjugal and productive relationships of the seventeenth century also suggest that the contract theorists could have extended the logic of their individualism to women without stepping completely outside their own world. We have emphasized the interrelationship of contract theory and the emerging capitalist, market economy, but the contract theorists and patriarchalists fought their battle in a period that lies at the beginning of the long process of social change that brought liberal society into being. In the seventeenth century world we have lost, the family was still the main unit of economic production. Although fathers exercised authority within the family, the relationship of husband and wife within this productive unit presents a striking contrast to the conjugal relationship which we assume is proper and "natural" today.

Historians, like political theorists, have concentrated almost exclusively on men in their analyses, and, with the important exception of Clark's *Working Life of Women in the Seventeenth Century*, there is little material available about the position of women in this period. Nevertheless, the broad picture is clear enough. Three centuries ago there was "strong prejudice against bachelors and masterless men."[5] Marriage "was the entry to full membership" in society, and it constituted "the creation of a new economic unit as well as a life-long association of persons previously separate and caught-up in existing families."[6] Within marriage, however, "the idea is seldom encountered that a man supports his wife."[7] In all classes of society women are engaged in productive work and were economically independent of their husbands: "The wife was subject to her husband, . . . but she was by no means regarded as his servant."[8] Even humble households had servants (of both sexes) so that wives were not exclusively occupied with domestic tasks as we think of these today. In the seventeenth century "able business women" were common, and the wives of tradesmen and farmers were their husband's economic associates and partners.[9] On the death of a husband, "surprisingly often, the widow, if she could, would herself carry on the trade."[10] Women could also engage in trade on their own account; the "early Customs of the Boroughs," and the by-laws of some corporations, allowed married women to trade as *femme sole*, with "certain proprietary and legal rights independent of their husbands."[11] Moreover, some trades and professions, notably brewing and midwifery, were the exclusive preserve of women. Even if the husband was a wage laborer, his wife fed and clothed the family; women "can hardly have been regarded as mere dependants on their husbands when the clothing for the whole family was spun by their hands."[12]

In the seventeenth century both women and men could "shift for themselves," and thus there was a sound socio-economic basis for both sexes being regarded as, or abstracted into the state of nature as, "free and equal individuals." The contract theorists were well aware that their starting point of "natural" individual freedom and equality had implications for the family as well as for political authority. If (like Hobbes) they contrived to remain silent about the status of wives in the family in civil society, or (like Locke) they capitulated to the patriarchalists, they nevertheless knew that there was a *problem* about the position of married women. Today, political theorists no longer acknowledge that such a problem exists; the authority of husbands over wives is excluded from theoretical scrutiny. To understand why this is the case it is necessary to examine the impact of the consolidation of capitalism in the eighteenth and nineteenth centuries on the socio-economic position of married women. We shall discuss this in more detail in the final section of this paper. At this point, it should be noted that as the development of capitalism separated economic production from the household, the relationship of husband and wife was transformed. They were no longer economic associates and partners, but either competed with each other in the market for individual wages, or the wife became her husband's economic dependent. This was an ironic, and tragic, development for women since at one and the same time, and as part of the same social process, liberal individualist ideas emerged that held out a promise of freedom and equality for women, yet socio-economic changes denied that promise and reinforced patriarchy.

Hobbes and the One-Parent Family

In order to treat Hobbes as a patriarchal thinker it is necessary to see his state of nature as inhabited by families, with fathers at their head. At times, Hobbes' statements provide support for this view, but to interpret his state of nature in this fashion is inconsistent with his radical individualism which, in turn, is a logical consequence of his scientific method. Furthermore, to present Hobbes as a patriarchalist is to ignore his repeated denial that generation entails authority, and his insistence that all authority relationships are based on consent. It is also to ignore his scathing rejection of the argument from testimony and example on which the patriarchalists rested their case.[13]

In *Leviathan*, Hobbes begins his argument from an imaginative "resolution" of a commonwealth into the physiological entities, or machines in perpetual motion, that are its component parts. He then builds these entities into recognizable human individuals by attributing various "natural" characteristics to them. Hobbes' method thus leads him to a radical, abstractly individualist conception of the state of nature and its inhabitants. It is not an historically realistic condition, but a logical fiction in the most complete sense. In the state of nature each individual has an equal right of freedom to secure everything that is judged necessary for self-preservation. All are naturally equal because each one is strong enough, and has sufficient prudence, to kill another if required for survival. Hobbes's natural condition is asocial; it lacks a common moral language that provides a stable meaning for "good" or "bad" or "justice"; it is without property, law, or "Dominion"—and it has "No Matrimoniall lawes."[14] Hobbes's atomized individuals have no "natural" connections with each other, and, in their mutual competition and war for survival in the state of nature, settled and ordered relationships, such as those in the patriarchal family, are extremely unlikely to exist. It is precisely because of Hobbes's singular picture of the natural condition that his "view of the family subverts patriarchal attitudes."[15]

When each "individual" is considered completely abstractly, in separation from others, its sex is irrelevant. In Hobbes's state of nature, female individuals are as capable of protecting themselves as male individuals: he writes that "the inequality of their natural forces is not so great, that the man could get . . . domination over the woman without war."[16] There is, therefore, no reason why a free and equal female individual should always place herself under the protection, or authority, of a male. In the Hobbesian natural state there are no "natural" relationships of authority. When all individuals are free and equal to each other, relationships of authority must be based on convention or consent. Hobbes pushes this argument to its limit and challenges every aspect of the patriarchal thesis. According to Hobbes, even an infant consents to the rule of a parent. In this particular argument, as in the rest of his political theory, Hobbes is helped by his conception of "consent." He identifies "consent" with submission, or the "voluntary" acceptance of protection in return for life, whether the submission is given by the subject in the face of the conqueror's sword, by a victim to a robber with a gun, or by a child to a parent who has the power to expose or abandon it.[17] In the latter case the "parent" who has this power is the mother who gives birth to the child, and it is to her authority and protection that the child gives its "consent." In Hobbes's state of nature, "every woman that bears children, becomes both a *mother* and a *lord*.[18] The procreative powers of the father are irrelevant to authority over children:

> it cannot be known who is the Father, unless it be declared by the Mother: and therefore the right of Dominion over the Child dependeth on her will, and is consequently hers. Again, seeing the Infant is first in the power of the Mother, . . . is therefore obliged to obey her, rather than any other; and by consequence the Dominion over it is hers.[19]

A mother can lose the right to authority over her children if she is taken prisoner, when they too come under the rule of her captor. She may also consent to a man exercising authority over her children, although a covenant between a man and a woman does not always have this consequence. If the mother enters a contract "for society of bed only" she retains dominion over her children; if it is a contract "for society of all things" then "sometimes the government may belong to the wife," notably if she is a queen.[20]

Like the patriarchalists, Hobbes sees authority as all of a piece throughout society, but as grounded in convention, not nature. The "Rights and Consequences" of parental domination and sovereignty by institution (contract) and acquisition (conquest, which is to say, submission or "consent") are all the same.[21] Hobbes is theoretically consistent enough to present the family as an "artificial" or entirely conventional institution. He sees it "strictly in rational terms": "It is a 'civil person' by virtue of jurisdiction, not by virtue of marriage or biological parenthood."[22] The family, Hobbes argues, rests not on the natural ties of generation or sentiment, but is, like the state, grounded in the consent of its individual members and is "united in one Person Representative."[23] But which parent exercises jurisdiction in the family in civil society; which parent is the "Person Representative"? The doctrine of indivisible sovereignty is a cornerstone of Hobbes's political theory, but in the state, although he prefers a monarch, he allows that sovereignty could be exercised by an assembly. Given the equality between the sexes, it would seem logical that the mother and father should rule jointly, as an "assembly," in the family in civil society. However, as shown in his discussion of covenants between men and women, Hobbes insists that only *one* of the parents can govern. Within the "matrimonial laws" of civil society he also assumes, although both mothers and fathers have the right of dominion, that it is the father who will exercise jurisdiction within the household. Most of Hobbes' commentators see nothing surprising in this: indeed it is offered as an example of his patriarchalism. Even Chapman, who emphasizes that the mother has an equal right to govern in the family, fails to discuss the status of the husband or wife who is ruled. Yet the precise status of this parent is extremely obscure, the more so if it is the status of the father that must be explained.

The problem is revealed in Hobbes's definition of a "family." The striking feature of his definition is that the mother silently fades from sight. In *Leviathan*, Hobbes refers to the "family" as "a man and his children; or . . . a man and his servants; or . . . a man, and his children, and servants together."[24] At first sight, in *The Elements of Law*, his definition is conventional; Hobbes writes of the family as "the father or mother, or both," together with the children and servants.[25] However, he concludes the sentence by stating that "the father or master . . . is sovereign of the same; and the rest (both children and servants equally) subjects." But what has happened to the mother? Similarly, he argues in *De Cive* that a "*father* with his *sons* and *servants*, grown into a civil person by virtue of his paternal jurisdiction, is called a *family*."[26] Again, this leaves a large question to be answered about the status of the "disappearing" free and equal individual who is the mother. One possibility is that the wife has the same status as a servant. This is unlikely, however, for the master-servant relationship, like slavery, originates in force.[27] The master makes a contractual grant of "corporall liberty" to a servant, whereas marriage is a contract between two individuals of equal status, both of whom, in principle, have the right of dominion in the household. In addition, as we have shown, wives were economic associates of their husbands, not their servants, in this period. Chapman argues that Hobbes took his model of the "artificial" family from ancient Rome.[28] This suggests that the wife's status might be that of a child. Either she would remain under the jurisdiction of her father, or, if the marriage was with *manus*, she would become part of her husband's household but have the position of a daughter in regard to property rights.[29] But this is hardly a plausible solution to the problem; everyone knew in the seventeenth century that wives and husbands were part of one family. Moreover, Hobbes's conception of the family follows logically from his theoretical individualism, so it is unnecessary to look to ancient Rome.

In fact, there is no solution to the problem of the "disappearing parent" within Hobbes's political theory. He must remain silent about the status of wives and mothers in civil society if the inconsistency of his capitulation to the patriarchalists is not to be brought to the surface. The only "argument" that he offers to justify the role of fathers within the family is that "for the most part Common-wealths have been erected by the Fathers, not by the Mothers of families."[30] When discussing the problem of succession to the sovereign in the state, he says that it will usually pass to a male child, because "generally men are endued with greater parts of wisdom and courage,"[31] and they are "naturally fitter than women, for actions of labour and danger."[32] He also argues that children should be taught, as part of a process of political socialization designed to secure the absolute rule of the sovereign, that it is fathers who have instituted commonwealths.[33] All this is not only in blatant contradiction to his attack on patriarchal claims, but ignores his own strictures against arguments that rely on history and the "Practise of men" rather than reason.[34]

The problem of the status of the "missing parent" arises from Hobbes's refusal to allow that married individuals might rule jointly within their families. Because he falls back on patriarchal assertions about the "natural" fitness of males to govern, the problem has gone unnoticed. The "disappearance" of the mother in his definition of the family, and its implication that women always have good reason to submit to (consent to) the authority of men, seems unremarkable today after three centuries of liberal accommodation to patriarchy. Hinton has argued that there is an "inherent dilemma" in patriarchalism:

> for if kings are fathers, fathers cannot be patriarchs. If fathers are patriarchs at home, kings cannot be patriarchs on their thrones. Patriarchal kings and patriarchal fathers are a contradiction in terms. The patriarchalist therefore walks a tightrope. On the one hand he wants to emphasize sovereignty in kings and obedience in subjects, but on the other hand he has to preserve the father's property and freedom.[35]

This dilemma arises because the patriarchalists argue that authority structures are homologous throughout society. Hobbes argues with them on this point, although he insists that all authority relationships are based on convention, not nature. But Hobbes avoids the dilemma; his radical individualism leads him to argue that just as family cohesion depends on the jurisdiction of a single "person representative," so socio-political cohesion depends on the sword of an absolute monarch. If the security provided by the sword is to be maintained, then no father can have "*an absolute Propriety in his Goods; such, as excludeth the Right of the Soveraign.*"[36] Hobbes's theory, like patriarchalism, is thus ideologically inadequate for a developing liberal, market society. It was Locke who led the way forward, who argued against an homologous structure of authority, distinguishing between paternal and political rule, and who also showed how patriarchal claims about women could be neatly fitted into a liberal theoretical framework.

"He for the Market Only, She for the Market through Him"[37]

If, in Hobbes's theory, the lady vanishes, women have their place in Locke's argument from the beginning of the *First Treatise,* where he accuses Filmer of ignoring God's command that both mothers and fathers should be honored. In part, Locke escapes Hobbes' peculiar difficulties over the position of wives in the family in civil society because his individualism is more moderate and so more anthropologically and sociologically adequate. But he also avoids the problem of the "disappearing parent" because he has no quarrel with the patriarchalists about the status of wives and husbands. Locke retains all the patriarchal claims about the "natural" authority of fathers, but hidden beneath a gloss of "consent." In this respect, as in others, his theory is "fully as much a defense against radical democracy as an attack on traditionalism."[38] However, just as some theorists wish to see Hobbes as a patriarchalist, so Locke is presented as an anti-patriarchalist. Schochet, for example, argues that Locke "more fully than anyone else, analyzed the patriarchal political theory and tried to put something in its place," and "by asking all the right questions" he rejected "the presumptions on which patriarchalism rested."[39] Hinton makes the extraordinary comment that "Locke countered the patriarchalist case almost too effectively."[40] Such arguments are plausible only if attention is exclusively concentrated on Locke's attack on absolute monarchy, his distinction between "paternal" and "political" power, and his insistence that mature male children are as free as their fathers. They are most implausible if Locke's arguments about wives and mothers are also considered.

At first sight women appear to fare well in Locke's *Two Treatises.* He argues against Filmer that God gave Adam no political power over Eve; the curse on Eve "only foretels what should be the Womans Lot." Locke argues that a woman might be free from subjection to her husband "if the Circumstances either of her Condition or Contract with her Husband should exempt her from it" (I; 47).[41] The crux of his attack on Filmer is contained in the distinction between political and other forms of authority: "the Power of a *Magistrate* over a Subject may be distinguished from that of a *Father* over his Children, a *Master* over his Servant, a *Husband* over his Wife, and a *Lord* over his Slave" (II; 2). Political rule is distinguished by the right to impose the death penalty. Neither parents nor husbands have the right to exercise this ultimate power over children or wives. Under certain circumstances a wife may even be at liberty to leave her husband (II; 82, 86). Parents have a natural authority over their children, but this does not, Locke argues against the patriarchalists, derive from procreation. Rather, it is a consequence of the parents' duty to care for and educate children while they are in their nonage and incapable of shifting for themselves (I; 52–3: II; 58, 65). Locke repeatedly states that the mother "hath an equal Title" with the father to authority over children, and this form of authority should therefore be called "parental" not "paternal" (e.g. II; 52). In his discussion of conquest he even suggests that a wife might own property by virtue of her own labor (II; 183).

All this appears to imply that Locke regarded women as well as men as free and equal individuals, and that his picture of the state of nature reflected women's productive role in the seventeenth century. However, this is only one side of Locke's argument and the least important. He sweeps away all that his individualism appears to promise women. It is no accident that Locke persistently forgets his own distinction between "parental" and "paternal" authority, and usually refers to the father and paternal rule in the Second Treatise. An examination of Locke's discussion of the natural right to appropriate private property, and his account of the origins of government, reveal that patriarchal assertions about the "natural" authority of fathers are basic to his political theory.

In his discussion of Adam and Eve, Locke takes the sting out of his attack on Filmer by adding that a wife's subjection to her husband has "a Foundation in Nature" (I; 47). A husband's authority rests on contract, not nature, but Locke assumes that a free and equal female individual will always enter a marriage contract that places her in subjection to her husband. The extent of a wife's subjection may appear to be strictly limited, for Locke states that she has her own "peculiar Right." However, this refers to the right she has to her life, and her right to share in the exercise of authority over children. Her "peculiar Right" excludes her from the crucial area of decision-making about family property. Notwithstanding his discussion of conquest, it is clear that Locke regards the labor of a wife, like that of a servant, as contributing to the property appropriated by her husband, or a master (II; 28). The authority of a husband, father and master, does not extend to the property that members of the household have in their lives, but paternal and political authority have one important feature in common; in both forms the locus of authority must be placed somewhere determinate. Locke argues that the rule of one man is no longer justified in political life but, within the family, it is precisely this form of authority which must prevail. The power of decision-making in the family, or "the last Determination, *i.e.* the Rule," will "naturally" belong to the father because he is "the abler and the stronger." His right, unlike that of his wife, reaches "to the things of their common Interest and Property" (II; 82). The father is the "Proprietor of the Goods and Land." and "his Will take(s) place before that of his wife in all things of their common Concernment" (I; 48).

Locke's picture of the state of nature offers an excellent illustration of the integral connection between political concepts and theories and specific forms of social life. It reflects the social relationships of an emerging capitalist, market economy and, in his conjectural history of the state of nature. Locke provides a moral justification for these relationships.[42] In addition, he provides an account of the origins of government. His commentators have often overlooked the fact that Locke's state of nature contains government—the government of fathers. Once this is taken into account the distinction between "political" and "paternal" authority becomes exceedingly fine. Schochet makes the important point that discussions of social contract theory usually fail to differentiate between the contract and consent.[43] Locke is able to meet the patriarchalist objection to his principle of individual freedom and equality, that an original contract cannot bind future generations of sons. He argues that they consent to the political arrangements made, through the contract, by their fathers. A sharp contrast thus seems to exist between Locke and Filmer; a Lockean father will rule by consent, not by virtue of his generative powers. But how far does Locke's argument about consent actually undermine patriarchal assertions? Pitkin has argued convincingly that Locke's conception of "consent" is of hypothetical consent; he argues that if a government is legitimate then consent ought to be given.[44] Indeed, Locke goes much further and argues that, given a legitimate government (such as that instituted through the social contract), then consent is given, or, at least, that it can always reasonably be inferred or hypothesized that it is given.

In the Lockean state of nature, male children who are out of their nonage remain under the authority of their father. God has "appointed" government to enable humans to live peacefully together (II; 105, 13). The "first" fathers in the state of nature become rulers through an "insensible change," a change in which the "first" mature male children give a "tacit and scarce avoidable consent" to them becoming monarchs (II; 76,

75). Locke says nothing about wives and mothers in this context, but he obviously takes it for granted that the marriage contract involves the wife's "consent" to her husband's transmogrification. Such a reconciliation of liberal contract theory and patriarchal theory was made all the easier because patriarchalists, too, had recourse to ideas of contracts and consent.[45] For example, Dudley Digges, in the 1640s, claimed that the "King hath paternall powers from the consent of the people." If this is a "curious union of consent with patriarchalism,"[46] it is no more curious than Locke's "consent" which gives kingly power to fathers in the face of his own argument that paternal and political power must be distinguished.

It might be objected that, even if there is little difference between a Lockean and a patriarchal account of the origins of government, Locke's argument in the *Second Treatise* for limited, representative government marks a complete break with patriarchal theory. It is true that Locke argues that, at a certain stage of the historical development of the state of nature, a single father-monarch is no longer able to provide adequate security for property, and that government must be reconstituted. He also adds that "at best an Argument from what has been, to what should of right be, has no great force" (II; 103); but there is an important continuity between what "has been" in Locke's conjectural history and what "should be." Locke's history shows why it is rational for individuals to enter the social contract through which the new, liberal government of representatives is instituted.[47] Given this justification for the liberal state, it can then be inferred that succeeding generations "consent" to this political act of their fathers. There is no separation of Locke's conjectural history from his theory of government; he does not turn the history "into a descriptive and politically neutral anthropology and then [insert] his own theory of consent . . . in place of the moral patriarchalism Filmer had improperly derived from history."[48] Locke's conjectural history is neither merely descriptive nor politically neutral. It provides the necessary basis for his brilliant justification of the liberal, constitutional state as the only form of government appropriate to a developing capitalist society. Furthermore, it provides a new contractual dress for the patriarchal assertion that wives are "naturally" subordinate to their husbands, and legitimizes the exclusion of women from political life.

The "individuals" who enter Locke's social contract and establish the liberal state are the fathers of families. They act to secure their property, whether this consists of estates or merely the "property" that members of the family have in their lives, liberty and labor. In so acting, they also secure the 'property' that they have in their own position of authority within the family. Locke states that "no rational Creature can be supposed to change his condition with an intention to be worse" (II; 131). During the change from the state of nature to civil society, inequalities of property and all the social relationships of the natural condition are preserved (indeed consolidated), including the authority relationships within the family. The *Second Treatise* offers no reason to suppose that Locke would have disagreed with James Tyrrell, his friend and fellow critic of Filmer, who argued that consent to government "needed no Compact of all the People of the world, since every Father of a Family . . . had a power to confer his Authority of governing himself and his Family upon whom he pleased"; and who added that women were "concluded by their Husbands."[49]

The emergence of patriarchal theory in the seventeenth century was, Schochet argues, a "direct result" of the differentiation of political from other forms of authority.[50] But this distinction is also crucial to the accommodation of social contract with patriarchal theory. It enables Locke to assume that women are "naturally" fit only for a restricted role within the family. Men alone can make the transition to political life; it is they who are the "individuals" who have the capacity to enter the social contract and to be authors of their own subjection in political life. A striking and sad corollary of this assumption is that women are seen as lacking in the rationality required to take these steps. The "moderate and sensible"[51] character of Locke's theory has been challenged by Macpherson who argues that Locke regards propertyless males as less than fully rational. He concludes his discussion of Locke's theory with these words:

> the greatness of seventeenth-century liberalism was its assertion of the free rational individual as the criterion of the good society; its tragedy was that this very assertion was necessarily a denial of individualism to half the nation.[52]

But Macpherson has completely overlooked *literally* "half the nation" for whom the development of liberal, capitalist society, which compounded and reinforced (while transforming) patriarchy, was an even greater tragedy. We would argue that for Locke every male, whether owning material property or not, is rational and an "individual." Every male is assumed to be sufficiently rational, or "naturally" to have the capacity, to govern a family. Rationality, it can be said, comes not just with age, but with the tying of the conjugal knot, and with fatherhood. In Locke's theory, it is women who are seen as "naturally" lacking in rationality and as "naturally" excluded from the status of "free and equal individual," and so unfit to participate in political life.

Liberalism and Feminism

The claim that women are lacking in rationality and unfitted for political life is still widely accepted; indeed, in 1978, this is frequently presented as one of the "natural" differences of character and attributes between the sexes. That it can seem unremarkable for women to be so regarded when today, as *citizens*, they are formally equal to men and have the same opportunities for political participation open to them, can be explained only by taking account of *both* the reconciliation of liberal and patriarchal theory and the economic changes that forced married women into dependence on their husbands. The failure of more recent liberal theorists, with the honorable exception of J. S. Mill, to extend their principles to one half of humankind remains unchallenged because it is now seen as "natural" for married women to be economic dependents, and so "naturally" unfree and unequal.

In the eighteenth century, economic independence (especially as exemplified in property ownership) became the major criterion for citizenship. Kant, listing all those unfit to vote because of their dependence and subordination, remarked that they had "no civil personality and their existence is, so to speak, purely inherent." He included in this group "women in general."[53] Women could be lumped into one undifferentiated group, forever dependent, whereas males might be able to transcend their position as "mere auxiliaries to the commonwealth." During the nineteenth century they began to do so. The fight for manhood suffrage had the advantage that all men, even the propertyless, were seen as able to govern within their families. Consequently, it was not implausible to claim that they had the capacities required for citizenship in the liberal state.

Richards has pointed out that the impact on women of the development of capitalist industry in England, from the seventeenth into the twentieth century, provides an extremely interesting comparison with the current effects of industrialization and the expansion of wage-labor in the developing countries. In both cases the participation rates of women decline as development proceeds.[54] From the end of the seventeenth century in England women's economic independence and legal status began to be undermined. Business women were less prominent by the end of the century and, although married women continued to participate in trades and crafts well into the eighteenth century, more and more avenues of employment became closed to them. Men began to organize themselves into professional and trade associations from which women were excluded; even from brewing, which was once a female trade. Women also lost control of dairying, midwifery and medicine.[55] Summing up the effects of capitalist development upon the wives of tradesmen and craftsmen, Clark writes that,

> it seems probable that the wife of the prosperous capitalist tended to become idle, the wife of the skilled journeyman lost her economic independence and became his unpaid domestic servant, while the wives of other wage earners were driven into the sweated industries . . .[56]

We have earlier drawn attention to the importance for married women of the gradual divorce of home and work and the expansion of wage-labor. On the land and in the new workplaces, men and women had to compete for an individual wage, and wages for women were rarely sufficient for them to feed and clothe themselves and their children.[57] Moreover, the employment of women (and children) in the textile factories was an atypical development. From the beginning of the nineteenth century in existing and newly developing industries, opportunities for employment of women declined: "the loss of employment in the traditional lines was probably greater than the creation of new opportunities."[58]

These economic changes were also accompanied by a deterioration in the legal status of women. Legal customs which had favored women were abrogated in favour of common law focused on the individual male. By the mid-nineteenth century when "the range of [economic] opportunities for . . . women was tragically restricted,"[59] the formal status of married women had also reached its lowest point; their position reflected Blackstone's Common Law doctrine of "unity of person." He wrote, "a man cannot grant any thing to his wife, or enter into covenant with her, for the grant would suppose her separate existence."[60] Women were deemed incapable of acting for themselves or assuming responsibility for so doing; that was a burden that husbands carried. Mothers had lost the authority over their children of which Locke had made so much, and a husband could legally imprison his wife in the matrimonial home to prevent her from leaving him.[61] It is not surprising that so many of the early champions of women's rights were abolitionists, or that married women were frequently compared to slaves, for legally and civilly they did not exist. Their social, political and economic dependence upon, and subordination to, their husbands was virtually complete.

Neither liberal theorists' acceptance of the dependence and subordination of wives to husbands as "natural," and so theoretically irrelevant, nor feminists' response to this view, can be fully understood in the absence of an appreciation of this historical background and of the integral connection between political and social concepts, theories and ideas, and specific forms of social life. Ideas are not merely automatic reflections of socio-economic developments, but nor do they exist in an independent timeless world of their own. The nineteenth and early twentieth century feminist movement was a response to the social, legal and economic position of women, and to the failure of theorists and men of affairs to grant that women were "individuals" capable of exercising civil rights. It was a largely middle-class movement, a class which included large numbers of women who could not be "concluded by their husbands" for they had no husbands, and few means of supporting themselves.[62] The consolidation of capitalist production had fostered a sharp class division between women. Many working class women continued to work from necessity, especially, of course, in domestic service (although the ideal of the non-working wife had spread to "respectable" households of all classes by the middle of the nineteenth century).[63]

> The narrow limits of acceptable and accessible female employment in the mid-century provoked from some women—almost entirely middle-class in origin—a response which generated fuel for the feminist developments of the age. . . . The real origins of the "emancipation of women" (in the modern sense of economic opportunity and independence) must be sought in the shifting balance of the occupational framework which began to emerge in the last quarter of the 19th century.[64]

The assertion that they too were rational was central to the earlier feminists' fight for women's emancipation. It is central to women's formal recognition as free and equal individuals capable of enjoying legal and civil rights; the vote, the right to enter economic contracts and control property, the right to education, and to work in the professions, and the right to dispose of the property they have in their persons. In a *formal* sense the battle is more or less over. In the last quarter of the twentieth century, the principle of individual equality and freedom, which the social contract theorists used to attack patriarchalism, is now being institutionalized in the liberal democracies—for both males and females. This could be seen as the last stage of the bourgeois revolution; yet, far from fulfilling the promise of liberalism, this formal recognition of women as individual human persons has served to highlight the contradiction between women seen formally as free and equal individuals, and women as wives and mothers within the family. The theoretical embarrassment that women posed to seventeenth century theorists, reluctant or unwilling to question the authority of husbands and fathers within the family, has now returned as a practical contradiction between institutionalized liberal individualism and the authority structure of the twentieth-century family.

The new feminist movement of the last decade has been particularly concerned with the private world of the family, rather than the public world that preoccupied their predecessors. This concern, too, can be related to economic developments. Since the Second World War there has been a dramatic increase in the participation rate of married women in the paid workforce. This increase is a result of new employment created by the rapid growth of the tertiary sector of the economy.[65] Married women now have the opportunity for economic independence and all that it implies for social and political life. Or at least this is true for educated middle-class women with special skills, who can compete for work that pays enough for them to be self-supporting.[66] The jobs open to most working-class women are very poorly paid, and many women are once more, perhaps have always been, in a position of interdependence in the family. In many cases their families can survive only through the combined incomes of husband and wife.[67]

However, many current feminist arguments and slogans fail to take account of the different positions of wives in the middle and working classes. Unlike liberal theorists they are concerned with women; but like those theorists they implicitly appeal to an abstractly individualist liberalism that ignores socioeconomic and historical realities and developments, and their importance for the married woman question. Some feminist aims and demands constitute a mirror-image of the abstractly individualist conception of social life, or resemble the liberal picture of the atomistic classless state of nature. Such a response leads to a politics of negation that is encapsulated in the popular slogans "the personal is the political" and "smash the family," and in the claim that "nature" is the oppressor and must be abolished.[68] Firestone, for instance, argues that women will only be free through artificial means of human reproduction.[69] Because so many women are now constrained by the burden of two jobs (paid and unpaid), it can easily appear as if the family must be "smashed" if women are to be independent, and the three centuries old promise of liberalism is to be achieved. Feminists have implicitly attacked Locke's always fragile separation of paternal and political authority and argue that males rule in an identical fashion in the family and in the state; "the personal is the political." Like Hobbes and the patriarchalists, they see authority relationships as all of a piece, and, ideally, as conventional. Once the family is "smashed" there will be no "natural" restrictions on the ability of equal individuals freely to interact; even "all adult-child relationships will [be] mutually chosen."[70] With these feminist arguments, the wheel has turned full-circle, back to Hobbes's radical abstractly individualist, and conventionalist, attack on patriarchy.

But if the liberal accommodation to patriarchy is to be broken, we must move forward, not backward, in both theory and practice. It is necessary to look beyond the abstract categories of liberal theory that have assisted the consolidation and transformation of patriarchy, to a theoretical perspective explicitly grounded in the present socio-economic realities. As we have shown, the social place of married women is not "natural" and unchanging, but forms part of specific socio-economic and political relationships. Nor is the family an unchanging social entity or an eternal, timeless enemy of women. The relationship between the class structure of advanced liberal-capitalist societies and the status of married women within the family is only just beginning to be investigated, and much work remains to be done. In this paper our aim has been to perform some of the groundwork necessary for this wider task. To show how and why married women pose an acute problem for liberal political theory and practice, and how popular beliefs about women's place, and the feminist attack on these, are bound up with the historical development of the capitalist economy and the liberal state.

Notes

An earlier version of this paper was presented to the Annual Meeting of the Australasian Political Studies Association, Sydney, 1976. We would like to thank the participants at the Conference and also the referee for *Political Studies*.

1. G. J. Schochet, *Patriarchalism in Political Thought* (Oxford, Blackwell, 1975), 19 and 55–56.

2. R. W. K. Hinton, "Husbands, Fathers and Conquerors: II" *Political Studies* 16 (1968): 58.

3. We have no space here to explore the opportunities opened up for women by the religious dimension of individualism. See, for example, K. V. Thomas, "Women and the Civil War Sects," *Past and Present*, 13 (1958); and C. Hill, *The World Turned Upside Down* (London, Temple Smith, 1972), ch. 15. The Reformation also reinforced patriarchy as fathers took on priestly tasks, see Schochet, *Patriarchalism in Political Thought*, 57.

4. In Rawls' revival of contract theory it is significant that he says of his original position that "we may think of the parties as heads of families." J. Rawls, *A Theory of Justice* (Oxford, Oxford University Press, 1972), 128. The veil of ignorance may be intended to hide the parties' knowledge of their sex, but it is unlikely that Rawls could make so many appeals to "our" intuitions and considered judgements if, for example, the heads of families are not seen in conventional terms as fathers.

5. Thomas, "Women and the Civil War Sects," 42.

6. P. Laslett, *The World We Have Lost* (London, Methuen, 1965), 11–12 and 90.

7. A. Clark, *Working Life of Women in the Seventeenth Century* (London, Frank Cass, 1968), 12. First published in 1919.

8. Clark, *Working Life of Women in the Seventeenth Century*, 41.

9. Clark, *Working Life of Women in the Seventeenth Century*, 35.

10. Laslett, *The World We Have Lost*, 8.

11. Clark, *Working Life of Women in the Seventeenth Century*, 151; R. Thompson, *Women in Stuart England and America: A Comparative Study* (London, Routledge and Kegan Paul, 1974), 163.

12. Clark, *Working Life of Women in the Seventeenth Century*, 145.

13. Hobbes argues that the authority of the Bible rests only on the authority of the church, which, in turn, derives from the Commonwealth and its head; and "hath the head of the Commonwealth any other authority than that which hath been given him by the members?" Cited from (*Liberty, Necessity and Chance*), in P. Riley, "Will and Legitimacy in the Philosophy of Hobbes: Is He a Consent Theorist?," *Political Studies* 21 (1973): 504.

14. T. Hobbes, *Leviathan* (Harmondsworth, Penguin Books, 1968), edited by C. B. Macpherson, XIII, p. 188; XX, p. 254.

15. R. A. Chapman, "*Leviathan* Writ Small: Thomas Hobbes on the Family," *American Political Science Review* 69 (1975): 77.

16. T. Hobbes, *De Cive* (New York, Anchor Books, 1972), edited by B. Gert, IX, 3, p. 213. And see *Leviathan*, XX, p. 253.

17. P. King, *The Ideology of Order* (London, Allen and Unwin, 1974), ch. 15, overlooks Hobbes' general conception of "consent" when he argues how implausible it is to speak of an infant's "consent." Hobbes' notion of "consent" is discussed in detail in C. Pateman, *The Problem of Political Obligation* (Chichester, Wiley, 1979).

18. Hobbes, *De Cive*, IX, 3, p. 213.

19. Hobbes, *Leviathan*, XX, p. 254; compare his views in T. Hobbes, *The Elements of Law* (London, Frank Cass, 1969), edited by F. Tönnies (second edition), Pt. 2, IV, 3, p. 132.

20. Hobbes, *The Elements of Law*, Pt. 2, IV, 5–6, p. 133; and see *De Cive*, IX, 5–7. The reference to "queens" suggests a social state of nature—or is Hobbes referring to civil society here?

21. Hobbes, *Leviathan*, XX, p. 256.

22. Chapman, "*Leviathan* Writ Small," 78; 80.

23. Hobbes, *Leviathan*, XXII, p. 285.

24. Hobbes, *Leviathan*, XX, p. 257; see Chapman, *Leviathan* Writ Small", 80.

25. Hobbes, *The Elements of Law*, Pt. II, IV, 10, p. 135.

26. Hobbes, *De Cive*, IX, 10, p. 217.

27. Hobbes, *Leviathan*, XX, pp. 255–56; *The Elements of Law*, Pt. II, ch. 3; *De Cive*, ch. 8.

28. Chapman, "*Leviathan* Writ Small," 82–84.

29. S. B. Pomeroy, *Goddesses, Whores, Wives and Slaves: Women in Classical Antiquity* (New York, Schocken Books, 1975) especially 152; 162. In ch. 8, Pomeroy shows that male relatives, especially fathers, retained considerable power over married women, even if married with *manus*.

30. Hobbes, *Leviathan*, XX, p. 253.

31. Hobbes, *The Elements of Law*, Pt. II, IV, 14, p. 136.

32. Hobbes, *Leviathan*, XIX, p. 250; and see *De Cive*, IX, 16, p. 219, where Hobbes states this is "for the most part" and that it has "grown a custom."

33. Hobbes, *Leviathan*, XXX, p. 382.

34. Hobbes, *Leviathan*, XX, p. 261.

35. R. W. K. Hinton, "Husbands, Fathers and Conquerors: I" *Political Studies* 15 (1967): 294.

36. Hobbes, *Leviathan*, XXIX, p. 367.

37. C. Hill's felicitous phrase.

38. S. Wolin, *Politics and Vision* (London, Allen and Unwin, 1961), 294.

39. Schochet, *Patriarchalism in Political Thought*, 245: 268.

40. Hinton, "Husbands, Fathers and Conquerors: II", 66.

41. References in brackets in the text refer to paragraphs of the "First Treatise" and the "Second Treatise" in J. Locke, *Two Treatises of Government* (Cambridge, Cambridge University Press, 1967), edited by P. Laslett (second edition).

42. The conjectural history is discussed in more detail in C. Pateman, "Sublimation and Reification: Locke, Wolin and the Liberal Democratic Conception of the Political," *Politics and Society*, 5 (1975).

43. Schochet, *Patriarchalism in Political Thought*, 9; 262.

44. H. Pitkin, "Obligation and Consent," in P. Laslett, W. G. Runciman, Q. Skinner, eds., *Philosophy, Politics and Society* (Oxford, Blackwell, 1972), fourth series.

45. Hinton, "Husbands, Fathers and Conquerors: II," 62, comments that "Hobbes's patriarchalism was for Locke the strongest patriarchalism because it was based on consent: . . ." For a detailed discussion of the use of the marriage contract as an analogue of the social contract by both royalists and republicans in the seventeenth century, see M. L. Shanley, "Marriage Contract in Seventeenth Century Political Thought," Paper presented to the Annual Meeting of the American Political Science Association, 1976.

46. Cited by Schochet, *Patriarchalism in Political Thought*, 104.

47. This argument is developed further in Pateman, "Sublimation and Reification."

48. Schochet, *Patriarchalism in Political Thought*, 259.

49. Cited by Schochet, *Patriarchalism in Political Thought*, 202. It should be noted that although all fathers take part in the contract, only a few propertied fathers become politically relevant members of civil society, who can act as, and choose, representatives.

50. Schochet, *Patriarchalism in Political Thought*, 55.

51. J. Plamenatz, *Man and Society* (London, Longmans, 1963), 1:241.

52. C. B. Macpherson, *The Political Theory of Possessive Individualism* (Oxford, Oxford University Press, 1962), 262.

53. I. Kant, *Kant's Political Writings* (Cambridge, Cambridge University Press, 1971), edited by H. Reiss, 139.

54. E. Richards, "Women in the British Economy Since About 1700: An Interpretation," *History* 59 (1974): 337–57.

55. Clark, *Working Life of Women in the Seventeenth Century*, especially ch. 6. On male trade and professional organizations and their effect on women's employment, see also H. Hartmann, "Capitalism, Patriarchy and Job Segregation by Sex," 1 (1976): 3, part 2. On women's economic role, see also I. Pinchbeck, *Women Workers and the Industrial Revolution, 1750–1850* (London, Routledge, 1930).

56. Clark, *Working Life of Women in the Seventeenth Century*, 235.

57. Clark, *Working Life of Women in the Seventeenth Century*, 92; 145; 304; also Thompson, *Women in Stuart England and America*, 241.

58. Richards, "Women in the British Economy Since About 1700," 345–46.

59. Richards, "Women in the British Economy Since About 1700," 347.

60. Sir W. Blackstone, *Commentaries on the Laws of England* (London: Sweet, Maxwell, Stevens and Norton, 1844) twenty-first edition, Volume I, Book I, Ch. XV, p. 442. The *Commentaries* were first published in 1765–69. Blackstone (p. 444) adds that ". . . even the disabilities the wife lies under, are for the most part intended for her protection and benefit. So great a favourite is the female sex of the laws of England."

61. See the examples in J. O'Faolain and L. Martines (ed.), *Not in God's Image* (New York, Harper, 1973), 318–28.

62. See R. McWilliams-Tullberg, *Women at Cambridge* (London, Gollancz, 1975), 21. In 1861, 46 percent of women aged 20–34 were unmarried.

63. See for example, the comments in G. Stedman-Jones, *Outcast London* (Harmondsworth, Penguin, 1976), 83–84; and D. Thompson, "Women and Nineteenth-Century Radical Politics: A Lost Dimension," in J. Mitchell and A. Oakley (eds) *The Rights and Wrongs of Women* (Harmondsworth, Penguin, 1976), 136–37.

64. Richards, "Women in the British Economy Since About 1700," 350–51.

65. Richards, "Women in the British Economy Since About 1700," 348; 354–57.

66. There is considerable (if sometimes unconscious) resentment of this potential independence, revealed in the current attacks on married women for depriving male school-leavers and other males of jobs in a period of high unemployment. Such attacks also reveal a considerable ignorance of the sexual structuring of the labour market. In fact women are usually channelled into sectors of the economy in which men (including male school-leavers) are unwilling to compete. On the structure of the labor-market see M. Reich, D. M. Gordon and R. C. Edwards, "A Theory of Labor Market Segmentation," *American Economic Review*, Papers and Proceedings, 63 (1973).

67. The economic interdependence of working-class women and men, as opposed to the potential economic independence of middle-class women, is discussed in T. Brennan, "Women and Work," *The Journal of Australian Political Economy* 1 (1977).

68. It is also reflected in the proposals for "contract" marriages. See, for example, L. J. Weitzman, "Legal Regulation of Marriage: Tradition and Change," *California Law Review* 62 (1974): 1169–288.

69. S. Firestone, *The Dialectic of Sex* (London, Paladin, 1972), 187 ff.

70. Firestone, *The Dialectic of Sex*, 222.

Afterword

Mere Auxiliaries to the Commonwealth in an Age of Globalization

Carole Pateman and Teresa Brennan

This chapter is in two sections, written respectively by Carole Pateman and Teresa Brennan, but this was not our intention. In the summer of 2002, Teresa and I had begun to write an afterword to our article "Mere Auxiliaries to the Commonwealth," originally published in 1979, to accompany its reprinting. I was going to join Teresa over Christmas 2002 and along with the celebrations we were to complete our piece. Our holiday never took place. On December 10 she was mown down, while on foot, by a hit-and-run driver in Florida. She passed away on February 3, 2003. What she had written to that point for our "afterword" comprises the second section. It draws on her (posthumously published) *Glob-*

alization and Its Terrors.[1] One can see some seeds of that book in "Mere Auxiliaries."

Her passing was also a severe personal blow. I had known Teresa for nearly thirty years, and "Mere Auxiliaries," my first exercise in feminist political theory, owed a good deal to her creative, agile mind. Teresa was a good comrade, a vivid and unforgettable personality, and she forged her own path through the thickets of theory.

This piece serves as a small memorial to Teresa and to those sunny good old days in Sydney.

Teresa Brennan 1952–2003 RIP

(Carole Pateman)

A book devoted to feminist readings of Locke, itself part of a series devoted to feminist scholarship on the classic texts, would have seemed a far-fetched idea when Teresa Brennan and I were working on "Mere Auxiliaries." In the mid-1970s feminist political theory was in its infancy, and as our footnotes indicate, there was little on which we could draw. Our article was published in 1979, a year that, in retrospect, is something of a landmark in reinterpretation of the classic texts, still a major part of feminist scholarship in political theory. For example, Lorenne Clark and Lynda Lange's collection, *The Sexism of Social and Political Theory*, Mary Shanley's "Marriage Contract and Social Contract in Seventeenth-Century English Political Thought," and Susan Okin's *Women in Western Political Thought* were all published in that year.[2] At that point we did not know that we had been preceded by early modern feminist critics of Hobbes and Locke, and curiously, their contribution was ignored by political theorists, including feminists, until the 1990s.

It is extraordinarily gratifying to have contributed to the beginning of this new scholarship. As Wordsworth so famously wrote, "Bliss was it in that dawn to be alive," and three decades later when both the intellectual and political climates have changed so completely, it is very difficult to convey the sheer excitement of the 1970s and the impact of the revelations in the first pamphlets, papers, and books to come out of the Second Wave of the feminist movement. When we wrote our article, I was digesting this material, and wrestling with the issue of what it all might mean for my own academic work. The broader implications were not immediately obvious to me. It took time to appreciate that a new way of looking at the world had changed irrevocably the way in which famous texts could be read, and that a feminist perspective challenged the central assumptions of theories on which I relied.

I was already writing a critical analysis of the arguments of theorists of an original contract, including Locke, and *The Problem of Political Obligation* was also published in 1979.[3] In both "Mere Auxiliaries" and my book the target is "liberal" theory, but unless the meaning of "liberal" is specified, I now see this as a misleading label. Defenses and criticism of liberalism are more ubiquitous than ever in political theory, but "liberalism" is a broad tent that can include theories that are at odds with each other. Most of my feminist work on the classic texts has been focused not on liberalism but, much more specifically, on theories of original contracts.

In my discussion of Locke in *The Problem of Political Obligation* I note that his assumptions about men and women pose a problem for arguments about consent and obligation, but I got no further than signaling the existence of the problem.[4] That is not surprising, since my book was about the social contract, namely, the justification of government in, and obligation of (male) citizens to, the modern (democratic) state. I had not yet grasped that the idea of an original contract included more than the social contract. Nor had I grasped how central the institution of marriage was to political theory and the construction of the modern state. I was lucky that Teresa had been my student; she took the initiative that led to us working together on "Mere Auxiliaries." The paper was a major step forward in the development of my ideas about theories of original contracts and, therefore, the sexual contract.

Two features in particular strike me on reading "Mere Auxiliaries" today. One is that it is very much part of the *marxisant* intellectual milieu of the time, and I shall come back to this. The second is that the major reason it has stood the test of time is precisely that we had worked out, as we state in the opening sentence, that wives were an embarrassment for political theory (or at least any nonconservative political theory). That is not to say that "the wife problem" is now always recognized. One obstacle is the still common practice of discussing theories of original contracts as "social contract theory," thus burying the sexual contract and the question of men's power over women. Another difficulty is that the institution of marriage is all too frequently subsumed into the category of "the family" (at times we slide between the two ourselves), and political theorists who vigorously criticize a variety of forms of power happily overlook conjugal power and the subordination of wives. The problem about wives was there plainly enough in the texts of the theorists of an original contract; they saw it and took pains to deal with it. But the standard interpretations in the political theory that I was taught in the 1960s, and that I initially began to teach myself, quickly passed over or ignored the relevant passages of the texts, and so their political significance remained unacknowledged. The subordination of wives had become politically invisible.

It took the literature of a political movement to concentrate the academic mind on the obvious question (already posed, though we did not know it in the 1970s, by Mary Astell in 1700). "Why is it," as we ask in "Mere Auxiliaries," that "a free and equal female individual should always be assumed to place herself under the authority of a free and equal male individual"? Until the legal reforms from the late 1970s onward in England finally eliminated coverture, to become a wife was to become a subordinate. This still remains true in law in many places round the world. Powerful antifeminist movements, especially in the United States, continue to attempt to shore up the social legitimacy of the husband as head of the household. Their efforts take a number of forms, such as generalized calls for "family values," policies designed to prod single mothers on welfare into marriage, movements like the Promise Keepers, or the declaration by the Southern Baptists in 1998, a congregation sixteen million strong, that a wife should "submit herself graciously" to the leadership of her husband, while he maintains her economic security for life.[5]

The problem about the power of husbands could not be avoided in theories of an original contract because stories of the pact derived from the premise, couched in universal language, of natural individual freedom, equality, and rationality. The very radical character of this premise is not always appreciated. The political constructs of the early modern theorists (except, partially, Rousseau) were designed to deflect the radical implications of their starting point, and they have too often been accepted at face value. The logic of theories of original contracts opened up a Pandora's box which then had quickly to be closed, and which feminist and other emancipatory political movements have continued to prise open, more and more widely, using the theoretical weapons provided by Hobbes, Locke, and their fellows.

The enormous political problem (or opportunity, depending on one's perspective) raised by the premise that "all men" are born free and equal is that all justifications for relations of power and authority are immediately rendered illegitimate—save for one. The only remaining justification for the government of one individual, or category of individuals, by another is that the governed have agreed to (contracted into, consented to) such an arrangement. Theorists of an original contract were, of course, concerned with the power of monarchs, arguments about the divine right of kings, and the establishment of parliaments, but as they and their political opponents knew very well, the same logic applied to all power relationships, including that between husband and wife. Indeed, as Shanley showed, the analogy between government in marriage and government in the state was stock-in-trade of the political battles of the period. Discussion of marriage was not merely an obscure or dispensable point in the texts.

That it became obscured and dispensed with in post–World War II political theory was in large part thanks to Locke's brilliant theoretical moves. Hobbes's theoretical usefulness was severely limited by his radically individualist and logically consistent conception of natural freedom, equality, and rationality, and his too rigorous conventionalism. In Hobbes's state of nature female individuals can be victors in the war of all against all just as often as male individuals. But he remains silent, as we noted in "Mere Auxiliaries," about the status of any men who come under women's power. We also emphasized his curious definitions of a "family" in which the mother disappears. There are no matrimonial laws in the natural condition, so the institution of marriage has to be created *ab initio* through the original contract, clearly raising the question of why in civil society it takes the familiar form in which "naturally" free and equal women become "wives," men's subordinates. That question is hidden away in Locke's theory. Hobbes lets too many theoretical cats out of the bag, and Locke stuffs them securely back in, so becoming the pivotal figure in the theoretical justification of the creation of a modern— patriarchal—state.

Locke's picture of the state of nature contains marriage, families, and patriarchal father-rulers. Despite his fuss and bother in response to Filmer about Adam and Eve and the Fifth Commandment, his daring argument that a marriage contract might be dissolved when children are grown, his support for girls' education, and his comment about a wife's property when he is discussing conquest, at the most crucial points Locke leaves no doubt that husbands exercise legitimate power over their wives. He rails against the rule of one man, yet he insists that there can be only one decision-maker in a marriage, and naturally that must be the husband: as "Proprietor" of their goods and land, "his Will take(s) place before that of his wife in all things of their common Concernment."[6] To be sure, Locke insists, against Filmer, that paternal power is not political power, and that the political power of a magistrate is unlike that that of a master, lord, or husband.[7] Nonetheless, the separation of paternal from political power *presupposes* that a husband exercises a legitimate power over a wife. Locke's division between private, conjugal power and public, political power has been taken for granted in contemporary "political" theory, and so the problem of the subordination of wives disappeared from view. The husband's power is brought from Locke's state of nature into civil society, but it is transformed. He no longer has the power of the father-monarch in (Locke's conjectural history of) the natural condition. He obtains a new conjugal power, naturalized and depoliticized, suited to a civil society—that is to say, a modern constitutional state—created through the original contract, a conjugal power that is the political fulcrum of his "right" to govern women within other major civil institutions.

This is my interpretation of Locke in *The Sexual Contract;* in "Mere Auxiliaries" we argued that Locke forged an accommodation between patriarchy and liberalism. The theorists of an original contract both dealt the deathblow to the classic patriarchal argument that political rule was paternal rule and laid the theoretical groundwork for a modern, contractual, patriarchal transformation.[8] Does this mean that I suppressed the ambivalences in Locke's theory that are present in "Mere Auxiliaries," and so repress what "has been and may be most useful to feminism," to produce an interpretation "of liberal political philosophy as oppressive to women"?[9] I plead not guilty. My more recent reading of Locke builds directly on "Mere Auxiliaries." One of the fundamental points in my book is that in theories of original contracts the freedom of women (wives) is necessarily at the same time denied and affirmed.[10] It is affirmed because women must be seen as free if they are to enter into the marriage contract, a contract which then denies their natural freedom.

The assumptions of theories of an original contract provided feminists with theoretical weapons with which to mount a systematic challenge to the legitimacy of conjugal power and the form of the marriage contract. But their efforts were made in a context in which the legal and social underpinning of husbands' power was strengthened between the mid-seventeenth and mid-nineteen centuries, attempts by the suffragists to appeal to the ancient rights and liberties of freeborn Englishwomen were rejected, and the modern constitutional (democratic) state was developed around the interconnections between the institutions of marriage, employment, and citizenship.

This brings me to the other feature of "Mere Auxiliaries" that particularly strikes me now. One of the strengths of our argument was that we put Locke's theoretical claims into a broader social context. That was hardly unusual when we were working on the paper. Economic and class-based analyses of capitalism (and political science), from which both Teresa and I drew many insights, provided the alternative in the 1970s to mainstream scholarly work. Marxist theory also provided a framework and a critical target for much feminist writing in the early years of the Second Wave. A good deal of time and energy went, for instance, into trying to decipher whether housework was productive labor and generated surplus value. Just to type that sentence brings home how far intellectual preoccupations and fashions have changed. The conjunction of the rise of poststructuralism, the hostility to anything seen as "socialist" following 1989, and the ideological triumph of neoliberalism have meant that the theoretical legacy on which we relied in our paper has had little influence in feminist theory for many years.[11]

While the new intellectual developments were invigorating, much of theoretical value has gotten lost, as Teresa's last books demonstrate. This is especially so at a time of increasing change and insecurity brought about by globalization, structural adjustment, the collapse of states and economies, mass population movements, and vicious wars with their massive civilian causalities. The outcome of this rapid transformation is far from clear. However, these new circumstances raise another question. Do Locke's arguments still have the same purchase today as they did in the world in which Teresa and I wrote "Mere Auxiliaries"?

Locke can be seen as standing at the beginning of changes that brought about the institutional and intellectual world that has been transformed since the late 1970s. We highlighted how Locke's arguments and theoretical categories were part of those first changes—the establishment of capitalism, representative government, and the modern state—and how his arguments fed into the long, and contested, process through which "separate spheres" was institutionalized by the mid-nineteenth century. More recent research confirms the general direction of the picture that we presented in "Mere Auxiliaries." Given the views about women's place with which we had been brought up, we were surprised to discover the economic role that women had played in the seventeenth century. During the early modern period it was not as "obvious" as it seemed later that women, even wives, should not participate in the new social order in the manner promised by the universal language of individual freedom and equality.

For instance, women were important in the emergence of the popular press and the development of freedom of expression; they used opportunities allowed by the constitutions of the East India Company and South Sea Company to turn to new forms of commerce,[12] and played a much bigger part in the Guilds than has been supposed.[13] The English courts in the seventeenth and eighteenth centuries had to admit, in a series of cases that concerned separated spouses and the Poor Law, that a wife was a legal individual.[14] That by the mid-nineteenth century the franchise had been reserved for men, a wife had disappeared as a legal and civil being under the "cover" of her husband, and women had been relegated to the peripheries of the economy came about because men took vigorous steps to enforce their rule, their prerogatives, and their monopoly of power, through political philosophy, popular writings, and political action. Men fought hard to consolidate their "right" to govern in the modern state, and to exercise power in the capitalist economy, in education, marriage, the household, and sexuality.

The epigraph to "Mere Auxiliaries" draws attention to the "peculiar" nature of women's subordination "in the modern family." The peculiarity, however, arose from the structure of the institution of marriage and the subordination that Locke had declared natural and politically irrelevant. The subordination of wives was a central political plank in the development of the modern state. To become a wife was not merely a private matter but vital for opportunities for employment and the rights of citizenship. From the 1840s in England paid employment became seen as properly performed by husbands, male "breadwinners," and the rights and benefits of citizenship became linked to male employment and marriage. In the twentieth-century welfare state most wives received benefits not by virtue of being citizens but indirectly through the employment of their husbands. The heyday of the "breadwinner" model lasted from the 1840s to the 1970s. Since then it has been crumbling under the weight of changes in law and in beliefs about masculinity, femininity, and marriage—testament to the impact of the feminist movement—and the elimination of jobs for male breadwinners in global economic restructuring. To what extent Locke's arguments remain salient in these new conditions depends on the future of the sexual contract: Will it be eliminated, or will it be rewritten in a new, but still recognizable, form for the twenty-first century? At present, in the midst of very rapid change, it is hard to give an answer.

Current political rhetoric and "the end of welfare as we know it" demand that all able-bodied adults should be in paid employment, even mothers with young children. Locke spends a good deal of time in his attack on Filmer emphasizing that mothers as well as fathers have authority over children, although that did not give them any political standing. It was deemed that women's task was to care for children, yet the labor they undertook as mothers was not seen as "work," a designation reserved for paid employment, nor was it seen as a contribution to citizenship. Yet, for example, as indicated by all the controversies over differential rates of population increase, and access to birth control and abortion, motherhood is an important political issue. We noted in passing in "Mere Auxiliaries" that there were parallels between the consolidation of capitalism and the introduction of wage labor from the seventeenth century in England and what was then happening to women in developing countries, and Teresa's discussion deals with these questions.

(Teresa Brennan)

Wage laborers needed to become "free" if they were to "choose" to be employed, but it followed that what was hitherto the main site of production, the household, ceased to be a productive unit. In household production, or petty commodity production as it is has been called, women's economically productive labor was not separated spatially from their work as mothers. One consequence was that married women had a stronger economic place, a direct role in production, and, we can add now, in selling. In Braudel's history of capitalism, the seemingly incidental references to women as vendors, up to and including the seventeenth century, are remarkable: they also reinforce our argument that women were visible as economic actors before industrialization. But these "market wives, more numerous than the men" disappear from the eighteenth century onward.[15]

Today, as we have noted, in rich countries most women are in some form of employment. Hobbes was worried about masterless men, but in the United States in particular masterless mothers are the cause for alarm. Contemporary cuts in social provision for single mothers on both sides of the Atlantic build on patterns which emerged in the seventeenth century. They do so not only in terms of political philosophy. These patterns also privilege space over time by focusing on the global speed of acquisition at the expense of social provision for reproduction. The deregulation of policies affecting the speed of acquisition through free trade is the other side of the denial of the time given to reproduction, by maternal labor and nature alike. In the case of nature, using up a local resource need not have consequences for the producers, provided they can acquire more of that resource elsewhere. In such cases they are not obliged to pay for the real time of the reproduction of those natural resources, if one accepts the idea that value should not only be conceived in terms of the energetic value labor adds in production, but in terms of the value added by all natural sources of energy.[16]

This works well enough for the biological, natural resources whose removal from one country to another constitutes the bulk of free trade. But it does not work in terms of the reproductive labor of mothers, which has to be, by definition, carried out locally. Now as in the seventeenth century, at the intersection between the spatial expansion of capitalism and the generational and daily reproduction of people, stand mothers, who suffer cumulatively from the direction capital has been traveling since its inception. The issue will come into focus if we return to the genesis of labor's mobility.

That labor power has to be free to sell itself in the marketplace is clear. Marx recognized long ago that, for capital, labor power could not be constrained by feudal obligation. If labor was constrained, it could not move from country to city, or factory to factory, nor could capital "bargain" with it to keep its cost down. Worse, capital would have to provide for labor when it was old; feudal obligations, formally at least, went both ways. Hence Marx's notion that the laborer's freedom and choice are ideological terms insofar as both these "rights" serve capital. What went underrecognized in Marx's critique is just how much "freedom" in fact means mobility. For this reason, in large part, Marxists and capitalists alike assume that capitalism as we know it "grew" out of small-scale, seventeenth-century petty commodity production. In other words, it is assumed that small producers accumulated capital, then increased the size of their enterprises, then gobbled up other small producers. At one level, this is self-evident. At another, the idea of natural growth from small to large obscures a central fact: production governed by natural time and production based on expansion through space and speed were and are actually in competition. Small businesses, such as the household-based production that dominated England up to the close of the eighteenth century, are in competition with larger production processes in that the latter acquire their raw materials and make their profits through spatial trade, while the former depend on time: the reproduction of those raw materials close to hand.

The explanation of profit based on this perspective presupposes that the conflict between the large and the small is ongoing, however latent that conflict has become. Hence in the South, as noted, the historical pattern just described continues to the present. Hitherto dependent on local production and subsistence agriculture, men leave their land (usually as a result of forced sales to agribusiness) and travel to cities in search of employment, as they did following the enclosure of common land in England. Like women of the seventeenth century, women of the South are less likely to leave their villages, holding onto subsistence agriculture where they can as a food source. If they do leave, as they know, they are less likely to be employed than the men. The industrialization or so-called development that globalization fosters invariably increases the poverty of women and decreases their social influence. Poverty spurs them to have more children. Some consolation might be offered the men, and a limited percentage of the women, by the fact that global corporations do offer *some* employment. They often relocate production to the South or third world, or former Eastern bloc, taking advantage of labor markets where they can pay less than the average $7.50 they are obliged to pay in the United States or Europe.

One of the additional evils of the recent welfare legislation in the United States is that while it stigmatizes migration as desertion, it ignores the fact that it is far harder for women with sole responsibility for children to be mobile. The ideological assumption that there are enough jobs in the United States, or Europe, for the number of unemployed if they were not too lazy to go looking for them is premised on the mobility of those unemployed. This ignores the need for locality in the rearing of a child, which in most cases cannot be schooled or cared for any distance from its home. But it is in the home itself naturally that most of the labor of childrearing is done. In this sphere nothing is more basic to human reproduction than the mother's labor, obviously in both senses of that term, but especially in terms of day-to-day work. This labor is recognized still to some degree in the provisions of the British welfare state (and even in the United States in the Family Dependents Act), just as it was recognized in the (until recently) unchallenged assumption that a child stayed with its mother in custody disputes. It only goes unrecognized when the rights based in labor give way to rights based on individual equality and abstract ascriptions. These rights have no relation to locality, or to labor. But they are suited to a world in which the mobility of labor becomes an increasing requirement as globalization proceeds. Individuals can take rights conceived independently of labor with them wherever they go.

Given that the business of substituting speed and spatial expansion for reproductive time has now spanned four centuries, it would be interesting to pursue facts suggesting that the economic position of women as mothers has deteriorated consistently with capitalism, and now globalization (which means that the women of the South are subject to overlapping circles of distantiation. They are subject to the mobility and separations contingent on the division into town and country, and the loss of land to agricultural business. They are also affected by the inter-country migration and tremendous traffic in biological resources, as well as minerals and fossil fuels, characteristic of globalization). The comparative and historical work on the feminization of poverty has only begun.

But it is clear now that the standing of women-as-mothers is linked to the time, or lack of it, accorded replenishment or reproduction in the most general sense. The division between household and workplace, and between town and country, mark the end of much petty commodity or household-based production. It is in household production that according to Lorenne Clark and others, women as mothers had a better economic place. This contrasts with the notion that the position of women has progressed in recent centuries. Instead women-as-mothers lose a place rooted in natural law, as well as a better economic place at the beginning of that uprooting when households struggle to be more than places of consumption, when production gets faster, and the problem of reproduction is solved by spatial expansion, except at the human level, where reproduction is slow, too slow to keep pace.

The real issue—as we have attempted to foreshadow—is the difference between formal contractual rights and rights-based-in-labor. Rights-based-in-labor have to presuppose a geographical proximity to the product of one's labor. The right to the product of one's labor is a right of the flesh, acknowledging that one has expended energy which is embodied in the product, including the child. It may or may not derive from natural law (one would need to write a reinterpretation of natural law to make this case). Contractual rights are based in property.

When Locke saw labor as founding a right to property, he did not mention the mother's labor in bearing and rearing the child (and doubtless would have assigned it, as he assigned the labor of servants, to the property of the master). But the idea that property is based on the rights conferred by labor survived until recently in the legal prejudice that gave mothers custody of their children, as well as the claims of socialism. At the level of political philosophy, we can see the history of the last four centuries as one wherein the formal, contractual rights of the individual to freedom and equality have increasingly eroded the natural rights of the flesh by presupposing an individual cut off from his or her roots in the physical world, as well as the patriarchal roots of Filmer's—and the Promise Keepers'—concern.

An interpretation of natural rights through labor differs from one based on the conventional (that is, not natural) rights of the individual. This denial begins with the appropriation of all creativity by the father in the interpretation of religion, an appropriation in which the mother's creative labor is invisible. That same invisibility afflicts her in terms of the recent trend in father's rights, which appear to be based in genetic or material property, rather than in labor expended. For instance, a father can now claim and win custody on the basis that he is better able to provide materially for a child the mother has labored to teach, train, and guard physically, for years. The denial of the mother's natural-law-based rights is, then, derivative of a denial of the rights of the flesh and labor more generally. First, the product is removed from the laborer, then the laborer is removed from the field of reproduction, by a similar fetishistic sleight-of-hand. An individual with individual rights must base those rights in abstractions, rather than physical connections with the environment and those in it. A right to a product based in labor is a right to a production system based in local production. This has to be the case. Once the laborer is separated from the product geographically, or the working mother from her child, then the basis of rights can no longer lie in labor, for the links in the chain of separation between numerous divided producers and the product have become too many. Petty commodity—or household—production is not simply a progenitor of big capital. Where it is based on allowances for natural reproduction time, it is a system opposed to it.

The conquest of time and space is basic to capital's national and global interests. The numbers of women on welfare, and their increasing immiseration, should be viewed as exemplary of a trend with a much broader basis. Close to home, that trend is evident in the general increase of female single-headed households (which extends well beyond those of welfare recipients). If the situation of women-as-mothers is deteriorating economically, that deterioration accelerates to the extent that the household ceases to be an economic partnership. This caesura takes various forms: a commuting partner, a migrating one, no partner at all. Historically, when the household remained a site of production—an alternative to the household as the place of consumption—human needs, human biological needs, had priority for more people. This priority is reduced the more that spatial acquisition substitutes for natural reproduction. But because the communities, the people, and the natural resources broken up in this process in the North still had the South to turn to for the labor and natural reserves which the North had exhausted on its own terrain, there were safeguards for human needs, safeguards dependent on imperialism and the general exploitation of the South. But as the South cannot exploit the North, and cannot really exploit itself as the North is already doing so, there are no such safeguards protecting even in part the human needs of its peoples.

Cutbacks in health, education, social security, and pensions, all these suffer while the welfare of corporations flourishes. While they are the least significant in terms of expenditure cuts, the new financial strictures against unwed mothers and restrictions on migration are paradigmatic, indicative of the fact that keeping down the overall social cost of generational reproduction is critical to capital's logic of speedy reproduction and unfettered spatial expansion, just as the costs of day-to-day reproduction may be borne more and more by workers in a way that substitutes time for money, so that the wage appears higher than it is in real terms. At the same time, the fact that women and men are both subject to the rule of exchange value pressures the patriarchal relation that kept women dependent economically on men.

As far as we can see, this is the most important contradiction thrown up by the way global capital breaks apart traditional commitments. Its significance lies in the fact that it brings the situation of women as mothers and workers into sharp relief. Women can make money in the market place, but that activity is at odds with rearing children without fathers (a growing demographic reality where fathers change towns and/or partners). The fact that the solution to this situation has to be one in which women are economically empowered as mothers is directly tied to localization. Globalization leads to the breakup of communities and displacement in the North and South, but its most serious effects on human beings are on women.[17]

Returning to the epigraph for the original article, and the "peculiar" nature of women's inequality vis-à-vis men: we sort that peculiarity in a parallel between the manner in which the lady of the house vanishes with theoretical individualism's assumptions about the social contract, and the manner in which women as mothers are disadvantaged by the breakup of production based on households. The fact that four-fifths of the world's poor are women has led the United Nations to a recent "mainstreaming" of gender issues in addressing poverty. Had attention been given to the place of women as mothers sooner, the reason for that poverty might also have emerged.

Notes

1. Teresa Brennan, *Globalization and Its Terrors: Everyday Life in the West* (London: Routledge, 2003).

2. *The Sexism of Social and Political Theory: Women and Reproduction from Plato to Nietzsche*, ed. Lorenne Clark and Lynda Lange (Toronto: University of Toronto Press, 1979); Mary Shanley, "Marriage Contract and Social Contract in Seventeenth Century Political Thought," *Western Political Quarterly* 32 (1979): 79–91; Susan Moller Okin, *Women in Western Political Thought* (Princeton: Princeton University Press, 1979). Clark's article in her edited volume was originally published as "Women and John Locke: Who Owns the Apples in the Garden of Eden?" in the *Canadian Journal of Philosophy* 7 (1976): 699–724, but we had seen neither it nor Melissa Butler's "Early Liberal Roots of Feminism: John Locke and the Attack on Patriarchy," which was published in the *American Political Science Review* 72 (1978): 135–50. Our original article cited an earlier version of Shanley's essay that she presented as a conference paper in 1976.

3. Carole Pateman, *The Problem of Political Obligation: A Critical Analysis of Liberal Theory* (New York: John Wiley and Sons, 1979).

4. Ibid., 74–76.

5. Cited in J. Spinner-Halev, *Surviving Diversity* (Baltimore: The Johns Hopkins University Press, 2000), 157.

6. John Locke, *Two Treatises of Government*, ed. Peter Laslett (New York: Cambridge University Press, 1960), 1.48. As Clark so pertinently asked, "Why, given Locke's assumptions, does not Eve own her own apples?" Clark, "Women and John Locke," 38.

7. Locke, *Two Treatises*, 2.2.

8. For the classification of traditional, classic, and modern patriarchy, see Carole Pateman, *The Sexual Contract* (Stanford: Stanford University Press, 1988), chap. 2

9. Kate Nash, *Universal Difference: Feminism and the Liberal Undecidability of "Women"* (New York: St. Martin's Press, 1998), 40.

10. Which is, I take it, an example of the "undecidability" of women with which Nash is concerned. Leaving aside issues about "liberalism" here, it would be hard to make a case about its "oppressive" character without discussing Wollstonecraft or J. S. Mill, who are outside of an argument about theories of original contracts.

11. Hence I am also charged with seeing political theory as merely "reflexive of socio-economic change," with no openings left for feminist alternatives. Nash, *Universal Difference*, 65. In "Mere Auxiliaries" we noted that the idea of natural freedom and equality was necessary if individuals were to be seen as capable of pursuing their interests and making exchanges and contracts in the market. But such ideas are also a condition for the development of the conception of the "free market" and "the economy" as a separate area of social life, subject to its own laws.

12. See Lois Schwoerer, "Women's Public Political Voice in England: 1640–1740," and Susan Staves, "Investments, Votes, and 'Bribes': Women as Shareholders in the Chartered National Companies," in *Women Writers and the Early Modern British Political Tradition*, ed. Hilda Smith (New York: Cambridge University Press, 1998).

13. Hilda Smith, *All Men and Both Sexes: Gender, Politics and the False Universal in England, 1640–1832* (University Park: Pennsylvania State University Press, 2002), chap. 2.

14. Barbara Todd, "'To Be Some body': Married Women and *The Hardships of English Laws*," in Smith, *Women Writers*.

15. Fernand Braudel, *The Wheels of Commerce*, trans. Siân Reynolds, vol. 2, *Civilization and Capitalism, 15th–18th Century* (Berkeley and Los Angeles: University of California Press 1992), 36. On the disruption of Parisian traffic "on market days [by] several women and stallholders, from the fields as well as from the city," see 31–32.

16. See Teresa Brennan, *Exhausting Modernity: Grounds for a New Economy* (New York: Routledge, 2000).

17. For empirical details of this and other unattributed references to the impact of globalization, see Brennan, *Globalization and Its Terrors*.

3

Early Liberal Roots of Feminism: John Locke's Attack on Patriarchy

Melissa A. Butler

The seventeenth-century conflict between patriarchal and liberal political thought grew out of a shift in views on human nature and the nature of society. This shift eventually led to new perspectives on the nature, role and status of women as well. Though the question of how political theorists handle the subject of women is rarely explored, it may be supposed that the way theorists treat half of humanity should have some consequences for their theories. Yet a theorist's comments on the status of women are usually treated as matters of antiquarian interest only; their significance for a full understanding of a theorist's work is seldom recognized. This was not always the case. In the past, theorists' discussions of women have had important implications for the acceptability of entire theories. The position of women has been used as a critical tool in evaluating theories. The clash between patriarchal and liberal theories serves as a case in point.

Though it is impossible to date the precise origin of the shift in collective consciousness which gave rise to the sexual revolution, it is clear that the revolution itself was (and is) directed against patriarchy. Simply defined, patriarchy is the rule of women by men, and of young men by older men.

Most feminists will agree that economic, social, psychological, political and legal structures are today quite patriarchal in practice. The weight of these structures is particularly oppressive since the theoretical justifications offered in their behalf have been bankrupt for centuries. This bankruptcy became evident, not with Marx or Engels, nor with John Stuart Mill, but with still earlier liberal attacks on the political theory of patriarchy. The vestiges of patriarchalism that survive in contemporary social practice are but remnants of a much more complete form of patriarchalism.

In early seventeenth-century England, patriarchalism was a dominant paradigm, a world view, a weltanschauung.[1] For many Englishmen, it represented the truth of their time and all time. It was a fully articulated theory which expressly accounted for all social relations—king-subject, father-child, master-servent, etc.—in patriarchal terms. Sir Robert Filmer and other patriarchal writers insisted that the king ruled absolutely, the divinely ordained father of his people. No one was born free; everyone was born in subjection to some patriarchal superior. Each individual human being could find his or her proper place by consulting patriarchal theory. Places were not matters of individual choice but were assigned according to a divinely ordained pattern set down at the Creation.

By the end of the seventeenth century, the patriarchal world view had crumbled. It was replaced by a new understanding of human nature and of social and political organization. Whigs such as Sidney, Tyrrell, and Locke grounded political power in acts of consent made by free-born individuals. Contract and individual choice supplanted birth and divine designation as crucial factors in social and political analysis. These changes raised problems concerning the status of women in the new order. At first, liberal theorists resisted the suggestion that the old assigned position of women might have to be abandoned. The champions of consent theory saw no need to secure the consent of women. Yet their critics insisted that excluding women violated the very theory of human nature on which liberalism was based. Eventually, liberals would be forced to bring their views on women into line with their theory of human nature. This changing image of women certainly played a part in that shift in consciousness which paved the way for the sexual revolution.

The Statement of Patriarchy: Sir Robert Filmer

While the appearance of full-blown patriarchal political theory was occasioned primarily by the turbulence of seventeenth-century English politics, patriarchal ideas and intimations could be found in political writings long before they received more systematic theoretical expression in the writings of Sir Robert Filmer.[2]

In that era of "divine right kings," the legitimacy of a monarch's claim to absolute rule could be proved if the source of a divine grant of power could be found. Patriarchal political theory satisfied this need. It offered an explanation of the historical origins of the king's political power and of the subject's political obligation. By tracing the king's power back to Adam, the theory provided more than mere historical justification; it provided divine sanction.

The explanation derived its effectiveness from a general awareness of the obvious truth which patriarchalism told.[3] The patriarchal family experience was universal. The family in the seventeenth century was a primary group in every sense of the term. Life was lived on a small scale and the family was at its center. The family patriarch was a universally-acknowledged authority figure with immense power. By linking the authority of the king with the authority of the father, a theorist could immediately clarify the nature of a subject's political obligations. Moreover, monarchical power grounded in patriarchal power took on the legitimacy of the least-challengeable social institution, the family. Patriarchal concepts found in catechism and sermon literature enhanced the king's legitimacy in the eyes of the masses. Finally, the linkage of paternal and monarchical power provided a means for transcending any residual or intermediate loyalties a subject might have. Absolute, patriarchal, monarchical power was vested in the king. It was to the king, not to the local nobility, that loyalty and obedience were rightfully owed.

Patriarchalists insisted that God, nature and history were on their side.

For proof, one need only consult the one true account of Creation, namely, the Book of Genesis. Not only was Genesis divinely inspired, it was also the oldest possible historical source and the best guide to man's nature.[4] There, in the Genesis account, was the evidence that God had created Adam in His image—patriarch and monarch He created him.

The gradual unfolding of biblical history showed that the basic institution of patriarchy, the patriarchal family, had always been a fundamental feature of society. Throughout Judeo-Christian society, family life, bolstered by marriage and divorce laws, primogeniture and property rules, continued thoroughly patriarchal down to the seventeenth century.[5]

During the English Civil War, both divine right monarchy and the patriarch theory which helped support it were severely challenged. Republicans declared that the power of the king was limited. Leveller tracts espoused social contract doctrines. Thomas Hobbes, though himself eager to uphold the power of a strong sovereign, insisted that political power did not originate in a divine grant from God to Adam, father of the race. Instead, Hobbes maintained that political power was the result of an agreement, a covenant among men. In reaction to these novel and dangerous doctrines, Sir Robert Filmer penned the best-known treatises in defense of the patriarchal position.

Filmer was himself something of a model patriarch.[6] He was the eldest son in a family of seventeen children, a landholder, a squire of Kent. He married a child heiress in 1610, but did not cohabit with his wife until 1618. Knighted by King James I in 1619, he took over the duties of head of the large Filmer household in 1629. Most of his father's family was dependent on him.

During the Civil War, Sir Robert was seen as a Loyalist. He spent many months in prison and suffered a sizable property loss. After his imprisonment, Filmer published several political tracts including *The Anarchy of a Limited or Mixed Monarchy* (1648), *The Freeholder's Grand Inquest* (1648), and *Observations Upon Aristotle, Touching Forms of Government* (1652). The work for which he is best known, *Patriarcha*, was begun around 1640, but was published posthumously in 1680.[7] Filmer's later political writings often drew on the ideas expressed in this earlier, unpublished manuscript.

To elaborate his patriarchal theory of politics, Filmer turned to both classical and constitutional sources. But Filmer's most important, most authoritative source was always scripture. Aristotle could be used as a commentary; but whenever disagreement arose between Aristotle and

Filmer, or Aristotle and scripture, Sir Robert would summon the force of scripture behind his own arguments, reminding that "heathen authors" were ignorant of the true facts of creation and the beginnings of government (F.W. 187).

The scriptural arguments for monarchy illustrate the most literally patriarchal aspects of Filmer's thought. In brief, his account of the biblical origins and justifications of patriarchy was a follows:

> God created only Adam, and of a piece of him made the woman; and if by generation from them two as parts of them, all mankind be propagated: if also God gave to Adam not only the dominion over the woman and the children that should issue from them, but also over the whole earth to subdue it, and over all the creatures on it, so that as long as Adam lived no man could claim or enjoy anything but by donation, assignation, or permission from him (F.W. 241).

Again and again throughout his works Filmer recalled the divine grant of paternal, monarchical power to Adam. Filmer drew upon the Book of Genesis, specifically Genesis 1:28, when he claimed that "the first government in the world was monarchical in the father of all flesh. Adam being commanded to multiply, and people the earth and subdue it, and having dominion given him over all creatures, was thereby the monarch of the whole world" (F.W. 187).

As critics from Filmer's own century were only to happy to observe, Sir Robert had erred in his biblical analysis. Filmer had assigned all power to Adam, but God had given dominion to Adam and Eve. The divine grant of power in Genesis 1:28 was made to "them," ostensibly the male and female whose creation had been announced in the preceding verse. Sir Robert had to tamper with the text because the original grant of power detailed in Genesis 1:28 was not, as he maintained, an exclusive grant of private monarchical dominion given to Adam, the patriarch. On the contrary, the blessing was given to both the male and the female.

If evidence of the patriarchal theory could not be found in God's blessing, perhaps it could be found in His curse. Conceivably, Filmer might have agreed that the original prelapsarian grant had been made to Adam and Eve jointly, and might still have salvaged his patriarchal theory. He could have maintained that the lines of patriarchal authority were established only after the Fall. Genesis 3:16 could have been offered as proof: "Thy desire shall be to thy husband, he shall rule over thee."

Indeed, in the *Anarchy*, Filmer did refer to these lines as proof that "God ordained Adam to rule over his wife . . . and as hers so all theirs that should come of her" (F.W. 283). Nevertheless, it is clear that Sir Robert preferred the Genesis 1:28 passage. By using that text, he could show that patriarchal order was in accord with man's original nature, not simply with his fallen nature. Filmer hoped to show that the human hierarchy was established in the *very* beginning. Every moment that passed risked the introduction of a custom which might lend credence to the anti-patriarchal case.[8] Each passing second made monarchical power appear less natural, and shared dominion more legitimate. Consequently, Filmer preferred to insist that Adam was monarch of the world from the very first moment of creation:

> By the appointment of God, as soon as Adam was created he was monarch of the world, though he had no subjects; for though there could not be actual government until there were subjects yet by the right of nature it was due to Adam to be governor of his posterity: though not in act, yet at least in habit. Adam was a King from his creation: and in the state of innocency he had been governor of his children; for the integrity or excellency of the subjects doth not take away the order or eminency of the governor. Eve was subject to Adam before he sinned; the angels who are of a pure nature, are subject to God (F.W. 289).

Filmer's analogy here is striking. The qualitative difference between man and woman, between king and subject, is virtually infinite; indeed, it parallels the qualitative difference which exists between God and the angels.

Genesis was not the only biblical source of patriarchal theory. The Decalogue, too, served to support patriarchal political authority, according to Filmer: "The power of the government is settled and fixed by the commandment of 'honour thy Father'; if there were a higher power than the fatherly, then this command could not stand and be observed" (F.W. 188). Filmer's omission is obvious. In service of political patriarchalism, the last half of the fifth commandment was dropped. All honor due to mother was forgotten.

Filmer and the Contract Theorists

Filmer's habit of selective quotation was not overlooked by his critics. In the 1680s Whigs severely attacked *Patriarcha* by dredging up one biblical reference after another to prove Sir Robert had flagrantly abused scriptural texts to support his theory. Lengthy criticisms were written by Edward Gee, a contemporary of Filmer's, and by later Whig theorists including Algernon Sidney, James Tyrrell, and John Locke.[9] Biblical criticisms constituted a major part of their attack of patriarchal theory. Indeed, Filmer's critics actually did far more biblical exegesis than he did.[10] Later commentators saw Filmer's opponents' efforts as little more than intellectual overkill. The commentators failed to realize that Filmer's thought was part of a pervasive pattern which had had a tight grip on the minds of many Englishmen.

Filmer's critics had to attack him by striking at the theological-scriptural base of the theory since scripture was by far its most important source. Filmer used scripture as the ultimate weapon, guaranteed to clinch any argument. In the eyes of his fellow Englishmen who shared his world view, the only way Sir Robert could be refuted was by destroying his scriptural base.[11]

In the course of the seventeenth century, standards of evidence and styles of argument changed dramatically. Forms of argument which had been perfectly acceptable, indeed even indispensable, in earlier political discourse were rejected in favor of newer "rational" arguments. Although John Locke would champion the new mode of thought, the old form still had a hold on him. Locke took Filmer's biblical arguments seriously, as challenges to be met and overcome. Locke's attack on Filmer, though incomplete, gives the impression that once the biblical criticism was finished, he believed Filmer stood refuted and the attack on contract theory rebutted. This was not necessarily true.[12]

Filmer staunchly insisted that man was not by nature free. Rather, man was born to subjection:

> Every man that is born is so far from being free-born that by his very birth he becomes a subject to him that begets him: under which subjection he is always to live, unless by immediate appointment from God, or by the grant or death of his Father, he becomes possessed of that power to which he was subject (F.W. 232).

By looking to the Garden of Eden, Filmer thought he could demonstrate the truth about natural man and his natural forms of association, but his contention that patriarchal monarchy was the natural and only legitimate form of government did not receive its force solely from the scriptural account. Sir Robert also relied on constitutional and classical sources to complement his biblical evidence. More importantly, however, the claims he made were strengthened by their apparent empirical relevance. The paternal power of the father and of the king was evident to all who would but look about them. The experience of patriarchalism in family life was a constant, natural feature of daily life. So too, paternal power in a kingdom would remain constant: "There is and always shall be continued to the end of the world, a natural right of a supreme Father over every multitude" (F.W. 62).

So persuasive was the use of patriarchy was a legitimating concept that Filmer maintained that even God exercised power by right of fatherhood. Filmer's argument takes on a circular character at this point. Nevertheless, it is clear that there was absolutely no room in patriarchal theory for free-born individuals. Government could not begin with an act of consent made by free and equal individuals in a state of nature. Filmer insisted that such government could be based on no more than myth. Furthermore, he insisted that contract theories which advanced such a myth would be replete with contradictions and logical fallacies.

Filmer offered a theory which was truly comprehensive and coherent, one which provided a place for every individual in society. His opponents, on the other hand, were far less able to provide a satisfactory accommodation for all the individuals and groups which made up seventeenth-century English society.

At least part of the difficulty which his adversaries encountered stemmed from their inability to dismiss patriarchalism completely in all its manifestations. They wished to destroy the patriarchal base of monarchy, and sever the connection between patriarchalism and divine-right politics, yet they were unable to reject less comprehensive forms of patriarchalism as basic organizing principles of government and society. They developed a new theory of human nature, but did not foresee or develop the impilications of that theory. This point can be illustrated specifically by examining the position of women in their theories.

Whig theorists such as Tyrrell and Sidney certainly believed that whole classes of people were plainly unfit to exercise political power and plainly incapable of giving their own consent to government. Sidney spoke harshly of forms of government which granted power without regard to age, sex, infirmity or vice.[13] Tyrrell wrote, "There never was any Government where all the Promiscuous Rabble of Women and Children had Votes, as being not capable of it."[14]

Edward Gee would have founded his "democracy" on fatherly authority. Those who lacked political significance (i.e., women, children, servants) would be "involved" in their patriarchal superiors.[15] James Tyrrell indicated that he found a similar arrangement acceptable at the foundation of a commonwealth.[16] In accepting this sort of "democracy" these theorists were not very far from Filmer. Sir Robert permitted the patriarchal heads of families to gather together to decide who among them would become supreme father when the king died without an heir (F.W. 288). Filmer, Gee, Tyrrell, and Sidney all agreed on one thing: women and children need have no part in these political decisions.

Despite their criticisms of patriarchalism and their arguments based on consent, neither Tyrrell nor his friend, John Locke, was willing to allow participation to all comers. Tyrrell wished to limit participation to male property owners. Locke, as MacPherson argues, would have limited participation to the demonstrably rational (read "acquisitive") classes.[17] But these limitations were swept away by historical actualities over the next two centuries. Rights to political participation were gradually extended to all men and subsequently to all women. Indeed, Filmer, rather than Locke or Tyrrell proved the better predictor of the historical course plotted by the liberal logic when he wrote of government by the people:

> If but one man be excluded, the same reason that excludes one man, may exclude many hundreds, and many thousands, yea, and the major part itself; if it be admitted, that the people are or ever were free by nature, and not to be governed, but by their own consent, it is most unjust to exclude any one man from his right in government (F.W. 211).

No one could be excluded from political participation if contract theorists were to remain true to their principles. Filmer understood that in speaking of "the people" and their natural liberty, one had to talk about all mankind.

Though contract theorists came to consider their theories as logical or moral rather than as historical, Filmer used the historical problems of the social contract in an attempt to undermine the logical and moral status of the theory. Filmer insisted that the state of nature and the social contract became logically and historically unacceptable doctrines if "the people" were to be equated with "all mankind." Furthermore, he believed that contract theorists themselves would recoil when faced with the full implications of their theory.

Filmer demanded to know the details of the great meeting where the contract was approved. When did the meeting occur? Who decided the time and place? More importantly, he wanted to know who was invited. Filmer saw these as serious problems for consent theorists since:

> Mankind is like the sea, ever ebbing or flowing every minute one is born another dies; those that are the people this minute are not the people the next minute, in every instant and point of time there is a variation: no one time can be indifferent for all of mankind to assemble; it cannot but be mischevious always at least to all infants and others under the age of discretion; not to speak of women, especially virgins, who by birth have as much natural freedom as any other and therefore ought not to lose their liberty without their consent (F.W. 287).

Filmer's attack was no longer simply historical; it was now logical and moral as well. It was clear to him that if the "natural freedom" of mankind was to be taken seriously, obviously the natural freedom of women and children would have to be considered. If women and children were free, they would have to be included in any sort of compact. "Tacit consent" was an impossiblity, and was rejected by Filmer as "unreasonable" and "unnatural" (F.W. 225). Simply to "conclude" the votes of children, for example, in the votes of parents would not be adequate:

> This remedy may cure some part of the mischief, but it destroys the whole cause, and at last stumbles upon the true original of government. For if it be allowed that the acts of the parents bind the children, then farewell the doctrine of the natural freedom of mankind; where subjection of children to parents is natural there can be no natural freedom (F.W. 287).

Filmer would probably have agreed that the same line of reasoning could be used to analyze the relationship of women to the social contract.

Filmer's technique in this instance was one of his favorites—reductio ad absurdum. Natural freedom and political participation of women and children were obviously absurd to all living in that patriarchal world. Thus, Filmer's case against natural freedom and the social contract stood proved. His aim was to show the absurdity of the concept "consent of all the people." He insisted that "all the people" must be taken at face value. It must include groups of people obviously unfit for such decision making, that is, children, servants and *women*. Each of these groups had been accorded a place within the social and political theory of patriarchy. Each group's place was in accord with a traditional evaluation of its status.

Those who asserted the natural freedom of all mankind upset the applecart. If men were born free and equal, status could not be ascribed at birth, but would have to be achieved in life. If Filmer's opponents were to be consistent, new political roles would have to be opened up for those previously judged politically incompetent. This consequence was never fully clear to Filmer's critics. Though Tyrrell and Sidney criticized Filmer's patriarchalism, they were by no means ready or willing to break with all the trappings of patriarchy. Consequently, they faced additional difficulties when they tried to account for the political obligation of the politically incompetent.

Tyrrell attempted to base the political obligation of women and children on the debt owed for their "breeding up and preservation." At first glance, this formula may seem to resemble Locke's doctrine of "tacit consent." A closer look will reveal that Tyrrell's version is far more extensive than Locke's. Tyrrell demanded much more from women and children than simply the passive obedience required of sojourners who were not parties to the compact:

> They may well be lookt upon as under an higher Obligation in Conscience and in Gratitude to his Goverment, than Strangers of another Contry, who onely staying here for a time to pursue their own Occasions and having no Right to the same privileges and advantages of the Commonwealth do onely owe a passive obedience to its laws.[18]

The obligation of disenfranchised groups stemmed from their nurture, from the debt of gratitude owed to the government for their upbringing and education. They had no actual voice. They themselves were never expected to give free consent to their government. Yet still they were held to be obliged—out of gratitude.

This sort of obligation theory is not far removed from Filmer's. The natural duties of Filmer's king were "summed up in a universal fatherly care of his people" (F.W. 63). The King preserved, fed, clothed, instructed, and defended the whole commonwealth. Government by contract would do the same things for those who were not part of the contract. In return for these services alone, political nonparticipants owed "a higher Obligation in conscience and gratitude." No participation, no express consent was necessary to put an end to their natural freedom.

A third problem was created for both Filmer and his critics when the questions of participation and monarchical succession were considered together. Filmer did not use patriarchal theory to challenge women's claims to the throne. His critics, especially Sidney, seized upon his silence, protesting that Filmer would allow even women and children to rule as patriarchs. Patriarchal theory enthroned "the next in Blood, without any regard to Age, Sex or other Qualities of the Mind or Body."[19]

Whig theorists did not render Filmer's arguments less damaging to their cause, but they did turn them back on patriarchal theory. To Filmer, contract theory was absurd because it entailed the participation of politically unfit groups in the formation of government and society. To Whigs, the patriarchal position was outrageous because it risked giving a single, similarly incompetent individual absolute unchecked dominion.

To summarize, both Whig and patriarchal theorists used the position of women as a critical tool in evaluating competing theories. Both Whig and patriarchal theorists had to find places for women in their theories. Each criticized the other for the role and status eventually assigned to women.

In patriarchal theory, women held a distinctly subordinate position. Their inferior place in family, state and society was justified on the basis of scriptural exegesis. But scripture was frequently twisted in service of patriarchalism.

The errors and excesses of Filmer's theory were pointed out gleefully by his critics, yet many of these critics rejected only political patriarchalism, and that only in a limited way. Whigs stripped Genesis of its political import. They freed both men and women from subjection to a supreme earthly father. The social implications of Genesis were not completely rejected, however. The story of the Creation and Fall was still used to show the general inferiority of women to men. In practical terms, Whigs initiated no real attack on Filmer's discussion of women. They attacked the theorological-historical justifications for political patriarchy, but basically supported the institutional arrangements promoted by patriarchy where women were concerned.

The issue of women's political participation created problems for both Whigs and patriarchs. Patriarchalism was a conservative theory aimed at legitimation of the reigning monarch. Patriarchal legitimacy was founded in an argument which was inherently antifemale. Yet English law permitted women to reign as sole monarchs. Patriarchal theorists found no really satisfactory escape from this dilemma.

Whigs upheld the natural freedom of all mankind yet maintained that women's consent to government could be "concluded" in that of their husbands or fathers. Whigs rejected the biblical basis for political subordination of women, but accepted empirically-based arguments which showed women naturally unfit for political life.

In effect, Whigs substituted a community of many patriarchs for Filmer's supreme patriarch. Filmer, the patriarch, realized immediately that this simple substitution alone was much less than was required by the doctrine of natural freedom of all mankind. Slowly, over the next two centuries, even liberal thinkers would be drawn to the same conclusion.

Locke's Attack on Patriarchy

While other Whig writers simply declared that their theories necessitated no new roles for women, John Locke treated the problem somewhat differently. He was among the first to sense the inherent contradiction in a "liberalism" based on the natural freedom of mankind, which accorded women no greater freedom than allowed by patriarchalism. New places had to be opened to women. This is not to claim that John Locke planned or even foresaw the feminist movement. It does seem true, however, that Locke took his individualist principles very seriously, even when they entailed an admission that women, too, might have to be considered "individuals."

Clearly Locke was not interested in creating a world in which all were equal; in his view, there would always be differences among individuals. The key question here concerns the extent to which a Lockean society would discriminate on the basis of sex. Would the fact that some are more equal than others be determined by traditionally-assigned sex roles?

In the first of his *Two Treatises of Government*, Locke showed little interest in the constitutional or classical arguments offered by Filmer. Doubtless he believe that these arguments were simply not at the heart of Filmer's theory. Instead, Locke charged that the scripture-based arguments were unproved, not because he doubted the truth of the Bible, but because he realized Filmer had distorted that truth. Locke's attack stemmed from no impious disregard for Filmer's evidence, but from a different method of construing that evidence. As Laslett suggests, Locke had broken the bounds of Filmer's world of biblical politics by introducing rationalist arguments.[20]

Since Filmer's patriarchal theory included a particular view of the status of women, based on biblical arguments, Locke's refutation also had to deal with that view. Concerning the benediction of Genesis 1:28, Locke noted that it was bestowed on "more than one, for it was spoken in the Plural Number, God blessed *them* and said unto *them*, Have Dominion. God says unto *Adam* and *Eve*, Have Dominion" (T.T., I, 29). This argument introduced the possiblity that Adam's dominion was not exclusive but was shared with Eve. Further, Eve's subjection to Adam need not have prevented her from exercising dominion over the things of the Earth. Eve, too, might have property rights.

In the fifth chapter of the *First Treatise*, Locke argued against "Adam's title to Sovereignty by the Subjection of Eve." There, Locke had much more to say about the patriarchal conception of women. He took issue with Filmer's use of Genesis 3:16 ("And thy desire shall be to thy Husband and he shall rule over thee"). Those words, Locke objected, were a "punishment laid upon Eve." Furthermore, these words were not even spoken to Adam. The moment after the great transgression, Locke noted, "was not a time when Adam could expect any Favours, any grant of Priviledges from his offended Maker." At most, the curse would "concern the Female Sex Only," through Eve, its representative (T.T., I, 45–47).

Here, Locke argued that Genesis 3:16 offered no evidence of a general grant of power to Adam over all mankind. By limiting the curse to Eve and to women, Locke effectively removed males from the sway of the patriarchal monarch. But he went even further, and suggested that the arguments for the subjection of women based on the Genesis 3:16 passage could be faulty.

First, the subjection of women carried no political import. The curse imposed "no more [than] that Subjection they [women] should ordinarily be in to their Husbands." But even this limit on women's freedom was not immutable and could be overcome:

> There is here no more Law to oblige a Woman to such a Subjec-
> tion, if the Circumstances either of her Condition or Contract
> with her Husband should exempt her from it, then there is, that
> she should bring forth her Children in Sorrow and Pain, if there
> could be found a remedy for it, which is also part of the same
> Curse upon her (T.T., I, 47).

Nevertheless, Locke largely accepted the empirical fact of women's inferiority and saw it grounded in nature as ordered by God. He attempted to avoid the conclusion that Adam became Eve's superior or that husbands became their wives' superiors, yet his effort is fairly weak:

> God, in this Text, gives not, that I see, any Authority to Adam
> over Eve, or to Men over their Wives, but only foretells what
> should be the Woman's Lot, how by his Providence he would
> order it so, that she should be subject to her husband as we see
> that generally the Laws of Mankind and customs of Nations have
> ordered it so; and there is, I grant, a Foundation in Nature for it
> (T.T., I, 47).

Locke was principally interested in refuting the idea of a divine grant of authority to Adam. He lived in a world in which the subjection of women was an empirical fact and was willing to yield to the contemporary view that this fact had some foundation in nature. His tone was hesitant, though. Locke seemed to wish that God had not been responsible for women's inferior status. He tried to cast God in the role of prophet rather than creator. God merely "foretold" what women's lot would be. Locke found it difficult to keep God in the role of innocent bystander, however. Where Locke admitted the use of divine power, he tried to remain tentative: God, in his Providence, "would order" social relations so that wives would be subject to their husbands. But God did not give men any kind of rightful authority over women. Locke implied that God merely suggested one empirical relationship which was subsequently adopted by mankind and reinforced by the laws and customs of nations. That these laws and customs were largely established by males did not, in Locke's opinion, damage the case. It did not seem to bother him that such laws and customs offered proof of the authority which men exercised over women. Locke simply wished to deny that male authority was exercised by virtue of some divine grant. At this point, he had no need to reject the customary exercise of such authority. It was enough to show only that it was human and not divine in origin.

Peter Laslett notes that "Locke's attitude towards the curse on women in childbearing is typical of his progressive, humanitarian rationalism."[21] But Locke's views on women were also evidence of his individualism. Though Locke believed there was a "foundation in nature" for the limitations on women, he remained faithful to the individualist principles which underlay his theory. In his view, women were free to ovecome their natural limitations; each woman was permitted to strike a better deal for herself whenever possible.

In conjunction with his attack on Filmer's use of Genesis 3:16, Locke touched another of patriarchy's soft spots. He sensed the weakness of Filmer's insistence on the inferiority of women in a nation where women had worn the crown. Locke made no sustained analysis of this point, but remarked, instead, "[will anyone say] that either of our Queens *Mary* or *Elizabeth* had they Married any of their Subjects, had been by this Text put into a Political Subjection to him? or that he thereby should have had Monarchical Rule over her?" (T.T., I, 47)

Locke also accused Sir Robert of performing procrustean mutilations of "words and senses of Authors" (T.T., I, 60). This tendency was most evident in Filmer's abbreviation of the fifth commandment. Filmer had cited the command in several places throughout his works, but always in the same terms, "Honour thy Father." Locke noted this fact and then complained that "and Mother, as Apocriphal Words, are always left out." Filmer had overlooked the "constant Tenor of the Scripture," Locke maintained. To bolster his position, Locke produced well over a dozen scriptural citations showing the child's duty to father and mother. A mother's title to honor from her children was independent of the will of her husband. This independent right, he argued, was totally inconsistent with the existence of absolute monarchical power vested in the father (T.T., I, 63). Ultimately, Locke denied that the fifth commandment had any political implications at all (T.T., I, 65).

In this analysis, Locke broke with one of patriarchy's strongest traditions. Political obligation had been justified through the fifth commandment. In seventeenth-century sermon literature and catechism texts, the subject's duty of obedience was firmly rooted in this command. Locke refuted these arguments, not by criticizing the use of scriptural evidence, but by analyzing the interpretations supposedly based on that source.

This completed the destructive part of Locke's case. His attack rent the fabric of Filmer's theory. Since patriarchalism represented a complete, integrated theory of society, an adequate successor-theory would have to replace all its shattered parts. If all social relations could no longer be understood through the patriarchal paradigm, how could they be understood? Locke's answer came in the *Second Treatise*. There he made his positive contribution to the understanding of social relations.

Social Relations in the Second Treatise

For Filmer and his sympathizers there was only one type of power: paternal power. This power was, by its nature, absolute. Filmer's simplistic, uncluttered view of power fit in perfectly with his analysis of social relations. Filmer admitted only one kind of social relationship: the paternal relationship. Each member of society was defined by his or her relation to the patriarchs of the family and of the nation.

Locke, however, maintained that there were many kinds of power and many types of social relations. He analyzed several nonpolitical relationships including those of master-servant, master-slave, parent-child, and husband-wife.[22] Each of these forms of association was carefully distinguished from the political relationship of ruler-subject. Two of the nonpolitical relationships, namely the parental and the conjugal, reveal a great deal about the status of women in Lockean theory.

From the very outset of the discussion of the parent-child relation, Locke rejected the terminology of patriarchy, claiming that "[paternal power] seems so to place the Power of Parents over their Children wholly in the Father, as if the Mother had no share in it, whereas if we consult Reason or Revelation, we shall find she hath an equal Title. . . . For whatever obligation Nature and the right of Generation lays on Children, it must certainly bind them equal to both the concurrent Causes of it" (T.T., II, 52).

The basic argument at the root of his terminological objection was one familiar from the *First Treatise*. Patriarchal theory could not stand if power were shared by husband and wife. As Locke argued in the *Second Treatise*, "it will but very ill serve the turn of those Men who contend so much for the Absolute Power and Authority of the *Fatherhood*, as they call it, that the *Mother* should have any share in it" (T.T., II, 53). Nevertheless, Locke was not consistent in his own use of the term he introduced. He reverted to the use of "paternal" to describe the relationship he defined as "parental." Yet it is clear from this discussion as well as from the analysis of the fifth commandment that Locke was willing to elevate women's status if he could overthrow the patriarchal monarch.

Locke's examination of the conjugal relationship demanded a more extensive analysis of the roles and status of women in society. He described conjugal society as follows:

> *Conjugal Society* is made by a voluntary Compact between Man and Woman: tho' it consist chiefly in such a Communion and Right in one anothers Bodies, as is necessary to its chief End, Procreation; yet it draws with it mutual Support and Assistance, and a Communion of Interest too, as necessary not only to unite their Care, and Affection, but also necessary to their common Off-spring, who have a Right to be nourished and maintained by them, till they are able to provide for themselves (T.T., II, 78).

Conjugal society existed among human beings as a persistent social relationship because of the long term of dependency of the offspring and further because of the dependency of the woman who "is capable of conceiving, and *de facto* is commonly with Child again, and Brings forth too a new Birth long before the former is out of a dependency" (T.T., II, 80). Thus the father is obliged to care for his children and is also "under an Obligation to continue in Conjugal Society with the same Woman longer than other creatures" (T.T., II, 80).

Though the conjugal relationship began for the sake of procreation, it continued for the sake of property. After praising God's wisdom for combining in man an acquisitive nature and a slow maturing process, Locke noted that a departure from monogamy would complicate the simple natural economics of the conjugal system (T.T., II, 80). Though conjugal society among human beings would be more persistent than among other species, this did not mean that marriage would be indissoluble. Indeed, Locke wondered "why this *Compact*, where Procreation and Education are secured, and Inheritance taken care for, may not be made determinable, either by consent, or at a certain time, or upon certain Conditions, as well as any other voluntary Compacts, there being no necessity in the nature of the thing, nor to the ends of it, that it shall always be for life" (T.T., II, 81). Locke's tentative acceptance of divorce brought him criticism over 100 years later. Thomas Elrington commented that "to make the conjugal union determinable by consent, is to introduce a promiscuous concubinage." Laslett notes that Locke was prepared to go even further and suggested the possibilities of left-hand marriage.[23] In Locke's view, the actual terms of the conjugal contract were not fixed and immutable:

> Community of Goods and the Power over them, mutual Assistance and Maintenance, and other things belonging to *Conjugal Society*, might be varied and regulated by that Contract, which unites Man and Wife in that Society as far as may consist with Procreation and the bringing up of Children (T.T., II, 83).

Nevertheless, Locke described what he took to be the normal distribution of power in marital relationships:

> The Husband and Wife, though they have but one common Concern, yet having different understandings will unavoidably sometimes have different wills, too; it therefore being necessary, that the last Determination, *ie.* the Rule, should be placed somewhere, it naturally falls to the Man's share, as the abler and the stronger (T.T., II, 82).

Clearly all forms of patriarchalism did not die with Filmer and his fellows. Here, the subjection of women is not based on Genesis, but on natural qualifications. Nature had shown man to be the "abler and stronger." Even James Tyrrell, while denying any need to obtain women's consent in the formation of civil society, thought it possible that, in some cases, women might actually be more fit to act as household heads and final decision makers. Unlike Tyrrell, Locke did not equivocate on this point. Rule must be placed somewhere, so he placed it in the husband. Locke's patriarchy was limited, though. The husband's power of decision extended only to those interests and properties held in common by husband and wife. Locke spelled out the limits on the husband's power:

> [His power] leaves the Wife in the full and free possession of what by Contract is her Peculiar Right, and gives the Husband no more

power over her Life, than she has over his. The *Power of the Husband* being so far from that of an absolute monarch that the *Wife* has, in many cases, a Liberty to *separate* from him; where natural Right or their Contract allows it, whether that Contract be made by themselves in the state of Nature or by the Customs or Laws of the Country they live in; and the Children upon such Separation fall to the Father or Mother's lot, as such contract does determine (T.T., II, 82).

In addition, Locke distinguished between the property rights of husband and wife. All property in conjugal society was not automatically the husband's. A wife could have property rights not subject to her husband's control. Locke indicated this in a passage on conquest: "For as to the Wife's share, whether her own Labour or Compact gave her a Title to it, 'tis plain, her Husband could not forfeit what was hers" (T.T., II, 183).

There were several similarities between the conjugal and the political relationship. Both were grounded in consent. Both existed for the preservation of property. Yet conjugal society was not a political society because it conferred no power over the life and death of its members. In addition, political society could intervene in the affairs of conjugal society. Men and women in the state of nature were free to determine the terms of the conjugal contract. But in civil society these terms could be limited or dictated by the "Customs or Laws of the Country."

The extent to which the participants in the parental and conjugal relationships could also participate in political relationships remains to be considered. We may gain some insight into the matter by following Locke's route, that is, by tracing the origins of political power from the state of nature.

To Locke, the state of nature was a "state of perfect Freedom" for individuals "to order Actions and dispose of their Possessions, and Persons, as they think fit." Furthermore, Locke also described the state of nature as:

A *State* also of Equality, wherein all the Power and Jurisdiction is reciprocal, no one having more than another: there being nothing more evident, than that Creatures of the same species and rank promiscuously born to all the same advantages of Nature and the use of the same faculties should also be equal one amongst another without Subordination or Subjection, unless the Lord and

Master of them all should by any manifest Declaration of his Will set one above another (T.T., II, 4).

Because of certain inconveniences (the lack of an authoritative executive power, the potential for injustice where men judged their own cases, etc.), men quit the state of nature to form civil society through an act of con-sent. It was in criticizing the formation of society by consent that Filmer's theory was most effective. Indeed, Locke found it difficult to show how free and equal individuals actually formed civil society. Ultimately he was forced to admit that the first political societies in history were probably patriarchal monarchies. He described the historic origins as follows:

> As it often happens, where there is much Land and few People, the Government commonly began in the Father. For the Father having by the Law of Nature, the same Power with every Man else to punish his transgressing Children even when they were Men, and out of their Pupilage; and they were very likely to submit to his punishment, and all joyn with him against the Offender in their turns, giving him thereby power to Execute his Sentence against any transgression . . . [the] Custom of obeying him, in their Childhood made it easier to submit to him rather than to any other (T.T., II, 105).

In this passage, Locke lumped paternal power and natural power to-gether, allowed for the slightest nod of consent, and—presto—civil soci-ety emerged. Even in the state of nature, it appeared that paternal (parental?) power could be effective. Children growing up in the state of nature were under the same obligations to their parents as children reared in civil society. What of natural freedom and equality? Locke confessed:

> *Children* are not born in this full state of *Equality*, though they are born to it. Their parents have a sort of Rule and Jurisdiction over them when they come into the World, and for some time after, but 'tis but a temporary one. The Bonds of this Subjection are like Swadling Cloths they are wrapt up in and supported by in the weakness of their Infancy. Age and Reason as they grow up, loosen them till at length they drop quite off, and leave a Man at his own free Disposal (T.T., II, 55).

Of course, once children reached maturity in the state of nature they no longer owed obedience to their parents, but were simply required to honor them out of simple gratitude. At this stage, however, Locke introduced another sort of power to support the father's claim to his child's obedience—namely that power which accrued to every man in the state of nature, the power to punish the transgressions of others against him. But the father's power was reinforced by the fact that his children would have a long-standing habit of obedience to him. In the state of nature, the father's commands to his mature children received added weight and legitimacy because he *was* their father. His children would recognize this legitimacy and would join their power to his to make him lawmaker. At this point, it seems, the father's former paternal power and his existing natural power were transformed by consent into political power.

Locke's account of the origins of political power raised problems. First of all, it seemed that the consent of free and equal individuals came about more as a result of habit than of mature, rational deliberation. Secondly, Locke's reconstruction fell prey to one of the difficulties he saw in Filmer: namely, the problem of accounting for monarchy as the form of government growing out of *parental* power. Against Filmer, Locke had protested repeatedly that the honor and obedience due to a father was due also to a mother. Both reason and revelation insisted upon this, he claimed. If "paternal" power actually meant "parental" power, that is, the power of father *and* mother, why should the form of government growing out of that power be the government of one, not two? By the time Locke had reached this stage of his discourse, he had apparently abandoned the earlier line of argument, just as he had abandoned the usage of "parental" for "paternal." The father as "abler and stronger" would rule.

In this discussion, Locke was willing to concede the historical or anthropological case for patriarchalism. He was not ready to concede the moral case, however. Filmer had tied his moral and historical arguments together by using the Book of Genesis as the source of both. Locke split the two cases apart. Locke's biblical criticisms were intended to demonstrate the weakness of the moral conclusions which Filmer had drawn from the Genesis creation account. Thus, at best, Filmer was left with only an historical case. But, Locke insisted, history was not the source of morality. He wrote that "an Argument from what has been, to what should of right be, has no great force" (T.T., II, 103). Instead, he broke with history and based his moral theory on a new understanding of human nature. In doing so, however, he reopened questions closed by

Filmer's theory. Locke had to deal with the political roles and status of women, children and servants. He was somewhat sensitive to Filmer's criticisms concerning the place of these politically unfit groups within contract theory. He certainly tried to make a consistent explanation of the relationship of children to civil society: "We are *born Free*, as we are born Rational; not that we have actually the Exercise of either: Age that brings one brings with it the other too. And thus we see how natural *Freedom and Subjection to Parents* may consist together and are both founded on the same Principle" (T.T., II, 61). No immature child could be expected to take part in the social compact. Yet children's inability to participate in politics would not preclude their right to consent to government when they reached adulthood. Locke indicated the necessity of each person giving consent as a condition of full political rights and full political obligation. Grown sons were free to make their own contract as were their fathers before them. An individual could not be bound by the consent of others but had to make a personal commitment through some separate act of consent.

But what of women? Unlike Tyrrell and Sidney, Locke remained silent on the question of their participation in the founding of political society. Of course, it is possible Locke referred to the role of women in the lost section of the *Treatises*. Or, perhaps Locke understood that explicit exclusion of women seriously weakened a theory grounded in the natural freedom of mankind. Yet Locke was also a good enough propagandist to have realized how deeply ingrained patriarchalism was in everyday life. Locke had criticized Filmer's use of the fifth commandment—"Honor thy father"—as a basis for political obligation. If the command were taken seriously, he charged, then "every Father must necessarily have Political Dominion, and there will be as many Sovereigns as there are Fathers" (T.T., I, 65). But the audience Locke was addressing was essentially an audience of fathers, household heads and family sovereigns. Locke had freed them from political subjection to a patriarchal superior—the king. He did not risk alienating his audience by clearly conferring a new political status on their subordinates under the patriarchal system, that is, on women. Nevertheless, in the absence of any sustained analysis of the problem of women, we may draw some conclusions from an examination of Locke's scattered thoughts on women.

Though Locke gave the husband ultimate authority within conjugal society, this authority was limited and non-political. Yet when Locke's account of the husband's conjugal authority was combined with his account of the historical development of political society, several questions occur which were never adequately resolved in Locke's moral theory. Did not the award of final decision-making power to the father and husband (in conjugal society) result in a transformation of "parental power" into "paternal power"? Was the subsequent development of political power based on paternal power a result of that transformation? What was woman's role in the establishment of the first political society? Since her husband was to be permitted final decisions in matters of their common interest and property, and since political society, obviously, was a matter of common interest, would her voice simply be "concluded" in that of her husband? If so, then Filmer's question recurs—what became of her rights as a free individual? Did she lose her political potential because she was deemed not as "able and strong" as her husband? If this were the case, Locke would have had to introduce new qualifications for political life.

Locke portrayed political society as an association of free, equal, rational individuals who were capable of owning property.[24] These individuals came together freely, since none had any power or jurisdiction over others. They agreed to form a civil society vested with power to legislate over life and death, and to execute its decisions in order to protect the vital interests of its members, that is, their lives, liberties, and estates. Yet John Locke was certainly no believer in the absolute equality of human beings. Indeed, on that score, he was emphatic:

> Though I have said . . . *That all Men by Nature are equal*, I cannot be supposed to understand all sorts of *Equality; Age* or *Virtue* may give Men a just Precedency: *Excellence of Parts and Merit* may place others above the Common Level; *Birth* may subject some and *Alliance* or *Benefits* others, to pay an Observance to those whom Nature, Gratitude, or other Respects may have made it due (T.T., II, 54).

But these inequalities in no way affect an individual's basic freedom or political capacity, for Locke continued in the same passage:

> . . . yet all this consists with the *Equality* which all Men are in, in respect of Jurisdiction or Dominion one over another, which was the *Equality* I there spoke of, as proper to the Business in hand, being that *equal Right* every Man hath, *to his Natural Freedom*,

without being subjected to the Will or Authority of any other Man (T.T., II, 54).

If "Man" is used as a generic term, then woman's natural freedom and equality could not be alienated without her consent. Perhaps a marriage contract might be taken for consent, but this is a dubious proposition. Locke had indicated that a marriage contract in no way altered the political capacity of a queen regnant (T.T., I, 47). While decision-making power over the common interests of a conjugal unit belonged to the husband, Locke admitted that the wife might have interests apart from their shared interests. Women could own separate property not subject to their husbands' control. If a husband forfeited his life or property as a result of conquest, his conquerors acquired no title to his wife's life or property.

Did these capacities entitle women to a political role? Locke never directly confronted the question; nevertheless, it is possible to compare Locke's qualifications for political life with his views of women. Locke used the Genesis account to show that women possessed the same natural freedom and equality as men. Whatever limitations had been placed on women after the Fall could conceivably be overcome through individual effort or scientific advance. Furthermore, women were capable of earning through their own labor, of owning property and of making contracts.

Locke and the Rational Woman

The one remaining qualification for political life is rationality. For Locke's views on the rationality of women it will be necessary to turn to his other writings, notably his *Thoughts on Education*.

In the published version of his advice on education, Locke mentioned that the work had been originally intended for the education of boys; but he added that it could be used as a guide for raising children of either sex. He noted that "where difference of sex requires different Treatment, 'twill be no hard Matter to distinguish."[25]

The *Education* was first written as a series of letters to Locke's friend, Edward Clarke, concerning the upbringing of Clarke's eldest son. Locke's intent was to provide a guide for the education of a gentleman. His attention was not focused directly on a lady's education, although later he offered the Clarkes guidance on the education of their daughter. From the latter advice we may discover just where Locke thought "difference of sex required different treatment."

Locke felt that his advice concerning a gentleman's education would have to be changed somewhat to fit the needs of Clarke's daughter. However, in a letter to Mrs. Clarke, Locke tried to convince her that his prescriptions were appropriate for girls and not necessarily harsh.[26] On the whole, Locke believed that except for "making a little allowance for beauty and some few other considerations of the s[ex], the manner of breeding of boys and girls, especially in the younger years, I imagine, should be the same."[27]

The differences which Locke thought should obtain in the education of men and of women amounted to only slight differences in physical training. While Locke thought that "meat, drink and lodging and clothing should be ordered after the same manner for the girls as for the boys," he did introduce a few caveats aimed at protecting the girls' complexions.[28]

Locke introduced far fewer restrictions in his plan for a young lady's mental development. In a letter to Mrs. Clarke he wrote: "Since, therefore I acknowledge no difference of sex in your mind relating . . . to truth, virtue, and obedience, I think well to have no thing altered in it from what is [writ for the son]."[29]

Far from advocating a special, separate and distinct form of education for girls, Locke proposed that the gentleman's education should more closely resemble that of young ladies. For example, he favored the education of children at home by tutors. Modern languages learned through conversation should replace rote memorization of classical grammars. In addition, Locke suggested that young gentlemen as well as young ladies might profit from a dancing master's instruction.

Taken as a whole, Locke's thoughts on education clearly suggest a belief that men and women could be schooled in the use of reason. The minds of both men and women were blank slates to be written on by experience. Women had intellectual potential which could be developed to a high level.

Locke's educational process was designed to equip young men for lives as gentlemen. Since the gentleman's life certainly included political activity, a young man's education had to prepare him for political life. If a young lady were to receive the same education, it should be expected that she, too, would be capable of political activity.

Locke's personal relations also may have reinforced his view of female rationality. Though he was generally secretive about his personal life, Locke did have a well-known close relationship with Damaris Cudworth Masham. She was a brilliant woman, a "theologian and correspondent of the intellectuals of her day," and perhaps, as Laslett suggests, "the first bluestocking of them all."[30] Locke described Damaris to a friend in glowing terms:

> The lady herself is so well versed in theological and philosophical studies and of such an original mind that you will not find many men to whom she is not superior in wealth of knowledge and ability to profit by it. Her judgment is excellent, and I know few who can bring such clearness of thought to bear upon the most abstruse subjects, or such capacity for searching through and solving the difficulties of questions beyond the range, I do not say of most women, but even of most learned men.[31]

What effects did Locke's relationship with Damaris Masham have on his views about women? Obviously this is a highly speculative matter. Locke had met Damaris some time before he began to advise Mrs. Clarke on the upbringing of her daughter. Damaris herself championed the cause of female education. In one of her (anonymously) published works, she castigated those English gentlemen, who, destitute of knowledge themselves, derived a sense of superiority from depriving women of knowledge. She realized that learned ladies risked becoming "a subject of ridicule . . . and aversion." Only a few "vertuous and rational persons" would rise above the conventional prejudice.[32] Surely Damaris Masham believed John Locke was among these exceptional individuals.

Locke wrote the *Treatises* before he met Damaris. While it is tempting to suggest that his relationship with Damaris caused him to move away from the somewhat more patriarchal sentiments of the *Second Treatise* toward the ideas of greater sexual equality found in his thoughts on education, to claim this would be to claim more than the evidence warrants. Locke's various views on women as expressed in the *Treatises* and his educational writings are not really incompatible. At most, we can maintain that Locke's acquaintance with Lady Masham reinforced his views on women—views already heavily influenced by his belief in individualism.

In summary, it does appear that Locke was a part of a shifting collective consciousness which made the sexual revolution a possibility. He did not totally reject all forms of patriarchalism but in many respects his thoughts on women anticipated such noted feminists as John Stuart Mill.

Locke did hold that there might be a foundation in nature for the subjection of wives to husbands. The pain of childbirth, the duration and frequency of pregnancy and the long dependency of the children helped dictate the form of conjugal society. In conjugal society, the final decision-making power belonged to the husband as the "abler and stronger." Locke was certainly not interested in abolishing what many feminists today see as the chief institution of modern patriarchy—the family. The form of conjugal society among human beings grew out of peculiarities in the human life cycle and in human nature. Human beings matured slowly and were acquisitive. These two factors shaped the character of the human family. Nevertheless, family relations—parent-child, and husband-wife—were not immutable or indissoluble as patriarchal theorists had claimed. The conjugal relationship was based on consent and the terms of the conjugal contract could be varied by the uniting couple. There was no inherent reason why the relationship had to be lifelong. Wives could have a right to separate from their husbands. When separations occurred, child custody could be granted to either parent.

Locke's views on women, as noted above, exemplified his individualism. While he believed that women did suffer from some natural weaknesses, he had a classic liberal faith in the ability of individual women to overcome these natural obstacles. The program of education he designed for young ladies attested to that faith and his own experience with Damaris Cudworth Masham confirmed it. Doubtless feminists today would find fault with the "concessions to female beauty" in his educational program. Yet his overall plan went far in breaking down traditional sex roles in education.

Locke believed that women shared the basic freedom and equality characteristic of all members of the species. Women were capable of rational thought; in addition, they could make contracts and acquire property. Thus it appeared that women were capable of satisfying Locke's requirements for political life. Yet Locke was never explicit about women's role in the formation of civil society. He gave no separate account of women's political obligation. He registered no protest over the rule of Queens Elizabeth or Anne or Mary; but he never stated whether he, like Tyrrell and Sidney, would have excluded the "whole multitude of women" from any form of political life.

Finally, 300 years ago, Locke offered a "liberated" solution to a controversy which still rages in religious circles—the question of the fitness of women to act as ministers. In 1696 Locke, together with King William, attended a service led by a Quaker preacher, Rebecca Collier. He praised her work and encouraged her to continue in it, writing, "Women, indeed, had the honour first to publish the resurrection of the Lord of Love; why not again the resurrection of the Spirit of Love?"[33] It is interesting to compare Locke's attitude here with the famous remark made by Samuel Johnson on the same subject in the next century: "Sir, a woman's preaching is like a dog's walking on his hindlegs. It is not done well; but you are surprized to find it done at all."[34]

Perhaps a similar conclusion might be reached about the roots of feminism in Lockean liberalism. In a world where political anti-patriarchalism was still somewhat revolutionary, explicit statements of more far-reaching forms of anti-patriarchalism were almost unthinkable. Indeed, they would have been considered absurdities. Thus, while Filmer had presented a comprehensive and consistent patriarchal theory, many of his liberal opponents rejected political patriarchalism by insisting on the need for individual consent in political affairs but shied away from tampering with patriarchal attitudes where women were concerned. John Locke was something of an exception to this rule. Though his feminist sympathies certainly did not approach the feminism of Mill writing nearly two centuries later, in view of the intense patriarchalism of seventeenth-century England, it should be surprising to find such views expressed at all.

Notes

I would like to express my gratitude to John Langton and Enid Bloch for their helpful comments and suggestions and to Mark Moore and Karen Berry for valuable technical assistance.

1. On patriarchalism as a world view, see Gordon J. Schochet, *Patriarchalism and Political Thought* (New York: Basic Books, 1975); also, W. H. Greenleaf, *Order, Empiricism, and Politics* (London: Oxford University Press, 1964), chs. 1–5; Peter Laslett, "Introduction," *Patriarcha and Other Political Works of Sir Robert Filmer* (Oxford: Basil Blackwell, 1949), 26; and John W. Robbins, "The Political Thought of Sir Robert Filmer" (Ph.D. dissertation, The Johns Hopkins University, 1973).

2. Patriarchal strains may be found in the literature of the sixteenth century including John Knox, *First Blast of the Trumpet Against the Monstrous Regiment of Women* (Geneva, 1558). Knox argued that women were incapable of ruling a kingdom. The tract was inspired less by Knox's fear of female rule than his fear of *Catholic* female rule. Counterarguments were introduced by John Aylmer in *An Harborowe for Faithfull and Trewe Subjects against the Late Blown Blast* (Strasborowe, 1559). Patriarchal political theory also influenced James I in *The Trew Law of Free Monarchies* (1598); he

noted that "Kings are also compared to Fathers of families: for a King is trewly *Parens Patriae*, the politique father of his people." Richard Field insisted in *Of the Church* (1606) that the political power of Adam as monarch could be derived from his power as father to the whole human race. Patriarchal theorists among Filmer's contemporaries included John Maxwell who wrote *Sacro-Sancta Regum Majestas or the Sacred and Royal Prerogative of Christian Kings* (Oxford, 1644); and James Ussher, *The Power Communicated by God to the Prince, and the Obedience Required of the Subject* (written ca. 1644, first published 1661, 2nd ed., London, 1683); and Robert Sanderson, in his preface to Ussher's work.

3. Peter Laslett, *The World We Have Lost* (New York: Scribner's, 1965), passim; Greenleaf, 80–94; Peter Zagorin, *A History of Political Thought in the English Revolution* (New York: Humanities Press, 1966), 198–99.

4. On the use of scripture in historical argument see J. G. A. Pocock, *The Ancient Constitution and the Feudal Law* (Cambridge: Cambridge University Press, 1957), 188–89.

5. See especially Greenleaf, 89; also Julia O'Faolain and Laura Martines, eds., *Not in God's Image* (New York: Harper Torchbooks, 1973), 179–207; and Schochet, 16.

6. Laslett, "Introduction," and Laslett, "Sir Robert Filmer: The Man Versus the Whig Myth," *William and Mary Quarterly*, 3rd ser., 5 (1948): 523–46.

7. Sir Robert Filmer, *Patriarcha and Other Political Writings of Sir Robert Filmer*, ed. Peter Laslett (Oxford: Basil Blackwell, 1949). This volume will be cited in the text as "F.W."

8. Pocock, 189–90.

9. See, for example, Edward Gee, *The Divine Right and Original of the Civil Magistrate from God* (London, 1658); [James Tyrrell], *Patriarcha Non Monarcha* (London: Richard Janeway, 1681); and Algernon Sidney, *Discourses Concerning Government* (London, 1698).

10. Greenleaf, 89.

11. Arguments had to be structured to persuade the widest possible audience. For an exploration of this general problem, see Mark Gavre, "Hobbes and His Audience," *American Political Science Review* 68 (December 1974): 1542–56.

12. Laslett concluded that "neither Locke nor Sidney nor any of a host of others who attacked *Patriarcha* ever attempted to meet the force of [Filmer's] criticisms [about political obligation], and that none of them ever realized what he meant by his naturalism." Introduction, 21.

13. Sidney, 2–4, 34–35.

14. Tyrrell, 83.

15. Schochet, 233.

16. Tyrrell, 74.

17. C. B. MacPherson, *The Political Theory of Possessive Individualism* (London: Oxford University Press, 1962), ch. 5; and MacPherson, "The Social Bearing of Locke's Political Theory," *Western Political Quarterly* 7 (March 1954): 1–22.

18. Tyrrell, 78.

19. Sidney, 4.

20. Peter Laslett, "Introduction," to *Two Treatises of Government*, written by John Locke, ed. Laslett (Cambridge: Cambridge University Press, 1960), 69. References to Locke's *Treatises* will be made to "T.T." with the treatise and section numbers indicated.

21. Laslett, ed., *Two Treatises*, 210n.

22. See especially R. W. K. Hinton, "Husbands, Fathers, and Conquerors," *Political Studies* 16 (February 1968): 55–67; Geraint Parry, "Individuality, Politics and the Critique of Paternalism in John Locke," *Political Studies* 12 (June 1964): 163–77; and MacPherson, *Possessive Individualism*.

23. Laslett, ed., *Two Treatises*, 364n.

24. See MacPherson, *Possessive Individualism*, ch. 5. MacPherson argues that Locke assumed a class differential in the distribution of these qualities. Full membership in political society would be limited to those who fully demonstrated them. The question under consideration here is the extent to which this class differential might also be a sex differential.

25. John Locke, *Some Thoughts Concerning Education*, sec. 6; also, see Locke to Mrs. Clarke, Jan. 7, 1683/4, in *The Correspondence of John Locke and Edward Clarke*, ed. Benjamin Rand (Cambridge, Mass.: Harvard University Press, 1927).

26. Locke to Mrs. Clarke, Jan. 7, 1683/4, in Rand, 121.

27. Locke to Clarke, Jan. 1, 1685, in Rand, 121.

28. Locke to Mrs. Clarke, in Rand, 103.

29. Locke to Mrs. Clarke in Rand, 102–3; while Locke admitted no difference between the sexes in their ability to grasp truth, he did realize that women had less practice in using that ability. He asked a friend to help him revise a Latin text of the *Essay Concerning Human Understanding*. Locke wanted assistance in "paring off superfluous repetitions . . . left in for the sake of illiterate Men and the softer Sex, not used to abstract Notions and Reasonings." Locke to William Molyneux, Apr. 26, 1695, in A. Bettesworth and C. Hitch, *Some Familiar Letters between Mr. Locke and Several of His Friends*, 3rd ed. (London, 1837), 88.

30. Peter Laslett, "Masham of Otes: The Rise and Fall of an English Family," *History Today* 3 (August 1953): 535–43, at 536. See also Maurice Cranston, *John Locke: A Biography* (London: Longmans, Green, 1957).

31. Locke to Limborch, Mar. 13, 1690/91, reprinted in H. R. Fox Bourne, *The Life of John Locke*, Vol. 2 (New York: Harper, 1876), 212–13.

32. [Damaris Cudworth Masham], *Occasional Thoughts in Reference to a Virtuous or Christian Life*, in George Ballard, *Memoirs of British Ladies* (London: T. Evans, 1775), 262–69, at 267.

33. Locke to Rebecca Collier, Nov. 21, 1696, reprinted in Fox Bourne, 453.

34. E. L. McAdam and George Milne, eds., *A Johnson Reader* (New York: Pantheon Books, 1964), 464.

Afterword

Roots and Shoots—Revisiting Locke's Attack on Patriarchy

Melissa A. Butler

It was the spring of 1973. I was completing my graduate course work and still had no idea for a dissertation. The concern weighed on my mind as I prepared for the last meeting of my last seminar. Our reading for the week included *Civilization and Its Discontents*. By the time I had finished the book, I had my topic. Over years of reading the canon of political theory, I had adopted the practice of simply accepting "man" as a generic term. Of course I realized that most writers had indeed meant "men" by "man," but it had never occurred to me that in an era when we were "beyond all that," we couldn't simply assume inclusivity (i.e., that "by 'man,' of course, we mean women, too!"). But there I was, confronting

Sigmund Freud for the first time and discovering that the strategy of extending to women an explanation written to apply to men flatly would not work. Gender was a central part of Freud's theory, and men and women were not interchangeable. His account of civilization's origins in men's renunciation of their desires to put out fire (by urinating on it) could never be read to include women.[1] One could not simply "add women and stir" in the Freudian account. I wondered if this might, in fact, be true of other thinkers as well. I asked, "What if one focused on those places where political theorists had specifically discussed women?" What if I reread the canon assuming that "man" meant *males?*

Today, it's hard to imagine how such obvious questions could have been a "eureka" moment. Let me supply the rest of the story. Several months later, I met with a distinguished senior professor to ask if he would be willing to direct a dissertation tentatively titled "Images of Women in Political Theory." During our conversation, he made it clear that he could not imagine what I would write about, since there simply were no images of women in political thought. My topic was a *non-topic!* Frustrated, I turned to a young female assistant professor to serve as my dissertation director. But her areas of interest in political theory were far different from mine. And so, concerned that I needed more feedback from scholars closer to my material, I packaged the first two completed chapters under the heading "Early Liberal Roots of Feminism: John Locke and the Attack on Patriarchy" and shipped them off to the *American Political Science Review*. I thought, naively, no doubt, that since the *APSR* was the most prominent journal in the field, that would be where I would get the best criticism. Six months later, a letter arrived from the editor saying, in effect, "make it shorter [the manuscript I sent out was in the vicinity of ninety pages!], and we'll take it."

The article was unusual in appearing in a journal that published relatively little theory and that, up to that time, had published little about women. Indeed, almost two years after it appeared, Berenice Carroll surveyed the literature of political science seeking studies about women. In the optimistic part of her report she noted that "although the number of books has been small, over 85 articles were published between 1976 and 1978 in over forty scholarly journals or serials." Oddly, from my point of view, she added a "less encouraging" observation that "many journals published only one relevant article and the *American Political Science Review* (APSR) published no article specifically on women in the three year period."[2] While I still quibble with her counting rules and her conclusion that the focus of my article "is not primarily on women," her basic point holds. In the 1970s, research about women was only beginning to percolate into the mainstream literature of political science.

In publishing "Early Liberal Roots of Feminism," my purposes (aside from trying to establish the validity of my dissertation topic!) were fourfold. I wanted to show that

1. Taking gender seriously shed new light on political theory.
2. That this approach wasn't so new—gender had been a critical concept in political theory before, specifically in the contest between patriarchalism and liberalism.
3. That the liberal emphasis on consent, individual rights, and equality contained the seeds of feminism and that these implications were *not* unforeseen, even in the seventeenth century.
4. That John Locke, while being somewhat ambiguous in parts, appeared to embrace an individualism that was conducive to the realization of goals of liberal feminism.

The first two points are now well established. Since the piece appeared, hundreds, if not thousands, of articles and books have appeared dealing with aspects of my original topic—retrieving lost works of forgotten women writers, reexamining works of male contributors to the canon, or adding original contributions to political theory with women's liberation as a guiding principle. The vibrancy and vitality of scholarship in this area over the last quarter century suggests that the first point is now unarguable. In 1980, Carole Pateman noted that the idea that "women and the relationship between the sexes are of no special relevance to political theory" represented a "contemporary consensus."[3] But as she and other scholars questioned the authors of the mainstream tradition, it became crystal clear that the writers they studied, as Diane Coole put it, "had a great deal to say about women and the family. It is only their exegetes who have ceased to pay attention to such topics."[4] Finally, the chapters of this book, indeed the very existence of the book itself, support my first two claims.

The last two points are more controversial. Can there be such a thing as a "liberal feminist," and, if so, was John Locke one? In the *Sexual Contract*, Pateman argues that "liberal feminism" is really an oxymoron. Liberalism simply took the oppression of women underground, as it were, through a kind of sleight of hand. While *political* patriarchalism may have ended, liberalism nurtured, even required, the subjection of women in the private sphere. Conjugal society, even though founded on contract, removed women from the political sphere, leaving fathers of families to form political associations. And contract theorists were sneaky about this. Relying on the public/private distinction, they "contrived" and "concealed" the exclusion of women from participation in the political order. And Locke was so successful at this that "ever since, most political theorists, whatever their view about other forms of subordination, have accepted that the powers of husbands derive from nature and, hence are not political."[5] Commenting on "Early Liberal Roots of Feminism," she saw it as "an almost perfect example of an uncritical liberal interpretation of Locke . . . [which] tells us more about the repression of the story of the sexual contract than about the way which Locke and Filmer dealt with sexual relations."[6] In laying the blame on Locke, Brennan and Pateman presented an interesting and challenging reading, but not a necessarily conclusive one. Their arguments were bold and critical but not always convincing or careful.

In the first section of chapter 6 of the *Second Treatise* ("On Paternal Power"), Locke shows an awareness of the problems that linguistic imprecision can create: "It may perhaps be censured an impertinent criticism in a discourse of this nature to find fault with words and names that have obtained in the world. And yet possibly it may not be amiss to offer new ones when the old are apt to lead men into mistakes."[7] Yet many readers have faulted Locke for not being clearer. One commentator after another has pronounced Lockean texts "ambiguous," and this ambiguity has promoted a variety of alternative readings concerning his views on women. Was John Locke a feminist or a closet patriarchalist bent on continuing the oppression of women? Researchers have placed him just about everywhere along a continuum between these two extremes.[8] Those who see him as some sort of feminist or "protofeminist" are likely to draw broadly on his works in economics, education, and epistemology in addition to his *Two Treatises of Government*. They frequently discuss his personal relationships with women, notably Damaris Masham. Those who see him as subtly endorsing the subordination of women tend to stick more closely to the *Two Treatises*, especially to two passages, one dealing with his comment that there was a "foundation in nature" for a husband's rule over a wife, the other concerning his discussion of the transformation of paternal power into political power through consent.[9]

Among the critics, Brennan and Pateman (and others as well) draw on the "foundation in nature" passage as clear evidence that Locke had not strayed very far from Filmer. Far from seeing women as free, equal individuals, Locke insisted on women's natural inferiority and based women's subjection and exclusion from the polity on it. Pateman later asked "why a [marriage] contract is necessary when women's subjection . . . is natural," but ignored the obvious answer: a contract was necessary precisely because the "foundation in nature" was not enough to obviate women's equal right to freedom from domination without consent.[10] Fur- thermore, "foundation in nature" may have meant something very differ- ent to Locke than it meant to Filmer. That phrase has been read, as Clark, Brennan and Pateman, and others have read it, as an absolute, necessary and comprehensive judgment, or it may be read as I read it, as a more tentative, variable, and contingent statement. Chris Nyland, ar- guing against Pateman's interpretation, develops an interesting alterna- tive reading. Nyland claims that not only did Locke *not* share Filmer's justification for women's subservience, he "aided women in their struggle to free themselves from the binds of a theological determinism which decreed they were forever fated to a condition of subservience to men."[11] In this reading, the "foundation in nature" to which Locke alluded does not deny women's natural liberty or undermine their claim to fundamen- tal equality. After all, equality in Locke's state of nature does not mean "all sorts of equality."[12] Locke recognized that individual differences in age, merit, virtue, and so on could give some a "just precedency." Yet he explicitly states that these inequalities do not negate one's equal right to freedom from domination. Locke recognized that men were usually stronger than women, Nyland notes, and cites material showing an em- pirical basis for Locke's claim. More recently, other empirical evidence has been developed that further bolsters Nyland's claims. Joyce Burnette's study of farm wages in eighteenth-century England (though not exactly contemporary with Locke), suggests that wage differentials between men and women were traceable to differences in productivity rooted in differ- ences in strength rather than gender *per se*.[13] On the whole, men's strength provided a natural advantage over women in earning power and as a result, in the negotiation of the marriage contract. Thus Nyland maintains, "contract, bargaining, relative productivity, utility and oppor- tunity cost: these were the critical elements in Locke's explanation of men's superior social position."[14]

After positing the "foundation in nature" as the basis of an immutable, inescapable division of power within the family, Brennan and Pateman asserted that "Locke assumes that a free and equal female individual will *always* enter a marriage contract that places her in subjection to her husband."[15] If that is true, then liberals didn't really count women as free and equal individuals. But Pateman's question itself assumes something not in evidence, namely that Locke and other liberals did, indeed, *always* make that assumption. Yet Lockean texts provide clear counterevidence. Indeed, right in the "foundation in nature" passage, Locke points out that no one thinks that a queen who marries a subject has been put into political subjection to him.[16] Clearly, Locke, unlike Tyrell and other antipatriarchalists, did not believe that a marriage contract *necessarily* stripped away a woman's political capacity. Locke's arguments follow Tyrell and others quite closely, but deviate from them in answering the patriarchal complaint that women, if free and equal, would have to be party to government-by-contract. Tyrell replies that the issue of obtaining women's consent was no problem at all, for they are "concluded" in their husbands. Locke, by contrast, is silent. Ordinarily, I would agree with Schochet that a theorist's silence on a point may be taken for tacit endorsement of a prevailing practice or as a signal that he or she is oblivious to the presuppositions of the argument. But how is that dictum to be applied in dealing with a failure to weigh in on either side of a debate? To what does Locke's silence give consent? Tyrell's parry or the patriarchalists' thrust? Did he recognize Tyrell's response as a bad argument that undermined the very basis of emergent liberal theory? I don't know, and so far, I'm not convinced that anyone else does either.[17]

Another point used to show that, from a feminist perspective, Locke was simply another warmed-over patriarchalist, is his pseudohistory, from which women appear to be absent. In these passages (which Peter Laslett note *do* bring Locke perilously close to Filmer's arguments) Locke tries to respond to one of the patriarchalists' more compelling points—that the arrangements they describe are grounded, not only in scripture, but in observable, empirical reality as well. Locke responded in two ways—first, by asserting that just because something has happened, doesn't make it right and, second, by offering an explanation for how it was consistent with his account that "people that were naturally free . . . generally put the rule into one man's hands."[18] Locke noted that the first kings might well have been fathers of families. He argued, however, that these fathers-turned-kings owed their right to rule to their children's consent, not to some natural right created by fatherhood. Pateman summarizes the situation as follows: "The sons agreed that no one was fitter . . . than the father who had cared for them. . . . Locke stresses that the father became a monarch through the consent of his sons, not by virtue of his father-hood."[19] Pateman observes that the mother was not included in this con-tract between father and sons. As she explains, Locke had no need for the mother's consent because the sexual contract ("the original political right") already bound her through her husband and placed her in subjec-tion to him. Furthermore, Pateman argues, the consent of sons to their father's rule bound their wives. Yet that wasn't quite what Locke said. Not only were there issues about what the "foundation in nature" implied in terms of necessary subjection of a wife to a husband, but there was a further problem as well. The consent Locke described was the consent, not of sons specifically, but of "children." Throughout sections 74–76 of the *Second Treatise*, where Locke describes consent, he describes it as the consent of "the children." A Lockean subterfuge that a critical reader should see through? Perhaps. Pateman could argue that the only people he really counted as "children" were sons. On the other hand, one might just as easily argue that his use of "children" shows more care and atten-tion to the requirements of an individualist argument.

But where does this leave us with Locke, liberalism, and feminism? Did Locke champion women's political equality? No. Was it a "missed opportunity" or part of a conspiracy to deny women their natural right to self-determination? I think more the former than the latter. It was no part of Locke's agenda to empower women politically. Yet, all things considered, I'm still surprised at how far Locke did go in accepting women as free, rational, and independent individuals. What about liberalism? On one hand, the public/private split provided a powerful tool for delay-ing the integration of women into political life, as many have com-mented. Nonetheless, whether intentionally or not, other Lockean ideas loosed on the world—natural equality, freedom, and individualism—carried with them a compelling logic of their own. As Pateman herself admits, the "apparently emancipatory potential of contract doctrine" did not go unnoticed, but it did long go unrealized.[20] Patriarchal theorists saw it in the seventeenth century. Mary Astell saw it in the eighteenth cen-tury. The women who convened at Seneca Falls, New York, saw it in the nineteenth century. The first-wave, equal-rights feminism was grounded in these concepts. Ultimately, the liberation of women was not liberal-ism's failure, but its flowering.

Notes

1. "It is as though primal man had the habit, when he came in contact with fire, of satisfying an infantile desire connected with it, by putting it out with a stream of his urine. The legends we possess leave no doubt about the originally phallic view taken of tongues of flame as they shoot upwards. Putting out fire by micturating . . . was therefore a kind of sexual act with a male, an enjoyment of sexual potency in a homosexual competition. The first person to renounce this desire and spare the fire was able to carry it off with him and subdue it to his own use." Sigmund Freud, *Civilization and Its Discontents*, translated and edited by James Strachey (New York: W. W. Norton, 1961), 37, no. 1.

2. Berenice Carroll, "Political Science, Part I: American Politics and Political Behavior," *Signs* 4 (1979): 290.

3. Carole Pateman, "Women and Consent," *Political Theory* 8 (1980): 149.

4. Diana Coole, "Re-reading Political Theory from a Woman's Perspective," *Political Studies* 34 (1986): 129.

5. Carole Pateman, "'God Hath Ordained to Man a Helper': Hobbes, Patriarchy and Conjugal Right," *British Journal of Political Science* 19 (1989): 462.

6. Carole Pateman, *The Sexual Contract* (Stanford: Stanford University Press, 1988), 21.

7. John Locke, *Two Treatises of Government*, ed. Peter Laslett (New York: Cambridge University Press, 1960), 2.52.

8. See, for example, Lorenne Clark, "Women and Locke: Who Owns the Apples in the Garden of Eden?" in *The Sexism of Social and Political Theory: Women and Reproduction from Plato to Nietzsche*, ed. Lorenne Clark and Lynda Lange (Toronto: University of Toronto Press, 1979); Teresa Brennan and Carole Pateman, "'Mere Auxiliaries to the Commonwealth': Women and the Origins of Liberalism," *Political Studies* 27 (1979): 183–200; B. Hansen, "Zur feministischen Kritik der politischen Theorie von John Locke," *Österreichische Zeitschrift für Politikwissenschaft* 22 (1993): 477–86; M. E. Kann, "John Locke and the Political Economy of Masculinity," *International Journal of Social Economics* 19 (1992): 95–110; Chris Nyland, "John Locke and the Social Position of Women," *History of Political Economy* 25 (1993): 39–63; S. O'Donnell, "My Idea in Your Mind: John Locke and Damaris Cudworth Masham," in *Mothering the Mind: Twelve Studies of Writers and Their Silent Partners*, ed. R. Perry and M. W. Brownley (New York: Homes and Meier, 1984); Kathy Squadrito, "Locke on the Equality of Sexes," *Journal of Social Philosophy* 10 (1979): 6–11; and Susan Moller Okin, *Women in Western Political Thought* (Princeton: Princeton University Press, 1979).

9. Locke, *Two Treatises*, 2.47, 2.74–76.

10. Pateman, *Sexual Contract*, 93.

11. Nyland, "John Locke and the Social Position of Women," 58.

12. Locke, *Two Treatises*, 2.54.

13. Joyce Burnette, "An Investigation of the Female-Male Wage Gap During the Industrial Revolution in Britain," *Economic History Review* 50 (1997): 257–81.

14. Nyland, "John Locke and the Social Position of Women," 58.

15. Brennan and Pateman, "Mere Auxiliaries," 193. In a variation on this elsewhere, Pateman asks "why a free and equal female individual should *always* be assumed to place herself under the authority of a free and equal male individual." Pateman, "Women and Consent," 153.

16. Locke, *Two Treatises*, 1.47.

17. Gordon Schochet, "The Significant Sounds of Silence: The Absence of Women from the Political Thought of Sir Robert Filmer and John Locke (or, 'Why Can't a Woman Be More Like a Man')," in *Women Writers and the Early Modern British Political Tradition*, ed. Hilda Smith (Cambridge: Cambridge University Press, 1998).

18. Locke, *Two Treatises*, 2.112.

19. Pateman, *Sexual Contract*, 93.

20. Ibid., 90.

4

Models of Politics and the Place of Women in Locke's Political Thought

Gordon Schochet

The family has long been used to explain the political order. In *The Republic*, Plato said that the Guardians should refer to one another as brother, sister, mother, and father—that is, by the names of family members—to establish affective bonds among them. Aristotle argued that the household experiences of ruling and being ruled were fundamental prerequisites to effective political participation and, correspondingly, that the family was the teleological source of politics. And Cicero similarly described marriage as "prima societas"—the "first society"—and called the household "principium urbis et quasi seminarium rei publicae"—the "seedbed [or nursery] of the commonwealth."[1] In the early modern period, this Aristotelian teleology was transformed into a developmental pseudo-anthropology, and the primitive family was seen as the structural as well as the ideational precursor of the political order. The familial model that provided the basis for this sort of political thinking was the traditional or conventional patriarchal household that had long characterized Europe, and the best-known proponent of what has come to be called "patriarchal politics" was, as is well known, the seventeenth-century English royalist, Sir Robert Filmer. It was Filmer's doctrines, of course, that were the overt and primary targets of the political theory of Locke's *Two Treatises*. Locke's announced aim was to subvert the patriarchalism of Filmer and to replace it with a conception of politics rooted in what he called "consent."

Nonetheless, it is hardly news that the participating members of the "civil society"[2] Locke envisaged in his *Two Treatises* were adult males. Even though he was not explicit about their exclusion, he left no place for women in the public life of his polity, as he would have to have done to make the point to his contemporaries. The parties to the "compacts" and "agreements" that established private ownership of land, the use of money, and ultimately the state itself as well as those who subsequently incorporated themselves and their possessions into states by various acts of "consent" were invariably men, often the heads of households, and certainly people with "estates" and goods that needed the protections afforded by the state. What is interesting, however, is that while Locke did see an altered status for women in the household or family, he accorded it no political significance.

Locke's silences did not attract significant scholarly attention until the 1970s, until, that is, feminist scholars took up the issue. In his editions of Filmer (1949) and Locke (1960), Peter Laslett said nothing about these silences, but he did note Locke's "concessions" to patriarchalism.[3] However, his references direct the reader only to those places in the *Second Treatise* where Locke discussed the development of the state from its anthropological beginnings in the family (pars. 74–76, 105–12, and 162). He did not in this context point out Locke's often explicit acceptance of various aspects of the divinely ordained, natural, and socially instituted female inferiority; he did not raise the issue of the place of women in Locke's civil society; and he did not include Locke's chiding of Filmer for having left "mother" out of his reading of the Fifth Commandment and then himself almost immediately switching from "parental" to "paternal."

C. B. Macpherson's *Political Theory of Possessive Individualism* (1962) did not mention women;[4] and I had relatively little to say about the gap in my *Patriarchalism in Political Thought* (1975).[5] In 1977, Lorenne M.G. Clark, endorsing Macpherson's reading but without apparently appreciating his implicit collapse of gender into class, published a sharply critical account that tied the absence of political women to Locke's "two major objectives, the legitimizing of inequality of property . . . and the legitimizing of an exclusive male right to control and dispose of familial property."[6] The next year, Melissa A. Butler argued that there were no inherent conceptual differences between men and women for Locke, even though he did not overtly express that position and did establish institutional differences between them.[7]

Lest it seem strange that these readings were so late in coming, it should be kept in mind that it was not until 1977 that Joan Kelly opened up the entire question of the relative status of women in early modern Europe with her challenging article "Did Women Have a Renaissance?" a work that remains relatively unknown to social scientists and philosophers. Kelly's conclusion—that they did not—implicitly manifested in Locke's political theory, was that as the bourgeois state became a more prominent feature of the European landscape, the political status of women was diminished. Part of the cause, she argued, was that the Renaissance replaced the medieval ideal of courtly love and the close relationship of the public and private worlds that actually enhanced the status of women with a conception that pushed women back into the private realm of the household and into a greater dependence on men.[8] To her account should be added the recently rehabilitated notion of the emergence of "individualism" and "voluntarism" or, in the somewhat sanitized Kantian vocabulary that seems to be preferable, "autonomy,"[9] a sense of self to which Locke made substantial contributions.

Because Locke's *Two Treatises* were conceptually aimed at the political doctrines of Sir Robert Filmer, much of the structure of Locke's argument followed patterns that Filmer dictated. The subjection of women and their exclusion from civic membership and apparent social significance played important, but largely implicit, roles in Filmer's patriarchal political theory. His politics rested upon an extremely oppressive, patriarchal conception of familial authority, but he said little explicitly about the status of women. He argued from what he presumed to be their divinely ordained subjection in their natural statuses as wives and the equally natural and divine subjection of children (sons as well as daughters) and servants to their natural, male superiors—husbands, fathers, and masters—to the divinely natural and patriarchal character of politics. Kings, he insisted, and all who occupy positions of authority, rule by a natural, patriarchal entitlement that had been instituted by God at the Creation even before the expulsion of Adam and Eve from Paradise. The political order for Filmer was a macrocosmic recreation of this patriarchal household. But Locke's confrontation of Filmerian patriarchalism reveals something further about women—no surprise here: there are very few seventeenth-century conceptions of women outside the household; they were wives and daughters. With the very important exceptions of roles women played in religious sects,[10] they were not viewed as "people" or "persons" in ways that made their statuses resemble those of men.

This differentiation is precisely what we should expect in a "naturalistic" world where status and identity are *given* to people rather than conventionally *created* for or by—especially by—them. The gradual displacement of that naturalistic world by a conventional one—the transition that we generally recall in the prosaic words of Henry Sumner Maine as the movement "from status to contract"—is one of the rarely appreciated marks of modernity; it signals one of the primary differences between ourselves and our ancestors. This is not to claim that we live today in a world where every person has the capacity to shape her own identity even in the so-called democratic West—far from it. But the ease with which we point to denials of that ability as failures to achieve our objectives suggests that the moral, albeit abstract, entitlement of people to participate in the shaping of their own lives is an important part of our belief systems. However much we might dishonor it in the breach, we are generally ideologically committed to some notion of human freedom and dignity that was not available to our forebears. The movement from them to us—from then to now—was not the result of a sudden rupture. Social change and especially changes in ideas rarely occur in that way, and Maine's somewhat hyperbolic description could have been made only toward the end of transformational process, when it was possible to look back and recognize that a change had indeed occurred.

My claim, hardly unique on its face, is that Locke played an important role in that redirection and that he did so, in the first instance, by calling into question the prevailing view of the political order as an integral part of the natural and seamless cosmos. Again, Locke did not invent this "new" worldview; no one can be credited with that. Its roots can be traced back through Hobbes, Grotius, the *Vindiciae contra Tyrannos*, and

Renaissance humanism to a reworking of the Thomistic doctrine of *potentia*—itself derived from Aristotle—stripped of the metaphysics of teleology. The fulcrum on which the modern version of this theory turned was, loosely, the twined doctrines of contract and consent, the only means by which people—male people—who were otherwise politically free could legitimately be subjected to the power of the state.

Only Hobbes was as systematic and as thorough as Locke in expressing this understanding. But Hobbes had used the conventional theory and its contract-consent corollary to reach an understanding of political *practice* that was virtually identical to that of Filmer, as Filmer himself readily appreciated, and in this instance, Hobbes produced a theory that was far more coherent than anything Locke would later present. Hobbes had been engaged in a theoretical struggle with the Levellers and their ilk for possession of this political conventionalism; his goal had been to demonstrate that generalized freedom, far from being the protector of the people's entitlements, was their worst enemy and, therefore, that it was only rational for people voluntarily to surrender their original liberty. Locke's genius in this respect was to recapture voluntarism and conventionalism for the constitutionalism he defended and to turn it against the patriarchal naturalism of Sir Robert Filmer.

The subjection of women and their exclusion from civic membership and apparent social significance was important, but largely implicit, in Filmer's theoretical apology for Stuart absolutism. His case rested upon an extremely oppressive, patriarchal conception of familial authority, and accordingly, there is something puzzling, if not downright astounding, about the fact that he says so little about the status of women. He argued from what he presumed to be the divinely ordained subjection of women in their natural statuses as wives and the equally natural and divine subjection of children (sons as well as daughters) and servants to their natural, male superiors—husbands, fathers, and masters—to the divinely natural and patriarchal character of politics. Kings, he insisted, and all who occupy positions of authority, rule by a natural, patriarchal entitlement instituted by God at the Creation even before the expulsion of Adam and Eve from Paradise. Although children and servants appear frequently in his reasoning, Sir Robert's theory was constructed with hardly any mention of women.

Filmer's relative indifference toward women invites two related inferences, which, together, diminish the puzzlement: first, that—however unwittingly—he accepted the practices and beliefs of his society about the status of women and tacitly built his theory around if not directly on these conventions, which, to his mind, were fully in accord with nature, and second, that the exclusion by silence effectively rendered women invisible in his scheme. The family, of course—pun and all—is inconceivable without women, who are its biological and social progenitors, so the result of Filmer's silence is a powerful paradox in which the central and foundational figures are never mentioned. Women are not even off-stage characters who are alluded to but make no appearance; they are altogether missing from the overt story.

Locke had rather more to say about women. His comments had the effect of enhancing their status within the household: he granted them considerable authority over servants, at least gave them a share of the power over children, and defended their right to divorce. But like Filmer, he did not call for their inclusion in the political community; also like Filmer, he was relatively silent about their general social status. He left women pretty much as he had found them in Stuart society, but by framing his answer to Filmer with a shift in the focus of politics from the patriarchal *father* to the rational, rights-bearing *individual*—who, in the world of the *Two Treatises*, remained an adult male—Locke created the theoretical possibility of full political membership for women. That move, to be sure, was not to be made until many years after the publication of the *Two Treatises*.

It is my ultimate claim that Locke's substitution of a political voluntarism rooted in individual rights for Filmer's conception of the state as an integral part of divine nature was one of the crucial steps in the development of modern understandings of justice and politics. Without Locke—or at least without that particular shift—twenty-first and late twentieth-century discussions of authority, rights, and the status of women would be very different from what they are today.

This essay seeks to contribute both to our understanding of the differences between Filmer and Locke on the question of the social and civil status of women and to the twentieth and twenty–first-century continuation of that debate. These objectives are closely related. The extension of effective, participating membership in society to classes of people who have traditionally been excluded is among the most pressing concerns of the modern world, and the place of women—who are arguably the most universally and readily identifiable excluded group—within that membership is of primary importance. In the English-speaking world, the derogated status of women is a lingering manifestation of the perspectives championed by Sir Robert Filmer. Thus, the inherent and historical interest that Locke's attack on patriarchalism arouses is no more significant than the implications of that attack for the twenty-first century. Traditional patriarchalism, along with much else, is part of that heritage we are struggling to overcome. Success in that struggle requires that we understand what we are fighting against and that we realize that while Filmer and seventeenth-century patriarchal political thought are not our contemporary foes, they are certainly among the progenitors of the world we are still seeking to overthrow.

Filmer is fascinating and important in several respects. His conscious and intentional articulation of the patriarchal doctrine is a clue to the existence of some disturbance in the way Stuart society understood itself—that is, in its ideology—and probably an indication that the structural bases of that society were being pressured as well. Filmer apparently felt that it was necessary to defend a set of beliefs and principles that European culture had taken for granted almost without exception for nearly two thousand years. Now, suddenly it seems, that ideology was in trouble.

Further, because he brought patriarchalism fully into the open as a political theory, Filmer is extremely helpful as a source of information about how early modern English society implicitly conceived of itself. As Peter Laslett shrewdly observed, "Filmer, for all his brash naïveté and his obviously amateur outlook, was that extremely rare phenomenon—the codifier of conscious and unconscious prejudice."[11] While he was not particularly profound or complex—not "deep" in the way we conventionally use the term to characterize thinkers—Filmer was virtually alone in his realization that the foundations of English society and social structure were being challenged. Moreover, he seems to have grasped this situation—however intuitively—before anyone else did. It is precisely that awareness and the process of defending that raises foundations to the level of consciousness and therefore opens them to debate. In a sense, then, Filmer unintentionally gave rise to the discussion that, over the next three hundred or so years, would subvert the traditional patriarchal household.

We cannot make a direct inference either from Filmer to the social structural beliefs of Stuart England or from what we presume those beliefs to have been to Filmer's underlying assumptions; the correspondence is not exact. The most we can say is that there was a relationship such that the ideas and the structure supported each other. But we cannot determine which one came first and "gave rise" to the other and where crucial changes must have occurred. When we reach this level of the ineradicably ideological component of Filmer's political thought, our ability to determine precisely what he believed are severely limited. Thus, unless there is a reason to the contrary—such as an overt rejection of or quarrel with received opinion (which we do not find in Filmer)[12]—and so long as the analysis yields a reasonable degree of coherence, we must be permitted to *presume* that he accepted the standards and practices of his society.

In the world of the seventeenth century, people were generally presumed to have been born into statuses that were dictated and preserved by nature and God. The world was conceived largely as a harmonious, tightly organized structure in which every creature was assigned a place. In some sense, this is rather an exaggeration, for the view of the world as naturally and rigidly hierarchical had been under serious challenge at least since the fourteenth century. But the *ideal* view was one in which nature, God, socioeconomic status, and political hierarchy were all comprehended as parts of the same, relatively seamless whole.

It was not a question of how or whether people could possibly "escape" the deprivations of their lowly statuses or avoid the benefits and responsibilities of privilege but of embracing the places that God and nature had provided. Again, extrapolated to the level of norms and expressed in something approaching a modern vocabulary, to the extent that there was a sense of "secular justice," it was an offshoot of the classic notion of giving each person her or his due. Thus, the crucial question was not *why* people occupied particular statuses but *what* their statuses were and what, accordingly, they were due.

Widows and daughters were allowed to inherit—in fact, the law preferred the direct line of a daughter to a collateral line of a brother[13]—but married women had little standing as civil persons for most purposes, and were considered "*to bee one person*" with their husbands,[14] who represented them to the outside world.[15] Although women were not permitted to sit in Parliament, queens regnant were an obvious exception, and England had twice been ruled by a queen in the sixteenth century. Filmer never commented on this apparent anomaly and referred to Elizabeth's and Mary's gender only once, noting that they, "by reason of their sex, being not fit for public assemblies," stopped the practice of formally meeting with Parliament.[16] He refers to Elizabeth with some frequency, but scarcely mentions Mary, presumably because she was Roman Catholic.

Thus, Filmer was not nearly so extreme as the Presbyterian reformer

John Knox who, in 1558, had railed against what he called "the Monstrous Regiment of Women" in his attack on the Roman Catholic queens Mary of England and Mary of Scotland. "To promote a woman to bear rule, superiority, dominion or empire above any realm, nation or city is repugnant to nature," Knox declared, "contumely to God, a thing most contrarious to His revealed will and approved ordinance, and finally it is the subversion of good order, of all equity and justice."[17] These words could easily have been written by Filmer, for they are fully compatible with his derivation of all political power from God's grant of absolute, patriarchal authority to Adam, but he avoided the entire matter, apparently content simply to presume that women were like children and servants in their lack of civil status. The only roles for women that Filmer's argument appears to allow are wife and mother, and it is the latter that makes fatherhood possible. Thus, it is not unreasonable—especially from the perspective of the twentieth century—to conclude with Carole Pateman that despite his explicit silence on the matter, "the genesis of political power [for Filmer] lies in Adam's sex-right or conjugal-right, not in his fatherhood. Adam's political title is granted *before* he becomes a father."[18]

When we look to the ideological and structural world around him—a world that Filmer showed no signs of rejecting—we see a patriarchal structure and a presumption of the inherent, natural inferiority of women.[19] But we have to qualify this judgment somewhat, for the derogation or suppression of women was not an overt, intentional part of Filmer's design.[20] Rather, it was part of the unconscious prejudices on which his society's view of the world was built. However necessary it may have been to that view and however accessible all the components of a fully antifeminist political theory may have been, there is no evidence to suggest that Filmer put these pieces together. On the other hand, numbers of his contemporaries do seem to have been overtly and self-consciously antagonistic to the granting of full civil status to women. Inherent female inferiority was generally understood to be part of nature, and the principal reason for calling attention to a legitimate status that everyone can be presumed to know about and accept is to justify enforcing it—or imposing the appropriate penalties—on people who violate its requirements.

None of this is meant to deny the existence of what could be called "institutional sexism," to minimize its deleterious consequences for women, or to claim that in early–modern England women were treated with a kind of benign indifference. Quite the contrary, for my point, rather, is that institutional sexism operated somewhere beneath the level of consciousness where it was important in maintaining social order and could be called upon when that social order was threatened.[21] And that is precisely what Filmer did despite the fact that he showed little concern for the restrictions against women entailed by traditional European patriarchalism.

For Filmer and his contemporaries, no less than for us in the twenty-first century, it was very difficult to reject prevailing doctrines that are imbedded in the self-conception of a society. Overcoming the constraints of one's own social structure requires enormous self-consciousness and strength of will as well as the perspicacity to see that prevailing standards are in some way inappropriate because they no longer properly reflect the society's changing standards or needs or do not correspond to the conceptual organization of the world. Part of the rhetorical structure of such challenges is the claim that the "old" arguments were incorrect to begin with and were themselves based on misunderstandings of those governing principles. Rarely is the equivalent of "that may have worked in the past, but it is not the way we do things around here now" asserted in behalf of a new set of claims. Conceptual innovations are seldom presented for what they are, reformulating pointers to the future; rather, they are firmly tied to the present, and sometimes to the past as well.

In the final analysis, what was at issue in the mid-seventeenth-century political debates to which Filmer contributed was the possession and control of the state. That problem was itself rooted in questions that the English had been able to avoid at least since Henry VIII's Reformation had succeeded in making the religious establishment an arm of the polity. Thanks to the convenient but ultimately broken-backed myth that England was ruled by the "king-in-parliament," a tacit if uneasy constitutional accommodation had permitted the question of "fundamental law" to be sidestepped until king and Parliament finally found themselves theoretically at loggerheads and physically at war in 1642. Like all deep, conceptual conflicts that are not abandoned, this one had to be settled by force rather than principle.[22]

Among the important subdisputes were the questions of whether politics and the state were natural or the results of human artifice and, closely related, whether political origins were to be found in familial, patriarchal organization or in a so-called state of nature, and if the latter, what made people sufficiently free to establish civil society. The patriarchal response, in the short run, was much the easier of the alternatives, and Filmer attacked the notions of "natural freedom" and individual "rights" that the state of nature and contract theories presupposed as "a New, Plausible and Dangerous Opinion" that "was first hatched in the Schools for good Divinity."[23] The effect of his remark in terms of the civil identity of women is that only a radical transformation in the way the social and political worlds were conceptualized could alter the status of women; nothing short of an overthrow of the nature-based political theory that had undergirded European self-consciousness since the time of Plato and Aristotle would do the job.

The starting point of Locke's argument against Filmer was the insistence that power over children was not due to fatherhood but was a consequence of the law of nature. All parents since Adam and Eve had been placed *"under an obligation to preserve, nourish, and educate the Children,* they had begotten, not as their own Workmanship, but as the Workmanship of their own Maker, the Almighty, to whom they were to be accountable for them."[24] It followed that "the *Power,* then *that Parents have* over their Children, arises from that Duty which is incumbent upon them, to take care of their Off-spring during the imperfect state of Childhood." "It [i.e., parental power] is but a help to the weakness and imperfection of their Nonage, a Discipline necessary to their education."[25] Accordingly, the child was bound to obey whoever maintained and cared for it whether that person was the natural parent or not.[26]

Familial authority belonged to both parents, Locke asserted, and he chided Filmer for ignoring the fact that the Fifth Commandment named both parents, not just the father.[27] Thus, even if parental power did come from generation, "This would give the *Father* but a joynt Dominion with the Mother over them [the children]. For no body can deny but that the Woman hath an equal share, if not the greater, as nourishing the Child a long time in her own Body out of her own Substance" (*Two Treatises,* 1.55). It followed, according to Locke, that paternal power ought "more properly [to be] called *Parental Power.* For whatever obligation Nature and the right of Generation lays on Children, it must certainly bind them equal to both concurrent Causes of it" (2.52). But Locke violated his own injunction almost immediately, reverting to the phrase *"Paternal Power"* (2.69), and subsequently suggested that the terms could be interchanged.[28]

In general, Locke treated the husband as the superior mate, but left a realm of freedom to the wife:

> But the Husband and Wife, though they have but one common Concern, yet having different understandings, will unavoidably sometimes have different wills too; it therefore being necessary that the last Determination, *i.e.* the Rule, should be placed somewhere; it naturally falls to the Man's share, as the abler and the stronger. But this reaching but to the things of their common Interest and Property, leaves the Wife in the full and free possession of what by Contract is her peculiar Right, and gives the Husband no more power over her Life than she has over his. (*Two Treatises*, 2.82)

What was more, this conjugal power did not provide the basis for civil government. If God's command to Eve that "thy Desire shall be to thy Husband, and he shall rule over thee" (Genesis 3.16)

> must needs be understood as a Law to bind her and all other Women to subjection, it can be no other Subjection than what every Wife owes her Husband, and then if this be the *Original Grant of Government and the Foundation of Monarchical Power*, there will be as many Monarchs as there are Husbands. If therefore these words give any Power to *Adam*, it can be only a Conjugal Power, not Political, the Power that every Husband hath to order the things of private Concernment in his Family, as Proprietor of the Goods and Land there, and to have his Will take place before that of his wife in all things of their common Concernment; but not a Political Power of Life and Death over her, much less over any body else. (*Two Treatises*, 1.48)

Quite simply, the complex society of the household, with its conjugal, parental, and master-servant relations "wherein the Master or Mistress of it had some sort of Rule proper to a Family, . . . came short of *Political Society*" (2.77).[29] But the basic structure of the family remained essentially patriarchal, and the members of civil society were men who were heads of households or otherwise enjoyed an economic and social independence. In this, Locke—with Hobbes—did not depart from the Filmerian understanding of the world. The important departure—also shared with Hobbes—was the movement out of nature and into convention. Locke's state, however, was the antithesis of all that Hobbes had defended; it was the constitutional, limited polity instituted to protect and maximize the rights and liberties of its members and derived from their consent that Hobbes had attacked in the *Leviathan*.

The derivation of politics from a conception of rights and liberty, while certainly not original to Hobbes and Locke, was the theoretical target of Filmer's patriarchalism and a denial of his political naturalism. Filmer used the term "rights" throughout his writings, but he generally intended a kind of entitlement that came from and was attached to superior status.[30] Rarely did he mean the natural or personal rights that belonged equally to each individual; he was aware of this meaning, and his criticism of Grotius was designed to condemn that usage by stressing its incompatibility with political authority.

The early–modern appeal to individual rights suggested voluntarism and conventionality, a world in which each rights-bearing person had the capacity to make and be responsible for his—and ultimately *her* as well—own place. These notions are altogether absent from Filmer, whose theory was a kind of divine-right naturalism; he looked to nature and the structures created by God for standards. But he appreciated the *logic* of the rights argument and saw that it would have to extend much further than its advocates intended.

Grotius had departed from the natural and original equality and common ownership of the state of nature and had endorsed the existence of private property and status in civil society. In a pointed criticism of Grotius that is applicable to all natural law theories, Filmer said: "Dominion . . . was brought in by the will of man, whom by this doctrine Grotius makes to be able to change that law which God himself cannot change, as he saith. He gives a double ability to man; first to make that no law of nature which God made to be the law of nature: and next to make that a law of nature which God made not; for now that dominion is brought in, he maintains, it is against the law of nature to take that which is in another man's dominion."[31]

His arguments against the fictitious contract of government that ended the state of nature were telling and recognized that the exclusion of women would violate the law of nature. The majority cannot bind any but itself, he said; all who dissented from the pact would have to retain their original liberty. Anything short of this would violate the putative natural right of liberty. Second, it is inconceivable, he wrote, that a multitude of people freely living without the constraints of society should come together to make such an agreement.[32] Not only that, but "infants and others under the age of discretion; not to speak of *women, especially virgins, who by birth have as much natural freedom as any other, . . . therefore ought not to lose their liberty without their own consent."*[33] Locke certainly knew of this argument but did not refer to it. However, his friend James Tyrrell inserted the following "Advertisement" to the first of the thirteen dialogues that comprised his *Bibliotheca Politica* (1691–94): "*I Desire always to be understood, that when I make use of the word People, I do not mean the vulgar or mixt multitude, but in the state of Nature the whole Body of Free-men and women, especially the Fathers and Masters of Families; and in a Civil State, all degrees of men, as well the Nobility and Clergy, as the Common People.*"[34]

If Tyrrell was aware of the problem, Locke should have seen it as well. At some level, he should have accounted for the relative absence of women from his conception of civil society and explained why women apparently did not have rights. Hobbes had forthrightly acknowledged that women's rights had been extinguished by men. Locke seems to have ignored the question altogether, which his conventional theory of political society should have prevented. As we shall see, there is a way of accounting for Locke's silence here, and that has to do with his understanding of the differences between "society" and politics.

In the end, of course, women were no more accorded civil status by Hobbes or Locke than they were by Filmer. In Filmer's case there were at least the excuses that his naturalistic conception of politics did not leave space for women and the fact that, in the final analysis, no one but the sovereign was a civil person. Even the patriarchal heads of households from whose God-given powers political power was derived did not enjoy civil status under the absolute monarchy Filmer envisioned.

Another important ingredient in the structure of Filmer's political theory is the *way* the household was used to prefigure politics. We are accustomed to regarding doctrines such as Filmer's analogically or metaphorically, such that the family *suggests* or *implies* things about the state, which can be seen as somehow *like* the household. Analogical reasoning is one of the standard modes of argument, and metaphors are among our principal means of assimilating and making sense of that which we might not otherwise understand or perhaps even perceive. The new or unfamiliar is presented as resembling or being a somewhat deviant instance of something that is already known to us, and we are "persuaded" to comprehend and eventually to accept it. This manner of arguing leaves room for discussion and debate about the ways in which the things in question do and do not resemble one another. In these terms, one might want to

claim that while the modern state resembles the family in some respects—say, the existence of determinate responsibilities and expectations—it is sufficiently different in others—the absence of kinship ties,
perhaps—to invalidate the comparison.

Initially, Filmer's argument would not be touched by such a response,
for his theory was based upon *identity* not *similarity*. Accordingly, the
family *was* a polity, and the polity *was* a household, and the patriarchal,
biblical family was not a prototype but the wellspring of politics. Theoretically, there are two ways of responding to an argument from strict identity. One may either accept it, as Hobbes did, and then go on to claim
that both institutions are conventional, or, with much greater difficulty,
one may deny the identity altogether. Locke took the latter course and
insisted that civil society was conventional and that the family was theoretically irrelevant to it, thereby avoiding even the question of the extent
to which they were related. While this also freed him from the need to
attack most of the prevailing social structural conceptions and beliefs of
his day, it left an important opening for Mary Astell, who said of Locke's
notion of natural rights, in effect, that women did not have them and
because women were no less human than men, no one did.[35]

Only these two moves could have provided the opening that was necessary for the emergence of women as politically visible. Both loosened
the stranglehold that patriarchal naturalism had on the politics of early-
modern Europe and replaced divine-right absolutism with a political conventionalism derived from personal and natural rights. The fact that
Locke himself did not carry his argument to the necessary next step and
fully incorporate women into his political doctrine is altogether separate
from the implications of that argument. The effect was that Locke accepted a significant part of the patriarchal structuring of Stuart society;
he endorsed its exclusion of women from the political process, but at the
same time prepared the way for the eventual admission of women to the
category of citizen. His omissions called attention to unresolved issues
and placed them on the political agenda of the English people.

A large part of what is involved in all this is Filmer's rather anxious
attack on *convention*.[36] It is probably the case, however, that Filmer did
not so much understand "modernity" as he defended the stable but de-
clining traditional, natural order against the challenges of precarious institutions and practices that were subject to human will. It is in the nature
of architectonic theories to reject uncertainty, and here, as elsewhere,
Filmer provides an illuminating example of the kinds of ideological and

structural changes that would be necessary before women could emerge into civil personhood.

Filmer stood for a conception of society in which whatever identities women were afforded were effectively derived from the males on whom they were dependent. Their statuses as wives and daughters rendered them radically different from men; they could never attain the familial headship that had been a prerequisite to functioning membership in civil society at least since the time of Aristotle. From the standpoint of the politics of the twenty-first century, it is ironic to realize that women in early–modern society needed a kind of *individualism* that would give them identities that were not *inherently* distinct from those of men. The transition to this modern outlook was already under way when Filmer was writing, but it was to be a protracted process of change, and Filmer stood somewhere near its beginnings.

One of the targets of Filmer's criticisms was the specter of discord, conflict, breakdown of government, and finally anarchy of Philip Hunton's *Treatise of Monarchy*.[37] Claiming that the government of England was a mixture of monarchy, democracy, and aristocracy, Hunton believed—as Locke would some forty years later—that the political process could not solve all the problems it confronted. When the moderation, accommodation, forbearance, and implicit trust that were essential to government broke down, Hunton reasoned, politics itself had reached an impasse that could only lead to revolutionary conflict. On that, Filmer and Hunton agreed, but Filmer placed the blame on the mixture itself, which he saw as an altogether improper and eventually disastrous form of rule.

Implicitly, Hunton accepted the modern conceit that authority is socially and culturally constructed and therefore controllable. One consequence of this view, which Hunton certainly did not embrace, is the assertion that the roles assigned to women are no less conventional and artificial than politics itself. More so perhaps than anyone else in the early–modern period, Hobbes represents that view. He is one of the most thoroughgoing social constructivists in history of Western thought,[38] and we have already seen how he applied this perspective to the status of women. In the end, however, the Hobbesian conventionalism did not emancipate women. In the first place, no one but the sovereign was free; rather more to point, however, Hobbes left women in a condition of subjection to their male superiors, so their inferiority—however conventional it may have been—was one layer deeper than that of men.

Locke stood somewhere between Filmer and Hobbes on this issue. He embraced that part of the conventionalist argument that applied to politics, but he was silent about the status of the family. What he did accomplish was the separation of politics from society, thereby foreclosing any attempt to infer the nature of the state from the household. The fact that the powers of a father and a civil ruler were sometimes resident in the same person was purely contingent, Locke insisted, in an effort to undermine Filmer's contention that because people are the natural subjects of their parents, they can never acquire enough freedom to be the authors of their own political obligations. The granting of Locke's point sets the stage for rendering all political relations indeterminate. His long-run contribution to political philosophy is the liberty that is required for humans to control their own destinies, and it is precisely that liberty that Filmer resisted.

Conclusion

It has been the genius of modern feminism to insist upon a place and identity for women independent of their memberships in households or families. For political as well as conceptual reasons, it has been a long and arduous struggle—the end of which is not yet in sight—but for what might be the first time in recorded history, we are able to talk of women apart from their traditional roles as wives, mothers, and daughters. This change is related to the growing dissatisfaction—itself part of the twentieth and twenty-first centuries' distrust of metaphysical speculation—with "essentialist" formulations in general. And all this, in turn, is related to the malaise that is sometimes said to accompany the contemporary world's readjustment of long-standing identities and relationships. While it is far too early to determine precise causal connections, it is certainly clear that feminism has had something important to do with generating and perpetuating this entire series of complaints.

What makes all this difficult is that the stakes are very high; the members of modern society are being asked—and not only by their feminist critics—to reconsider some of their most fundamental self-understandings and to alter the relationships and social structures that have sustained the distributions of power and social advantage at least since the Reformation. Metaphysics, the essentialist conceptions of the self to which it gives rise, and the role-assignments that result function like "totalizing" institutions—society-wide, conceptual prisons that contain and restrain the guards as well as the inmates, both of whom appear to have some interest in maintaining the system. For the "guards," the benefits are status, privilege, and power; for the "inmates," they are the psychological security of identity and stability.

All of which is to say that it is often painful and usually costly to bring about alterations in the characteristic ways societies have of describing themselves and their members. Resistance to such proffered changes is generally grounded in attempts to retain status and power, but even those who might benefit from the changes can be reluctant to adopt or endorse innovations they find too unsettling. The entire process rarely occurs at this level of consciousness, but desires to retain status and anxieties about potential dislocations help explain the unwitting motives people frequently have for preserving social order without in any way denying their possible sincerity.

In many respects, modern feminism has been unusually successful, for one of the most conspicuous consequences of the contemporary debate is that the meaning of *woman* (and of *man* too, for that matter) is no longer stable. While this meaning is not quite up for grabs, as it were, it does appear to be on its way to being "lost" in the sense intended by James Boyd White, who following Thucydides, remarks, "An alteration in language of the kind I mean is not merely a lexical event, and it is not reversible by insistence upon a set of proper definitions. It is a change in the world and the self, in manners and conduct and sentiment."[39] It is now possible—and not merely plausible—to talk about women outside the structures of the family. What is more, our understanding of the family has been altered, partially in response to feminist criticisms and partially because the institution itself has changed. Although these reconceptualizations continue to be resisted by many people, they have fairly secure places in the social vocabulary of the Western world. These alterations continue to reverberate throughout society rather like an earthquake and its aftershocks, for the traditionally conceived household, with its hierarchical arrangements, is part of the bedrock on which the whole of modern social structure rests.

There is something fascinating about the entire business, for in the adult lifetimes of many of us, a set of linguistic conventions and their surrounding, supporting, and dependent institutions and practices that have held sway for more than five hundred years have all been successfully modified as a result of the conscious efforts of feminist political reformers. It is an astounding phenomenon—better yet, accomplishment—when apprehended from that perspective. This success would have been altogether lost on Sir Robert Filmer, for it represents the ultimate victory of his most profound critic, John Locke.

I should be very clear about what is being claimed here, both *about* Locke and *for* modernity. Locke's conception of the polity is certainly not one of nongendered participation. He was not an egalitarian on any grounds, hardly least among them, sexual. Nonetheless, his theory considerably widened the category of the political person even though it retained the traditional restriction of that status to males. Pateman is correct in her implicit protestation that the very important separation of the social from the political that Locke made—a separation that was essential to his state of nature, social contract, and natural rights reply to Filmer[40]—allowed him to endorse (or potentially blinded his readers to) the continued oppression of women and their exclusion from politics.

This criticism can be carried much further. A distinction of this sort entails that Locke's civil society was built on top of a set of not merely non- but determinedly *pre*-political arrangements. The resulting polity reflects, is sustained by, and itself sustains those non- or pre-political arrangements that have gone into its existence. In these terms, the deep danger of so-called liberal political neutrality in which the state evinces no interest in the outcome of the conflicts it mediates—as Anatole France pointedly observed in his well-known comments about sleeping under the bridges of the Seine—is that it is officially blind to *social* injustice and virtually prides itself on that fact by insisting upon this state/society (or public/private) separation.

At the same time, it can be argued that it is precisely and exclusively that perspective of social justice denied—on what grounds can we justify the fact that one person or class of people is deprived of what someone else has?—that permits the removal of undue burdens.

What Locke did accomplish in these terms—almost as if to show the problematic and ultimately unstable nature of his own distinction—the recognition that women had a level of *interest* that permitted them to engage in the contractual relationship of marriage. Historically and conceptually, this move opened doors to a wider and more overtly political participation that is founded upon social visibility and voice. That this is insufficient is beyond question, but it is also part of the historical story that must be told in order to account for the movement from Filmer, through Blackstone, to the twenty-first century within a continuous line of political development. What is not clear is whether the limitations on women that Locke retained and which have been passed on to subsequent ages *necessarily* sustain a sexual oppression that cannot be overcome or today provide a negative standard to be overthrown and which reveals the failings of our own social and political practices.

My position is that in all relevant respects, men and women are already indistinguishable and that once we understand that fact, it is up to us to remove the obstacles to the actual achievement of that equality. More important—and this is an argument that must be made elsewhere[41]—this achievement is most likely to occur through the realization of the conception of rights that is the central part of the Lockean legacy that frames much of our politics.

Notes

1. Cicero, *De officiis* 1.17.54.

2. Lest I be misunderstood, I should make it clear that I interpret Locke's "civil society" as a synonym for "political society"—what we might call the "state"—not a forerunner of the later "civil society" that is generally understood as a "mediating space" between the "political" and "private" realms. Locke made this clear in chapter 7 of the *Second Treatise* ("Of Political, or Civil Society"). *Civil* is the Latinate word that corresponds to the Greek-derived *political;* it did not acquire a separate meaning until the late eighteenth century.

3. Peter Laslett, introduction to his edition of John Locke, *Two Treatises of Government*, Cambridge Texts in the History of Political Thought (Cambridge: Cambridge University Press, 1988), 68. All subsequent references to Locke's *Two Treatises of Government* will be to this edition.

4. Nor, for that matter, did any of the other significant works on Locke published in that period, in particular Martin Seliger, *The Liberal Politics of John Locke* (New York: Praeger, 1969), and John Dunn, *The Political Thought of John Locke: An Historical Account of the Argument of the "Two Treatises of Government"* (Cambridge: Cambridge University Press, 1969).

5. I attempted to make amends for my omission in a pair of articles published in the late 1990s: "De l'idée de sujétion naturelle à l'indifférenciation par convention: les femmes dans la pensée politique de Sir Robert Filmer, Thomas Hobbes, et John Locke," in *Encyclopédie Politique et Historique des Femmes: Europe, Amérique du Nord*, ed. Christine Fauré (Paris: Presses Universitaires de France, 1997), and "The Significant Sounds of Silence: The Absence of Women from the Political Thought of Sir Robert Filmer and John Locke (or, 'Why Can't a Woman Be More Like a Man?')," in *Political Writings, Political Women: Early-Modern Britain in a European Context*, ed. Hilda Smith (Cambridge: Cambridge University Press, 1998), but by that time, Lorenne Clark and Melissa Butler had already made the point (see notes 6 and 7).

6. Lorenne Clark, "Women and John Locke; or, Who Owns the Apples in the Garden of Eden?" *Canadian Journal of Philosophy* 7 (1977): 721.

7. Melissa A. Butler, "Early Liberal Roots of Feminism: John Locke and the Attack on Patriarchy," *American Political Science Review* 72 (1978): 135–50. Reprinted herein as Chapter 3.

8. Joan Kelly, "Did Women Have a Renaissance?" originally published in *Becoming Visible: Women in European History*, ed. Renate Bridenthal and Claudia Koontz (Boston: Houghton Mifflin, 1977), reprinted in her *Women, History, and Theory: The Essays of Joan Kelly*, ed. Blanche W. Cook et al. (Chicago: University of Chicago Press, 1984).

9. See in particular J. B. Schneewind, *The Invention of Autonomy: A History of Modern Moral Philosophy* (Cambridge: Cambridge University Press, 1998), and some of the essays in *Reconstructing Individualism: Autonomy, Individuality, and the Self in Western Thought*, ed. Thomas C. Heller et al. (Stanford: Stanford University Press, 1986).

10. See in particular Keith Thomas, "Women in the Civil War Sects," *Past and Present* 13 (1958): 34–62, reprinted in *Crisis in Europe*, ed. Trevor Aston (New York: Basic Books, 1965), and Patricia Crawford, "'The Poorest She': Women and Citizenship in Early-Modern England," in *The Putney Debates of 1647: The Army, the Levellers, and the English State*, ed. Michael Mendle (Cambridge: Cambridge University Press, 2001), 197–218.

11. Peter Laslett, introduction to Sir Robert Filmer, *Patriarcha and Other Political Works*, ed. Laslett, Blackwell's Political Texts (Oxford: Blackwell, 1949), 41. All references to Filmer, unless otherwise indicated, will be to this edition, cited only by the name of the individual work itself. I have prepared a new edition of this work (to be published by Transaction Press), with a new introduction and two additional tracts by Filmer; otherwise, the pagination will remain the same.

12. However, in two works that have been omitted from the Filmerian canon since the seventeenth century—*An Advertisement to the Jurymen of England, Touching Witches; Together with a Difference Between a Hebrew and an English Witch* (London, 1652) and *Quaestio Quodlibetica, or, A Discourse Whether It May Be Lawful to Take Use for Money* (London, 1653)—Sir Robert did challenge prevailing doctrines. In the first—rather uncharacteristically if his political writings are the standard—he substituted reason for biblical superstition and denied that the accused witches of his day satisfied the requirements of the Hebrew Bible; in the second, he defended the charging of interest for loans. Both tracts are included in my forthcoming second edition of the Laslett edition of Filmer's *Political Works*.

13. See *The Lawes Resolutions of Womens Rights: or, The Laws Provision for Women* (London, 1632), 9–10. This work is generally but erroneously attributed to one "T.E.," who signed the preface in which he (presumably) said, "By whom this following Discourse was Composed I certainly know not" (sig. ar). For a general discussion of *The Lawes Resolutions*, see W. R. Prest, "Law and Women's Rights in Early Modern England," *The Seventeenth Century* 6 (1991): 169–87. Authorship and the identity of "T.E." are discussed on 172–75.

14. *The Lawes Resolutions*, 116; see also 119.

15. This limitation extended well into the eighteenth century. As William Blackstone noted in his *Commentaries*:

> By marriage, the husband and wife are one person in law: that is, the very being or legal existence of the woman is suspended during the marriage, or at least is incorporated and consolidated into that of the husband: under whose wing, protection, and *cover*, she performs every thing; and is therefore called in our law-french a *feme-covert*; is said to be *covert-baron*, or under the protection and influence of her husband, her *baron*, or lord; and her condition during her marriage is called her *coverture*.

William Blackstone, *Commentaries on the Laws of England* (1765–69), 1.15.3; text from the four-volume facsimile edition by Stanley N. Katz (Chicago: University of Chicago Press, 1979), 1:430. Carole Pateman quotes a portion of this same, well-known passage in *The Sexual Contract* (Stanford: Stanford University Press, 1988), 91.

16. Filmer, *The Freeholder's Grand Inquest, Touching Our Soveraigne Lord the King and His Parlia-*

ment (1648), 154. Cf. 163 and 178, where Filmer specifically referred to the "duty . . . to obey the Queen" and to Elizabeth's warning to Parliament "not to meddle with the Queen's Person."

17. John Knox, *The First Blast of the Trumpet against the Monstrous Regiment of Women* (1558), as reprinted in Knox, *On Rebellion*, ed. Roger Mason, Cambridge Texts in the History of Political Thought (Cambridge: Cambridge University Press, 1994), 8. Although his book was directed at the two Marys, it was Knox's misfortune to have published it the same year that the Protestant Elizabeth succeeded to the throne of England, for his general arguments applied to her with equal force. The *First Blast* provoked a considerable literature, for which see my *Patriarchalism in Political Thought: The Authoritarian Family and Political Speculation and Attitudes especially in Seventeenth-Century England* (Oxford: Blackwell, 1975; 2nd ed., New Brunswick, N.J.: Transaction Books, 1988), chap. 3.

18. Pateman, *Sexual Contract*, 87.

19. In this, I agree with Anthony Fletcher's analysis of what he calls "the God-given naturalness of the patriarchal order" and its presumption that "women were inferior." Fletcher, "The Protestant Idea of Marriage in Early Modern England," in *Religion, Culture, and Society in Early Modern Britain: Essays in Honor of Patrick Collinson*, ed. Anthony Fletcher and Peter Roberts (Cambridge: Cambridge University Press, 1994), 161–81, quotations from 175. Cf. Susan Dwyer Amussen, *An Ordered Society: Gender and Class in Early Modern England* (Oxford: Blackwell, 1988), for an interpretation that sees the society as somewhat less repressive of women.

Fletcher's argument has been incorporated into his *Gender, Sex, and Subordination in England, 1500–1800* (New Haven: Yale University Press, 1995), the thesis of which is that "patriarchy," which is defined as "the institutionalized male dominance over women and children in the family and the subordination of women in society in general," was "an outstandingly significant feature of English society between 1500 and 1800" (xv).

20. Cf. Margaret J.M. Ezell, *The Patriarch's Wife: Literary Evidence and the History of the Family* (Chapel Hill: University of North Carolina Press, 1987), 129–44 and 169–90.

21. For accounts and explanations of that invocation, see Amussen, *An Ordered Society*, chaps. 2 and 5, and Lena Cowen Orlin, *Private Matters and Public Culture in Post-Reformation England* (Ithaca: Cornell University Press, 1994), esp. chap. 2.

22. See Gordon Schochet, "The English Revolution in the History of Political Thought," in *Country and Court: Essays in Honor of Perez Zagorin*, ed. Bonnie Kunze and Dwight Brautigam (Rochester: University of Rochester Press, 1992), and J.G.A. Pocock and Gordon Schochet, "Interregnum and Restoration," in *The Varieties of British Political Thought, 1500–1800*, ed. Pocock, Schochet, and Lois G. Schwoerer (Cambridge: Cambridge University Press, 1994). For the constitutional background, see Margaret A. Judson, *The Crisis of the Constitution: An Essay in Constitutional and Political Thought in England, 1603–1645* (originally published 1949), reprinted with a forward by J. H. Hexter (New Brunswick: Rutgers University Press, 1988). The same period is covered with rather different emphases by J. P. Sommerville, *Politics and Ideology in England, 1603–1640* (London: Longman, 1986), and Glenn Burgess, *The Politics of the Ancient Constitution: An Introduction to English Political Thought, 1603–1642* (University Park: Pennsylvania State University Press, 1993).

23. Filmer, *Patriarcha: A Defence of the Natural Authority of Kings Against the Unnatural Liberty of the People* (written c. 1630–40; first published, 1680), 53.

24. Locke, *Two Treatises*, 2.56; see also 2.60.

25. Ibid., 2.58 and 65.

26. Ibid., 1.100 and 2.65.

27. Ibid., 2.6, 11, and 60–66; see also 2.52–53.

28. See ibid., 2.170 and 173.

29. I have discussed this latter passage and its significance in greater detail in *Patriarchalism in Political Thought*, chap. 13; in my essay on Locke in the *Oxford History of Political Thought*, ed. Steven Kahn (Oxford: Oxford University Press, 1998); in " 'Guards and Fences': Property and Obligation in Locke's Political Thought," *History of Political Thought* 21 (2000): 369–89; and in "From Nature to Politics and Back Again: John Locke on Civil Society and the State of Nature," forthcoming.

30. See, e.g., Filmer, *Patriarcha*, 59–61.

31. Filmer, *Observations Concerning the Originall of Government* (1652), 266. Although Locke never cited this criticism, the attempt to meet it is probably the source of his doctrine of property and his refinement of the Grotian argument by the implicit use of a scholastic conception of *potentia*. See also Schochet, "'Guards and Fences.'"

32. Filmer, *The Anarchy*, 286.

33. Ibid., 287; emphasis added. Filmer carried this argument even further, saying that consistency would require that "children and servants [who] are far a greater number than parents or masters" be permitted to participate, which would lead to a "most unnatural" conclusion by giving "the children the government over their parents" (ibid.).

34. [James Tyrrell], *Bibliotheca Politica: or, An Enquiry into the Ancient Constitution of the English Government . . . in Thirteen Dialogues* (London, 1691–94), sig. A4v; italics in original. The dialogues were originally published separately but with continuous pagination. A *General Alphabetical Index* was published in 1694; it was bound with all thirteen dialogues, and the collection was published as a single book, also in 1694, with a "second edition" in 1701. A fourteenth dialogue was published in 1702, and new editions of the enlarged work were published in 1717 and 1727.

Tyrrell was a competent if undistinguished Whig historian and controversialist. He had been a colleague of Locke's during his undergraduate career at Oxford, and their association continued throughout Locke's life. Although there are frequent references to him in works on the political thought and ideology of the 1680s and 1690s, Tyrrell is relatively obscure. His best-known work is an attack on Filmer, *Patriarcha non Monarcha*, written at about the same time that Locke was composing the *Two Treatises* and published anonymously in 1683. For further discussion, see Julia Rudolph, *Revolution by Degrees: James Tyrrell and Whig Political Thought in the Late Seventeenth Century* (London: Palgrave, 2002), and J. W. Gough, "James Tyrrell, Whig Historian and Friend of John Locke," *Historical Journal* 19 (1976): 581–610.

35. Mary Astell, *Reflections upon Marriage* (1700), reprinted in *Political Writings*, ed. Patricia Springborg (Cambridge: Cambridge University Press, 1996), 18.

36. I have discussed some of this, but without extensive references to Filmer, in "Patriarchalism, Naturalism, and the Rise of the 'Conventional State,'" in *Categorie del Reale e Storiografia: Aspetti di Continuità e Transformazione nell' Europa Moderna*, ed. F. Fagiani and G. Valera (Calabria, Italy: Franco Angeli, 1986), which was also published in *Materiali period Una Storia della cultura Guiridica* 14 (1984). See also, Schochet, "Constitutionalism, Liberalism, and the Study of Politics," in *NOMOS XX: Constitutionalism* (1979), as well as *Patriarchalism in Political Thought*, chap. 14.

37. Hunton's *Treatise of Monarchy* was published anonymously in 1643 (and republished in 1680 and 1689) and immediately became the center of an extensive debate. Hunton responded to some of his critics in A *Vindication of the Treatise of Monarchy* in 1644.

38. See, e.g., Thomas Hobbes, *Philosophical Rudiments Concerning Government and Society* (1651), an English translation of *De Cive* (1642), Preface, paragraph 3: "*for as in a watch, or some such small engine, the matter, figure, and motion of its wheels, cannot well be known, except it be taken in sunder, and viewed in parts; so to make a more curious search into the rights of States, and duties of Subjects, it is necessary, . . . they be so considered, as if they were dissolved.*" Text from Hobbes, *De Cive: The English Version*, ed. Howard Warrender (Oxford: Oxford University Press, 1983), 32; italics in original.

39. James Boyd White, *When Words Lose Their Meaning: Constitutions and Reconstitutions of Language, Character, and Community* (Chicago: University of Chicago Press, 1984), 4.

40. I have discussed this in *Patriarchalism in Political Thought*, chap. 13, and in a forthcoming essay on Locke's state of nature theory.

41. See my *Rights in Contexts: The Historical and Political Construction of Moral and Legal Entitlements* (Lawrence: University Press of Kansas, 2007).

5

Intersectionality Before Intersectionality Was Cool

The Importance of Class to Feminist Interpretations of Locke

Nancy J. Hirschmann

Twenty-first-century feminists repeatedly invoke the holy trinity of gender, race, and class (sometimes squaring it off with sexuality) as the categories most central to political analysis and identity. Kimberle Crenshaw's theory of "intersectionality" suggests that feminists need to attend to these different vectors of identity and power simultaneously in order to generate intellectually plausible and politically effective theories. When theorizing about "women," she argued, feminists cannot afford to ignore the fact that, because of their race, black and white women experience similar phenomena—such as domestic violence—differently.[1] Crenshaw's argument resonated with feminists, at least in theory, for many feminists proclaim the need to follow her recommendations.

Few, however, actually accomplish this. When dealing with the history of canonical political thought in particular, it is extremely uncommon to find any of these various categories considered at all, much less in concert. Even feminist analysis of the canon tends to deal with "women" as an undifferentiated category; although we declare the importance of race, class, and sexuality in contemporary analysis, once feminists reach back before the late twentieth century, once again "all the women are white,"[2] not to mention middle class.

The ostensible reason for this could be that the majority of women in canonical political thought *are* white and middle class: the wives and daughters of the men who were the primary subjects of political theory. Thus, for instance, it is rare to find a single comment made about men of color, much less women of color, in the works of many Enlightenment theorists. Kant made some brief references to Native American women in his *Anthropology*, Mill an oblique reference to African-American female slaves in his *On the Subjection of Women*.[3] Rousseau made passing mention of "savages" in *The Origin of Inequality* and argued that people from southern, warmer climates—who were also likely to be darker-skinned—were more indolent, less industrious, and therefore not appropriate subjects for democracy, any more than were women from any climate.[4] References in Locke's work to Africans of either sex are extremely scarce, thus causing a number of scholars to abandon the attempt to develop a definitive argument about Locke's views on slavery.[5] Even the work that historians—and very few of them, at that—have offered attests more to the milieu in which theorists like Locke wrote, rather than to any definitive claims about the theorists' lives and experiences themselves.[6] Just as it may be the case that women's failure to show up on a theorist's radar screen is due not to women's absence from history but to the theorist's inattention, contempt, and dismissiveness toward women, so it is possible that a theorist's inattention to race is the mark of his racism, for he does not even see race as worthy of his notice, despite its political, economic, and social significance to the late seventeenth-century Western world. It is thereby understandable, however, that feminist political theorists have not addressed the possible intersections of race and gender in the canonical works of political theory: there is frequently too little material to work with.

However, class issues were considered at somewhat greater length by theorists such as Mill and Kant, and less overtly, though no less significantly, by Locke, as a number of commentators have shown us. Foremost among these was C. B. Macpherson, whose idea of "possessive individualism" held that people in the social contract theories of Hobbes and Locke (as well as figures in between such as Harrington and the Levellers) were focused on acquisition. The supposedly natural individuals at the heart of Hobbes's and Locke's theories were, Macpherson argued, the white, propertied, middle-to-upper-class individuals of emerging capitalism.[7] By locating these theories at the dawn of capitalism, possessive individualism theorizes an ontology for a new historical era and world order. People are constructed as "individuals" in the most extreme sense of the term, as innately separate from other people, even hostile and antagonistic to them. In the interest of challenging hierarchical, agnatic obeisance, these theorists deny any and all natural bonds of community; relationships can be established only by formal agreement, the result of individual choice. Hence government can be legitimately founded only by a "social contract," or an explicit agreement between governments and the people they are to govern.

The theory of possessive individualism gave feminists a useful entry point for considering gender, because of course the white propertied possessive individuals of which Macpherson spoke were decidedly male. In this sense, Macpherson provided a sort of template for feminist analysis: by arguing that underneath the language of "free and equal" individuals in a state of nature lay very unequal beings, who were not at all universal or natural but rather situated in particular social and economic relationships in a particular historical era, Macpherson showed us that Locke's argument about the state of nature masked a class bias. Feminists subsequently argued that this language also masked a gender bias. If "all men" were not actually free and equal to each other in Locke's theory, despite his assertions to the contrary, women were nevertheless their unconditional inferiors. When it came to gender, feminists found, freedom and equality were unilaterally masculine.

But feminists tend to leave out Macpherson's central argument about class, developing a "parallel" argument rather than an "intersecting" one. For instance, Melissa Butler, in one of the earliest feminist critiques of Locke, explicitly wondered about "the extent to which this class differential might also be a sex differential."[8] But she made no attempt to bring these two vectors together, instead moving on to consider "women" as a generic, and largely bourgeois, category. This limited conceptualization of gender has dominated feminist scholarship on not only Locke but the entire modern Western canon for the past thirty years. When subsequent feminists appropriated possessive individualism, they turned it into a broader notion of "abstract individualism," as feminists focused on the relationship handicaps these natural men seemed to have. The term "abstract individualism" was coined by Marxist-feminist Nancy Hartsock, who argued that the competition and hostility that characterizes Macpherson's possessive individualism was a feature of ancient political theory as well, just exacerbated in the era of capitalism. Such hostility and aggression are not only an inherently contradictory foundation for relationship, she said, but betray severe psychological insecurities in the masculine psyche; "the individual" of state of nature theory is not only founded on historically based masculine interests in preserving gendered power and the gender division of labor, but also feeds into the perpetuation of gendered differences in self-conceptions and self-other relationships.[9]

Other feminist critiques employed similar arguments that focused on the relational difficulties that the "natural" individuals of political theory seemed to exhibit. Feminists critiqued the fact that families did not appear to exist in the state of nature,[10] as well as the fact that women's subordination was construed as the product of women's voluntary agreement. This last point was obviously key to feminist critiques of "social contract" theorists, for feminists saw in this paradox an entire ontology for liberal capitalism. Feminists argued that taking the contract as the template for relationships of all sorts, including adult sexual partnerships ("the marriage contract") masked the economic basis of women's subordination within the patriarchal family and denied not only the reality of reproduction but also basic human emotional and psychological needs for connection.[11]

The notion of abstract, rather than possessive, individualism particularly influenced Lockean analysis, as feminists tended to focus on the apparent contradictions Locke offered on bourgeois married women. Women were owed equal respect and obedience by their children, independent of the husband's will, but the husband had to have the final say in familial decisions because he was "abler and stronger." Women, as human beings, presumably had "property in the person," yet the major things they were supposed to produce—namely children—did not belong to them, but to God; and the fruits of household production belonged to their husbands or fathers who owned the materials to which women added their labor. Women freely contracted to marry, and could separate from their husbands once their children were grown, yet they did not really have much choice about whether or not to marry, or much say in the specific terms of the marriage contract, since they did not own property.[12]

These arguments were important in opening up Locke's work to gender analysis, and to seeing the gendered foundations of the liberal state. But rarely, if ever, did feminists attend to Locke's remarks about female servants in the bourgeois family, for instance, or about requiring poor women on parish relief to work. This may be because feminists have tended to focus on the *Two Treatises*, where Locke's remarks are not only decidedly ambiguous about women but also locate women in the bourgeois family, as Macpherson at least indirectly revealed by identifying the possessive individual as the bourgeois capitalist. But there were other women in Locke's world besides bourgeois women, particularly poor and working-class (presumably white) women.[13] These women are generally ignored in feminist analysis of Locke. I suggest that attending to what Locke says about them not only deepens and supports the standard arguments made about bourgeois women, but provides important insights into the significance and place of gender in Locke's theory.

Class would thus seem to provide some potential for allowing feminists to address the "intersectionality gap" in canonical theory, and in Lockean scholarship more specifically. In this chapter I will consider the relationship of gender and class by comparing texts that feminists usually ignore—particularly Locke's "Essay on the Poor Law," *Some Thoughts Concerning Education*, and *Of the Conduct of the Understanding*. None of these texts is primarily about women; indeed in *Education* girls and women are given decidedly short shrift. But by looking at the relatively straightforward relationship between property and reason that Macpherson first identified, as well as the far more ambiguous relationship that women have to both, which feminists have long debated, I hope to shed some new light on the relationship between gender and class in Locke's work, and the need for feminists to attend to the latter in modern canonical theory in order to fully appreciate the former. This argument thus offers in part a substantive reading of Locke's theory. But I also hope to make a case for greater methodological attention to the "intersectionality" that is much touted by feminists, but infrequently enacted when we consider the modern canon.

Locke and the Poor Law

Though Macpherson's interpretation of the *Second Treatise* built an elaborate argument about its hidden class biases, Locke's lesser-known "Essay on the Poor Law" addresses class issues more directly. In this essay, Locke worried that dependency on parish relief was growing too common, creating unreasonably severe tax burdens on the middle class, and even on the working poor. Locke sought a more efficient and regulated system of poor relief because "the multiplying of the poor, and the increase of the tax for their maintenance, is so general an observation and complaint that it cannot be doubted of," and "it has been a growing burden on the kingdom these many years." Growing taxes, and the fact that increasing numbers of the indolent were living off the hard work of others, was a highly objectionable state in need of reform.[14]

Even more alarming than the cost, however, was the corruption that spurred such dependency. The "Essay on the Poor Law" was written in 1699, the last of Britain's "seven barren years," a period in which pauperism was extremely common and two percent of the British population owned 65 percent of the land.[15] But even so, Locke claimed that poverty resulted not from a lack of economic opportunities—"not from scarcity of provisions, nor from want of employment for the poor, since the goodness of God has blessed these times with plenty." Rather, it resulted from laziness and corruption, "the relaxation of discipline and corruption of manners; virtue and industry being as constant companions on the one side as vice and idleness are on the other."[16] In other words, Locke blamed poverty on the moral corruption of the poor, not on systematic economic inequality: or rather, the inequality was systematic only insofar as it revealed differences in moral health.

The parish relief system, rather than alleviating poverty, actually worsened it, because it was set up to encourage people to believe that they could get something for nothing, and hence contributed to their moral corruption. The poor were provided relief through parishes funded by the levying of a "poor rate," or tax on parish members. Locke sought to replace this ad hoc system of control by individual parishes with a more centralized and consistent system where groups of parishes would be coordinated and governed by corporations.[17] For Locke believed that the increase in pauperism, and the accompanying taxation it wrought, demonstrated the failure of existing poor laws, or more specifically, their improper execution. The "relief" that the poor laws were intended to provide, Locke claimed, was to provide work; but instead parish relief tended toward direct payments, resulting in "the maintenance of people in idleness, without examining into the lives, abilities, or industry, of those who seek for relief."[18]

Such a situation is "to the shame of Christianity" because it actually violates the ideals of charity. That is, defining "charity" as direct payment goes against God's will; God has given us property in the person and rationality, as Locke argued in the *Second Treatise*, and to use neither is to waste God's gifts. But parish relief does encourage people to waste them. How one demonstrates true charity, therefore, is by enacting discipline; just as the loving parent must be able to discipline the child for its own good, so must the parish discipline the poor and direct them to a better way of life. Specifically, the parish must "encourage" the poor to work: "the true and proper relief of the poor . . . consists in finding work for them, and taking care they do not live like drones upon the labour of others."[19] Locke conceded that there are some on parish relief, such as the ill and infirm, who are genuinely unable to support themselves. And indeed, he argued that certain workers who became disabled in the Irish linen trade should receive double the normal relief allowance.[20] He also recommended permits for begging—which for the most part he believed was just another corrupt form of trying to get something for nothing— acknowledging that some were entitled to do so, just as some were entitled to parish relief, because they were genuinely unable to work. But most poor people could support themselves, either entirely (particularly in the case of able-bodied male drunkards) or at least partially (such as destitute widowed mothers of small children). Forcing such people to labor was essential, for they were clearly able to work, just unwilling to do so, or at best ignorant of how to organize themselves to obtain appropriate employment.

Accordingly, Locke suggested that begging be punished by forced labor until the vagrant could be set aboard a ship to work for a period of three years "under strict discipline." Women caught begging had it a bit easier, being fined or put to work for three months; children under fourteen for six weeks. Making a clear parallel that dispelled any doubt about his attitude toward the poor, in the very same paragraph Locke maintained that anyone seeking parish relief because they claimed to be unable to find employment should be forced to work under similarly indentured conditions. Specifically, the claimant would be offered by the parish minister at the Sunday service to members of the parish for work "at a lower rate than is usually given"; and if no parishioner voluntarily hired him, then parishioners would take turns employing him at this below-usual wage. Such a policy would motivate the poor to seek work on their own, since the pay would be better, and they would, at least in the theory of free market labor, have some degree of control over the kind of work they did and the wages they were able to bargain for.[21]

My use of the masculine pronoun in the previous sentences should not occlude the fact that Locke also believed that women on parish relief suffered from laziness and corruption, and he insisted that women work as well, including mothers. Though childrearing is burdensome enough to prevent women from working out of the home full time, Locke maintained, it does not completely fill their days: women have many "broken intervals in their time" during which they "earn nothing" and "their labour is wholly lost."[22] Feminist readers of the Second Treatise will, of course, see a convenient shift in argument in the "Essay on the Poor Law." For in the former, Locke argues that the rigors of childbirth actually disable women from participation in the same activities as men; a human female, unlike animal females, is "capable of conceiving" almost immediately after giving birth, "and de facto is commonly with Child again, and Brings forth too a new Birth long before the former is out of a dependency." This reason is used in that text to support the argument that men have obligations of fidelity to the family, to support their wives and children, being "under an Obligation to continue in Conjugal Society with the same Woman longer than other creatures."[23] By contrast, in the "Poor Law" Locke argues that since "more than two children at one time, under the age of three years, will seldom happen in one family," then women are not normally overly burdened by pregnancy and childcare.[24] This change in views about reproduction could reflect a change in Locke's thinking about women in general, or it could reflect his views about the civilizing effects of the social contract; once familial forms are more fully regularized and regulated under the social contract, women would somehow gain more control over their sexual relations and fertility. This latter argument is highly speculative, of course, and I think a stronger case can be made that this shift in Locke's views about reproduction reflects a class bias: the Two Treatises, with its central concern of property, refers explicitly to bourgeois women, who should, presumably, dedicate all their time and attention to the well-being of their husbands and their children.

By contrast, the "Poor Law," fairly obviously, refers explicitly to the propertyless. Locke believed that the fact that poor families have too many children contributes to their poverty; "a man and his wife, in health, may be able by their ordinary labour to maintain themselves and two children."[25] Most poor families have more than two, however; if the social contract's civilizing effect gives bourgeois women greater control over their fertility, poor women and men would seem to be closer to the state of nature where women are continually pregnant. Part of the project of helping the poor, then, would be to discipline them into civilization proper. Locke seeks a solution that will enable poor women seeking parish relief to be productive; in-home piecework might be one solution, particularly since that was the primary means of textile production until the nineteenth century, though the rise of the linen factory in Ireland may have encouraged the prescient Locke to view production in more industrialized terms.[26] Rather, the solution that Locke hit on was to take children out of the home altogether.

In particular, Locke recommended that children aged three to fourteen be placed in "working schools," which were basically wool-spinning factories.[27] Doing this would accomplish several things at once. First, it would enable both parents to work for wages, particularly mothers, by freeing them of caretaking responsibilities. Second, it would further reduce the cost to the parish of supporting these "excess" children, since they would be contributing to their own upkeep by producing wool. Third, it would provide direct support for these children, which they otherwise would not obtain from their impoverished parents, for the children would not be paid in wages—which would only be lost to drunken fathers—but in food, specifically, bread and water, and "in cold weather, if it be thought needful, a little warm water-gruel." For, the efficient Locke noted, "the same fire that warms the room may be made use of to boil a pot of it."[28]

If *Oliver Twist* comes to mind—"Please sir, I want some more"—we might not be far off the mark; for just as Dickens satirized the hypocrisy of poor laws that made it impossible for the poor to escape poverty and then blamed them for their plight, Locke's recommendation would seem to contradict its supposed ethical foundations. That is, if poverty breeds bad character, one would think that giving people the means to escape poverty—such as meaningful education and training in skilled trades— might be a better answer than indenturing poor children. But Locke seems to assume that there would be no point in this. Yes, it was important to change habits in the poor to enhance their industry and rationality, but there were limits to how far it was worthwhile to pursue this endeavor. Seventeenth-century society demanded a large number of laborers, and laboring required great expenditures of time and energy. Locke was not a Leveller, he was only interested in making everyone fill their place in a divine "architecture of order"[29] more efficiently, and thereby more "contentedly." Indeed, as John Marshall notes, Locke saw inequality as a necessary corollary of maximally efficient production.[30]

But more is at stake for Locke than protecting the property rights of the wealthy and middle class, or even maximizing capitalist efficiency. Rather, it is character that is at issue, specifically, the development of industry and rationality, or rather their lack of development in a particular segment of the populace. Not only did the existing form of parish relief rob the industrious who paid the poor rates, it also robbed those on relief. For by not working, such individuals' reason would deteriorate (or never develop) from lack of use; by living "upon the labour of others" they would become "drones," less than human.[31] Such a state was an affront to God and to Christianity, for it violated the divine order that God decreed by which all should use the gifts He gave man—freedom, equality of right, and property in the person—to better themselves and thereby honor Him. Through their labor, by contrast, laborers would develop reason sufficiently to know that working hard is the right thing to do, that work is key to achieving as much contentment out of life as their lot will allow. So they would be "reasonable" beings, sufficiently rational to know to follow their leaders and obey the law, even if they were not rational enough to be express consenters and active parties to the social contract.

Locke did not see himself as hostile to poverty and the poor, then. Rather, he was hostile to laziness and corruption, whether it manifested itself in the poor or rich. Indeed, he is quite scornful of those who take their inherited wealth as an excuse for idleness.[32] By contrast, he seemed to express respect for hard-working laborers who, when all was said and done, might not be that much better off economically than those on parish relief, but had superior moral character. If those dependent on parish relief were poor because they were lazy and corrupt, then the cure for poverty was to change their characters. In adults, this was a hard business, because their characters were already largely formed; hence the requirements of forced labor. But in children, the secret was establishing the correct "habitudes." Hence the point of the working "schools" in

Locke's view is not to punish, but rather to build health, mental discipline, reason, and strength of character.

Working schools would habituate poor children to work and teach them its value: "the children will be kept in much better order, be better provided for, and from infancy be inured to work, which is of no small consequence to the making of them sober and industrious all their lives after."[33] If parents on parish relief habituate their children to sloth and indolence, then by accustoming poor children to work, working schools would break the cycle of dependency on parish relief by creating a new generation of rational, reliable workers. At the same time, an added bonus is that their parents, and particularly mothers, through the combination of work requirements and their new freedom from parenting responsibilities, will also learn the same lessons of industriousness (though obviously these lessons would not be as deeply ingrained in adults). For the true evil that needs to be rooted out, according to Locke, is not poverty per se, but irrationality, which leads to poverty. Locke linked industry and rationality very closely such that industry—the use of property in your person (labor) to acquire property in the form of land or goods—was taken as evidence of rationality, and a lack of property was evidence of a lack of rationality. Hence those on parish relief, who were by definition not industrious (because otherwise they would be self-supporting), were also not rational.

Gender, Class, and Reason

The issue of rationality is central to Locke's theory; it is tightly linked to the law of nature, and in many of his major writings, such as the *Two Treatises*, he maintains that reason is a natural capacity. We are guided by the "law of reason," which is the ultimate mark of human equality and the only legitimate limitation on freedom, defined by the ability to do what one wants "within the bounds of the Laws of Nature." Reason is what prevents us from harming or killing others, from taking more than we need, and indeed from the state of war more generally. Of course, reason also is what leads us into the state of war, particularly when money changes the terms of rationality; that is, once money is introduced, it becomes rational to take more than you can use, for as long as spoilage is obviated, it is rational to save up against harder times. Though money produces a greater abundance of available wealth, so that there is more to go around, it also produces greater opportunity for conflict and makes the need for a social contract more apparent.[34]

Reason is also a theme that relates to both gender and class, in terms of the relative (in)equality of women and the poor to propertied white men. Macpherson's thesis of "differential rationality" posited that the poor were *naturally* less rational than the wealthy; the reason that some people are wealthy and others are poor is that the former have superior powers of rationality that the latter lack. Hence poverty was a sign of a natural inequality in reasoning ability.[35] Feminists have made similar interpretations of Locke's views of women's reason; not that one's level of rationality determined one's gender, of course, but rather that women's subordination stems from inferior natural reason. Furthermore, since those who owned estates were likely to be rational, and those without were not, or at least less so, then women's ability—or rather, their inability—to hold property has generally been taken as evidence of their reasoning (dis)ability. After all, why would you not live your life in such a way as to be industrious and acquire property unless you were simply not sufficiently rational to understand the desirability of saving up nonperishable goods to protect against leaner times?[36] The fact that neither laborers nor women owned much, if any, property is only the most obvious evidence that they are on a par in terms of reason; and most feminists have argued that Locke denied women natural rationality altogether.[37]

Of course, laboring men were not prohibited from owning property, as at least married women were.[38] Furthermore, some notable exceptions, such as Rogers Smith and Melissa Butler, have maintained that Locke grants women equal rationality, and their arguments have some persuasive force. As Smith argues, Locke never explicitly says in the *Two Treatises* that women lack reason.[39] Smith's point takes on added significance when it is acknowledged that Locke does explicitly identify "Innocents which are excluded by a natural defect from ever having" reason, madmen, "Lunaticks and Ideots" as naturally deficient in reason, and therefore in need of "the Tuition and Government of others."[40] The fact that women are not mentioned here implies that they do have natural reason.

Butler makes a stronger case, maintaining that Locke's belief in women's reason is unequivocal. In fact, given the role of education in developing reason, she argues that Locke advocated equal education for girls, with "minor" modifications that had primarily to do with protecting their complexions from the sun. She notes that in a letter to Mrs. Clarke

(Locke's *Education* originated in a series of letters to her husband, Edward Clarke, concerning the education of their son), Locke wrote, "Since, therefore I acknowledge no difference of sex in your mind relating . . . to truth, virtue and obedience, I think well to have no thing altered in it from what I have writ" for the son to be applied to daughters. From this, as well as from the fact that education should take place in the home with tutors rather than in schools, hence following what Butler calls a "ladies" model of education, she concludes that Locke believes that "men and women could be schooled in the use of reason. . . . Women had intellectual potential which could be developed to a high level." Furthermore, since gentlemen had to be educated in politics, women would receive the same education, and thereby be equipped for "political activity."[41]

It is true that a number of recommendations Locke makes apply to daughters that are in keeping with contemporary progressive beliefs, such as clothing that does not bind, for girls as well as boys, thus permitting freedom of movement; lots of play outdoors, where boys roam fairly freely (girls, to avoid the negative cosmetic effects of the sun, should be allowed to do this only at sunrise and sunset); few rules (because children should learn by example); encouragement rather than force in pursuit of virtuous activities such as reading. There is much gender equity in these recommendations; indeed, Locke explicitly says that "the nearer they [girls] come to the hardships of their brothers in their education, the greater advantage they will receive from it all the remaining parts of their lives."[42] But this is said in the context of Locke's recommendations for physical health, which occupies the entire first third to half of *Education*, concerned with eating habits, "costiveness" (constipation) and regularity, health and hygiene, guidelines for recreation, and the methods and philosophy of punishment. Locke seemed to have a particular passion for the strengthening benefits of cold wet feet, for he suggests that boys should wear shoes that leak, and be encouraged to traipse around marshes in the rain, and have their feet washed in cold water at night. Recognizing the limits of girls' gallivanting, he recommended that water be put inside their shoes during the day, as well as washing their feet in cold water every night.

As bizarre as such measures seem—indeed, the kind of thing that only a childless bachelor like Locke could come up with—reason is the endpoint of his physical prescriptions; Locke opens the essay with Juvenal's "a sound mind in a sound body." But I believe Butler is too generous to

Locke in concluding that he grants girls full equality in reasoning ability. For physical "health and hardiness" do not automatically translate into reason, they merely set its stage. Reason itself, to be developed in its full flower, requires the learning of substantive subjects such as Greek, Latin, and particularly mathematics: "in all sorts of reasoning, every single argument should be managed as a mathematical demonstration," though "not so much to make them mathematicians as to make them reasonable creatures."[43] And although Locke clearly states that these subjects, particularly mathematics, are largely the province of the propertied classes—only "those who have the time and opportunity" should learn it[44]—there is no evidence in Locke's writings that girls would learn the same academic material as boys. The letter to Mrs. Clarke that Butler cites, for instance, refers only to females' "truth, virtue, and obedience," not to their reason or intellectual capacities.

As Butler notes, Locke claims that "where the Difference of Sex requires different Treatment, 'twill be no hard Matter to distinguish."[45] But given the widespread acceptability of gender inequality among Locke's contemporaries, it is not obvious how the requirements of "the Difference of Sex" will direct his readers. Indeed, considering that Locke's greatest concern for girls appeared to be protecting their complexions from sunburn, one wonders how unconventional his program really is for females. The apparent gender neutrality with which Locke presents many of his recommendations camouflage conventionally gendered assumptions. For instance, although parents must get their "children" into the "armor" of "Fortitude," which is "the guard and support of the other virtues," courage is defined in explicitly gendered terms, as "the quiet possession of a man's self and an undisturbed doing his duty, whatever evil besets or danger lies in his way. . . . Without courage a man will scarce keep steady to his duty and fill up the character of a truly worthy man."[46] By contrast, Locke repeatedly associates the term "effeminate" with the worst character traits, such as weakness, crying, complaining, and whining.[47]

Even the "truth, virtue, and obedience" he mentions to Mrs. Clarke as qualities that females share are hardly the stuff of reason: as Kant later put it, they are the "beautiful" virtues of sensibility and intuition, not the "sublime" ones of reason.[48] Furthermore, although *Two Treatises* suggests in various places a rough equality between the sexes, and indeed implies women's rationality through its reiteration of the commandment to honor one's father and mother (why would God grant both parents equal respect if they were not equally rational?), Locke's other works are less generous to women. In *The Reasonableness of Christianity*, for instance, Locke explicitly says that laborers and "those of the other sex" can only understand "simple propositions," suggesting a natural limitation on reason.[49]

Locke's ambiguity on the question makes it, I think, safe to say that he believes that women have *less* rationality than men. But whether this is by nature or artificial design is the more important question than "how much" rationality Locke grants women. Once again, comparing gender and class is instructive, for the "differential" that Macpherson correctly observed in the rationality of various classes clearly can be applied to women as well: Locke thought that the poor and women were less rational than propertied males. However, contrary to Macpherson and most feminists, I maintain that this difference is not natural, but rather artificially constructed through the social relations of labor and the sexual division of labor.

This is clearest in *Of the Conduct of the Understanding*, where Locke explicitly says that "defects and weaknesses in men's understandings, as well as other faculties, come from want of a right use of their own minds. I am apt to think the faculty is generally mislaid upon nature, and there is often a complaint of want of parts, when the fault lies in want of a due improvement of them."[50] Similarly, Locke says, "We are born to be, if we please, rational creatures, but it is use and exercise only that makes us so, and we are indeed so no farther than industry and application has carried us."[51] Even in the *Second Treatise*, where he seems to make the strongest case for the naturalness of freedom, Locke actually acknowledges the constructed quality of reason. Though he declares "we are *born Free*, as we are born Rational," he also says, immediately following, "not that we have actually the Exercise of either: Age that brings one, brings with it the other too." Of course, in this passage, reason could still be natural, something that develops with age, like secondary sexual characteristics, a deeper voice, and body hair. But Locke links "Age" with "Education" as the things that "brought him [man] Reason and Ability to govern himself, and others." In other words, differential rationality is not natural, but socially constructed.[52]

The distinction Locke employs is subtle. As Locke argues in *Of the Conduct of the Understanding*, "We are born with faculties and powers capable almost of anything, such at least as would carry us farther than can easily be imagined: but it is only the exercise of those powers which gives us ability and skill in anything, and leads us toward perfection."[53] In other words, we must distinguish between capacities, defined as the natural potential to think rationally if people receive adequate education, and abilities, that is, what one actually can do given the education one has received and the cultural milieu in which one lives. Hence, he says, "Every man carries about him a touchstone, if he will make use of it, to distinguish substantial gold from superficial glitterings, truth from appearances. And indeed the use and benefit of this touchstone, which is natural reason, is spoiled and lost only by assumed prejudices, overweening presumptions, and narrowing our minds. The want of exercising it in the full extent of things intelligible, is that which weakens and extinguishes this noble faculty in us."[54]

This distinction between natural capacity and learned ability is key to making sense of Locke's views of reason. After all, without a belief that the *capacity* to reason is natural, Locke's "white paper" theory of education would not make sense. There would be no point in making "the right marks" on a piece of paper if the paper were unable to receive the marks. But this capacity must be developed in order to work; those marks must be made.

Hence, the poor do not have a diminished capacity for reason. Rather, they have less ability, and Locke clearly explains that this differential reason is a practical matter, not one of nature: "What then, can grown men never be improved or enlarged in their understandings? I say not so, but this I think I may say, that it will not be done without industry and application, which will require more time and pains than grown men, settled in their course of life, will allow to it."[55] The development of full reason requires learning a wide range of scholarship such as philosophy, theology, Latin, and particularly mathematics, all of which require time that the laboring classes do not have.[56] Thus, most laborers would never have the opportunity and means to develop their reason to the same level as a gentleman; as Locke argues in the *Conduct*, the "constant drudgery to their backs and their bellies" means laborers have insufficient time and energy to develop reason. Moreover, because laborers have not been trained in the higher use of reason, they will be unlikely to seek to train themselves. Hence "knowledge and science in general is the business only of those who are at ease and leisure."[57] Accordingly, in the "Poor Law," Locke explicitly argues that poor children will not receive the kind of education that will produce full-blown reason; rather, they will learn industriousness.

That does not mean laborers are entirely devoid of reason, however; they can, if they choose, develop their capacity into an ability to a limited extent. After all, he notes, even laborers have Sundays off, and can apply themselves to the attainment of knowledge, at least of religion. For theology is "one science . . . incomparably above the rest."[58] However, this does mean that laborers are very unlikely to develop "right reason," and the fullness of the reasoning capacity with which God endows (most) humans. Moreover, it is not necessary that they develop it, Locke believes; through their labor—and possibly the study of theology on Sundays—laborers will develop reason sufficiently to know that working hard is the right thing to do, that work is key to achieving as much contentment out of life as their lot will allow.

Those on parish relief were a different matter, of course, because their idleness meant that they failed to develop reason to even this rudimentary level. The poor were not poor because they were *constitutionally* irrational; such a condition would require the rational wealthy to take pity on them as members of the first (and smallest) category of those on relief, viz. those who are genuinely unable to support themselves (and who would therefore, under Locke's schema, also be granted licenses to beg). Rather, for most of the poor on relief, poverty was evidence of a failure to *develop* and *use* their God-given rationality. The irrationality of the poor was not set in stone, but rather was the product of habits acquired through poor living, which must be corrected for their own good, as well as the good of society. This was hard to accomplish in adults, who had become used to sloth and indolence, and that was why they needed to be forced to work. Children were more likely prospects and had this capacity as undeveloped future potential, but only if they were taken away from the corrupting influence of their parents. The need to bring them up and educate them properly so as to develop reason appropriately to their station in life meant that while poor children in working schools may learn only a low-grade skill, the more important lesson they learn is industry and productivity: they learn how to work, and how to value work.

This class differentiation is not even limited to relatively poor laborers; Locke makes further distinctions between the bourgeois gentleman and the middle-class tradesman or merchant. Thus he says that although "Latin . . . is absolutely necessary to a gentleman," it is "ridiculous . . . that a father should waste his own money and his son's time in setting him to learn the *Roman language,* when at the same time he designs him for a trade, wherein he having no use of *Latin* fails not to forget that little which he brought from school."[59] Since such sons are evidently capable of learning Latin—Locke is, after all, ridiculing the "common custom"—such middle-class men must be capable of reason and learn to exercise it. But this reasoning ability must atrophy somewhat once the student graduates and enters a trade, for the subjects that he learned in school which Locke associates with right reason are not drawn on and utilized. It is really only gentlemen who have the time to keep up with Latin and Greek, and therefore only they who can exercise full reason.

The fact that Locke explicitly attributes class differences in reason to the pragmatic realities of laboring life would seem to include women. In the "Poor Law" Locke suggests that poor women are as corrupt as poor men and must be forced to work just like poor men. Locke makes no distinctions between girls and boys in the working schools, and we know that he approved of females' participation in the Irish linen trade.[60] But Locke's argument about the time-consuming demands of labor also raises the analogous possibility for bourgeois females who must run a home and manage servants in addition to bearing and raising children, leaving little time or energy for studying scholarly subjects. As Sara Mendelson and Patricia Crawford suggest, running a household in the upper classes in seventeenth-century England was a demanding job, including accounting skills and management, particularly considering that wealthy families often maintained two households, a house in the city and an estate in the country.[61]

Furthermore, if there is little point in teaching Latin, Greek, and mathematics to laborers, or even to middle-class tradesmen, because they would have no use for them, why teach them to women? Women could not enter the clergy or become doctors or Oxford lecturers like Locke. Some women of the middle classes engaged in trades as *feme sole*, including some married women still living with their husbands, but most wives engaged in trade did so as *feme covert* and "had no legal right dispose of the commodities they produced, nor spend the cash they had inherited or earned." Those who engaged in the same trade as their husbands were legally required to do so as "servants."[62] But further, most women so engaged had not even been able to apprentice, and thus were not solidly identified with a particular profession. They could not be major merchants, or businesswomen, much less members of Parliament; they could not even vote, since at the end of the seventeenth century—before Locke wrote *Education*—Parliament had expressly barred women from voting, after a number of women had tried to do so in prior decades.[63] So what rational purpose could it serve to teach them the necessary subjects?

One purpose, at least for mothers in families of the landed gentry, might have been the education of their sons. Again, Locke may not be saying that women are incapable of learning Latin; for indeed, in section 177 of *Education* (not long after saying that fathers who intend their sons for trades should not waste time or money on Latin), Locke suggests that women could assist in their sons' learning of Latin, and indeed thereby learn it themselves:

> His mother may teach it [Latin] him herself if she will but spend two or three hours in a day with him and make him read the Evangelists in *Latin* to her: for she need but buy a *Latin* Testament and, having got somebody to mark the last syllable but one, where it is long, in words above two syllables (which is enough to regu-late her pronunciation and accenting the words), read daily in the *Gospels*, and then let her avoid understanding them in *Latin* if she can. And when she understands the Evangelists in *Latin*, let her in the same manner read Æsop's *Fables*, and so proceed on to Eutropius, Justin, and other such books.[64]

I believe Locke argues this, however, not to argue that girls or women *should* be taught Latin per se, but rather to establish that Latin is not as difficult a subject as others make it out to be. For this argument sits in the middle of a discussion of the appropriate qualifications of a tutor; Locke wishes to emphasize that Latin is far from the primary credential of a suitable tutor, who "should be one who thinks *Latin* and *language* the least part of education . . . [and] who, knowing how much virtue and a well-tempered soul is to be preferred to any sort of *learning* or *language*, makes it his chief business to form the mind of his scholars and give that a right disposition."[65]

Thus earlier in *Education*, with Locke's characteristic ambiguity, he hints that it would serve no purpose for women to know Latin; and in-deed seems to undercut his apparent recommendation that women should assist in teaching their sons Latin. In section 164, Locke argues that the male student is to learn French and Latin "by speaking and reading nothing else with his tutor." But he must "not forget to read English, which may be preserved by his mother or somebody else hearing him read some chosen parts of Scripture or other English book every day."[66] The implication here is that mothers do not know Latin—and possibly even French—because they were not taught them.[67] Or at the least, he suggests that they would be inferior teachers of Latin and French, when compared to a tutor. This suggests that the later passage, in section 177, claiming that even mothers could learn Latin readily if provided with appropriate texts, is a rhetorical point to illustrate the easiness, as well as relative unimportance, of Latin rather than a substantive point about women's reason. Again, because women have the capacity of reason, they have the capacity to learn Latin; but for the most part, it would serve little purpose for them to develop that capacity into an ability.

Thus it is likely that the more rigorous academic subjects of Greek and mathematics, if not Latin, so key to the development of right reason, are among the aforementioned things that "will not so perfectly suit the Education of Daughters."[68] If reason is the product of education, and if women are not educated like men, then they will not be able to think as rationally as educated men. This would again fit Locke's "white paper" theory of education; if we are all blank slates at birth, with no innate ideas, and girls are taught embroidery, music, and household management rather than mathematics and Greek, then it should not be surprising that women do not fully develop their rationality, as Locke's contemporary Mary Astell argued.[69] But, like propertyless men, that does not mean that women completely lack the capacity to reason; and in contrast to theorists like Rousseau and Kant, who seemed to take women's frivolity as a function of their nature, Locke seems to believe that women could behave rationally. The question was, how rational should they be?

Character at the Corner of Class and Gender

To answer this question, we should begin by noting that the majority of Locke's *Education* is not devoted to intellectual subjects but to character formation, to developing the right "habitudes" in children so that they could develop reason as they grew older. Indeed, as bizarre as many of Locke's recommendations for physical health may seem, the point of these, too, is to strengthen character. The goal of education is to achieve mastery over inclination and habituate children to the correct behaviors, values, and attitudes: "The great thing to be minded in Education is, what Habits you settle." For "Great Care is to be had of the forming of Children's Minds, and giving them that seasoning early, which shall influence their Lives always after."[70] Hence long before teaching boys philosophy, mathematics, Latin, and Greek, Locke is concerned with building character in the pupil, and most of his recommendations aim to the end of building a strong foundation for the acquisition of civic moral talents. Hence in the passage cited earlier concerning the qualities of a good tutor, being skilled at teaching Latin is less important than being able to develop "virtue and a well-tempered soul" in the child.

This is not to say that the tutor can be academically incompetent, of course, for it is important to develop the natural capacity for reason as the fundamental building block of character. Indeed, the reason that Locke favors education in the home with a tutor over public schools is that the latter favor academic subjects at the expense of teaching virtue and character; character in public schools is thus forged by interaction with peers, who, equally unguided, simply display "rudeness and ill-turned confidence." By contrast, education in the home combines academic subjects with the full development of all human capacities, the most important one being a virtuous character. Similarly, what he lauds about education in the home for girls is the "retirement and bashfulness which . . . daughters are brought up in" and which hardly "make them less knowing or less able women. Conversation, when they come into the world"—not, it should be noted, Latin or Greek—"soon gives them a becoming assurance."[71] Character is not unrelated to reason and intellectual matters, but if push comes to shove, the latter can be sacrificed to the former, and in some cases may need to be.

In this project of education-cum-character-development, the disciplining of desire is key. Hence, "contrary to the ordinary way, Children should be used to submit their Desires, and go without their Longings, even from their very Cradles. The first thing they should learn to know should be, that they were not to have any thing, because it pleased them, but because it was thought fit for them."[72] Gaining control over desire is central to the ability to think rationally, for humans are too often tempted by the immediacy of desire and thereby act contrary to their true interests. To prevent this, and to foster reason, parents must teach children to "stifl[e] their Desires" and "master their Inclinations."[73] In this regard, poor children might seem to have a natural advantage over their bourgeois counterparts, for "those of the meaner sort are hindered by the straitness of their fortunes from encouraging intemperance in their children by the temptation of their diet of invitations to eat or drink more than enough." And of course their shoes are likely to leak without any special assistance. But Locke points out that such deprivations do not build character because the parents' "own ill examples, whenever plenty comes in their way, show that it is not the dislike of drunkenness and gluttony that keeps them from excess, but want of materials."[74] Thus, although technically the poor were used to deprivation, this did not qualify them to be considered worthy of educating into right reason because they did not develop a disciplined character, but rather wantonness.

Similarly, the generous reading of Locke that Butler offers—that girls not only received the same education as boys, but that "Locke introduced far fewer restrictions in his plan for a young lady's mental development" than he did for young gentlemen[75]—might be technically correct insofar as less was at stake in educating them, and less could be expected of them because of the inferior rationality both required and nurtured by sex-role differences. Furthermore, to the extent that education's primary goal in the younger years is to instill discipline and shape habits, I would not only agree that Locke's educational recommendations are applicable to girls but also argue that girls needed more careful scrutiny and discipline, for they posed a greater danger of unruliness. After all, the "family" in which education takes place is the bourgeois patriarchal family, where gender relations are structured to serve the ends of property and inheritance. If girls are to grow up to be responsible wives and mothers on whom inheritance can be based, developing their reason is not particularly productive; being able to argue rationally with one's father or husband is hardly healthy for stable patrilineal inheritance. Hence, girls must learn obedience.

Indeed, amid Locke's repeated warnings against the use of corporal punishment, which is to be reserved for particularly "stubborn" and "obstinate" children who display an independent nature, the only illustration of it Locke offers in *Education* is of "a prudent and kind Mother" who is

> forced to whip her little Daughter, at her first coming home from Nurse [which would make the child at most two or possibly up to three years old] eight times successively the same Morning, before she could master her Stubbornness, and obtain a compliance in a very easie and indifferent matter. If she had left off sooner, and

stopped at the seventh Whipping, she had spoiled the Child for ever; and, by her unprevailing Blows, only confirmed her *refractoriness*, very hardly afterwards to be cured: But wisely persisting, till she had bent her Mind, and suppled her will, the only end of Correction and Chastisement, she established her Authority throughly [*sic*] in the very first occasion, and had ever after a very ready Compliance and Obedience in all things from her Daughter. For as this was the first time, so, I think, it was the last too she ever struck her.[76]

The mother is "forced" not because her husband is making her do this, of course, but rather by the rational necessities of the child's welfare. Uday Mehta highlights this passage to show that Locke's "anxiety of freedom" is an almost incapacitating one, in response to which he builds an authoritarian edifice that will bear no breach. Admittedly, Mehta's argument may be overly reflective of late twentieth-century views that label physical punishment of any kind as child abuse. For Locke actually is fairly restrained in his recommendations for physical punishment. Although he admitted it was necessary for "obstinate" children, he recommended that it be used only rarely, and to the end of inflicting not pain, but shame. Thus, rather than frequent spankings, which he thought would only generate fear, and thus not change children's habits and inclinations toward things that are bad for them (but only make them more devious about pursuing them), he advocated the use of physical punishment rarely, but thoroughly, to impress upon the child the severity of his (or her) transgression. Moreover, the punishment should never be given when the parent is in an emotional state of anger, but rather must demonstrate reasoning and rationality.[77]

But there are several feminist points that are worth noting in Locke's views which Mehta's interpretation highlights. In the first place, it is notable that a girl is Locke's case of particular obstinacy, and the mother is the parent inflicting the whipping. For Locke paints the whipping in colors of dispassionate rationality, thus suggesting that women can be equally authoritative and rational in dealing with children, rather than uselessly emotional and indulgent. Indeed, the whipping is almost bureaucratic, as the mother simply administers the punishment that the rational interests of the child require her to inflict. As Locke points out in the *Two Treatises*, mothers and fathers are fairly equal within the family, or at least in regard to the children.[78] What girls need is discipline;

and since this disciplinary education is to occur in the family, saying that children owe obedience to mothers as well as fathers serves a utilitarian purpose, for Locke has doubled his disciplinary force.

The purpose of granting such power to women is to the benefit of children's reason, however, not women's equality; after all, how can sons be taught discipline if their sisters are allowed to misbehave? And the fact that women may act as bureaucratic administrators does not mean they can exercise executive decision-making. After all, Locke also maintains servants should do the whipping rather than fathers (so as to minimize the possibility that the child will associate the father's disapproval with the fear of violence), suggesting a possible equivalence between mothers and servants in terms of their status and importance in the educational process.[79] So the dispensing of such discipline to girls does not mean that they will eventually be able to take over their own lives for themselves sufficient to the needs of citizenship and political participation. Mehta in fact suggests just the opposite, pointing out "one can only wonder why, in one of the very few examples in the *Thoughts* of a mother and her daughter, the latter should serve as a metonymy for a form of defiant alterity in the face of which liberalism deploys the weapons of absolutism, brandished by the mother with a horrifying but precisely calibrated tenacity and certainty."[80]

Indeed, given that all children love "power and dominion" even more than liberty, and that such love of dominion must be curtailed, physical punishment would seem particularly directed to girls. For girls must learn submission even more than boys, since they have to accustom themselves to submitting to their husbands. And given that the love of dominion often takes the form of the desire for "property and possession," in a system of patrilineal inheritance that depends on monogamy girls might naturally be more resistant, since they foresee a future of foreshortened possibilities, in contrast to their privileged brothers.[81] In that light, it is also worth noting in Locke's exemplary story that the punishment has effected a complete "cure" of the child's obstinacy, suggesting perhaps terror in the child's mind rather than "compliance." Mehta comments, "One can only guess what gesture of her little body revealed her mind's refractoriness, what particular shrillness of the screech, following the eighth whip, now made clear her compliant will and her 'bent' mind."[82] Such terror would seem to be at odds with the methodical and rational application of the rod that Locke recommends in this story.

At the same time, Locke's use of the punishing mother in this example serves as a significant counterpoint to his remarks elsewhere in *Education* that mothers' indulgence poses a serious danger to children's education and their development of right reason. The "fond mothers" in *Education* are criticized for spoiling their children and for worrying too much about their frailty, which Locke feared would undermine his more unconventional recommendations (particularly the leaky shoes).[83] He criticizes both parents for letting their natural affection for their children degenerate into "fondness" which results in harmful indulgence: "Thus parents, by humoring and cockering them when little, corrupt the principles of nature in their children, and wonder afterwards to taste the bitter waters, when they themselves have poisoned the fountain."[84] But his examples of such lax indulgence always refer to mothers, who dress their children in fine clothes and fawn over them.[85] This feeds the gender imbalance in circular ways; for parents must distinguish between "wants of fancy and those of nature," responding to the latter and curbing the former. Natural wants are those which "reason alone, without some other help, is not able to fence against," whereas reason is a reliable safeguard against wants of fancy, thinking they are wants of nature. But if women's reason is not developed, then it follows that women are not able to discern the one from the other; hence their tendency to indulge their children in wants of fancy. By the same measure, however, this means that mothers themselves are unable to discriminate among their own desires, and must be subject to some other guiding force, presumably their husbands or fathers. Indeed, indulgence in wants of fancy will "effeminate [children's] minds and make them fond of trifles."[86] Though Locke says this about "children," the gender of his intended target is logically boys, since they are the beings for whom "effeminacy" is something to be avoided.

More specifically, his target is upper-class boys, since Locke similarly complains of servants, who tend to undermine children's training by giving in to their wants of fancy. Just as bourgeois mothers' emotionalism and sentimentality threatens to undermine Locke's rigorous program, so does Locke repeatedly despair of servants, who harm children actively as well as indirectly. Servants, "those foolish flatterers . . . undo whatever the parents endeavor to establish" in the development of children's reason by encouraging children to take "strong drink, wine, fruit" and other unhealthy foods, fawning over them and turning their heads with flattery, sneaking them treats and sympathy when they have been punished, and encouraging children in the belief in ghosts and goblins.[87] More indirectly, though perhaps even more profoundly, servants harm children simply by the proximity of their poor character. For "the company they converse with" is the single most important factor in forming children's character, and servants are generally poor company. Most servants are "clownish or vicious," poorly educated and ill bred.[88]

In this sense, Locke may arguably have greater ambivalence about gender than he has about class; for although bourgeois mothers are at times the agents of developing children's reason and at other times the enemies, servants always apparently harm children. But the underlying issue, concerning the level of reason that women and the lower classes can or should develop, is remarkably similar. This does not mean that Locke believes all women are the same, for indeed, class is an important element in differentiating among women. For instance, the enthusiasm with which he outlines his plan for working schools to enable poor mothers to work hardly translates into a program for professional upper- (or even middle-) class women. Locke does not ask whether middle- or upper-class women are good mothers, or whether full-time mothering is good for children; families who can afford to support women in the idle, unproductive "intervals" that housewives inevitably experience are certainly justified in doing so. Even here, class differentiates gender, for in *Education*, Locke assumes that middle- and upper-class women are more likely to fill these intervals productively without external prompting. The mothers in *Education* are criticized for spoiling their children, and for worrying too much about their frailty, but they are not criticized for idleness, nor are they seen by Locke as unproductive layabouts: presumably running a household and overseeing servants are legitimate expressions of "industry." After all, in the passage cited earlier, it is the bourgeois mother who is the disciplinarian, she has not farmed out the responsibility to any of her servants, despite the apparent equivalence between them. Rather, Locke seems to believe that full-time mothering is the preferred arrangement for women in the family, all things considered equal. But for those asking for parish relief, things are not equal, and the differing circumstances of the different classes produces Locke's reconfiguration of gender along class lines.

Conclusion

The link between gender and class is more than a mere parallel, then. Rather, gender and class mutually interact and constitute each other, as attention to class helps deepen and complicate the standard feminist reading of Locke's view of women and gender. Certainly, if gender were not relevant at all as a category for differentiation, then the question of women's reason should be answered by reference to class: poor women, like poor men, have little reason; that is why they are poor. This lack of reason is a function, in circular fashion, of the fact that they are poor, and not industrious. If they were industrious, they would not be (as) poor. Laboring women, like laboring men, have sufficient reason to understand the importance of their work, but not enough to participate in lawmaking or voting. On this reading, bourgeois women should have reason equal to bourgeois men. But the likelihood that they do is slim, for the reasons I have previously offered. This suggests that the explanation for why laboring-class women might have equal reasoning abilities with laboring-class men is that the latter themselves have so little that any differential caused by gender would be barely noticeable. Attending to the similarities and differences among women by virtue of class, therefore, reveals that Locke's notion of reason is decidedly a function of gender, as well as class.

But considering gender through the lens of class reveals that reason is a function of these characteristics not because of natural incapacities; rather, women (of all classes) and the poor (of both sexes) are explicitly prevented from developing reason to the same extent as bourgeois males. Locke creates a reasoning disability by structuring education in ways that produce the very thing that he presupposes: laboring men and women do not have the time, energy, and inclination to develop reason because the process of education is so incredibly time-consuming, taking years of careful preparation of the canvas before an equally painstaking application of paint. And since what is learned must be continually practiced, such elaborate education is pointless for any but the economically privileged, who have the sustained leisure to support it. Poor men and women on parish relief were fairly beyond hope in terms of canvas preparation, so the application of paint was pointless: hence Locke recommends forced labor to make them behave *as if* they had reasoning ability. If, in the process, they develop enough reason to understand the benefits of working, so much the better, but coercion is at least necessary to get them started. Similarly, their children have absolutely no hope of receiving the kind of character training Locke outlines in *Education*; if they did, after all, their parents would not have to be forced to work. Hence Locke recommends for them working schools rather than academic education.

Whatever one might think of the efficiency of Locke's poor law recommendations, and whether they simply provided an excuse for class hatred and disdain, Locke's prescriptions do suggest that poor women were more on a par with poor men than women of the gentry were with men of their class, and that class intersects with gender in subtle but complex ways. Poor women could readily develop the same rudimentary level of reason that poor men could develop, since that level would seem to be necessary to living an independent (i.e., of parish relief) life, and since that level could be obtained through work itself. It is only girls and women of the gentry who would *need* to have their natural capacity for reason less developed than their male peers. Indeed, since women of the gentry did not work out of the home like poor women did, they might be even less rational than female laborers, though one assumes that the tasks of household management could be as productive of reason as spinning wool. But perhaps that link between labor, industry, and reason is also why it was desirable that poor women work but not wealthy women; the class division in social roles coheres with the class division in reasoning skills. That is, not only do poor women *need* the same basic level of reason that poor men need, but their developing it does not threaten the divine "architecture" of order, as Kirstie McClure puts it, for neither poor men nor poor women would have sufficient reason to be political agents, only enough to see the wisdom in labor and obedience. By contrast, upper-class women were potentially in a position to challenge their second-class status, if they could only access the resources of education and the development of right reason that existed under their very roofs. In order to make sure that what they learn is obedience, therefore, bourgeois women's education must be curtailed by comparison with males of the same class.

Given the significance of class to critical readings of Locke, the inattention to it in the majority of feminist work on Locke is rather puzzling. Some of it may be chalked up to the unconscious racism and classism of white academic women that I discussed at the start of this essay; white middle-class academic women are, like most other people, concerned with the problems that their own experience generates. But as the popularity of the idea of intersectionality attests, if feminism is a movement dedicated to the welfare of all women, then it cannot focus only on a limited sample. As I have already suggested, when dealing with canonical figures, the ability to consider "all women" is obviously curtailed by the fact that many canonical theorists themselves did not even bother to think about nonwhite, nonbourgeois women. If such women are entirely absent from canonical texts, critiquing those texts along these other vectors of analysis is virtually impossible. But those canonical figures who did offer us thoughts on lower-class women, such as Locke, provide rich material that feminists should exploit.

Notes

1. Kimberle Crenshaw, "Mapping the Margins: Intersectionality, Identity Politics, and Violence Against Women of Color," *Stanford Law Review* 43 (1991): 1241–99.

2. *All the Women Are White, All the Blacks Are Men, But Some of Us Are Brave: Black Women's Studies*, ed. Gloria T. Hull, Patricia Bell Scott, and Barbara Smith (Old Westbury, N.Y.: Feminist Press, 1982).

3. Immanuel Kant, *Anthropology from a Pragmatic Point of View*, trans. Mary J. Gregor (The Hague: Martinus Nijhoff, 1974); John Stuart Mill, "On the Subjection of Women," in Mill, *On Liberty and Other Essays*, ed. John Gray (London: Oxford University Press, 1992). It should be noted that Mill mentioned American slavery only so that he could contrast the situation of black slaves with the plight of white married women in England, who according to him were even worse off because they had no "right" to refuse sex to their husbands.

4. Jean Jacques Rousseau, "The Origin of Inequality," in Rousseau, *The Social Contract and Discourses*, ed. G.D.H. Cole (London: J. M. Dent and Son, 1973).

5. See Wayne Glausser, "Three Approaches to Locke and the Slave Trade," *Journal of the History of Ideas* (1990): 199–216, and James Farr, "So Vile and Miserable and Estate: The Problem of Slavery in Locke's Political Thought," *Political Theory* 14 (1986): 263–89.

6. Peter Fryer, *Staying Power: Black People in Britain Since 1504* (Atlantic Highlands, N.J.: Humanities Press, 1984); Joan Tucker, *Resistance, Change and Continuity: Britain and the Black Peoples of the Americas, 1550–1930* (London: JET, 1992); Folarin Shyllon, *Black People in Britain, 1555–1833* (Oxford: Oxford University Press, 1977); James Walvin, *Black and White: The Negro and English Society, 1555–1945* (London: Penguin, 1973).

7. C. B. Macpherson, *The Political Theory of Possessive Individualism: Hobbes to Locke* (Oxford: Oxford University Press, 1962).

8. Melissa Butler, "The Early Liberal Roots of Feminism: John Locke and the Attack on Patriarchy," *American Political Science Review* 72 (1978): 147 n. 24. Reprinted herein as Chapter 3.

9. Nancy Hartsock, *Money, Sex and Power: Toward a Feminist Historical Materialism* (Boston: Northeastern University Press, 1984).

10. Jane Flax, "Political Philosophy and the Patriarchal Unconscious," in *Discovering Reality*, ed. Sandra Harding and Merrill B. Hintikka (Boston: Kluwer Academic, 2003).

11. Carole Pateman, *The Sexual Contract* (Stanford: Stanford University Press, 1988); Nancy J. Hirschmann, *Rethinking Obligation: A Feminist Method for Political Theory* (Ithaca: Cornell University Press, 1992); Christine Di Stefano, *Configurations of Masculinity* (Ithaca: Cornell University Press, 1991); Mary O'Brien, *The Politics of Reproduction* (Boston: Routledge and Kegan Paul, 1981).

12. Lorenne Clark, "Women and John Locke; or, Who Owns the Apples in the Garden of Eden?" *Canadian Journal of Philosophy* 7 (1977): 699–724; Hirschmann, *Rethinking Obligation*; Pateman, *Sexual Contract*.

13. Obviously, the use of the term "working class" is historically anachronistic for this era, but efficient for my purposes here. Also obviously, there were African women in Locke's world, since

slavery was beginning to gain importance as a key to the emerging capitalist economy in Britain in the latter half of the seventeenth century. And Peter Fryer maintains that there is evidence of "free" African women in Britain, most likely prostitutes in Elizabethan London. Fryer, *Staying Power*, 9. By the first half of the eighteenth century, when the slave trade was in full swing, Fryer argues, slavery had been practiced in England by the wealthy for many decades. Locke, a stockholder in the Royal African Trade Company, was likely knowledgeable of the practice of slavery, and his notes on the constitution of the Carolinas is often offered as evidence that he supported the practice. But others maintain that he simply transcribed, rather than originally authored those notes, and so his views on slavery are even more ambiguous than they are on white bourgeois women. See Mark Goldie's introduction to "The Fundamental Constitutions of Carolina," in John Locke, *Political Essays*, ed. Mark Goldie (Cambridge: Cambridge University Press, 1997), 161. That makes Locke's views on black women particularly difficult to extract.

14. John Locke, "An Essay on the Poor Law," in John Locke, *Political Essays*, ed. Mark Goldie (Cambridge: Cambridge University Press, 1997), 183. See Nancy J. Hirschmann, "Liberal/Conservativism, Once and Again: Locke's "Essay on the Poor Law and Contemporary U.S. Welfare Reform," *Constellations* 7, no. 1 (September 2002). Portions of this section of the discussion borrow from that earlier paper.

15. Henry Richard Fox Bourne, *The Life of John Locke*, vol. 2 (London: Scientia Verlag Allen, 1969), 376; John Marshall, *John Locke: Resistance, Religion, and Responsibility* (New York: Cambridge University Press, 1994), 158.

16. Locke, "Poor Law," 184.

17. Though Fox Bourne surely exaggerates when he calls this an "immense state-machinery of work-houses." *Life of John Locke*, 391.

18. Locke, "Poor Law," 190.

19. Ibid., 189.

20. Fox Bourne, *Life of John Locke*, 367.

21. Locke, "Poor Law," 186, 188.

22. Ibid., 189.

23. John Locke, *Two Treatises of Government*, ed. Peter Laslett (Cambridge: Cambridge University Press, 1988), 2.80.

24. Locke, "Poor Law," 182.

25. Ibid., 191.

26. On the shift from piece work to factory production, see Arthur Francis, *New Technology at Work* (Oxford: Clarendon Press, 1986); on Irish linen production, see Fox-Bourne, *Life of John Locke*.

27. Locke, "Poor Law," 182, 192.

28. Ibid., 191.

29. My phrasing here borrows doubly from Kirstie M. McClure, *Judging Rights: Lockean Politics and the Limits of Consent* (Ithaca: Cornell University Press, 1996), who uses the terminology of architecture, and John Dunn, *The Political Thought of John Locke: An Historical Account of the Argument of the "Two Treatises of Government"* (Cambridge: Cambridge University Press, 1969), who discusses the notion of God's "divine order."

30. Marshall, *John Locke*, 174.

31. Locke, "Poor Law," 189.

32. John Locke, *Some Considerations of the Consequences of the Lowering of Interest and the Raising the Value of Money*, in *Locke on Money*, ed. Patrick Hyde Kelly (New York: Oxford University Press, 1991); also see Isaac Kramnick, *Republicanism and Bourgeois Radicalism: Political Ideology in Late Eighteenth-century England and America* (Ithaca: Cornell University Press, 1990).

33. Locke, "Poor Law," 190.

34. See Hirschmann, *Rethinking Obligation*, 46–47, for an argument linking the two dominant explanations for why men leave the state of nature, viz. money and "lack of a known judge."

35. Macpherson, *Possessive Individualism*.

36. Locke, *Two Treatises*, 2.61.

37. Clark, "Women and John Locke"; Pateman, *Sexual Contract*. See also Zillah Eisenstein, *The Radical Future of Liberal Feminism* (New York: Longman, 1981); Jean Bethke Elshtain, *Public Man, Private Woman: Women in Social and Political Thought* (Princeton: Princeton University Press, 1981); and Susan Moller Okin, *Women in Western Political Thought* (Princeton: Princeton University Press, 1979).

38. Sara Mendelson and Patricia Crawford, *Women in Early Modern England: 1550–1720* (Oxford: Clarendon Press, 1998).

39. Rogers M. Smith, *Liberalism and American Constitutional Law* (Cambridge: Harvard University Press, 1985).

40. Locke, *Two Treatises*, 2.60.

41. Butler, "Early Liberal Roots of Feminism," 148. See also letter, from John Locke to Mrs. Mary Clarke, Dec. 1683, in *The Correspondence of John Locke and Edward Clarke*, ed. Benjamin Rand (Oxford: Oxford University Press, 1927), 101, 103.

42. John Locke, *Some Thoughts Concerning Education*, in Locke, *Some Thoughts Concerning Education and Of the Conduct of the Understanding*, ed. Ruth Grant and Nathan Tarcov (Indianapolis: Hackett Publishing, 1996), secs. 8–14.

43. John Locke, *Of the Conduct of the Understanding*, in Locke, *Some Thoughts Concerning Education and Of the Conduct of the Understanding*, ed. Ruth Grant and Nathan Tarcov (Indianapolis: Hackett Publishing, 1996), secs. 7, 6.

44. Ibid., sec. 6.

45. Locke, *Education*, sec. 6.

46. Ibid., sec. 47.

47. Ibid., secs. 107, 113.

48. Immanuel Kant, *Observations on the Feeling of the Beautiful and Sublime*, trans. John T. Goldthwaite (Berkeley and Los Angeles: University of California Press, 1960). See Nancy J. Hirschmann, *The Subject of Liberty: Toward a Feminist Theory of Freedom* (Princeton: Princeton University Press, 2002), chap. 2, for a discussion of the similarities between Locke's and Kant's theories of education.

49. John Locke, *The Reasonableness of Christianity as Delivered in the Scriptures*, in John Locke, *"The Reasonableness of Christianity" with "A Discourse of Miracles" and Part of a "Third Letter Concerning Toleration,"* ed. I. T. Ramsay (Stanford: Stanford University Press, 1958), 76. At the end of *A Discourse of Miracles*, he takes another swipe at the intellectual capacities of "poor bricklayers," though does not mention women this time. Ibid., 86.

50. Locke, *Conduct*, sec. 4.

51. Ibid., sec. 6.

52. Locke, *Two Treatises*, 2.61, 63.

53. Locke, *Conduct*, sec. 4.

54. Ibid., sec. 3.

55. Ibid., sec. 6.

56. On the importance of mathematics, see Locke, *Conduct*, secs. 6, 7; on the time constraints of laborers, see secs. 3, 4, 6, and 7.

57. Ibid., sec. 7.

58. Ibid., sec. 23; see also sec. 8.

59. Locke, *Education*, sec. 164.

60. Fox Bourne, *Life of John Locke*.

61. Mendelson and Crawford, *Women in Early Modern England*.

62. Ibid., 219, 257, 330.

63. Mendelson and Crawford (ibid., chap. 7) indicate that women had tried to vote in Parliamentary elections in the 1640s and 1650s in particular; records show that their votes were declared

invalid, but since only disputed votes were recorded, they believe that some single women's votes must have been counted in some elections in the middle of the century, at least. By the end of the century, with the ascension of Mary II to the throne conjointly with her husband William of Orange, anxieties about female power and the contradictions between female sovereignty and subjection to husbands expressed itself, among other ways, in an official ban on female suffrage.

64. Locke, *Education*, sec. 177.

65. Ibid.

66. Ibid., sec. 164.

67. Mendelson and Crawford (*Women in Early Modern England*, 324) suggest, however, that daughters of the gentry needed to learn languages, as well as some basic mathematics so that they could maintain household accounts. Locke similarly says that it is absolutely forbidden to give children sweetmeats, "which whether they do more harm to the maker or eater is not easy to tell . . . and so I leave them to the ladies" (*Education*, sec. 20). Since "ladies" may be dismissed, then presumably denying these things to young girls cannot prevent their corruption as adult women, as the focus of these educational recommendations once again seems to be specifically boys.

68. Locke, *Education*, sec. 6.

69. Mary Astell, "Reflections upon Marriage," in *Mary Astell: Political Writings*, ed. Patricia Springborg (New York: Cambridge University Press, 1996).

70. Locke, *Education*, secs. 18, 32.

71. Ibid., sec. 70.

72. Ibid., sec. 38.

73. Ibid., sec. 107.

74. Ibid., sec. 37.

75. Butler, "Early Liberal Roots of Feminism," 178.

76. Locke, *Education*, sec. 78. On the likely age of the child, see James L. Axtell, *The Educational Writings of John Locke: A Critical Edition with Introduction and Notes* (London: Cambridge University Press, 1968), 129 n. 1.

77. Ibid., secs. 43, 47–51, 60, 62, 83, 112.

78. Locke, *Two Treatises*, 2.72, 79–84.

79. Locke, *Education*, sec. 83.

80. Uday Mehta, *The Anxiety of Freedom: Imagination and Individuality in Locke's Political Thought* (Ithaca: Cornell University Press, 1992), 148.

81. Locke, *Education*, secs. 103, 105.

82. Mehta, *Anxiety of Freedom*, 148.

83. Locke, *Education*, sec. 7.

84. Ibid., sec. 35.

85. Ibid., sec. 37.

86. Ibid., sec. 107.

87. Ibid., secs. 59, 69, 138; see also sec. 19 on the likelihood of servants encouraging children to drink strong liquor.

88. Ibid., secs. 67, 69. See also pp. 106–7, where "clown" is associated with "ill breeding," and "good breeding" is key to educating a "child" into a gentleman.

6

Gender and Narrative in Locke's *Two Treatises of Government*

Terrell Carver

In this chapter I use the "gender lens" to explore narratives in Locke's *Two Treatises of Government* that have become foundational for the documents and practices of liberal democracy. Working from established feminist concerns, and employing ideas from sociological and historical studies of men and masculinities, I review what has previously been conceptualized in commentary as the family and household, parental and filial obligations, the "sexual contract," patriarchy, the public/private "split," and gender-neutral concepts of "man."[1] The literature on men and masculinities starts from the feminist insight that men have presented an idealized image of themselves as generically human, and that this has had the effect of marginalizing women in practice and devaluing the activities with which they have been stereotypically associated.[2] Recent research in sociology and history has further demonstrated that this image of "man" is itself untrue to many men's experiences, and politically selective in its portrayal of an apparently singular masculinity.[3]

It is clear from feminist critique that the traditional conceptualization of "man" as generically human was certainly neither a woman nor subject to specifically female experiences. It was masculinized, rather than androgynous. However, it does not follow that this conception "man" represents the actual and potential experiences of men, or the range of masculinities, including practices of sex and sexuality, with any degree of subtlety beyond the merely stereotypical. More nuanced understandings are needed to drive critical and constructive theorizations of political issues concerning men, and therefore men in relation to women. These issues were salient in Locke's time, and are still so in ours. Texts such as Locke's exclude and devalue women, but they are also hierarchically validating with respect to some kinds of men, in terms of some kinds of masculinities. In short, they are normative constructs requiring deconstruction, and the new, feminist-inspired literature on men and masculinities represents an important resource for doing this.[4]

Feminist critique has identified generic "man" with a male body, that is, a body unable to give birth, and with a competitive and self-interested persona, rather than one attuned to nurturing and emotion. Feminists have also identified an apparent paradox in that generic "man" is also made to seem sexless, or de-gendered, a figure abstracted from sexual activity, reproductive attributes, and even the body itself. This, of course, fits well with . a public/private "split" that feminists have identified, namely that sex and reproduction are conceptualized as (somehow) "private," and so women (stereotypically associated with these activities) are then consigned to that realm in practice. Conversely men, operating in a "public" realm to which sex and reproduction (supposedly) do not belong, are conceptualized as apparently sexless and almost disembodied beings, monopolizing "public" powers for themselves. There is thus an *apparently de-gendered* narrative of "public man" through which political theory makes its most crucial claims about humanity, but in a falsely generic way.[5]

However, in Locke's *Two Treatises,* and in any theoretical account of the human community, there are also *overtly gendered* narratives. These include the association of women with reproduction and motherhood, and the relegation of those activities to a "private" (or domestic, non-public) realm that is presumed to be pre-political. That, of course, is the foil that makes "public man" seem apparently de-gendered, because gender issues are stereotypically defined as "private" and so out of the "public" realm. Yet the textual narratives of political theory do not maintain a consistent boundary line in this respect, since the "private" sphere is not exclusively reserved for females, nor are all gender issues overtly female-related. There are moments in those texts when men have a life as gendered beings in private and in public. Indeed, the public/private "split" tends to collapse at that point because it is an inherently patriarchal and antifeminist device deployed to marginalize women and the feminine side (as it were) of certain social activities.

The *overtly gendered* narrative relating to men in political theory gives them a generative role in reproduction, a husbandly role in marriage, a fatherly role in relation to children (especially sons), and a head-of-household role in relation to servants. In feminist thought this overtly gendered narrative about men has a sharply political edge, since feminism is by definition antipatriarchal. The men and masculinities perspective is a useful one, though, because it draws on the breadth and variety of men's experiences of *differences within masculinities*. In that way it establishes the dynamics of patriarchy more clearly, in relations between men as well as in relations between men and women, and also points up critical areas where diversity among men could be mobilized politically. This could be done in ways that feminists might find constructive.[6]

Locke is an exceptionally interesting theorist in this regard, because he was an adamant opponent of seventeenth-century "patriarchalism." He portrayed it as a dangerous doctrine, in which absolute monarchical authority was said to be the only correct theory of rulership. This was supposedly the case because God had granted that power (which was said to be the same as that of the husband, the father, and the householder) to Adam and his heirs, who were assumed to be males in male lines of descent. Patriarchal theories of that kind obviously relied on contemporary assumptions, doctrines, and laws that comprehensively privileged men over women.[7] In seeking to undermine contemporary claims to divine right and absolute authority, Locke attacked patriarchalism in terms that border on the burlesque. His contrary view concerning political power made bold claims for equality,[8] and he took delight in referring to women as contracting wives, parents, householders, and rulers. This was in specific rebuttal to the "truths" about men and women that patriarchalists had argued were natural, God-given features of human society and fundamental relationships.

However, Locke was concerned at certain points to limit his claims regarding equality in order to accommodate unequal power relationships already existing in society (*Two Treatises*, 2.54), provided that these did not touch (as he thought) on the fundamental dimension of political power with which he was principally concerned, and which he distinguished from the powers appropriate to other relationships (marriage, parenthood, householding). Thus he tempered his bold egalitarianism with a certain conventional hindsight, with respect to equality generally and male/female relations specifically (2.82), and so became perforce a patriarchal theorist in feminist eyes, or at least partly so. Locke would not, of course, have recognized his own residual patriarchalism as a serious fault, nor would he have seen the similarity with the partriarchalists he so despised. However, it is apparent that he used egalitarian arguments enthusiastically as a way of ridiculing patriarchalists, and hence their absolutist claims concerning a divine right of kings. Later in his discussions he reined in his egalitarianism, perhaps to avoid any charge of fomenting undue radicalism elsewhere in the social order, most particularly in marriage, parenthood, and the household.

My working definition of gender is "ways that sex and sexuality become political."[9] This is not supposed to legislate what gender is (always and already, as the phrase goes). Rather, it is intended to alert readers to how that term can be useful in identifying power-relations that are binary and hierarchical.[10] In my view, using gender to mean merely sex or M/F is in effect an attempt to erase or silence the complexities of sexuality, and to disguise the ways that these and other factors are constitutive of gender relations.[11] Highlighting sexuality in considering gender is not only a matter of adding marginalized sexualities to "the heterosexual matrix." Rather, we should also remember that heterosexuality is also a sexuality, albeit an undertheorized and underinvestigated one. It denies its own variousness. Much the same could be said with respect to men as gendered beings, and with "straight" men in particular.[12]

In common with other "mainstream/malestream" political theorists, Locke's narratives were about the "straight" men and patriarchal households presumed to be foundational for the polity. This set up hierarchies of disadvantage, marginalization, and exclusion that were both explicit and implicit. My aim is not to reveal that Locke's texts were written by "the straight mind" of a "straight man" but rather to engage critically with the argumentative strategies deployed there and continuously reap-

propriated in overt and covert gender politics since 1689.[13] This requires
a view of gender that deploys it to represent binaries and hierarchies
beyond the M/F distinction, including sexuality differences, as they are
framed within familiar "cleavages"—property, class, race/ethnicity, religion, language, and so on. It is through these concepts and practices that
marriage, parenthood, householding, and other "gradations of esteem" in
citizenship are defined and take effect.[14] In that way the "gender lens"
reveals not just that sex and sexuality relations are crosscut with other
kinds of social difference, but that those forms of difference may themselves be genuinely hybridized with sex and sexuality, and thus "gendered."

The *overtly gendered* narrative about men in Locke's *Two Treatises* "gen-
ders" power relations in society. I aim to draw out what he has to say
about rulership, householding, parenthood, and conjugal relations by
showing that there are effectively three kinds of dominant masculinities
at issue in his *Two Treatises*. One is related to the rational/bureaucratic
masculinity of modern commerce, which he endorsed, and another is
related to concepts of masculine tenderness and solicitude, of which he
also approved. The third is related to the warrior mode of absolutism,
conquest, and tyranny, which he deeply opposed. The advantage of reading Locke's text this way is that it shows how he reconciled a residual
patriarchy with his egalitarian principles of equality, legitimacy, and consent. He did this by drawing a strong contrast between an absolutist and
irrational masculinity, on the one hand, and a dual masculinity not just
of competitive individuality but of fatherly care, on the other. He deployed these historically in relation to archaic societies, and politically in
relation to contemporary society. Feminists are rightly critical of Locke's
residual patriarchy as regressive in practice with respect to his principles.
Liberals are today puzzling over how to reconcile egalitarian principles
with the practical exigencies of gender. This chapter argues that the literature on men and masculinities can be deployed to aid both those political processes.

Locke's *Two Treatises:* Overtly Gendered Narratives of Women and Men

Locke's *Two Treatises of Government* were published anonymously in a
single volume in 1689. The *Second Treatise* is probably the most successful

political tract of all time. It is often used to interpret the founding documents and later legislation of liberal democracies, and sometimes serves
as the raw material for judicial interpretations in the English-speaking
world. As a founding narrative it was translated (in part and anonymously) into French in 1691, and republished, for example, in Boston in
1773, just before the American Revolution. In any case, it is a reasonably
concise conflation of power/knowledge, served up in a discourse that now
sounds like "plain truths" about liberal democracy. Those "plain truths"
persist through cultural processes that do not reference the work explicitly, and Locke's ideas have thus entered democratic discourse generally.

The *First Treatise* has been explored by feminists because of its close
connection with patriarchalism, since Locke engaged directly and at
length with Sir Robert Filmer's *Patriarcha, or the Natural Power of Kings*
(written c. 1628–21, published by "divine right" monarchists in 1679–
80).[15] In "mainstream/malestream" political theory the *First Treatise* is
generally less read and cited than the *Second*. This is because "main-
stream/malestream" theory is not particularly interested in the divine
right of kings as such, or in the gender issues about women and women's
roles, and about men and men's roles, that patriarchalism raised explicitly.[16] In short, it lacks the "gender lens."

The *Second Treatise* became canonical for "mainstream/malestream"
theory, because it contained formulations of equality and legitimacy that
are foundational for liberal democracy. These employ a conception of
"public man" that effectively feminizes and so marginalizes gender issues,
a situation that "mainstream/malestream" theorists have found very normal, not least because their world is already organized that way. I make
use of both Locke's texts. Schochet rightly criticizes the literature on
Locke for taking his version of patriarchalism, and in particular of Sir
Robert Filmer's doctrines, on trust.[17] However, for my purposes, Locke's
version of Filmer is important because it represents the kind of patriarchalism from which he wished to distinguish himself very sharply, and
which functioned as a foil to his own residual patriarchalism when this
surfaced in his thinking.

Locke's text was not only *covertly gendered* in relation to "public man,"
as feminists have demonstrated, but also *overtly gendered* in relation to
women and men. This is because an account of human society and political community requires a narrative of reproduction, birth, infant care,
transition to adulthood, and many other things connected with an inter-
generational and continuing polity.[18] To do that, sex and sexuality must

be confronted out in the open (which is not to say that there is much subtlety about it in Locke's text—rather the opposite). So Locke discussed mammalian reproduction, conjugal society, marriage, husbands and wives, fathers and mothers, legitimate and illegitimate offspring, the care of children, the obligations of adult offspring to parents, and other gender and "gendered" relationships in the household and community, including class relations (as master/servant) and rulership (as magistracy).

Chapter 1 of the *Second Treatise* begins with an overtly gendered narrative, in the sense that not only is the sexual binary introduced, but the two sexes are also set hierarchically in relation to each other in very explicit ways. Locke was keen to distinguish the power of "magistrate over subject" from that of "a father over his children" and a "husband over his wife" (2.2). Of course Locke was not constructing his text as some theory or doctrine in isolation from contemporary politics, but rather still pursuing—in the *Second Treatise*, as well as in the *First*—a polemical riposte to Filmer's overtly gendered narrative of patriarchal authority. In Locke's reading, Filmer was arguing that political power arose from, and was in essence the same as, the patriarchal power attributed to fathers/husbands with respect to children/women (2.1). While Locke could have claimed merely that patriarchal and political powers were different in kind, without challenging fatherly/husbandly authority over children/women, he actually cited biblical teaching and contemporary practice to make an egalitarian-sounding case with respect to men and women—though he did not pursue this consistently. Thus in chapter 6 "Of Paternal Power" he appealed to biblical injunctions to obey both father and mother, or "parents" (2.52), mentioning that mothers had "a share" in this "parental authority" and then referring to "two persons jointly" as holders of it (2.53). This had already been argued out more fully and prominently in the *First Treatise*, beginning in chapter 2: "I hope 'tis no injury to call a half quotation a half reason, for God says, 'honour thy father and mother'; but our author [Filmer] contents himself with half, leaves out 'thy mother' quite, as little serviceable to his purpose" (1.6).

This passage continued with a scornful Lockean riposte to Filmer's identification of fatherly with regal power, again, making an egalitarian-sounding claim with respect to mothers and female rulers:

> [Filmer says] "to confirm this natural right of regal power, we find in the Decalogue, that the law which enjoins obedience to kings,

is delivered in the terms, 'honour they father', as if all power were originally in the father." And why may I not add as well, that in the Decalogue, the law that enjoins obedience to queens, is delivered in the terms of "honour thy mother," as if all power were originally in the mother. The argument, as Sir Robert puts it, will hold as well for one as t'other. (*Two Treatises*, 1.11)

The argument returned later in chapter 6 of the *First Treatise*, with what Locke intended as an ultimate *épater* to Christian patriarchalists: "For had our author set down this command without garbling, as God gave it, and joined mother to father, every reader would have seen that it had made directly against him, and that it was so far from establishing the 'monarchical power of the father,' that it set up the mother equal with him."

Thus noting scriptural equality between the sexes, Locke acidly mentions that scripture does not actually support exclusively patriarchal authority over children anyway: "The Scripture joins mother too in that homage, which is due from children, and had there been any text, where the honour or obedience of children had been directed to the father alone, 'tis not likely that our author [Filmer], who pretends to build all upon Scripture, would have omitted it."

And even better for Locke, in scripture mothers sometimes come first! "Nay, the Scripture makes the authority of father and mother, in respect of those they have begot, so equal, that in some places it neglects, even the priority of order, which is thought due to the father, and the mother is put first, as *Leviticus* 19:3" (1.61).

Thus in the *Second Treatise* section 53 establishes an apparently egalitarian concept of parental authority in "two persons jointly," yet the very next section explicitly qualifies the apparently unlimited egalitarianism of the preceding chapters 2–5 that has thrilled so many liberal readers, and indeed defined the liberal project. Locke mentions "age or virtue," "excellency of parts and merit," "birth," and "alliance or benefits" as significantly qualifying his opening salvo concerning the equality of all "men." To establish his initial egalitarianism at the opening of the *Second Treatise*, Locke first asserts the negative, namely that no man is bound to another by any natural tie of unfreedom. At the beginning of chapter 2 he states: "We must consider what state all men are naturally in . . . a state of perfect freedom to order their actions, and dispose of their possessions, and persons as they think fit . . . without asking leave, or depending upon the will of any other man."

He then continues by arguing that those relations among free men are also equal in a crucially important respect: "A state also of equality, wherein all the power and jurisdiction is reciprocal, no one having more than another: there being nothing more evident, than that creatures of the same species . . . should also be equal one amongst another without subordination or subjection" (2.4).

However, in section 54, where Locke qualifies his initial egalitarianism, he does not include inequality between husbands and wives, or fathers and mothers, or indeed men and women. Perhaps surprisingly the starkly gendered juxtaposition men/women does not seem to occupy him very much in his thinking in the text (though see the overtly procreative "male" and "female" in 2.79–80). Instead he carefully traces out the implications for children when their father dies, commenting that "everywhere" parental power is then exercised by the mother, and that children should fulfill their duties to her in exactly the same way as if the surviving single parent were the father.

That line of argument had the useful consequence that Locke could taunt his patriarchalist enemies by appealing not only to moments of apparent biblical egalitarianism but also to contemporary practice, in that widows did indeed exercise parental power and other powers as head of household, until remarriage. So keen was Locke on this argumentative tack that he also attempted (astonishingly) to undermine patriarchalist claims concerning the naturalism of the two-parent family by appealing in apparently factual terms to polyandry in unspecified places, and even to normalized practices of maternal single-parenting in America, presumably among "Indians" (2.65)!

Unsurprisingly Locke's own version of residual domestic patriarchy, namely, gender inequality between husbands/wives and fathers/mothers, comes back with a vengeance in the succeeding chapter 7 in the *Second Treatise*. There he reintroduces in section 82, as it were, a subordination of wife/mother to husband/father, the "sexual contract" with which Carole Pateman has been so productively occupied. Moreover, all Locke's examples of inheritance in the *Second Treatise* are of father to son (e.g., sec. 58), though in his own time daughters (of the right social class) certainly inherited, and many would-be husbands looked not merely for wives but for heiresses. Prior to the Married Woman's Property Act of 1882, of course, a husband became sole proprietor of what his bride had previously owned, and moreover a father had a clear right to custody over any children. This was legally superior to a mother's claim, a situation not modified until the Custody of Children Act of 1839.[19]

In the *Second Treatise* Locke does not consider female rulers explicitly, either by inheritance or by usurpation/conquest, as anyway the overall argument of the tract was to refute all theories of political power that derive rulership, not from consent, but from anything else, such as, for example, divine right to rule descending patriarchally from father to son (or exceptionally, descending to males only, but through the female line). However, female rulers were considered explicitly in the *First Treatise*, and in properly respectful terms. Locke refers to "our queens Mary or Elizabeth," arguing the absurdity of believing that their (presumably legitimate) monarchical authority would have been forfeited if they had married any of their subjects, *contra* Filmer's view that God's grant of authority to Adam over his wife Eve was part of Adam's grant of authority as absolute monarch over all peoples. Queenly marriage, of course, was a famous sixteenth-century political issue in both cases, viz. Mary's marriage to Philip II of Spain, and Elizabeth's presumed need to marry, both in relation to their personal will and in relation to their monarchical role.[20] Philip II was conspicuously absent during Queen Mary's marriage, and was never king of England anyway, and Queen Elizabeth remained notoriously and in the end deliberately unmarried in order to function as "prince."

Surprisingly, though, Locke goes on to argue that the curse of the Fall in Genesis not only gave Adam no monarchical authority over anyone, never mind any "succession," but also no authority over Eve, "or to men over their wives" (1.47). Locke portrays Eve as a "helper in the temptation, as well as a partner in the transgression," who "was laid below" Adam, giving him "accidentally a superiority over her, for her greater punishment." But then strangely Locke further argues that Adam, having "had his share in the fall, as well as the sin" was "laid lower" as "a day labourer for life." That wonderfully refuted Filmer by absurdly suggesting that God "in the same breath" should make Adam "universal monarch over all mankind" while condemning him "to till the ground" (1.44). But it also raised apparently irresolvable issues concerning gender (in)-equality in Locke—who is lower than whom? Rather similarly, the authority of "husbands over wives" was said by Locke to be both accidental (due to the Fall) (1.44) and "ordinary" in normal practice (1.47), and in any case strictly limited by the purpose of the association and also as specified in a marriage contract (2.82). Moreover, he argues that Genesis merely foretold "what should be the woman's lot," and did not actually establish a form of natural subjection: "But there is here no more law to oblige a woman to such a subjection [in marriage], if the circumstances either of her condition or contract with her husband should exempt her from it, that she should bring forth her children in sorrow and pain, if there could be found a remedy for it, which is also part of the same curse upon her" (1.47).

This is an unusually de-naturalizing argument in relation to women, interestingly viewing marital subjection as potentially remediable, like pain in parturition (and perhaps with a similar moral obligation to bring this amelioration about?). But before anyone today gets too excited about this passage, it has to be noted that Locke followed it with comments that "generally the laws of mankind and customs of nations have ordered it [i.e. wives subject to husbands] so; and there is, I grant, a foundation in nature for it" (1.47). This then reappears in the *Second Treatise* (at 2.82), where he identifies men as "abler and stronger" than women, and so apparently entitled to execute the last "determination" in any conflict of wills between husband and wife. Returning to his previous argument— that any subjection of wives to husbands has nothing to do with any "original grant of government and the foundation of monarchical power"—Locke explains that "conjugal power" is different: "the power that every husband hath to order the things of private concernment in his family . . . and to have his will take place before that of his wife in all things" (1.48). However, it is clear that for Locke "wife" and "woman," at least, were not necessarily the same, and in certain cases, neither were "queen" and "wife," whereas, according to him, they were all the same to Filmer.

The only other female ruler Locke mentions is Athaliah, "a woman, who reigned six years [over the Hebrews] an utter stranger to royal blood," *contra* Filmer's argument (as presented by Locke) that the succession of monarchical authority among the Hebrews could be reckoned consistently with an inheritance from father to son (1.161). (Rather predictably Locke's text at 1.93 and 1.98 wanders indiscriminately between "child" and "son" in discussing inheritance more generally.) Elsewhere Locke has considerable fun with Filmer's naïveté concerning the rules of monarchical succession, which marks a rare point at which "daughter," as well as "sister" and "widow," enters Locke's text explicitly. The discussion broadens out again from monarchy to reproductive relations, and marital (and nonmarital) relations, particularly those of consanguinity and inheritance, with interesting glances at the effects of reproductive technologies on naturalistic presumptions about birth order ("dissection of the mother," that is to say, Caesarian section, is mentioned later) and at nature's indifference to the whole customary (and Christian) apparatus of marriage and legitimacy:

> I go on then to ask whether in the inheriting of this paternal power, this supreme fatherhood, the grandson by a daughter, hath a right before a nephew by a brother? . . . Whether the daughter before the uncle? Or any other man, descended by a male line? Whether a grandson by a younger daughter, before a granddaughter by an elder daughter? Whether the elder son by a concubine, before a younger son by a wife? From whence also will arise many questions of legitimation, and what in nature is the difference betwixt a wife and a concubine? For as to the municipal or positive laws of men, they can signify nothing here. (*Two Treatises*, 1.123)

Locke is evidently taking a hard-headed doctor's view of human reproduction, evincing a remarkably unmoralized view of humanity that queried conventional presumptions concerning a supposed natural order of precedence by birth order and by matrimonial legitimacy. He then goes on to ridicule a strict patriarchalism as unworkable, again drawing on medical circumstances and legal conundrums: "Who has the paternal power, whilst the widow queen is with child by the deceased king, and nobody knows whether it will be a son or a daughter? Which shall be heir of two male twins, who by the dissection of the mother, were laid open to the world? Whether a sister by the half blood, before a brother's daughter by the whole blood?" (1.122).

Locke's overtly gendered engagement with women and men unsurprisingly covers issues of parental care, marriage, childbirth, legitimacy, widowhood, inheritance, householding, and rulership. Arguing inconsistently from both moralized and nonmoralized presumptions, he pursues his case against what he presents to his readers as Filmer's patriarchalism. Filmer's besetting sin, according to Locke, was an absurd insistence on absolute precedence for males and the male line, for which neither nature nor science nor scripture nor conventional practice could provide a justification. Filmer had rolled up fatherhood, husbandhood, householding, and rulership into one patriarchalist package, and had perforce produced a complementary view of motherhood, wifehood, and female subjection right across the board. In arguing against such ridiculous consistency, Locke produced any inconsistency with it that looked good at the moment, and in so doing promoted (unwittingly, of course) both the emancipation of women along gender-egalitarian lines *and* their continued subjection within a residual patriarchalism that he found comfortable (again, arguing from various inconsistent premises). Relentless in his pursuit of Filmer, Locke ventured into areas and issues that other political theorists merely touch on, or simply omit. In doing that he (inadvertently, no doubt) helped to push gender egalitarianism and political emancipation much further than he had in mind. However, he also provided us with a useful way into many issues that are of political importance today, precisely because he articulated so many "traditional" presumptions so thoroughly and so variously. At least in his texts they are out in the open, if one cares to look.

Locke's *Two Treatises:* Overtly Gendered Narratives of Men and Women

The terms of Locke's discussion of masculinized citizenship are only slightly archaic. The operation of the gender binary that he outlines is recognizable today with minimal translation. The apparently de-gendered (yet covertly gendered) narrative that makes women second-class citizens is visible now in Locke, and in practical politics, thanks to feminist analysis. The *overtly gendered* narrative in Locke does not cover only women as gendered beings. In those terms it certainly gives the lie, as we have noted, to his generically human egalitarianism (and his occasional egalitarian comments concerning women as parents, as contracting wives, and as rulers). The *overtly gendered* narrative in Locke also covers men as gendered beings. In those terms it makes explicit the political obverse to the subordination and exclusion of women. It positions some men over others in crucial ways with respect to power, property, and full citizenship, as well as over women generally.

Locke's text gives a portrait not just of patriarchy, but of dominant masculinities that privilege some men over others (as well as men over women).[21] Those dominant masculinities are heavily inflected (overtly or covertly) with race/ethnicity, class, religion, language, and numerous categories that appear to be other than gender. However, it is worth considering the extent to which those categories are already defined in gender terms, provided that gender is itself allowed to represent hierarchical differences *within* the sexual and sexuality binaries. Locke's privileged males, the ones who were not servants or foreigners or children and could thus become "perfect members" of the community (*Two Treatises*, 2.119), were propertied householders and fathers, precisely because they were marriageable. Marriage was an important way that property came to men, through marriage settlements (as husbands) and subsequent inheritance (as sons). It was just as important for Locke that some men dominate other men in certain social relationships, such as propertied/unpropertied in commercial society, master/servant in the household, "industrious and rational"/"wild Indian" territorially (2.26, 34), as it was that men in general dominate women. Marriageable men were the "men" of the *Second Treatise*, not because they were heterosexual rather than homosexual (in modern terms), but because marriage was the public face of sexuality, as well as the public face of property, and therefore a defining factor in the dominant masculinities of the time. Servants, foreigners, boys, and for example "several nations of the Americans" (2.41) all belonged to different and subordinate masculinities, and as such, were treated as inferiors, making them objects of domination, *within* the male gender order.

In particular, overt gendering of men in Locke reinforces a modern, rather commercial type of dominant masculinity, by contradicting an old-fashioned, rather Old Testament archetype of patriarchy. Locke's text thus marks a point where a rational/bureaucratic concept of masculinity overthrows (theoretically, at least) a "warrior" masculinity associated with physical force and lethal violence.[22] The latter masculinity appears in Locke's portrayal of the Filmerian patriarchal tyrant, absolute and arbitrary, as father, as husband, as householder, and as ruler. The Filmerian ruler as absolute monarch is portrayed by Locke as violent, aggressive, subhuman, animal-like in unpredictability and ferocity. Filmerian patriarchal powers were all of a piece, whether those of father, husband, householder, or ruler: "In absolute monarchies indeed . . . if it be asked, what security, what fence is there in such a state, against the violence and oppression of this absolute ruler? The very question can scarce be borne. They are ready to tell you, that it deserves death only to ask after safety." Locke cannot imagine "men" bargaining their way out of the state of nature only to set up so dangerous a tyranny: "This is to think that men are so foolish that they take care to avoid what mischiefs may be done them by polecats, or foxes, but are content, nay think it safety, to be devoured by lions" (*Two Treatises*, 2.93)."

The superior claim of some (presumptively) male agents over others in terms of a competitive, individualistic, and commercial cast of mind is famously and sweepingly announced by Locke in the *Second Treatise*: "God gave the world to men in common; but since he gave it them for their benefit, and the greatest conveniences of life they were capable to draw from it, it cannot be supposed he meant it should always remain common and uncultivated [i.e. unenclosed for commercial agriculture]. He gave it to the use of the industrious and rational, (and labour was to be his title to it); not to the fancy or covetousness of the quarrelsome and contentious" (2.34). The executive power of the law of nature, held (presumptively by males, and later transferred to magistrates as rulers, again presumptively male) fits into this pattern of orderly and bounded restraint: "And thus in the state of nature, one man comes by a power over another; but yet no absolute or arbitrary power, to use a criminal when he has got him in his hands, according to the passionate heats, or boundless extravagancy of his own will, but only to retribute to him, so far as calm reason and conscience dictates, what is proportionate to this transgression, which is so much as may serve for reparation and restraint" (2.8).

Lockean "masters" (of households, and over servants and laborers generally) were also defined in terms of this masculinized vision of rationality and industry. Note the positioning of (presumptively but not necessarily male) servants in this passage alongside their fellow (animal) laborers: "Thus the grass my horse has bit; the turfs my servant has cut; and the ore I have digged in any place where I have a right to them in common with others, become my property" (2.28). In terms of "conjugal society" between husband and wife, once again the orderly and purposive, contractual, and limited qualities of a relationship were contrasted with Filmerian absolutism. For Locke even the marriage relationship was not perpetual, and there was "no necessity in the nature of the thing, nor to the ends of it." A wife may be "in the full and free possession of what by contract is her peculiar right," and thus a husband has "no more power over her life, than she has over his," and indeed the "power of the husband" is "so far from that of an absolute monarch, that the wife has, in many cases, a liberty to separate from him" (2.81). In terms of parental relations, Locke argued similarly that fathers had paternal powers to guide and protect their charges, but no absolute power over their lives as such, and therefore no legitimate powers to destroy or disadvantage them (2.69).

The concepts of fatherhood, husbandhood, householding, and magistracy that Locke endorsed stand in contrast to the absolute, arbitrary powers of murder and enslavement that he rejected as "force without right" (2.19). He condemns those illegitimate powers in his portraits (explicit and implied) of tyrannical rulers, householders, husbands, and fathers. In his view they all pretend to a right that no one could ever have, namely, the right to harm others who are themselves innocent of any evildoing. The Lockean household thus comprises conjugal, parental, and master/servant relationships, none of which represent or assign "absolute power of the whole family," as Filmerian patriarchy was supposed to entail, and all of which reflect an "industrious and rational" form of dominant masculinity. Filmerian tyranny, Locke argued, would fall apart even in the domestic context, paralleling his later argument (2.222–26) that such tyranny in the political context is a standing invitation to rebellion and disorder: "If it [the family] must be thought a monarchy, and the paterfamilias the absolute monarch in it, absolute monarchy will have but a very shattered and short power, when 'tis plain, by what has been said before, that the master of the family has a very distinct and differently limited power, both as to time and extent, over those several persons that are in it" (2.86).

Locke argued that rulers acted legitimately when and only when they rule for the public good, and therefore have no such absolute powers as life and death over the community or individuals, independent of that justification (2.131). It follows that in his theory no one can consent to absolute and arbitrary power in a ruler, precisely because it would expose the citizenry to public evil, rather than good.[23] That situation, Locke noted, was one of slavery, and totally inconsistent with the freedom which only legitimate government could provide, as opposed to Filmerian absolutism. Locke's sole justification for slavery (*ad hoc* suspension of the death sentence for prisoners from an unjust war) was, of course, a situation in which an evil was rightly owed as punishment (*Two Treatises*, 2.23). This was carefully distinguished even from Old Testament slavery, which Locke said gave the master no right to kill those whom they (mistakenly) called slaves (2.24).

While arguing that legitimate government arises only from consent of the people, as would be true with the Old Testament Judges of the *First*

Treatise or the contemporary "magistrates" of the *Second Treatise*, Locke also felt that he needed to reconcile his theory of popular sovereignty with the historical existence of legitimate rulers who were *apparently* patriarchal monarchs, *contra* Filmer's general thesis that this was no mere appearance but a God-given reality for all time. However, arguing that patriarchal monarchy was not what it seemed then turned out to be a rather difficult task for Locke, in terms of evidence, and it also posed a problem vis-à-vis his theory of "express consent." His theory of "express consent" was a defining feature of the "perfect member" (2.119), that is to say, the marriageable householder, of his political society. In so far as Locke could solve his problems, he did so by again contrasting a different type of dominant masculinity of which he approved—the kindly father—with Filmer's "warrior" absolutism—which he was at pains to reject.

For Locke there was a masculinity of fatherhood that is gendered just as much masculine as feminine, and distinctly different from Filmer's "warrior" absolutism. Jointly as parents both men and women were said by Locke to have a similar authority to match their duty of care. It was, however, a power tempered with "suitable inclinations of tenderness and concern" for "the children's good" (2.63). Moreover, the power of fathers and mothers over children was temporary: "The bonds of this subjection are like the swaddling clothes they [i.e. babies] are wrapped up in, and supported by, in the weakness of their infancy" (2.55). Thus the "subjection of a minor places in the father a temporary government, which terminates with the minority of the child. . . . The nourishment and education of their children is a charge so incumbent on parents for their children's good, that nothing can absolve them from taking care of it" (2.67). Locke's portrait of the kindly father thus presents a contrast with its opposite, the Filmerian patriarch, imbued with "absolute, unlimited power" (2.61): "And therefore God Almighty when he would express his gentle dealing with the Israelites, he tells them, that though he chastened them, 'he chastened them as a man chastens his son' (Deut. viii. 5)—*i.e.*, with tenderness and affection—and kept them under no severer discipline than what was absolutely best for them, and had been less kindness to have slackened" (2.67).

Locke relied on a classical image of dominant masculinity that was not overtly in the warrior mode, namely the "nursing" father as lawgiver (2.110)—Moses, Lycurgus, Solon, and Numa Pompilius were the usual models. In the scholarship and literature of the time they were seen as carers for "their" peoples. Locke had no difficulties idealizing classical and Old Testament rulership when he could make it wise and kindly, because he saw it as functioning within the God-given moral frame, through which God's property in human life was preserved and promoted. However, he objected to the (presumed) Filmerian idealization of ruler-ship as fatherly and *absolute*, seeing absolute power as nothing to God's purpose and quite against reason. Filmer's patriarchalism thus promoted the wrong kind of masculinity, falsely identifying the fatherly role with the untrammeled powers of a "wild beast, or noxious brute." Men who behave in that way, even in war, are not welcome in Locke's moral uni-verse (2.177–80).

When Locke dealt with the historical problem of (apparently) patriar-chal monarchy, he shifted his ground on consent very considerably. "Ex-press consent" is the "actual agreement" and "express declaration" that binds all who make it "perpetually and indispensably" to the government (2.121) and makes each of them a "perfect member" (2.119) of the com-munity. But in archaic times the very consent that instituted legitimate rulership was (paradoxically) so utterly tacit as to be virtually impercepti-ble to the parties giving and receiving it: "Thus, whether a family by degrees grew up into a commonwealth, and the fatherly authority being continued on to the elder son, everyone in his turn growing up under it, tacitly submitted to it, and the easiness and quality of it not offending anyone, everyone acquiesced, till time seemed to have confirmed it, and settled a right of succession by prescription" (2.110).

That argument merely justified patriarchal rule by consent, but did not catch what was for Locke the point behind consent and legitimacy in the first place, namely "All for the public good" (2.131). To bring that in, but in the archaic context, he needed to add something further about the kind of fathers he had in mind: "Without such nursing fathers tender and careful of the public weal, all governments would have sunk under the weakness and infirmities of their infancy; and the prince and the people had soon perished together" (2.110). That way of forming legiti-mate government was ascribed to a distant but happy past when in simple societies "the people" moved effortlessly from filial obedience to political obligation, because of the excellent ministrations of their "nursing fathers." Those legitimated rulers presumably noted the difference be-tween one role and another, namely, their role as father with respect to children, and their role as magistrate with respect to consenting adults. Locke's "nursing fathers" were thus model males, not just fatherly, but fatherly in the right way. From the children's point of view such a father sustains them with his care and brings them up with a "tenderness for them all" (2.75). In the past those men had been so thoroughly accepted as excellent fathers, husbands, and heads of household that they were then ultra-tacitly legitimized as ruler-magistrates, a sequence that Locke said he could not then recommend to a more corrupt age, as material temptations for both sides were so much more prevalent (2.111).

Unfortunately, though, ultra-tacit consent of that sort makes Locke's concept of express consent—the only consent that makes one a "perfect member" (full citizen) of a modern community (2.119)—even more mysterious than it already is, as notoriously Locke never really envisions a practical process through which such contracts among "men" are drawn up and executed. Indeed, Locke himself was somewhat mystified about what counted as express and what counted as tacit in his imagined historical situation: "since without some government it would be hard for them [i.e. a family] to live together, it was likeliest it [i.e. some government] should, by the *express or tacit* consent of the children, be in the father" (2.74; emphasis added).

How can the consent that makes one a "perfect member" be an express declaration as a matter of principle (self-imposed obligation), and also an unstated understanding (which, being unstated, would not necessarily be the same for everyone)? The explicit and usual concept of tacit consent in Locke was really quite different in function and form. Tacit consent, as Locke explained in detail (2.119, 122), was very much parasitic on an existing "political society," and it could only arise when a binding obligation has been expressly incurred on the part of some "men" to be "concluded by the majority" (2.96). Those merely enjoying even minimal advantages of the life, liberty, and property that legitimate government secured, without consenting expressly, were then obliged to obey it, and were said to have consented tacitly. That, of course, did not give them the same status as "perfect members," although the obligations may apparently be similar.

How then could another form of tacit consent also flow from "the people" (namely, adult sons in the primitive familial society) to their erstwhile father, such that he was legitimized as magistrate in the imperceptible way that Locke wanted, and such that they became "perfect members" of a "political society"? Obviously there are two kinds of tacit consent at work here: tacit-express (an ultra-tacit consent in relation to "nursing fathers")" and tacit-tacit (a mere use of facilities in relation to political societies that have already been formed). Intriguingly, express consent and tacit-tacit consent occur in the *apparently* de-gendered narrative. Tacit-express consent occurs in an *overtly gendered* narrative concerned with "nursing fathers" who are legitimized as magistrate-monarchs. The "nursing" father version of dominant masculinity canceled out the need for marriageable males to make an explicit declaration of obligation to be "concluded" by the majority, which could then devolve government by majority decision to a smaller body or to an individual person. In Locke's view, the "sons" of the archaic era were evidently not up to making that kind of "rational" declaration in favor of a bureaucratic ruler who would act as magistrate. Rather, the kindly father salvaged the nexus between consent and legitimacy for all times, by contrast with the Filmerian patriarchy of absolute rule by a "warrior."

Locke's text was not, even in part, about genderless values (relating anyone and everyone equally to the "public good"). Rather, those values were expressed in his text through the construction of different dominant masculinities (along with their subordinate "others"). In the archaic world Lockean masculinity for rulers was that of the "nursing" father, tender and solicitous. In his modern world, Locke's preferred masculinity for rulers was rational/bureaucratic and contractual/commercial. In both worlds Locke's residual patriarchalism was effected through a unified portrait of fathers, husbands, and householders that mingled both those masculinities together. Fatherhood was more tender than contractual; husbandhood more contractual than commercial; and householding more contractual/commercial than tender. In none of those roles, however, was a Filmerian, tyrannical "warrior" male in evidence, holding absolute and arbitrary power over the very lives of children, wives, servants, and fellow citizens.

Thus Locke's principles of equality, articulated explicitly between men and women, and between some men and other men, were made to fit into a politics of preexisting masculinities. Locke was concerned to theorize society and politics that way round. Many of his readers, feminists especially, have been concerned to drive the argument in reverse, and to use the principles of equality to re-envision and reform the social relationships that Locke conceptualized as conjugal, parental, household and political. Given that feminists have an interest in just that kind of politics, it follows that overtly gendered narratives of masculinities, such as those that Locke reinforced as foundational, are very much an issue. All of the issues that Locke raised are issues today for men, as well as women, not because they are "male" issues in some sense, but because there are issues concerning how to perform properly in these relationships that turn on the different ways that dominant masculinities are defined.

Locke's *Two Treatises*: De-gendered Narratives

It is evident from the foregoing analysis that Locke's *Two Treatises* contain overtly gendered narratives about women and men, and about men and women, and that these narratives perform important tasks:

1. They disrupt patriarchal absolutism in marital relations, parenthood, householding, and rulership.
2. They explain away the problem of legitimate yet apparently patriarchal monarchy through tacit-express consent to "nursing fathers" in a happier age.
3. They subordinate women/wives/mothers/daughters in marriage, family, household, and political society through residual patriarchy.

Why then did Locke construct an *apparently* de-gendered narrative at all? The apparently de-gendered narrative in Locke fits with his ringing announcements of equality between "men," and his egalitarian line of attack on (his version of) Filmer's patriarchalism. His objections to patriarchalism were twofold: it empowered some *politically* through birth alone (via the supposed grant of kingship by God to Adam), and it misdefined *power* (as absolute and arbitrary, hence tyrannical and despotic). Locke's objections to absolute and arbitrary power were that it was not by definition morally framed within the public good, and that it did not involve some notion of consent from the governed as guarantor of this end. Both those were required by Locke to make government legitimate, and he spelled that out through his view that political power arises only when "men" have "made a community by the consent of every individual," wherein "the majority have a right to act and conclude the rest" (2.95).

The apparently de-gendered narrative tracks Locke's egalitarianism when he deployed it (at certain points) in discussing rulership, householding, parenthood, and marriage, and within those terms humanity appears, for a time, in a de-gendered light. Those parts of Locke's text have thus been useful for promoting egalitarianism of all kinds, as his general statements appear to cancel forms of entrenched discrimination.

Indeed, that is what makes his principles so attractive to liberals and democrats, including feminists. Whether Locke ever meant his text to be used in such ways is, of course, not the issue. His egalitarianism can simply be excerpted and turned to other purposes. One way of doing this was its appropriation by liberal feminists. Within the feminist literature that reading was then taken two ways: one emphasized the extent to which liberal egalitarianism was *covertly gendered*, because the overtly gendered narratives of women and men had not been critically interrogated;[24] the other emphasized the extent to which liberal egalitarianism could be used to produce genuine *gender equality*, because gendered relationships could be reformulated in theory and practice.[25]

Chapters 2–5 of the *Second Treatise* are consistent, so far as I can tell, in being *apparently* de-gendered. Locke uses "man" and "mankind" with reference to activities from which it is inconceivable to imagine excluding women. He said, *inter alia*, that "men" are "all the workmanship of one omnipotent, and infinitely wise Maker," and that the law of nature "obliges everyone" that "no one ought to harm another" (2.6). Given Locke's doctrinal and social background, it would seem that "men," "all," and "everyone" includes women in this originary moral frame. A category such as "thief" (2.18) was also surely de-gendered for Locke (to a point, anyway), and conversely he specifically cited the Old Testament Hebrews and their Judges, of which Deborah was a well-known example, in support of his concept of authority (2.21). Indeed he did this even more extensively in the *First Treatise* (1.163, 164), where his highly approving argument was that their authority had been neither monarchical in function nor hereditary in succession, but rather just the sort of authority— that of the legitimate magistrate—that he was concerned to promote over and against Filmer's patriarchal absolutism. This is not to say that Locke was imagining that women were included in all these activities on exactly the same terms as men. My point is not about Locke as some kind of protofeminist *malgré lui*, but about the kind of narrative that is apparently consistent with gender equality and can be selectively appropriated as such.[26] Ever adept at inconsistency, however, Locke tried to argue his way out of any difficulties without reconciling the contradictions that arise in his transitions between overtly gendered narratives and apparently de-gendered ones. Very similar strategies are at work in the constitutional, legislative, and judicial gender politics that feminists are familiar with today.

Even without the overt stimulus of a gendered theory from Filmer's relentless patriarchalism, gender would have played a huge and crucial role in Locke's thinking. That is because a theory of government must present a view of the community, acknowledging reproduction, parenthood, marriage, infant care, age-of-majority, householding, and inheritance in respect of "the people," not least in order to argue that political relationships are similar to, or different from, certain other relationships (Locke mentions father/children, master/servant, husband/wife, lord/slave), and to draw out similarities and differences accordingly (2.2). This is very much what Locke's text is about. In feminist terms, however, Locke's theory is masculinized, because it presents gendered relationships overtly for the wrong reasons (to get at Filmer), rather than for the right reasons (to present a nuanced conception of the activities essential within a polity). Moreover, Locke's theory is based on overt assertions of male superiority and female subordination. These define away the apparent equality of persons that he initially announces, and amount to a residual patriarchalism. That residual patriarchalism fits with Locke's versions of dominant masculinity (competitive, acquisitive, individualistic, but also tender, caring and solicitous), with his rejection of Filmer's alternative (absolute power in a regal male), his relegation of various male "others" to subordinate masculinities, and with his consignment of women to feminine subordination as such.

What is interesting for our purposes is that Locke's *apparently* de-gendered discourse of civil equality survived the intellectual and political confrontation with Filmerian patriarchy and served so well in another, namely that pursued by women in gaining rights in the political community equal to those of men, or perhaps more accurately, still trying to gain such rights in full. *Apparently* de-gendered discourse can be read in ways consistent with the sexual egalitarianism that many feminists have advocated, but it can also be read in ways consistent with the traditional gender hierarchies that Locke residually favored. The latter strategy defined "mainstream/malestream" political theory, precisely because, as with Locke, the gendered hierarchies of the domestic sphere were read back (overtly and covertly) into the *apparently* de-gendered world of the polity. Given the prevalent characterization of women as essentially domestic (wife/mother/daughter), it supposedly followed that persons in the public realm were "men" (though not husbands/fathers/sons as such).

Locke's narratives are universally inscribed into any understanding of liberal democracy. An egalitarian politics based on *apparently* de-gendered language like his is inadequate, in my view, unless it includes an account of reproduction, infant care, age-of-majority, parenthood, marriage, inheritance, householding, and the other important relationships from which gender in the community is constructed, and through which sex and sexuality become political. For a realization of gender equality, these relationships would all have to be reconceptualized along egalitarian lines, taking sex and sexuality into account, as indeed many feminists, gay theorists, and some men's studies writers have tried to do. Otherwise, inegalitarian assumptions start to leak back into the very definitions of the terms that are being used to conceptualize equality, and issues about power in community relationships do not get properly addressed. Indeed, it becomes impossible for anyone to make good sense of the egalitarian principles or policies that are proposed, because on the whole democratic egalitarianism addresses so few issues (bracketing off so much as "private") and offers such a limited identity (the genderless "citizen"). Existing gendered hierarchies of power are often only *apparently* disengaged by egalitarian claims, which is why "mainstream/malestream" liberals still produce texts that are far too much like Locke's. Turning the "gender lens" onto men and masculinities exposes crucial points at which residual patriarchy subverts egalitarian principles by deploying narratives of dominant masculinities in order to subordinate some men to other men, and women to men generally. This analysis suggests that a broad coalitional politics of gender egalitarianism is possible over and above the sexual binary through which feminism has generally been constructed.

Notes

1. The feminist literature on these issues is very large. With respect to Locke the foundational account is Carole Pateman, *The Sexual Contract* (Cambridge: Polity Press; Stanford: Stanford University Press, 1988). For some recent studies that I have found useful, see Mary Lyndon Shanley, "Marriage Contract and Social Contract in Seventeenth Century English Political Thought," in *The Family in Political Thought*, ed. Jean Bethke Elshtain (Amherst: University of Massachusetts Press, 1982); Sharon Cooney, "A Revolution in the Household: Locke's Reconstitution of the Family" (paper presented at the annual meeting of the American Political Science Association, Chicago, 1995); Peter C. Myers, "Locke on the Constitution of the Liberal Family" (paper presented at the annual meeting of the American Political Science Association, Washington, D.C., 1997).

2. Harry Brod, "Introduction" and "The Case for Men's Studies," in *The Making of Masculinities: The New Men's Studies*, ed. Brod (Winchester, Mass.: Allen & Unwin, 1987), 1–18, 39–62; Jeff Hearn, *The Gender of Oppression: Men, Masculinity and the Critique of Marxism* (Brighton: Wheatsheaf, 1987).

3. Peter Filene, "The Secrets of Men's History," in Brod, *Making of Masculinities*, 103–20; R. W.

Connell, *Gender and Power: Society, the Person and Sexual Politics* (Cambridge: Polity Press, 1987), and *Masculinities* (Cambridge: Polity Press, 1995); Jeff Hearn and David Collinson, "Unities and Differences between Men and between Masculinities," in *Theorizing Masculinities*, ed. Harry Brod and Michael Kaufmann (Newbury Park, Calif.: Sage, 1994), 97–118; Tim Edwards, *Erotics and Politics: Gay Male Sexuality, Masculinity and Feminism* (London: Routledge, 1994); Lynne Segal, *Slow Motion: Changing Masculinities, Changing Men* (London: Virago, 1990); Marysia Zalewski and Jane Parpart, eds., *The "Man" Question in International Relations* (Boulder, Colo.: Westview Press, 1998).

4. For a detailed discussion of these points, see Terrell Carver, "'Public Man' and the Critique of Masculinities," *Political Theory* 24, no. 4 (1996): 673–78.

5. Ibid., 676–79.

6. Terrell Carver, *Gender Is Not a Synonym for Women* (Boulder, Colo.: Lynne Rienner, 1996), 32–36.

7. Gordon J. Schochet discusses varieties of seventeenth-century patriarchalism, and hence gives a critical view of Locke's account of their theories, in his *Patriarchalism in Political Thought: The Authoritarian Family and Political Speculation and Attitudes Especially in Seventeenth-Century England* (Oxford: Blackwell, 1975).

8. John Locke, *Two Treatises of Government*, ed. Mark Goldie (London: J. M. Dent, 1993), 2.4–5.

9. This definition is discussed in Carver, *Gender Is Not a Synonym for Women*, 1–2.

10. Judith Butler, *Gender Trouble: Feminism and the Subversion of Identity* (London: Routledge, 1990), 16–34.

11. Terrell Carver, "Gender," in *Political Theory and the Concept of Politics*, ed. Richard Bellamy and Andrew Mason (Manchester: Manchester University Press, 2002). This is also discussed in Terrell Carver, "Sexual Citizenship: Gendered and De-gendered Narratives," in *Politics of Sexuality: Identity, Gender, Citizenship*, ed. Terrell Carver and Véronique Mottier (London: Routledge, 1998), 13–24, and in Terrell Carver, "A Political Theory of Gender: Perspectives on the Universal Subject," in *Gender, Politics and the State*, ed. Vicky Randall and Georgina Waylen (London: Routledge, 1998), 18–28.

12. Connell, *Masculinities*, 143–63; Jonathan Ned Katz, *The Invention of Heterosexuality* (New York: Dutton, 1995).

13. Monique Wittig, *The Straight Mind and Other Essays* (London: Harvester/Wheatsheaf, 1992).

14. For a study that defines and deploys this concept, see David T. Evans, *Sexual Citizenship* (London: Routledge, 1993).

15. See Goldie's bibliographical note in the glossary of his edition of Locke, *Two Treatises of Government*, 243.

16. See, for example, Richard Ashcraft, *Revolutionary Politics and Locke's "Two Treatises of Government"* (Princeton: Princeton University Press, 1986).

17. Schochet, *Patriarchalism in Political Thought*, 1–4.

18. Carver, "'Public Man,'" 679–82.

19. These issues are discussed in Mary Astell, *Some Reflections on Marriage* [1700], in *Perspectives on the History of British Feminism, The Wives: The Rights of Married Women*, ed. Marie Mulvey Roberts and Tamae Mizuta (London: Routledge/Thoemmes Press, 1994), 1–98.

20. John Guy, *Tudor England* (Oxford: Oxford University Press, 1988; repr., 1991), 226–49, 250–52, 268–71, 282–83.

21. Connell, *Masculinities*, 67–86.

22. Jean Bethke Elshtain, *Public Man/Private Woman: Women in Social and Political Thought*, 2nd ed. (Princeton: Princeton University Press, 1993), 100–131; Connell, *Masculinities*, 185–203; Charlotte Hooper, *Manly States: Masculinities, International Relations and Gender Politics* (New York: Columbia University Press, 2001), 64–76.

23. John Dunn, *The Political Thought of John Locke: An Historical Account of the Argument of the "Two Treatises of Government"* (Cambridge: Cambridge University Press, 1969), 131–47.

24. Pateman, *Sexual Contract*.

25. Zillah R. Eisenstein, *The Radical Future of Liberal Feminism* (New York: Longman, 1981; reprint, Boston: Northeastern University Press, 1986).

26. It is, of course, a further and much debated question whether gender neutrality is really possible and indeed, if it is, whether it would be desirable.

7

Recovering Locke's Midwifery Notes

Joanne H. Wright

The feminist literature on John Locke focuses on his political and, to a lesser extent, philosophical writings. These focal points are obviously warranted, for he is best known for his innovations in social contract theory and epistemology, and for advancing the cause of religious tolera-

Several people have given helpful comments at various stages of this article. My thanks to Gordon Schochet and John Sainsbury for their early suggestions; to David Bedford, Ross Rudolph, Donald Wright, Leah Bradshaw, and Ingrid Makus for their thorough readings; and to Christine Saulnier and Krista Hunt for their comments on an earlier version of this paper given at the Atlantic Provinces Political Science Association Meetings in St. John's, Newfoundland. Finally, my thanks to the editors of this volume for their helpful feedback.

tion. But there is also something to be gained by exploring Locke's extensive medical writings. Although he never received an M.D., Locke was a practicing physician, and medicine was one of the most enduring of his intellectual passions.[1] Of particular interest here are his notes on the subject of midwifery, which are dispersed throughout his medical journals and his correspondence. While early modern historians have identified an increase in the number of writings on midwifery during the latter part of the seventeenth century, particularly by men, Locke's notes are not counted as part of this trend because they were not published during his lifetime.[2] Indeed, his notes have been all but neglected by early modern historians and medical historians alike.

Locke's interest in medicine constituted a life-long pursuit.[3] From the extensive medical papers held in the Lovelace Collection at the Bodleian Library it is clear that he began to keep medical journals in the late 1650s while he was still at Oxford and that he continued to do so throughout his life.[4] Decades later, during his last years, he maintained a small medical practice in the town nearest to Oates, the residence of Lady Damaris (Cudworth) and Sir Francis Masham and home to Locke from 1691 to 1704.[5] While it is difficult to date precisely the beginnings of Locke's thoughts and writings on midwifery, his interest in the subject of reproduction is evident in the earliest of his medical commonplace books. In a book dating from about 1658, Locke took extensive notes on the "ovist" theory of human reproduction—which posits the existence of a preformed fetus in the female egg—from William Harvey's *Exercitationes de Generatione Animalium*.[6] By 1669, Locke was being consulted regularly—often by correspondence—for his advice on midwifery and infant care, advice that he continued to provide to friends and acquaintances for the rest of his life. In about 1695, Locke also wrote a short tract containing some of his ideas on the practice of midwifery that was published in 1954 by his primary medical biographer, Kenneth Dewhurst.[7] Locke's interest in midwifery was both scholarly and practical, and it extended throughout the better part of his medical career.

Debate persists over Locke's significance as a medical scholar and practitioner.[8] To some his "discoveries were negligible and his medicinal remedies . . . eccentric."[9] Patrick Romanell suggests that Locke might have been more discriminating in his choices of what to record in his voluminous medical notes, finding them copious to a fault.[10] Of course, it is unlikely that Locke agreed with the efficacy of every remedy or "physic" of which he made note, or that he accepted at face value the often bizarre medical accounts and anecdotes relayed to him by friends and acquaintances. But as G. G. Meynell rightly points out, even the more unusual entries should not be dismissed, for they are "a record of folk medicine or general experience written down at a time when no one knew what was important and what was not." In this sense, part of Locke's medical legacy is to have left behind these repositories of information—these microhistories—on the ideas and practices surrounding medical care in the late seventeenth century.[11]

Among the topics covered in the notes, midwifery is of greatest relevance to scholars interested in Locke's assumptions about gender. Part of my purpose in this chapter is expository: to recover Locke's notes on midwifery and to situate them within the contemporary English discourses on midwifery. As microhistories, Locke's notes on midwifery patch together his own opinions, along with those of his contemporaries, on a range of interconnected issues and practices: pregnancy, labor and delivery, maternity, and the care and feeding of infants, including breastfeeding and wet-nursing. Then, as now, discussions about midwifery and choices in infant feeding are imbued with political meaning; embedded within these discussions are a host of assumptions about the tension between midwifery and obstetrical medicine, the roles and meanings attached to maternity and infancy, and by extension, the nature and purpose of the family.

As a thinker, Locke both contributed to, and was writing on the cusp of, significant changes in the ideas about the family. Susan Moller Okin and Ruth Perry observe an eighteenth-century rise in sentimental rhetoric surrounding the family, on the one hand, and increased levels of ideological remuneration associated with motherhood, on the other. In her examination of seventeenth- and eighteenth-century thinkers on the family, Okin positions Locke as decidedly presentimental as compared to later thinkers such as Rousseau.[12] In "Colonizing the Breast," Perry uses attitudes and practices surrounding maternal breastfeeding and wet-nursing as indicators of the degree to which motherhood is viewed in sentimental terms. Perry argues that it was not until the mid-eighteenth century that motherhood was cloaked in the language of sentimentality and obligation. Prior to the mid-eighteenth century, in her view, there was an absence of obligatory rhetoric connected to maternal breastfeeding in Britain where wet-nursing was the common and accepted practice, at least among the upper classes.[13] Locke's status as a late-century writer raises the questions: Where do his notions about the family reside on the historical continuum of ideas about the family? Can we detect in his writings evidence of a shift toward sentimental notions of maternity?

In his political writings, Locke's conception of the family is not fully elaborated. Certainly, feminists are in general agreement that Locke is the clearest and perhaps earliest exponent of a gendered, (proto)liberal public/private dichotomy.[14] Moreover, his notion of the contractual matrimonial union represents a milestone in historical conceptions of the family.[15] Still, where Locke discusses the family, what he presents is not so much a *theory* of the family as an instrumental argument against the constitutional doctrine of patriarchalism. For seventeenth-century political writers, the family serves as an important analogy—or in Locke's case, a counterpoint—for the relations of the political sphere.[16] What he says about the family in this context may not represent his actual views or preferences on the subject.[17] In contrast, his notes and correspondence on midwifery provide a fresh source of material from which we can glean some of his assumptions about the family in a context that is set apart from his strategic argument against Sir Robert Filmer.

Upon examination, Locke's assumptions about the practices of wet-nursing and maternal breastfeeding found in his midwifery writings substantiate and enhance Okin's thesis. More than this, when Locke is compared with his contemporaries, the picture that emerges is that of a political philosopher and medical practitioner who is not only detached from the emerging discourse of sentimentality but stands distinctly outside and apart from the rise in rhetoric about proper maternal roles. Locke's notion of the family appears to be neither sentimental nor fully contractualist, but rather, traditionally hierarchical, oriented to propagating the human species and the passing down of property, and thus in keeping with aristocratic customs of the period.[18]

Introduction to Locke's Midwifery Notes

Locke's forays into the field of midwifery are connected with some of the most important relationships and events in his career, including his relationships with the first earl of Shaftesbury, and the English Hippocrates, Thomas Sydenham, and his experience of living in exile in Holland. Locke became acquainted with Lord Anthony Ashley Cooper, later the Earl of Shaftesbury, through Ashley's physician, David Thomas, who conducted experiments in medical chemistry with Locke. Locke subsequently joined the Cooper household as Lord Ashley's physician and, later, his personal secretary.[19] At Shaftesbury's behest, Locke assisted the Coopers in securing a third-generation heir to the title by finding a suitable marriage partner for the future second earl.[20] The woman who became Shaftesbury's daughter-in-law, Lady Dorothy (Manners) Cooper, was one of the many friends and acquaintances Locke advised on pregnancy, birth, and the care of infant children. Locke was particularly esteemed in this regard among members of the Cooper family after he assisted Lady Dorothy following her miscarriage in 1669.[21] He then saw her through her subsequent pregnancy and attended her confinement, an event that was customarily attended exclusively by midwives and a small community of women friends and family.[22] The care that he was asked to provide for Shaftesbury's grandson following the birth, along with the many other associations he had with the children of his colleagues and friends, particularly Mary and Edward Clarke, gave Locke a unique opportunity as a bachelor to experience infants and children firsthand and to develop his own theories concerning how they should best be treated and cared for.[23] His ideas on this subject constitute his essay *Some Thoughts Concerning Education*.

It was through his formative association with Shaftesbury that Locke made the acquaintance of the physician Thomas Sydenham. Sydenham was considered a medical heretic for his revival of the Hippocratic method of empirical observation in his clinical practice and for challenging the orthodoxy of orienting medical training around the study of natural philosophy and anatomy.[24] Sydenham prescribed treatment for disease from "his own carefully observed natural history of a patient's illness."[25] Locke accompanied Sydenham on his rounds, most notably when he was treating smallpox victims, recorded his observations in his medical notebooks, and collaborated with Sydenham on several essays.[26] Sydenham's influence is evident throughout Locke's medical notes.

In 1683, Locke sought political exile from England because of his association with the highly controversial politics of Shaftesbury.[27] In his six years of Dutch exile, he was sheltered by several Dutch physicians and participated in an informal, elite circle of Dutch medical men called the Collegium Privatum.[28] Here he learned a great deal from the members of his "private medical college" about midwifery and the "diseases of women," as this was an area of medicine in which his Dutch colleagues were highly regarded.[29] He took notes on tumors of the breast, abnormalities of menstruation, discharges before and after childbirth, the retention of afterbirth, pains after birth, and the treatment of the newly born.[30] Locke kept a separate medical journal recording his observations from this period, and over two-thirds of it is devoted to this branch of medicine.[31]

Examining Locke's Midwifery Notes

Pregnancy and childbirth were precarious experiences in seventeenth-century England. Becoming pregnant necessarily meant a confrontation with the possibility of death. In "A Child-Bed Womans Funeral Oration," Margaret Cavendish, Duchess of Newcastle, laments the unequal distribution of pain and suffering in reproduction: "Women do not only indure the Extremity of Pain in Child-birth, but in Breeding, the Child being for the most part Sick, and seldom at Ease; Indeed, Nature seems both Unjust and Cruel to her Femal Creatures." The woman who dies in child-bed is happy, she asserts, because "she Lives not to Indure more Pain or Slavery."[32] Although the maternal mortality rate has been estimated at only 1 percent for each birth, or 6 or 7 percent over the course of a woman's childbearing years, as Linda Pollock points out, "childbirth was a very conspicuous *single* cause of mortality and a fate which a prospective mother had several long months to contemplate."[33] Moreover, women calculated their risk, not with statistics, but with anecdotal evidence of the dangers; from early on in their lives, girls knew of women who had died in childbirth or had become ill afterward.[34]

That early modern pregnancy and childbirth were associated with a high degree of risk is evident in Locke's notes and letters. For example, in a letter to his friend Mary Clarke, wife of Edward Clarke, Locke wishes her well in her upcoming delivery: "Look you to yourself [and to the] great belly, which I desire you may lay down with as little danger and [trouble] as may be. As to any other concernment of your health there is nothing else now to be considered or meddled with. I hope I shall now speedily have news that you are well delivered of a lusty boy, and after that we will talk of other matters."[35] The hope for a boy is common in Locke's correspondence[36]—despite his obvious affection for the girl children of his friends—and it is typical for the upper classes of seventeenth-century England. Indeed, the desire to produce male heirs meant that, among the upper classes at least, great emphasis was placed on childbearing in general and the bearing of sons in particular.[37]

Not only does Locke wish Mary Clarke physical well-being, he is also attentive to her state of mind. The rest of the letter is a reassurance that her older daughter, who is staying with Locke at the Masham household, is well and loved and that her mother ought not to be concerned with anything else but her own health. Pregnancy often brought about a degree of melancholy in women as they contemplated what lay ahead.[38] Locke acknowledges these worries but certainly does not indulge them. Whereas some women would carry precautionary measures to an extreme, confining themselves to their chambers to await delivery,[39] Locke did not recommend excessive pampering or special precautions for most pregnant women. He is particularly skeptical of the practices of women "of quality" whose bodies are "kept lazy and without exercise," as compared to the "poor and labouring country women" who have a much lower rate of miscarriage in his view. For Locke's contemporaries, every pregnancy was susceptible to miscarriage,[40] but it seems that for Locke the pathology was not pregnancy itself but the measures that some women adopted in response to it. In his midwifery notes, he writes: "If she be with child let her not doe as is usual with women of condition shut herself up in her chamber for fear of miscarrying much less confine her self to her bed. This makes the body and spirits weak which is one great cause of miscarrage. . . . For the minde being kept in a constant apprehension of miscarrage every the least occasion turne that apprehension into a viall fright."[41] He recommends, very much in keeping with twenty-first-century advice, that a woman with child "continue her ordinary course of living and exercise as if she were not[,] without any apprehension."[42] Of course, everything in moderation: women should exercise moderately, drink little, and eat bland food. While society may have thought it normal for women of leisure to be "perfectly idle and lazy for ten months together," Locke implies that they would do well to, in effect, follow the course of "poor labouring people" and remain physically active. Since their class status relieves them of the work of necessity, they ought to replace actual work with "moderate exercise especially in the open air."[43]

In the instance where a woman has miscarried before, he gives specific instructions for venesection, or bloodletting, to be carried out just before the point of her previous miscarriage. Furthermore, "the same remedie of bleeding must be used in the same method if she finds the child at any time bustling and disordered," or if there has been a fright or fall that might lead to miscarriage.[44] Bleeding was a common remedy and was thought to relieve the body of the bad humors that were the source of fever, pain, and infectious disease. Lady Dorothy Cooper was bled immediately upon presentation of the signs of a second miscarriage (Locke having assisted her in her first). Beyond this, his treatment was essentially noninterventionist. Following Sydenham's advice, "nothing was done, but everything left to nature."[45] Locke's effective supervision of Lady Cooper was rewarded with the birth of the future third earl of Shaftesbury and with praise from the maternal grandmother, Lady Rutland, who believed Locke's midwifery care helped in "safely bringing that noble familie so hopefull an heire."[46]

Locke's noninterventionist approach to pregnancy, labor, and delivery is connected to Sydenham's revival of Hippocratic medicine and the concomitant faith that, if permitted, nature would work its own cure. He is critical of midwives for what he perceives to be their overly interventionist methods of assisting birth and instructs them not to be "too busy with her [the laboring woman]." "Those [midwives] for the most part are meddling but ignorant women who think they must be doing something that they may not appear useless and unskillful."[47] In fact, contrary to what twenty-first-century readers might expect, male practitioners generally regarded themselves as less interventionist than traditional female midwives.[48] Writing in 1671, William Sermon warns midwives about "being over-hasty to busy themselves in matters they know not."[49] William Harvey shared this concern and felt that those women who were "delivered in private without . . . any midwife" fared better.[50] In his Dutch journals, Locke records the advice his colleagues offer to midwives: "At the onset of the birth pains. . . . Do not put the patient at once on her seat nor force her to give birth."[51] Locke himself worries that if the woman "be too forward to put herself into labour," and yields to the midwife's attempts to hasten the process, she will have wasted her energy prematurely and might not have enough left to see her through a safe delivery.[52] In a passage that is thoroughly noninterventionist, Locke asserts that "the natural birth is a work only of nature which only knows when the fruit of the womb is full ripe, and if it be let alone till that time it drops as it were of it self it is certain it comes easiest."[53] He advises a woman in labor to avoid succumbing to the first pains, and to "decline the thought and ways of being relieved" as long as she can.

Despite their noninterventionist approach to birth, early modern medical practitioners tended to see the female body as a site of disease and malfunction, a view stemming from suspicions about the female reproductive processes.[54] Not so for Locke: although we know that he either owned or knew of Mauriceau's *Treatise on the Diseases of Women in Pregnancy and Childbirth,* and while his notes contain sporadic references to bizarre cases such as the "virgin in whom a failure of menstruation was made up for by a nosebleeding at every monthly period,"[55] there is no evidence to suggest that he regarded the female body as particularly pathological. For Locke, childbirth was an entirely natural event that possessed its own pace and rhythm and that ought not to be interfered with. Labor and delivery are of obvious medical interest, and in that sense they are medicalized events, but they are not pathologized. Unlike his Dutch journals, which record from his Dutch colleagues countless remedies for the ailments and delays associated with birth and refer to the laboring woman as the "patient," Locke's own midwifery notes refer only to "women" and "breeding women."[56] If anything, Locke's writing on reproduction is rigorously dispassionate and devoid of obviously normative judgments regarding the "quality" of the female body.

In keeping with his view that childbirth ought to progress naturally, Locke harbored a certain skepticism about the practices and rituals surrounding seventeenth-century childbearing. In early modern England, childbirth was an entirely female affair. As labor began, the midwife was summoned along with the female relatives and neighbors—gossips—who were chosen by the mother-to-be to comfort and assist her during her confinement.[57] The gossips aided in the preparation of the lying-in room and might also physically support the woman during her delivery. Locke seems dubious. In his view, midwives possessed insufficient skill and the utility of gossips was questionable. "At the time of labour," he writes, "let not the room be crowded with useless women; so many and no more as will be of use to the woman in labour are all should be there; all the rest hurt and hinder one another and spoil the air of the room which is the great refreshment of the woman in labour."[58]

These comments hint at the often tense relationship between medicine and midwifery, and on this subject, Locke is an interesting study. By the early eighteenth century, there is a trend away from the use of women midwives and toward male midwives, particularly in the aristocracy.[59] This is a transformation which has been represented rather crudely by early feminist interpreters who suggested that early modern midwives were also witches, and that the witch-craze was a campaign to wrest control of obstetrics out of the hands of traditional female healers.[60] While we cannot ignore the history of men trying to obstruct women's participation in the healing professions,[61] or Locke's possible collusion in this effort, Locke's notes on midwifery provide but one example of how the transformation from midwifery to obstetrics was more complicated and subtle than it might have once seemed.[62]

An indication of this complexity can be found in Jane Sharp's *The Midwives Book*, published in 1671. The only female-authored English instructional guide to midwives, it defends the preeminence of midwives as birth attendants against the encroachment of male professionals. Sharp saw that male midwives and practitioners had an advantage in being permitted to study medicine in the universities and thus were equipped with a superior knowledge of anatomy. In Sharp's view, however, university training did not necessarily give birth attendants the best preparation for the work that they must carry out, for in fact "farther knowledge may be gain'd by a long and diligent practice, and be communicated to others of our own sex."[63] Sharp also recognized, however, as did her fellow midwife Elizabeth Cellier, that midwifery expertise was not uniform among their colleagues and that a more consistent approach to the practice of midwifery would be beneficial to midwives themselves and to the women they were assisting.[64] For this reason, Elizabeth Cellier sought to establish a college of midwifery to train and license midwives, but her bid was unsuccessful. Sharp's *The Midwives Book* was intended to counter medical superiority by disseminating the accumulated knowledge of midwifery practice and providing some anatomical grounding to her female colleagues.

Locke is not among the men who defined themselves as man-midwives, or *accoucheurs* as they were called; nevertheless, his writings and notes document the beginnings of a transformation in the ideas and practices surrounding childbirth. Locke's perspective on contemporary midwifery practice is undoubtedly a reflection of an emerging professionalization in medical practice and his own rejection of the kinds of holistic approaches and theories that would have been the mainstay of practicing midwives. Locke wanted to separate medical science from traditional medical art; as Dewhurst explains, "Locke preferred dull facts to the vaguely mystical medieval glamour which still veiled the medical art."[65] Again, this is a carry-over from Locke's clinical apprenticeship with Sydenham, in which experience and bedside observation were valued over "the rules of the art of medicine."[66] On the surface, Locke and Sharp share a commitment to experiential knowledge that can be gained only through bedside observation. However, Locke is critical of contemporary midwifery as an art—an art that had not subjected its hypotheses to rational clinical observation.[67] His is not a benign critique, and it is important to situate him in the context of the early modern medical professionals who asserted their own status by distancing themselves from "ignorant" practitioners of all kinds.[68] Among medical men there existed a strong (and at least implicitly gendered) bias in favor of professional, university training—from which women were excluded—and Locke would have been hard-pressed to avoid assimilating such a bias during his years at Oxford. However, Locke's critique is neither directed at midwives *as women*, nor is it directed at midwives primarily or exclusively.[69] In other words, Locke's objections to midwifery need to be seen, not simply as part of a patriarchal usurpation of obstetrical practice, but as part of a historical move toward professionalization, a trend in which midwives themselves had an interest.

But if Locke is critical of midwifery practice from a newly professional medical standpoint, this standpoint has no moral overtones. The dispassionate tone of Locke's writings is demonstrated once again by the complete lack of extraneous social commentary about mother, infant, midwife, attending women, or gossips. What is not present in Locke is the kind of systematic attack against midwives that Percival Willughby launches in his *Observations in Midwifery*.[70] Locke claims that the ways in which midwives assist (and relieve) women's labor are faulty and perhaps even dangerous, for "Nature cannot be much hastened at least safely in this work."[71] But unlike William Sermon, for example, Locke seems entirely uninterested in the moral character of the midwife. While Sermon goes to some length to describe the proper midwife as "mild, gentle, courteous, sober, chaste," and to instruct midwives not to "report anything whatsoever they hear or see in secret, in the person or house of whom they deliver,"[72] Locke's primary concerns are efficiency and practicality—the easiest and safest way for a woman to deliver a baby—and he has little interest in the social rituals and strictures surrounding birth. His approach may be a reflection of an instrumental approach to medical inquiry and a function of the emerging discourse of professionalization.

To grasp the significance of Locke's silence on the moral rectitude of the midwife, it is essential to understand the social monitoring role that the midwife (along with the gossips) played in early modern England. Midwives served two functions: to oversee the birth and to observe and possibly testify later as to the legitimacy of the child. In a society anxious to regulate women's sexuality and reproduction, a midwife had to take an oath swearing that no false charges of paternity would be made, no babies would be swapped or hidden, no infanticide would be committed, and that all babies would be baptized in the Anglican Church.[73] Gossips were present first and foremost to comfort and support the laboring woman, but they, too, served as witnesses for the subsequent baptism of the baby.[74] In denouncing the presence and overabundance of "useless" gossips, Locke is implicitly downplaying the importance of their social function to monitor the birth and observe the legitimacy of what went on in the lying-in room. Locke's apparent indifference to the regulation of the lying-in ritual is made more unusual by his emphasis on the transference of property through generations, a transference that depended on strict rules of legitimacy. Locke appears to confine his concern with legitimacy to the act of conception, believing that the propagation of the species ought to occur within the "security of the marriage bed."[75] His lack of commentary on the moral standing of midwives indicates that while he may not agree with their clinical practices, he does not view them as the objects of suspicion that some of his contemporaries did.

Locke's critique of midwifery may also be connected to his disagreement with the then common practice of swaddling babies. Swaddling was the final birth ritual, and it was carried out or at least supervised by the midwife. After the baby was delivered, severed from the umbilical cord and washed, it would be wrapped tightly "lest it should move its hands and feet too freely, and thereby distort the bones, which are yet very flexible."[76] Although the practice was widely endorsed by midwives and medical practitioners alike, it was not without controversy. As Patricia Crawford notes, swaddling limited movement and prevented easy contact between parents or nurse and baby; there was also concern about how frequently the baby was unwrapped and changed.[77] Locke seems to admire the practices of other cultures and historical periods more than his own: he refers to the people of the Gold Coast who leave their babies unrestricted "on the ground so that you see them dragging themselves along like kittens on four paws" which accounts for "why they walk earlier than European infants."[78] He also praises Spartan nurses who brought up children without swaddling them, and "whose limbs were well made, their faces very pleasant, they were not dainty feeders, but content with any food before them."[79] For Locke, it seems that swaddling falls into the category of unproven and untested interventions carried out by midwives, interventions that stand in the way of the infant's natural development.

In the end, Locke is critical of midwifery but his criticisms do not lead him to suggest that male attendance at births would be an obvious and better alternative, or that male attendance would produce necessarily superior results. The presence of the female midwife, at least at this point in history, is still assumed. What is evident in Locke is an early sense of the interprofessional rivalry that was to emerge later but is not yet fully articulated, at least in his writings.

Locke on Wet-Nursing, Maternity, and the Pre-sentimental Family

If Locke was writing on the cusp of significant changes in the ideas and practices surrounding childbirth, he is also a transitional figure on the continuum of ideas about the family. Following in Hobbes's contractualist footsteps, Locke introduces the notion of a revocable marriage contract as a similitude for the contractually negotiable trust between the people and their government. Unlike Hobbes, Locke asserted the relatively equal maternal share of parental authority in the family to undermine Filmer and the patriarchalist argument for absolute and undivided paternal rule. Given the historical association of women with the private sphere, feminists have an obvious interest in dissecting the relationships in the family and the assumptions that justify these relationships. But what more is known about Locke's perspective on the constitution of the family? What kinds of familial relationships does he envision? Because he was not a theorist of the family his political theory is silent on these questions. Yet his midwifery writings and correspondence are not; they offer some important clues. Particularly useful are Locke's ideas on infant feeding, for as Ruth Perry implies, the question of *who* feeds the child *what* is overlaid with assumptions about the configuration and nature of familial relationships. Perry's interest is in the eighteenth-century turn away from wet-nursing in rhetoric and in practice and toward an increased emphasis on maternal breastfeeding as a "serious duty and responsibility."[80] Maternity, she and Susan Moller Okin concur, was privatized, domesticated, and given the new shine of sentimentality. Nowhere is this articulated more explicitly that in Rousseau's *Emile*, in which he elaborates on the importance of maternal breastfeeding—for the rejuvenation of morals in society and ultimately, for the nation:

> Let mothers deign to nurse their children, morals will reform themselves, nature's sentiments will be awakened in every heart, the state will be repeopled. This first point, this point alone, will bring everything back together. The attraction of domestic life is the best counterpoison for bad morals. . . . [F]rom the correction of this single abuse would soon result a general reform; nature would soon have reclaimed all its rights. Let women once again become mothers, men will soon become fathers and husbands again.[81]

Perry bases her argument regarding the eighteenth-century rise in sentimental maternal rhetoric on her belief that such rhetoric is absent in the preceding century. She uses the discourses of the previous century—Locke's century—to show the differences in the "cultural climate surrounding childbearing and breast-feeding." Wet-nursing was, for all intents and purposes, beyond question, she suggests, and "the controversy about breast-feeding focused not on who nursed the child . . . but on whether or not breast-feeding was preferable to artificial feeding."[82]

However, the seventeenth century cannot be so easily categorized. Although wet-nursing was indeed prevalent, the cultural static surrounding it was anxious. Locke and his contemporaries worried about the potentially negative influence of wet nurses on their nurslings. Some of Locke's contemporaries supported the eradication of the practice altogether and pleaded for a return to maternal breastfeeding. In an important corrective to Perry's argument, Toni Bowers points to a significant seventeenth-century literature codifying "the ideal of the tender, noble, self-sacrificial, and ever-nurturant mother" in contrast to the neglectful and dangerous practices of mercenary nurses.[83] Indeed, the subject of infant feeding is frequently addressed in midwifery, medical, and conduct writing in the seventeenth century.

Where did Locke stand in the emerging discourse of sentimentality and maternal obligation? By friends and acquaintances, Locke was sought after for his ideas about infant feeding, including his belief that children should not be fed meat until the age of six and that they should avoid fruit altogether.[84] As to what an infant should eat following birth, Locke suggests recipes for purging the meconium—a spoonful of honey and nothing afterward for three or four hours, or syrup of violets with almond oil[85]—and he refers to the hand feeding of pap, an experimental practice of feeding babies a mixture of flour and water or other ingredients. In fact, his medical writings contain considerable detail about the consumption of particular foods, on the one hand, and the purging of the body, on the other. But Locke rarely mentions breastfeeding, nursing mothers, or breastmilk at a time when babies were typically breastfed for at least the first year or eighteen months of their lives.[86]

His silence on this subject stems from his assumption that breastfeeding is the job of a wet nurse. Wet-nursing was a common practice in seventeenth-century England, particularly among the wealthy and the middle class, but also for parish children, foundlings, and orphans.[87] Royalty employed live-in nurses, but this was not the norm; infants were typically sent out to live in the home of the wet nurse, sometimes even out of town.[88] Reasons against maternal breastfeeding included women's concerns about the demise of their appearance as a result of nursing and husbands' desires to produce more male heirs and to have their wives sexually available.[89] Sending the child out to nurse meant that a woman's fertility was not compromised by breastfeeding, and it circumvented the widely accepted prohibition on sexual relations with a nursing mother. Wet nurses would sometimes come to collect the child after its baptism, within a week of its birth, or arrangements would be made for the child to make the journey to the home of the nurse.[90]

Locke's writings clearly presuppose the presence of a wet nurse. Given that he corresponded and associated with women who could afford to hire wet nurses to breastfeed their children, this is not surprising. Lady Dorothy Cooper, it seems, left her infant son, the future third earl, in Locke's care while she traveled with her husband to the home of her parents in Belvoir following her mother's death. In a letter she expresses her gratitude to Locke "for your letter and kind account; and care of my Deare one."[91] In the same letter, she complains of her current state of pregnant discomfort and laments Locke's absence, presumably because he could have provided her with some relief. Although the question of how this child was being fed in the absence of its mother was never addressed, it is likely that Lady Dorothy employed a live-in wet nurse.

Locke does not explicitly state his views on the use of wet nurses, or on maternal breastfeeding. However, considering the degree of influence that Locke enjoyed as the Shaftesbury household physician—recall his attendance to Lady Dorothy's miscarriage and subsequent confinement, and Lady Dorothy's express wish to be nearer to Locke during her pregnancy—it is probable that if he advocated maternal breastfeeding, or if he seriously disagreed with the use of wet nurses, he would have made his views clear to Lady Dorothy. If he did have a preference in one direction or the other, it does not surface in his midwifery writings.

That he did not object strongly to the use of wet nurses is confirmed in his letters to the Clarkes. In an unusually humorous missive, Locke teases his correspondent, Mary Clarke, that he expects a letter from her more often than once each confinement, for this would be a letter "but once a year."[92] Significantly, a woman whose children were put out to nurse could expect a pregnancy each year. He proceeds in the letter to explain that he has no objection to her choice of wet nurse for her new daughter, Ann. "In a former letter to Mr Clarke I told you that there appeard noe reason to me to apprehend that your nurses being rickety when she was a child should make her milke lesse wholsome now if she be otherwise healthy and of a good constitution now."[93] Locke takes the business of wet-nursing to be a matter of practical interest only, and his primary concern seems to be with the nursling's health. He does not discourage the use of a wet nurse even in the instance where a child has not been thriving in one's care. In an earlier round of correspondence, this time to Edward Clarke, he describes how Mary Clarke has resolved to transfer the care of her first daughter, Elizabeth, from one wet nurse to another, "because the thriveing of the child since your last seeing of it, argues some neglect in the nurse before." No criticism of the outgoing wet nurse is offered except that she ought to have provided the child with more tenderness, and that "'tis agreed that Nurse Edeling has very litle or noe milk."[94] In a significant passage, Locke explains that the new nurse has plenty of milk, so "if sucking agrees with her there she may have it. [sic] and if Feeding does better Nurse Trent can doe that as well as the other."[95] Feeding here indicates hand-feeding, an approach that probably had been tried with Elizabeth at her birth, but unsuccessfully.[96] Hand-feeding was a dangerous practice as it provided insufficient nutrition, and the lives of many babies, including the son of James II, were endangered because of it.[97] Nevertheless, Locke endorses hand-feeding a four month-old infant over returning it to the care—and breast—of its mother. He concludes his discussion of the subject with the hope that "this resolution . . . will be of good successe to the child and in the meane time put both your mindes at rest haveing donne that which upon consideration was thought best and most reasonable to be don." Locke's advice notwithstanding, Elizabeth Clarke survived infancy.

Locke's apparent reluctance to endorse maternal breastfeeding, and his relative complacency about the use of wet nurses, must be seen as a reflection of the emphasis placed by the upper class upon the ideal of an annual pregnancy. Among women of high rank, annual pregnancy was an expectation throughout their childbearing years, owing primarily to the upper-class desire to produce male heirs. Anecdotally, annual pregnancy is documented in Locke's advice to Dorothy Cooper (who had miscarried once and borne two children in the span of two calendar years) and Mary Clarke (from whom he wishes a letter more frequently than at her annual confinement). In his journal, as well, Locke records the story of Alice (Guise) George, who lived to be one hundred and eight years old: "she was married at 30 and had 15 children viz 10 sons and 5 daughters baptized besides 17 miscarriages."[98] Alice George would have been an extreme, with thirty-two pregnancies in as many years after thirty as she was fertile. Still, her experience was in keeping with the trend; as Dorothy McLaren explains, "if a marriage contained twenty child-bearing years for a mother," an aristocratic woman "was at risk for twenty pregnancies."[99]

Significantly, annual pregnancy was possible only with the reliance on wet nurses. Upon the completion of the lying-in period and, having put her infant out to nurse, an aristocratic woman, like a "brood mare" was ready for another pregnancy.[100] When we connect Locke's midwifery writings to his political thought, it becomes apparent that the ideal of annual pregnancy is vitally connected for Locke to the project of multiplying the human species in general and to transferring property within families. The goal of increasing the human population was widely shared by early modern thinkers: it was nature's intent; it was God's intent; and it was thought to expand national wealth.[101] In keeping with his contemporaries, in his *First Treatise*, Locke connected the dictate to increase the human population to nature's purpose for men: "God Planted in Men a strong desire also of propagating their Kind, and continuing themselves in their Posterity, and this gives Children a Title, to share in the Property of their Parents, and a Right to Inherit their Possessions."[102] To multiply, and to hand down to your children their inheritance: these are the raisons d'étre of the conjugal union. Although contractually based and revocable in theory, the conjugal union is driven by a God-given and natural purpose to sustain itself beyond the birth of one child "because the Female is capable of conceiving, and *de facto* is commonly with child again, and Brings forth too a new Birth long before the former is out of a dependency for support on his Parents help."[103] In these passages, the connections are made clear between Locke's presumption of annual pregnancy and his concomitant tacit acceptance of the use of wet nurses, on the one hand, and his beliefs in the importance of propagating the species and the natural right of inheritance, on the other.

Although Locke does not object to the use of wet nurses, he does disparage them and their practices throughout his medical and educational writings. He criticizes them for some of the same reasons that he criticizes midwives: they are superstitious, ignorant, and interfere too much with nature. In *Some Thoughts Concerning Education*, Locke takes them to task for straight-lacing, a practice of binding children tightly to force their limbs to grow straight. Straight-lacing contravenes nature, Locke argues, and "busie People" including "ignorant Nurses" should abstain from "medling in a Matter they understand not."[104] Locke also worried about alcohol consumption in infants, drink "being the Lullaby used by Nurses, to still crying Children." He reports that "Mothers generally find some Difficulty to wean their Children from Drinking in the Night, when they first take them home."[105] Servants in general are a "mean Sort of People" who drink to excess themselves and thus are "narrowly to be watched, and most severely to be reprehended, when they transgress" and offer children strong liquor.[106]

Locke's criticisms of nurses stem from their class status as servants. His voice contributed to the contemporary cultural prejudice about the base character and mean habits of wet nurses, as his contemporaries worried about their neglectful practices and the safety of their infants. At the same time that wet-nursing was so prevalent, parents were encouraged to visit their nurslings often and unexpectedly so that nurses could be caught off-guard.[107] While in Valerie Fildes's estimation the preponderance of evidence indicates that most wet nurses "served their family well, and were very fond of the children they nursed," concerns prevailed nonetheless about the quality of the milk that could be produced by women of such humble origins. Mercenary nurses, as Henry Newcome called them, "might transmit some desperate Contagion" into their nurslings, including venereal disease and deafness—a condition which, he believed, could be passed on by some vapor in the nurse's milk.[108] Nurslings might also derive bad spirits, poor character, and depraved manners from the mercenary's milk.[109] Although Locke worried about the contaminating effect of servant-class nurses upon children, the transmission of poor qualities or disease through actual breast milk was not one of his fixations.

Those of Locke's contemporaries who railed against the depravity of wet-nursing, also prescribed maternal breastfeeding and highlighted the importance of maternal sentiment.[110] Henry Newcome declares that a "Fruitful Wife is a Blessing, so when she Nurses her Children she is a double Blessing to a Family."[111] Mothers who "discard their Offspring from their own Breasts, and hire them out to be nursed by Strangers" are inhumane, degenerate, and slothful, whereas those women who assume their bodily and moral duty to breastfeed are "honourable Ladies who have had the Vertue and Courage" to ignore social custom.[112] Nursing one's own children, writes Newcome, "is a very proper and natural Testimony to *maternal Love*."[113] Richard Allestree, another seventeenth-century conduct writer, confesses: "I cannot but look with reverence upon those few Persons of Honor, who have broke thro an unreasonable Custom" to nurse their own children.[114]

Normative conceptions of maternity also appear in the educational writings of Locke's contemporaries. Obadiah Walker's *Of Education, Especially of Young Gentlemen*, praises the practice of the ancient Romans who, "when a child was born, put him not out to a hired Nurse, but brought him up in his Mother's chamber."[115] Jean Gaillard asserts that children are "by half, more obliged to Mothers who take these pains [to nurse them], than to those who do not; it being known that a Nurse is a second Mother." While a suitable nurse can be chosen, in Gaillard's view, she could not have "that care and true tenderness of Mothers who have carried them nine months in their Womb."[116]

Among the most famous writings on breastfeeding and wet-nursing in the seventeenth century is the maternal plea of Elizabeth Clinton in *The Countesse of Lincoln's Nursery*. Clinton addresses the text to her daughter-in-law to urge her not to follow her own example. A mother to eighteen children, not one of whom she breastfed, Clinton blames herself for bowing to the will of others who overruled her, and for not having considered this maternal office before it was too late to "put it in execution." Clinton urges her daughter-in-law to consider the example of Eve, "who suckled her sonnes Cain, Abel, Seth, & c. . . . which shee did not only of meere necessitie, because yet no other woman was created; but especially because shee was their mother, and so sawe it was her duty: and because shee had a true naturall affection, which moved her to doe it gladly."[117] Clinton establishes the relationship between good motherhood and the maternal obligation to breastfeed, for the "suckling of her own childe" is the "part of a true mother, of a just mother, of an honest mother, of a mother worthy of love."[118] Although published earlier in the century, and before motherhood was "defined as an ongoing, 'nurturing' relationship with one's own child," *The Countesse of Lincoln's Nursery* anticipates later depictions of motherhood, which are centered on the breast as the site of maternal devotion.[119] Along with the later-century conduct and educational writers who endorsed maternal breastfeeding, Clinton offers an important counterpoint to Locke's pre-sentimental conception of maternity.

For his part, Locke stands in relief to this maternal discourse: his writings are noticeably devoid of commentary about maternal obligation, and are, in fact, wrung dry of extraneous sentimental rhetoric. As we have seen, Locke simply does not recommend or even offer an opinion on maternal breastfeeding. At most there are brief references in his medical notes, such as a remedy from the countess of Monmouth for swollen breasts in a nursing mother (apply pieces of flannel which have been fried in unsalted butter).[120] His Dutch notes dictate that the new mother's diet ought to be "moderate if she is not suckling the child," and "even if she is suckling, she must not stuff herself with food."[121] Even where he is critical of wet nurses, he fails to make any connection between their inadequacies and a maternal obligation to breastfeed. Locke's distaste for wet nurses is not about their function as a stand-in for mothers, and it is not wrapped up in predetermined notions of sentimental maternity.

Rather, Locke's objection to wet nurses must be viewed in light of his overall concern with the proper breeding of children. A look at his discussion of the tutor provides insight into this point. For Locke, the tutor plays an important role in the development of a young boy in helping him master his own desires on the route to virtue. For this reason, the tutor must be chosen carefully and must be a role model in "Restraint of the Passions."[122] Locke places great emphasis on the impressionability of children: the behavior that they observe, they will mimic; the ideas to which their unwary minds are exposed will take hold, and be fastened by custom and education "beyond all possibility of being pulled out again."[123] In Locke's view, "the Tutor's Example must lead the Child into those Actions he would have him do." For this reason, then, the tutor must also protect him from bad influences, "especially the most dangerous of all, the Examples of the Servants; from whose Company he is to be kept."[124]

Unlike tutors, nurses are servants. As servants they have improper breeding themselves and thus expose their nurslings to, and inculcate in them, poor habits. While on the one hand the wet nurse is a stand-in for a mother in the same way that Locke sees the tutor as a stand-in for a father, the two are profoundly distinguished by their breeding. When the tutor's task is complete, the result is a well-bred young gentleman. When the child returns from the nurse's care, parents may well have a difficult time establishing their control. Locke feared that nurses did not adequately discipline the infants in their care. "A prudent and kind mother, of my acquaintance, was . . . forced to whip her little Daughter, at her first coming home from the Nurse, eight times successively the same morning, before she could master her *Stubbornness*."[125] The answer to this problem is not to return the child to the mother—as we have seen, Locke advocates hand-feeding over maternal breastfeeding—rather, the answer is to find a suitable wet nurse who will have as little negative impact on the child as possible.

In conclusion, Locke's medical writings remain obscure and—in the case of the midwifery writings—largely unpublished. But the microhistories contained in these notes shed light on his conceptions of childbirth and medical and midwifery practice in the seventeenth century. They are also significant for those interested in mapping the changing conceptions of the familial private realm over time. If seventeenth- and eighteenth-century notions of the family are placed on a continuum, among the most important conceptions would include the Filmerian patriarchal family ruled absolutely by the father; the contractual view put forth most starkly by Hobbes in which all human relationships are rendered rational and consensual; and the Rousseauean sentimental family. Despite his theoretical innovations in contractual thinking about the family, Locke is somewhat difficult to place.

Locke's shadowy conception of the family is given some illumination by the midwifery notes. It is clear from his notes, for example, that, unlike some of his contemporaries, Locke has not made the leap to, nor do we find in his writings early references to, the sentimental family. Among some of the late seventeenth-century conduct and educational writers, mothers are "insistently enjoined . . . to constant attendance on their children."[126] Similarly, in Rousseau's sentimental family, motherhood is woman's defining role. But the same dispassionate tone that governs Locke's writings about childbirth and the roles and shortcomings of the midwife infuses Locke's writings about the practice of wet-nursing and about maternity in general. Locke simply does not offer any sort of ideological remuneration to mothers who breastfeed, or to mothers for anything at all.

That Locke is more interested in parental duty in general than maternal duty specifically is relevant to our understanding of his overall purpose in discussing the family, and it assists us in the effort to place him on the continuum of ideas about the family. The new ideas of freedom and equality associated with the language of contractual familial relations had not yet made an appearance in practical conceptions of the family. That these ideas of freedom and equality had not infused the private realm of the family, had not yet seriously threatened Locke's traditional, aristocratic understanding of the family, means that he did not have any need for the sentimental rhetoric that later was called upon to repress them.

Indeed, Locke, like Hobbes before him, introduced contractual language only as a similitude for discussing political relationships. Once his purpose is served, and Filmer's argument defeated, he reverts back to customary assumptions about the natural basis for the difference in authority of mothers and fathers in families.[127] The midwifery notes confirm that Locke's real interest in the family is as a site for the proper breeding of children, the propagation of humankind in accordance with God's will, the "natural Right" of children to "inherit the Goods of their Parents," and the duty of parents, who are "taught by Natural Love and Tenderness to provide for [their children], as a part of themselves."[128] Locke is neither sentimetal, nor fully contractualist, but presupposes in his writings a traditionally hierarchical, aristocratic familial configuration founded upon the assumption of natural differences between the sexes.

Notes

1. John W. Yolton, A Locke Dictionary (Cambridge, Mass.: Blackwell Publishers, 1993), 135–36.

2. Valerie Fildes, Breasts, Bottles and Babies: A History of Infant Feeding (Edinburgh: Edinburgh University Press, 1986), 399.

3. The quantity and character of Locke's early notes indicate that he seriously considered choosing medicine as his vocation. While he did, in the mid-1660s, apply for dispensation to write the medical examinations at Oxford, it appears that he never followed through on his application. He was granted a bachelor of medicine in 1675 but did not pursue the matter further, apparently because of his own poor health. See J. R. Milton, "Locke's Life and Times," in The Cambridge Companion to Locke, ed. Vere Chappell (New York: Cambridge University Press, 1994); Yolton, Locke Dictionary, 136; and G. G. Meynell, "A Database for John Locke's Medical Notebooks and Medical Reading," Medical History 42 (1997): 473.

4. See Milton, "Locke's Life and Times," 6, and Kenneth Dewhurst, John Locke (1632–1704),

Physician and Philosopher: A Medical Biography; with an edition of the medical notes in his journals (London: Wellcome Historical Medical Library, 1963).

5. Yolton, *Locke Dictionary*, 136. For further discussion of this period in Locke's life, see Maurice Cranston, *John Locke: A Biography* (Toronto: Longmans, Green, 1957).

6. Dewhurst, *John Locke*, 27.

7. Kenneth Dewhurst, "Locke's Midwifery Notes," *Lancet*, September 4, 1954, 490–91.

8. William O. Coleman summarizes his achievements succinctly, including his contributions to the study of respiration, physiology, pharmacology, reproduction, digestion, and anatomy among others. See "The Significance of John Locke's Medical Studies for His Economic Thought," *History of Political Economy* 32, no. 4 (2000): 714.

9. Anonymous, quoted in Patrick Romanell, *John Locke and Medicine: A New Key to Locke* (Buffalo, N.Y.: Prometheus Books, 1984), 25.

10. Ibid.

11. Meynell, "Database," 476.

12. Susan Moller Okin, "Women and the Making of the Sentimental Family," *Philosophy and Public Affairs* 11, no. 1 (1981).

13. Ruth Perry, "Colonizing the Breast: Sexuality and Maternity in Eighteenth-Century England," *Journal of the History of Sexuality* 2, no. 2 (1991).

14. Teresa Brennan and Carole Pateman, "'Mere Auxiliaries to the Commonwealth': Women and the Origins of Liberalism," *Political Studies* 27, no. 2 (1979): 183–200; Jean Bethke Elshtain, *Public Man, Private Woman: Women in Social and Political Thought*, 2nd ed. (Princeton: Princeton University Press, 1993), chap. 3.

15. For discussion, see Mary Lyndon Shanley, "Marriage Contract and Social Contract in Seventeenth Century English Political Thought," *Western Political Quarterly* 32 (1979): 79–91.

16. For discussion of the family as a similitude in seventeenth-century political thought, see Gordon J. Schochet, *The Authoritarian Family and Political Attitudes in 17th Century England: Patriarchalism in Political Thought* (New Brunswick, N.J.: Transaction Books, 1988), and Mary Beth Norton, *Founding Mothers and Fathers: Gendered Power and the Forming of American Society* (New York: Alfred A. Knopf, 1996).

17. That Locke had "assumptions" about gender and the family is not to say that he entertained the question of gender relations as a topic unto itself. For discussion of the instrumental use of gender and the family, see Rachel Weil, *Political Passions: Gender, the Family and Political Argument in England, 1680–1714* (Manchester: Manchester University Press, 1999), and Joanne H. Wright, *Origin Stories in Political Thought: Discourses on Gender, Power, and Citizenship* (Toronto: University of Toronto Press, 2004).

18. For further discussion, see Weil, *Political Passions*, and Joanne Boucher, "Male Power and Contract Theory: Hobbes and Locke in Carole Pateman's *The Sexual Contract*," *Canadian Journal of Political Science* 36, no. 1 (March 2003): 23–38.

19. As a physician, Locke is probably most famous for overseeing an abdominal surgery that was performed on Lord Anthony Ashley Cooper, who later became the first earl of Shaftesbury. When Lord Ashley became seriously ill in 1668, it was Locke who orchestrated the surgery that would incise and drain the cyst on his liver and who kept detailed notes on the progress of his recovery.

20. Cranston, *John Locke*, 121.

21. Letter no. 242, from Frances Manners to Locke, January 31, 1670, in *The Correspondence of John Locke*, ed. E. S. DeBeer, vol. 1 (Oxford: Clarendon Press, 1976), 337.

22. Cranston, *John Locke*, 139.

23. See, for discussion, George H. Jackson Jr., "John Locke, Pediatrician," *American Journal of Diseases of Children* 36 (1928): 1250–56, and John W. Yolton and Jean S. Yolton, "Introduction," in John Locke, *Some Thoughts Concerning Education*, ed. John W. Yolton and Jean S. Yolton (Oxford: Clarendon Press, 1989).

24. Simon Schaffer, "The Glorious Revolution and Medicine in Britain and The Netherlands," *Notes Rec. R. Soc. Lond.* 43 (1989): 167–90, 181.

25. Dewhurst, *John Locke*, 35.

26. Debate continues over whether the philosophical essay "De Arte Medica"—which is written in Locke's hand—is properly attributed to Locke or Sydenham. See Milton, "Locke's Life and Times," 9, and Romanell, *John Locke and Medicine*, 115–20. Dewhurst credits Sydenham with authorship and includes the essay in Sydenham's medical biography, *Dr. Thomas Sydenham (1624– 1689): His Life and Original Writings* (Berkeley and Los Angeles: University of California Press, 1966).

27. In fact, by the time Locke fled to Holland in September 1683, Shaftesbury himself was dead. Shaftesbury left for Holland in early 1683 and subsequently died there. For a brief summary of these events, see Milton, "Locke's Life and Times," 14.

28. Schaffer, "Glorious Revolution," 169.

29. Kenneth Dewhurst, "John's Locke's Medical Notes During His Residence in Holland," *Janus* 50 (1963): 178. See also Dewhurst, *John Locke*, 226.

30. Dewhurst, "John Locke's Medical Notes," 226; Dewhurst, *John Locke*, 256–60.

31. While Dewhurst refers to these notes and to Locke's correspondence on midwifery, as do others, none of his interpreters subject his midwifery writings to any sort of analysis. Aside from Dewhurst, William Weston also refers to Locke's interesting commentary on midwifery, but does not explore the subject further in "John Locke, Household Physician and Personal Secretary to Ashley Cooper," *Journal of the South Carolina Medical Association* 66, no. 5 (May 1970): 149.

32. Margaret Cavendish, Duchess of Newcastle, *Orations of Divers Sorts accomodated to divers places* (London, 1662), 182–83.

33. Linda Pollock, "Embarking on a Rough Passage: The Experience of Pregnancy in Early-Modern Society," in *Women as Mothers in Pre-Industrial England*, ed. Valerie Fildes (New York: Routledge, 1990), 47. Adrian Wilson disagrees that parturition generated fear in women, arguing instead that women tended to fear childbirth only when a male practitioner had to be called in, as this often meant the performance of a craniotomy on their dead child. See Wilson, "The Ceremony of Childbirth and Its Interpretation," in Fildes, *Women as Mothers*, 50–51.

34. Sara Mendelson and Patricia Crawford, *Women in Early Modern England, 1550–1720* (Oxford: Clarendon Press, 1998), 153.

35. Letter no. 1554, from Locke to Mrs. Mary Clarke, October 31, 1692, in *Correspondence*, 560.

36. For example, see letter no. 774, from Locke to Mrs. Mary Clarke, [early February 1684], in *Correspondence*, 607. It is clear from Locke's correspondence that his wish for friends to have more boys is not a sign of his greater preference for them as companions; indeed, he professes a great affection for Mary Clarke's daughter, Betty, among other girl children.

37. Mendelson and Crawford, *Women in Early Modern England*, 150. See also Patricia Crawford, "'The Suckling Child': Adult Attitudes to Child Care in the First Year of Life in Seventeenth-Century England," *Continuity and Change* 1, no. 1 (1986): 28, and Letter no. 255, from Lady Dorothy Ashley to Locke, [July] 1, [1671], in *Correspondence*, 356.

38. Pollock, "Embarking on a Rough Passage," 47.

39. Ibid., 51.

40. Ibid., 50

41. From Dewhurst, "Locke's Midwifery Notes," 490.

42. Ibid.

43. Ibid., 491.

44. See ibid., and also Pollock, "Embarking on a Rough Passage," 51.

45. From Dewhurst, *John Locke*, 43.

46. Frances Manners, countess of Rutland, writes to Locke: "I am most thankfully acknowledg

gods great goodness to my deare daughter, and am obliged to your own justice. . . . The Lord's name be blest and praised for her well doeing . . . and safely bringing that noble familie so hopefull an heire, that early accosts ladies in bed and manages a weapon at 3 days olde to my wonder and joy." Letter no. 251, from Frances Manners to Locke, March 7, [1671], in *Correspondence*, 350.

47. From Dewhurst, "Locke's Midwifery Notes," 491.

48. For discussion of some of the dangers associated with midwifery interventions, see Audrey Eccles, *Obstetrics and Gynaecology in Tudor and Stuart England* (London: Croom Helm, 1982), chap. 10.

49. *The Ladies Companion*, excerpted in N. H. Keeble, *The Cultural Identity of Seventeenth-Century Woman: A Reader* (London: Routledge, 1994), 212.

50. Quoted in Wilson, "Ceremony of Childbirth," 72.

51. From Dewhurst, *John Locke*, 257.

52. There are different means by which the midwife might assist the birth that caused concern to Locke and his contemporaries. William Sermon worried that the midwife might "destroy poor women by tearing the membrane with their nails, and so let forth the water (at least) to the great danger and hurt not only of the woman but the child." See the excerpt from *The Ladies Companion* in Keeble, *Cultural Identity*, 212. "It is to be impressed on the midwife," writes Locke in his Dutch journal, that "while using her hands to assist the birth" she does not accidentally push the coccyx bone too far and "hinder the birth strainings." She also ought not to make any cuts, "especially if it is not yet certain whether the foetus is near the opening," nor should she pull out the afterbirth prematurely, for "it will slip out insensibly, just as a snake or other slippery body passes through a half closed hand." See Dewhurst, *John Locke*, 258.

53. From Dewhurst, "Locke's Midwifery Notes," 491.

54. Pollock, "Embarking on a Rough Passage," 45.

55. From Dewhurst, *John Locke*, 88, 200.

56. Ibid.

57. Male practitioners were called into the lying-in room only to assist the attending midwife in difficult deliveries. Occasionally a male practitioner might be called in advance to live in with the expectant mother, to advise her on her pregnancy, to see her through to the birth and perhaps even to attend the birth. As the household physician for Shaftesbury, Locke seems to have served in this latter role for Lady Dorothy Cooper; moreover, he performed some of these functions for other acquaintances by correspondence. See Adrian Wilson, *The Making of Man-Midwifery: Childbirth in England, 1660–1770* (London: University College London Press, 1995), 48.

58. From Dewhurst, "Locke's Midwifery Notes," 491.

59. Mendelson and Crawford, *Women in Early Modern England*, 316.

60. For discussion, see Diane Purkiss, *The Witch in History: Early Modern and Twentieth-Century Representations* (New York: Routledge, 1996); Deborah Willis, *Malevolent Nurture: Witch-hunting and Maternal Power in Early Modern England* (Ithaca: Cornell University Press, 1995); Elaine Hobby, "Introduction," in Jane Sharp, *The Midwives Book; Or the Whole Art of Midwifery Discovered*, ed. Elaine Hobby (New York: Oxford University Press, 1999); and Wilson, *Man-Midwifery*, 31.

61. See Elaine Hobby, *Virtue of Necessity: English Women's Writing, 1649–88* (Ann Arbor: University of Michigan Press, 1988), 177.

62. Further, see Mendelson and Crawford, *Women in Early Modern England*, 316.

63. Quoted in Hobby, "Introduction," xxiii. Elizabeth Cellier attempted unsuccessfully to establish a college of midwives that would train and license them and thus provide a greater consistency in midwifery skills. See Hilda L. Smith, *Reason's Disciples: Seventeenth-Century English Feminists* (Chicago: University of Illinois Press, 1982), 99–102.

64. Smith, *Reason's Disciples*, 98.

65. Dewhurst, *John Locke*, 51.

66. Ibid., 38.

67. Eccles suggests that, by the seventeenth century, a "number of midwives' customs and beliefs about the birth were already regarded as old wives' tales." See *Obstetrics and Gynaecology*, 93.

68. See Mendelson and Crawford, *Women in Early Modern England*, 316. Sydenham was among those who distrusted the unlearned ways of woman attendants at childbirth. See Samuel X. Radbill, "Pediatrics," in *Medicine in Seventeenth-Century England: A Symposium Held at UCLA in Honor of C. D. O'Malley*, ed. Allen G. Debus (Berkeley and Los Angeles: University of California Press, 1974).

69. For example, Locke cites two French medical authors in his notes who have catalogued "almost all the points about childbirth in which mistakes are usually made *both* by *women* and by *ordinary doctors*." See Dewhurst, *John Locke*, 136; emphasis added.

70. Percival Willughby, *Observations in Midwifery*, ed. Henry Blenkinsop (Warwick: H. T. Cooke and Son, 1863).

71. From Dewhurst, "Locke's Midwifery Notes," 491.

72. Sermon, *The Ladies Companion*, excerpted in Keeble, *Cultural Identity*, 211.

73. Hobby, *Virtue of Necessity*, 183.

74. Wilson, "Ceremony of Childbirth," 71.

75. Quoted in Weil, *Political Passions*, 29. Weil argues that, of the Whig thinkers of the period, "Locke seems to be the least interested in making a sustained argument about the inherent unknowablility of paternal identity." He is more interested, she suggests, "in the fact that children have two parents than in the fact that they can be certain of the identity of only one" (72).

76. John Pechey, quoted in Crawford, "The Suckling Child," 37.

77. Ibid., 38.

78. From Dewhurst, *John Locke*, 82. In the same way that Locke's writings serve as microhistories of changing midwifery practices, they also point to Locke's interest and role in the expansion of the British Empire. Locke was drawn into and benefited from the expansion into America through his close relationship with the earl of Shaftesbury, with whom he drafted the first constitution of colonial South Carolina. One can hardly fail to notice Locke's colonial mentality as it surfaces in his medical and midwifery writings—for instance, in the animal imagery evoked by his description of Gold Coast babies as kittens dragging themselves on four paws. For discussion, see Barbara Arneil, *John Locke and America: The Defence of English Colonialism* (Oxford: Clarendon Press, 1996); Charles W. Mills, *The Racial Contract* (Ithaca: Cornell University Press, 1997); and James Tully, *Strange Multiplicity: Constitutionalism in an Age of Diversity* (New York: Cambridge University Press, 1995).

79. From Dewhurst, *John Locke*, 141.

80. Perry, "Colonizing the Breast," 215.

81. Jean-Jacques Rousseau, *Emile, or On Education*, trans. Allan Bloom (New York: Basic Books, 1979), 46.

82. Perry, "Colonizing the Breast," 218.

83. Toni Bowers, *The Politics of Motherhood: British Writing and Culture, 1680–1760* (Boston: Cambridge University Press, 1996), 14–15.

·   84. Children fared best on a plain diet, with no spices, little sugar, no meat, and no fruit. See Locke, *Some Thoughts Concerning Education*, secs. 13, 14, and 20.

85. Dewhurst, *John Locke*, 207–8 and 259.

86. The age of weaning varied tremendously in the early modern period, but does seem to have declined during the eighteenth century. Fildes speculates that mothers who were, by this point, breastfeeding their own children, might have had less interest in prolonged breastfeeding than a woman who was being paid to nurse a child. See Fildes, *Breasts, Bottles and Babies*, 364.

87. Valerie Fildes, *Wet Nursing: A History from Antiquity to the Present* (New York: Basil Blackwell, 1988), 79.

88. Ibid.

89. Ibid., 83.

90. Ibid., 82. What is often left unspecified, however, is who fed the child in the intervening first week.

91. Letter no. 255, from Lady Dorothy Ashley to Locke, [July] 1, [1671], in *Correspondence*, 356.

92. Letter no. 774, from Locke to Mrs. Mary Clarke, [early February 1684?], in *Correspondence*, 607–8.

93. Ibid.

94. Letter no. 758, from Locke to Edward Clarke, February 22, 1683, in *Correspondence*, 582–83.

95. Ibid.

96. In his letter to Locke about the birth of this infant, Elizabeth, Edward Clarke explains that "the chyld is weake and Feeds verie little, soe that wee are at present under some difficultyes in that Particular, but I hope if the child bee not better by to morrow my Wife will bee content to try it with a Breast." Precisely whose breast will be tried is not mentioned. We can assume that the Clarkes attempted to hand-feed Elizabeth upon birth, that this was not a success, and that she was then put out to nurse, first with Nurse Edeling and then with Nurse Trent. Letter no. 739, from Edward Clarke to Locke, October 26, 1682, in *Correspondence*, 556.

97. Fildes, *Wet Nursing*, 91; Fildes, *Breasts, Bottles and Babies*, 288–91.

98. Quoted in Dewhurst, *John Locke*, 199.

99. Dorothy McLaren, "Nature's Contraceptive. Wet-Nursing and Prolonged Lactation: The Case of Cheshum, Buckinghamshire, 1578–1601," *Medical History* 23 (1979): 427–28. This number of pregnancies was "close to the physiological maximum for most women," and was lamented by many in the diaries they left behind (427–28). McLaren considers the question of why upper-class women produced larger families than poor ones, concluding that "the answer is to be found in their refusal to use nature's contraceptive, prolonged lactation" (430).

100. Ibid.

101. Weil, *Political Passions*, 28.

102. John Locke, *Two Treatises of Government*, ed. Peter Laslett (New York: Cambridge University Press, 1988), 1.88.

103. Ibid., 2.80.

104. Locke, *Some Thoughts Concerning Education*, sec. 11.

105. Ibid., sec. 18.2.

106. Ibid., sec. 19.

107. Fildes, *Wet Nursing*, 92.

108. Henry Newcome, *The Compleat Mother* (London: Printed for J. Wyat, 1695), 71–74.

109. Ibid., chap. 4.

110. English Puritans on the whole resisted the custom of the upper class and encouraged maternal breastfeeding. William Gouge, conduct writer and author of *Of Domesticall Duties* was among them. See R. V. Schuckner, "The English Puritans and Pregnancy, Delivery and Breast Feeding," *History of Childhood Quarterly* 1 (1974): 637–58.

111. Newcome, *Compleat Mother*, 21.

112. Ibid., 5.

113. Ibid., 42; italics in original.

114. *The Ladies Calling* (Oxford: At the Theatre in Oxford, 1673), 44.

115. *Of Education, Especially of Young Gentlemen* (Oxon: At the Theater, 1673), 18–19.

116. *The Compleat Gentleman; Or, Directions for the Education of Youth* (London: In the Savoy, 1678), 7–8.

117. Elizabeth Clinton, *The Countesse of Lincoln's Nursery* (Oxford, 1622), 3.

118. Ibid., 7.

119. Marilyn Luecke, "The Reproduction of Culture and the Culture of Reproduction in Eliza-

beth Clinton's *The Countesse of Lincoln's Nursery*," in *Women, Writing and the Reproduction of Culture in Tudor and Stuart Britain*, ed. Mary E. Burke, Jane Donawerth, Linda L. Dove, and Karen Nelson (Syracuse: Syracuse University Press, 2000), 241. In a social context that rhetorically endorses wet-nursing, if anxiously, Clinton "figuratively reconnects the breast to the female reproductive body, its functions and its fluids" (243).

120. Ibid., 286.

121. Ibid., 258.

122. Locke, *Some Thoughts Concerning Education*, sec. 89.

123. John Locke, *An Essay Concerning Human Understanding* (London: William Tegg, 1875), bk. 4, chap. 20, sec. 9, 601.

124. Locke, *Some Thoughts Concerning Education*, sec. 89.

125. Ibid., sec. 78.

126. Bowers, *Politics of Motherhood*, 157.

127. Locke, *Two Treatises*, 1.47.

128. Ibid., 1.97.

8

Locke, Adam, and Eve

Jeremy Waldron

Basic equality—the view that humans are fundamentally one another's equals and entitled accordingly to equal concern and respect—has not always been a reputable premise of social and political thought. When Sir Robert Filmer, the great proponent of patriarchalism and the divine right of kings wrote in the 1650s *"that there cannot be any Multitude of Men whatsoever, either great or small, . . . but that in the same Multitude . . . there is one Man amongst them, that in Nature hath a Right to be King of all the rest,"*[1] he was not teasing his audience with a counterintuitive hypothesis to liven up a quiet day in a dusty philosophy seminar. He was stating something on which he could reasonably expect implicit agreement from the consensus of educated and respectable opinion, and something that was evidently embodied in aspects of social, familial, political, and ecclesiastical organization that most of his contemporaries believed were or ought to be largely beyond question. It was the contrary position—the principle of basic equality—that seemed radical, disreputable, beyond reason, valid only as a philosophical hypothesis entertained for the sake of argument in a carefully controlled environment. Let it loose in politics and morality, and there was no telling the harm it would do. It was rather like communism in America in the 1950s. There was no denying that there were people who held this position, but they were widely regarded as unsound and dangerous to the point of incendiary, the last people respectable opinion would rely on for an account of the grounding or the reform of stable and effective political institutions.

John Locke, beyond doubt, was one of these equality radicals in the late seventeenth century. Today, many political theorists are skeptical about this characterization: they read Locke as someone who pretended to believe in equality, but who was really in favor of massive *in*equality between classes and between the sexes. But it is hard to see how the pretense is supposed to have been motivated. There was no particular advantage to Locke—as there might be for a sneaky authoritarian or patriarchialist or bourgeois apologist in the twenty-first century—in pretending to be a partisan of basic equality when he wasn't. Locke didn't have troublesome feminist students whom he needed to fool in order to get favorable teaching evaluations. If anything, political correctness argued the other way, and Locke knew perfectly well that neither the premise of his political philosophy—basic equality—nor the enterprise of figuring out its ramifications was a passport to political or philosophical respectability. Nevertheless, he evidently took the premise of basic equality very seriously. It was not just a preference or a pragmatic rule-of-thumb; nor was it simply a "dictate of reason," like Hobbes's precepts "that no man by deed, word, countenance, or gesture, declare hatred or contempt of another" and "that every man acknowledge another for his equal."[2] Locke accorded basic equality the strongest grounding that a principle could have: it was an axiom of theology, understood as perhaps the most important truth about God's way with the world in regard to the social and political implications of His creation of the human person.[3] God created all of us in what was, morally speaking, "a state . . . of equality, wherein all the power and jurisdiction is reciprocal, no one having more than another" (*Two Treatises*, 2.4), all of us lords, all of us kings, each of us "equal to the greatest, and subject to no body" (2.123). And anything that was said about the power of princes, generals, bishops, teachers, scholars, fathers, husbands, employers, landowners, colonists, or the masters of slaves had to be built up on that basis, and justified with reference to and under the discipline of this truth about basic equality.[4]

That is what I believe about the premise of Locke's political theory. But of course, it is one thing to articulate a premise; it is quite another to hold fast to it in the detail of one's social and political thinking. Reading Locke's mature political philosophy—by which I mean An Essay Concerning Human Understanding, the Two Treatises of Government, the four (or rather three and a half) Letters Concerning Toleration that he wrote in the 1680s and 1690s, and The Reasonableness of Christianity—we can see him grappling with the consequences of this radicalism. And we can watch him as he responds to the charge of radical unsoundness, sometimes holding fast to what he knew was a counterintuitive position, sometimes flinching a little from his underlying egalitarian commitment, but more often delighting in the fact that he was able to articulate the difference—which we still think it important to articulate—between equality as a premise and some particular egalitarian policy or distribution which he might or might not be in favor of.[5] It would be nice to be able to report that, one way or another, Locke remained steadfast in the basics of his egalitarianism. Unfortunately, I cannot. He flinched at a number of points, in particular in some parts of his discussion of women. But even on this topic—even in this area that has traditionally afforded such fertile ground for inegalitarian prejudice—John Locke did not flinch from the implications of basic equality as often or as comprehensively as some of his modern critics suppose.

Attacking Filmer's Inequality

What I would like to do in this chapter is chart John Locke's struggle to free contemporary thought—indeed to free himself—of the conviction that a difference as striking as the difference between men and women must be morally and politically salient in its own right, and that it must also prefigure and exemplify the general implausibility of human equality as a starting point for social and political thought. My initial focus will be on Locke's discussion of Adam and Eve and the circumstances of their creation and fall, in the first of his *Two Treatises of Government*.

Everyone knows that Locke's target in the *First Treatise* was the inegalitarianism of Robert Filmer. What is less often understood is that Filmer's rejection of basic equality consists less in a *general* inegalitarianism than in what I should like to call a *particularistic* theory of inequality. Filmer actually opposed what must have been in his day the most familiar philosophic defense of general inegalitarianism, namely Aristotle's theory of natural slavery. He did so quite firmly at the start of chapter 2 of *Patriarcha*:

> Also Aristotle had another fancy, that those men "which proved wise of mind were by nature intended to be lords and govern, and those that were strong of body were ordained to obey and be servants" (*Politics*, book I, chapter 2). But this is a dangerous and uncertain rule, and not without some folly. For if a man prove both wise and strong, what will Aristotle have done with him? As he was wise, he could be no servant, as he had strength, he could not be a master. Besides, to speak like a philosopher, nature intends all men to be perfect both in wit and strength. The folly or imbecility proceeds from some error in generation or education, for nature aims at perfection in all her works.[6]

Filmer's primary interest was in identifying specific individuals who have authority over others, rather than classes or types of individual in some general hierarchy. A theory of the divine right of kings is particularistic in this sense inasmuch as it purports to identify particular persons, like Charles Stuart or his brother James, as entitled to monarchical authority. A racist or a sexist theory by contrast would be a *general* inegalitarianism, implying as it does that all humans of a certain type are superior to all humans of some other type, but leaving it open who in particular was entitled to rule.

Now, of course, it was Filmer's particular inegalitarianism that Locke set out to refute. Locke wanted to show the absurdity of the Filmerian view that certain specific individuals had a natural right to rule over the rest. But in the course of his refutation of that particular inegalitarianism, Locke necessarily also took on certain propositions that were in his day (and are still sometimes in ours) cited as the basis of a more *general* inequality. Both aspects are present in his discussion of women. The biblical subordination of Eve to Adam that Filmer makes so much of can be seen as a privileging of Adam in particular and his particular (male) heirs, or it can be seen as a privileging of men generally over women generally, or husbands generally over wives generally. By seeking to undercut or diminish Filmer's particular inferences from the subordination of Eve to Adam, Locke inevitably undercut the appeal of the two broader positions as well. I do not think he was ever entirely comfortable with this, and the texts I am going to examine show him in two minds as to the position about women that he wanted ultimately to adopt. But there is little doubt where Locke's most fundamental premises were leading him, and the struggle that we can discern in the texts is his personal struggle to come to terms with the fact that women as much as men are created in the image of God and endowed with the modicum of reason that is, for Locke, the criterion of human equality.

Let me repeat my description of Locke's endeavor in regard to this matter of equality between men and women, for it flies in the face of a number of modern commentaries. There used to be a view—in certain circles, there still *is* a view—that something as striking as the difference between the sexes must be morally and politically salient in its own right, and also that difference between the sexes foreshadows the general implausibility of basic equality as a starting point for social and political thought. That view is very deeply rooted, and like all others in our culture, John Locke felt the force of it. But I believe he struggled in his philosophy to free himself of this conviction. He certainly sought to demonstrate its implausibility as a premise for a normative theory of politics. He tried as hard as he could to refute theories based on it, and he sought to develop an ethics and a politics that had no need of that hypothesis. He did not succeed in this to the satisfaction of modern feminists.[7] I am not sure he succeeded in it to his own satisfaction: the discussion of men and women and particularly marriage in Locke has an air of embarrassment about it, perhaps reinforced by his own lack of any firsthand acquaintance with the institution. Indeed the ambivalence and embarrassment is part of the reason I want to begin my discussion of equality with this issue. It is not an easy issue, and setting out the difficulties and inconsistencies in Locke's account helps us understand that basic equality is a demanding principle, one whose adoption can shake up a political theorist quite beyond our expectations.

Adam and Eve

There can be no doubt whatever about John Locke's intention in the *First Treatise* so far as the understanding of Adam and Eve is concerned. That Adam was furnished with God-given political authority over Eve, either by virtue of the circumstances of their creation, or by virtue of their punishment in the Fall, was the first of Filmer's positions on natural inequality that Locke set out to refute.

He tried to refute it in all its manifestations. The first version is a sort of argument from priority. Eve was created after Adam, therefore Adam is boss by virtue of seniority.[8] Locke is unconvinced. By the same token, he says, Adam was created after all the other animals, after the Lion for example: so "this Argument, will make the Lion have as good a Title to [dominion] as he, and certainly the Ancienter" (*Two Treatises*, 1.15). Locke does not say much to respond to Filmer's claim that "God created only Adam and of a piece of him made the woman."[9] But later he shows himself quite unimpressed by any argument that children are subordinate to their parents because they are created out of their parents' bodily material (1.52–55). If such an argument worked, he says it would establish the authority of mothers more than fathers, because "the Woman hath an equal share, if not the greater, as nourishing the Child a long time in her own Body out of her own Substance" (1.55). But Locke believed that these body-part arguments did not work at all, and that all credit for and authority arising out of the creation of any human being had to go to "God, who is *the Author and Giver of Life*" (1.55), not to the inadvertent donor of the raw materials. In the *Second Treatise*, the fact that "*Adam* was created a perfect man, his Body and Mind in full possession of their Strength and Reason" shows that he has a responsibility to look after his children, "who are all born Infants, weak and helpless," and "to supply the Defects of this imperfect State, till the Improvement of Growth and Age hath removed them" (2.56). But the telos and endpoint of that responsibility is the child's equality with his parent, not any continuing subordination traceable to the fact that the father was created complete and the infant not. In any case, though Eve may have been made out of a part of Adam, she too was created with her "Body and Mind in full possession of their Strength and Reason." There is just no room here for any inequality based on priority of creation or on ownership of the spare parts used in the process.

The bulk of Locke's argument about Adam and Eve is a response to Filmer's scriptural claim that God gave Adam general plenary authority over everything in His commandment (Genesis 1:28)—"Be fruitful, and multiply, and replenish the earth, and subdue it: and have dominion over the fish of the sea, and over the fowl of the air, and over every living thing that moveth upon the earth." Locke's refutation of this argument of Filmer's is quite devastating on scriptural grounds. "That this Donation was not made in particular to *Adam*, appears evidently from the words of the Text, it being made to more than one, for it was spoken in the Plural Number, God blessed *them*, and said unto *them*, Have Dominion. God says unto *Adam* and *Eve*, Have Dominion" (*Two Treatises*, 1.29). Since many interpreters think it significant, says Locke, "that these words were not spoken till *Adam* had his Wife, must she not thereby be Lady, as well as he Lord of the World?" (1.29). There then follows a passage of extraordinary importance for the argument about equality:

> God in this Donation, gave the World to Mankind in common, and not to *Adam* in particular. The word *Them* in the Text must include the Species of Man, for 'tis certain *Them* can by no means signifie *Adam* alone. . . . *They* then were to have Dominion. Who? even those who were to have the *Image* of God, the Individuals of that Species of *Man* that he was going to make, for that *Them* should signifie *Adam* singly, exclusive of the rest, that should be in the World with him, is against both Scripture and all Reason: And it cannot possibly be made Sense, if *Man* in the former part of the *Verse* do not signifie the same with *Them* in the latter, only *Man* there, as is usual, is taken for the Species, and *them* the individuals of that Species . . . God makes him *in his own Image after his own Likeness*, makes him an intellectual Creature, and so capable of Dominion. For wherein soever else the *Image of God* consisted, the intellectual Nature was certainly a part of it, and belong'd to the whole Species. (*Two Treatises*, 1.30)

This is the one place in the *Treatise* where Locke associates humankind in general with the Judaeo-Christian idea of *imago dei*, the image of God, in a way that makes it absolutely clear that that characterization applies to Eve (the only other member of the species around) as well as to Adam, to women as well as men.

Intriguingly (for us), this passage is also a meditation on pronouns—

"the word *Them* in the Text . . . can by no means signifie Adam alone"—
and on the meaning of the word "Man"—"*Man* there, as is usual, is taken
for the Species, and *them* the individuals of that Species." Now, as I said,
besides Adam the only other member of the species around at the relevant time was Eve. This passage makes no sense unless we assume that
"Them" includes Eve, that "Man" includes "Eve," and that even "him"
includes Eve in Locke's comment that "God makes him *in his own Image
after his own Likeness*, makes him an intellectual Creature" (*Two Treatises*,
1.16). The grant of dominion over the animals, says Locke, "was not to
Adam in particular, exclusive of all other Men," and his evidence for this
is that God "spoke to Eve also" (1.29). I am belaboring this point just
because it is so often and so carelessly assumed by modern commentators
that by "Man" or "Men" Locke means only males, whereas this whole
passage is completely unintelligible unless we assume that females are
included also.[10]

What about the role of Eve in the Fall, and the particular sentence
God imposed on her, as reported in Genesis 3:16—"Unto the woman he
said, I will greatly multiply thy sorrow and thy conception; in sorrow
thou shalt bring forth children; and thy desire shall be to thy husband,
and he shall rule over thee"? Locke's account of this is complicated. First
he notes that *both* Adam and Eve are being punished by their offended
maker, and that this would be an odd time for God to choose for vesting
"Prerogatives and Privileges" in Adam, when He was "denouncing Judgment, and declaring his Wrath against them both, for their Disobedience" (*Two Treatises*, 1.44). Certainly God's words do amount to a curse
on Eve "for having been the first and forwardest in the Disobedience"
(1.44). And it is a worse curse than Adam suffers: "As a helper in the
Temptation, as well as a Partner in the Transgression, *Eve* was laid below
him, and so he had accidentally a Superiority over her, for her greater
Punishment" (1.44). Yet Adam too had his share in the Fall, says Locke,
and he suffered along with Eve the most severe punishment of all: the
loss of immortality.[11] Adam also suffers the condemnation of having to
work for subsistence—"*In the Sweat of thy Face thou shalt eat thy Bread*,
says God to him, ver. 19" (1.45)—and Locke notes wryly that Adam is
definitely *not* given permission to sit back and let Eve do the spadework,
on account of her greater transgression.

Indeed the subordination of Eve is so much a matter of contingency—so much an optional extra, as it were—that the special curse
upon her may be read, Locke suggests, as a prediction rather than a pre-

scription: "God, in this Text, gives not, that I see, any Authority to *Adam* over *Eve*, or to Men over their Wives, but only fortels what should be the Womans Lot, how by his Providence he would order it so" (*Two Treatises*, 1.47). Now this is not all he has to say about the matter, as we shall see in a moment, and his introduction of the idea of "Providence" might seem to blur the line between prediction and prescription.[12] But it is worth noting that Locke says about this business of subjection exactly what he says about pain in childbirth. Though Genesis 3:16 predicts pain in childbirth—"in sorrow thou shalt bring forth children"—it does not prohibit anesthesia: and similarly in the condemnation of Eve to being ruled by her husband, "there is . . . no more Law to oblige a Woman to such a Subjection, if the Circumstances either of her Condition or Contract with her Husband should exempt her from it, th[a]n there is, that she should bring forth her Children in Sorrow and Pain, if there could be found a Remedy for it" (*Two Treatises*, 1.47).

One other point in this connection. Locke's views on the subject of original sin were always controversial—it was one of many grounds on which people accused him of Socinianism.[13] He tended generally to minimize the transmission down the generations from Adam and Eve of either sin or punishment. What was lost in the Fall, he wrote in *The Reasonableness of Christianity*, was immortality. Adam and Eve were created immortal in the image of God; "but Adam, transgressing the command given him by his heavenly Father, incurred the penalty; forfeited that state of immortality. . . . After this, Adam begot children: but they were 'in his own likeness, after his own image;' mortal, like their father" (*Reasonableness of Christianity*, 106). That, Locke suggests, is a genetic matter: as he puts it in a note to his paraphrase of Romans 5:12, "a mortal father. infected now with death, [was] able to produce noe better than a mortal race."[14] It is not a *punishment* imposed on all of Adam and Eve's descendants; God cannot be supposed to have committed the injustice of visiting the sins of the father upon the children. And, Locke adds in *The Reasonableness of Christianity*, "much less can the righteous God be supposed, as a punishment of one sin, wherewith he is displeased, to put man under the necessity of sinning continually."[15] It seems to follow from this that Locke is not in a position to accept any view about the subordination of women which supposes that they became especially corrupt, all the way down the human line, as a result of the Fall. If Eve sinned, that is true of Eve only. If Eve was subordinated to her husband by her greater transgression, that is true of Eve only. Throughout his work Locke is adamant that punishment is not vicarious: "Every one's sin is charged upon himself only."[16] It would make no sense in the Lockean scheme of things to attribute Eve's particular punishment to all of Eve's female descendants.[17]

Intriguingly, Sir Robert Filmer does not associate political power with the Fall either. Though he was happy to derive what he could from Genesis 3:16, his basic position set out in *The Anarchy of a Limited or Mixed Monarchy* was that Eve was subject to Adam before she sinned. Political authority, on Filmer's view, is not at all a postlapsarian remedy for sin, any more than the legitimate subjection of the angels to God before the fall of Satan.[18] Filmer goes on to acknowledge that Adam would have had no occasion to *coerce* Eve before the Fall, nor even to direct her "in those things which were necessarily and morally to be done." She would be disposed to do those things naturally in her original innocent condition. Yet there were things to be settled in the state of nature—Filmer calls them "things indifferent" (maybe the gardening schedule?) that depended merely on the free will of Adam and Eve—and in these, said Filmer, Eve "might be directed by the power of Adam's command."[19]

Now Locke does not respond directly to that passage of Filmer's, about Adam having a natural power of direction even in paradise over things that are otherwise indifferent. In view of his egalitarian premise, we might expect his response to be that *no one* has a power of direction over things indifferent—that's what natural *freedom* amounts to.[20] But the odd thing is that Locke in fact seems to agree with Filmer. This is where the hesitations and the contradictions begin.

A Husband's Authority

Remember I said earlier that Locke suggests we try reading Eve's subjection to Adam as a prediction rather than a prescription. But he also says that if you *want* to read it as a divine prescription, the words of Genesis 3:16 "import no more but that Subjection [women] should ordinarily be in to their Husbands" (*Two Treatises*, 1.47). Concerning the subjection of women, he says: "We see that generally the Laws of Mankind and customs of Nations have ordered it so; and there is, I grant, a Foundation in Nature for it" (1.47).

Now *that* is an alarming claim for a theorist of equality: *there is a foun-*

dation in nature for the ordinary subjection of a woman to her husband. And the claim is explicit in Locke's argument in the *Second Treatise*—quite outside the Adam and Eve context—in some notorious observations that he makes about marriage and about the location of final authority in what he calls "*Conjugal Society.*" The *Second Treatise* passage on this is pretty well known. It begins with equality of individual rights. The basis of marriage, says Locke, is "a voluntary Compact between Man and Woman" consisting "chiefly in . . . a Communion and Right in one another's Bodies." It includes also obligations of "mutual Support, and Assistance" and a "Communion of Interests" uniting their care and affection, and providing of course for their children (*Two Treatises*, 2.78). Intriguingly, in the posthumously published *Paraphrase and Notes on the Epistles of St. Paul,* Locke even produces an argument for reciprocity so far as rights in one another's bodies are concerned. Commenting in a footnote to his paraphrase of 1 Corinthians 7:4,[21] Locke observes that "the woman (who in all other rights is inferior) has here the same power given her over the mans body, that the man has over hers. The reason whereof is plain. Because if she had not her man, when she had need of him; as well as the man his woman when he had need of her, marriage would be noe remedy against fornication."[22] At any rate, having set up these reciprocal rights and duties in the *Second Treatise*, Locke then introduces a sickeningly familiar asymmetry, along the following lines: "But the Husband and Wife, though they have but one common Concern, yet having different understandings, will unavoidably sometimes have different wills too; it therefore being necessary, that the last Determination, i.e. the Rule, should be placed somewhere, it naturally falls to the Man's share, as the abler and the stronger" (*Two Treatises*, 2.82). "Naturally . . . the Man's share, as the abler and the stronger." What does this portend for Locke's egalitarianism?

It is pretty obvious that this position on marital authority sits uneasily with any principle of basic human equality. But where exactly does the inconsistency lie? It is hard to tell, because the meaning of the passage is unclear. We can read it in two ways. The reference to *strength*—"the abler and the stronger"—might suggest that what we have here is a relationship based on conquest and violence. I do not think that was what Locke meant. It would straightforwardly contradict his contractualist account of marriage. "Conjugal society," he says, "is made by a voluntary compact" (*Two Treatises*, 2.78), and there is no suggestion (as there is in *Leviathan*, for example) that the voluntariness of such an arrangement could be compatible with its being the upshot of coercion.[23] I think that Locke cannot plausibly be read as saying that the husband's matrimonial authority may be established by force, not only because it would embarrass the fundamentals of his contractualist account, but also—perhaps paradoxically—because Locke conceded that although this was likely to happen in fact, its happening in fact did not determine the right of the matter. I have in mind here the distinction between prediction and prescription which we talked about a little while ago.[24] Remember his comment about the prediction of pain in childbirth not prohibiting anesthesia: "There is here no more Law to oblige a Woman to such a Subjection, if the Circumstances either of her Condition or Contract with her Husband should exempt her from it, th[a]n there is, that she should bring forth her Children in Sorrow and Pain, if there could be found a Remedy for it" (*Two Treatises*, 1.47). In general Locke was quite careful to distinguish *de facto* probabilities from prescribed or legitimated outcomes.[25] In the *Letter Concerning Toleration*, for example, he was adamant that the physical ability of a magistrate to prevail over a subordinated minority did not make his prevailing right: "You will say, then, the magistrate being the stronger will have his will and carry his point. Without doubt; but the question is not here concerning the doubtfulness of the event, but the rule of right."[26] Might is not necessarily right; so the right of male rule is not established by the mere fact of male strength. (As an aside, let me say that I also disagree with John Simmons's suggestion that there is anything in common between Locke's argument here about male strength and his argument in the *Second Treatise* about majority rule—"it being necessary to that which is one body to move one way; it is necessary the body should move that way whither the greater force carries it" [2.96].[27] The only thing in common in the two situations is the need for a decision rule, and as I argued in *The Dignity of Legislation*,[28] the majoritarian argument does not really involve an appeal to physical strength at all.)

However, there is another way of reading this passage about the will of the husband prevailing. It is a more plausible reading, but it still involves a head-on challenge to the principle of basic equality. Locke's suggestion might be that male strength and male ability constitute an *entitlement* to authority—strength and ability in the sense of a superior capacity to carry out the tasks involved in the relationship. It is a distinction of authority based on an allegation about a distinction of merit.

Is this necessarily a problem for basic equality? Even in his most egali-

tarian moments, Locke does not deny that there are important distinctions in capacity among human beings—and hence functional
distinctions in merit. Actually he insists on the point: "Though I have
said above, Chap. II. *That all Men by Nature are equal*, I cannot be supposed to understand all sorts of *Equality: Age* or *Virtue* may give men a
just Precedency: *Excellency of Parts and Merit* may place others above the
Common Level" (*Two Treatises*, 2.54). The trouble is that Locke also
wants to insist that differences like these are consistent with basic equality *of authority*. The passage just quoted continues: "And yet all this consists with the *Equality*, which all *Men* are in, in respect of Jurisdiction or
Dominion one over another; which was the *Equality* I there spoke of, as
proper to the Business in hand, being that equal *Right*, that every Man
hath, *to his Natural Freedom*, without being subjected to the Will or Authority of any other Man" (2.54). But that is exactly what this business
about the superior ability of the husband denies. In the passage about
husbands and wives, Locke is not just noticing a difference in ability, he
is inferring a difference in authority from a difference in the capacities of
human beings; and that *is* fundamentally at odds with what he wants to
say generally about equality. The inconsistency is the more striking because, as far as I can tell, this is the only place in his mature thought
where Locke bases entitlement to authority on superior capacity.[29] He
does say in a few places that people might *choose* their ruler on the basis
of ability.[30] But in such cases consent is still the basis of authority; and
although the recognition of ability may be a reason for giving consent, it
does not trump or override it. Nowhere, except in this passage about
husbands and wives, does he say that ability confers authority in the
absence of consent or perhaps even in contradiction of consent.

True, Locke does talk about the power of parent over child as based on
the difference in their respective capacities. But there the point is that
the child really has no will or understanding of its own. In the case of
husbands and wives, the passage about the husband's ability is predicated
on the assumption that the husband and wife are both rational beings
and it is simply a matter of whose will is to prevail: "The Husband and
Wife, though they have but one common Concern, yet having different
understandings, will unavoidably sometimes have different wills too; it
therefore being necessary, that the last Determination, *i.e.* the Rule,
should be placed somewhere" (*Two Treatises*, 2.82). The issue is undeni-
ably one of authority, then—authority among beings who are without

question supposed to be one another's equals so far as authority is concerned.

Locke's Inconsistency

I wish Locke had not said this: it would make my life easier as an exponent of his theory of basic equality. But there is no way round it. The
position cannot be saved by saying, "Well, Locke just accepted the custom of his day." Locke was a consistent critic of the customs of his day
on all sorts of topics, and he was well aware of the "gross absurdities" to
which "the following of Custom, when Reason has left it, may lead" (*Two
Treatises*, 2.157). He was at least as capable of distancing himself from
the assumptions of his culture as we are from ours.[31] Moreover, in both
Treatises he talked about law and custom in regard to men and women,
and he made his argument about the "foundation in nature" for male
superiority explicitly as a point in addition to that. Or more precisely,
what he said was that there is a natural presumption in favor of husbands
that can be displaced either by the contract between husband and wife
or by some contrary custom or local law. But even the idea of a defeasible
natural presumption here is at odds with basic equality.

Nor can the consistency of Locke's overall position be saved by saying
that this is a subordination of wives in the specific circumstance of marriage, not a general proposition about the inequality of women. Strictly
speaking that is true, though Locke's point in the *Treatises* is that the
subordination of wives is based on the natural inferiority of women. Elsewhere in his writings, Locke describes women as the "weaker" and "the
more timid" sex.[32] He talks also in the *Essay Concerning Human Understanding,* of nurses and maids as sources of myth and disinformation.[33] In
the footnotes to his paraphrase of 1 Corinthians, Locke talks freely of
"the subordination of the sexes," the undesirability of setting "women at
liberty from their natural subjection to men," "the confessed superiority
and dominion of the man," and "this subordination which god for order's
sake had instituted in the world."[34]

In an excellent essay on Locke and feminism, Melissa Butler has observed the "hesitant" tone in which Locke talks about conjugal inequality.[35] He qualifies it, she says, and he does his best to mitigate it and limit
its impact on the rest of the theory. She is right—up to a point. Accord-

ing to Locke, the husband's authority affects only matters of common concern. It does not affect the wife's personal property. It may be offset by the contract between them or by municipal law. And it may be terminated by divorce, "there being no necessity in the nature of the thing, nor to the ends of it, that [this relationship] should always be for Life" (*Two Treatises*, 2.81).[36] And Butler is right in the further point she makes, about Locke's argument that a husband's authority has nothing to do with *political* power. It is, says Locke, at most, "only a Conjugal Power, not Political, the Power that every Husband hath to order the things of private Concernment in his Family, as Proprietor of the Goods and Land there, and to have his Will take place before that of his wife in all things of their common Concernment; but not a Political Power of Life and Death over her, much less over any body else" (1.48). Still, even this does not really reconcile the position to the principle of basic equality. Locke may insist on a verbal difference between conjugal and political society,[37] and even a difference in content—the husband has no power over the *life* of his lady, whereas the magistrate does. (And we must bear in mind Mary Astell's response: "What tho' a Husband can't deprive a Wife of Life without being responsible to the Law, he may however do what is much more grievous to a generous Mind, render Life miserable.")[38] But the fact is that Locke has built a difference of authority between two adult human wills on the basis of natural differences. And that in itself, being quite at odds with what he says about equality, is enough to cast doubt on the general premise—which is essential to his politics— that no such construction is legitimate. Locke's political theory depends on flattening out the traditional hierarchies within the human species, and he does that by denying that natural differences among humans give rise to basic differences of authority. Once that is compromised, as it certainly is in this instance, the credibility of the general position is shaken.[39]

A Consistent Patriarchalist?

Carole Pateman believes that a consistent position *is* salvageable if we take seriously the propositions we have just been examining about women and conjugal authority. What we have to realize, says Pateman, is that for Locke the issue of *political* power over women does not arise. In Locke's scheme of things political power is a relation between free and equal individuals; conjugal power on the other hand is a relation between a free individual and a creature that is something less than a free individual. It is a form of "natural subjection," and it is simply unregulated by the equality-oriented principles associated with politics. Hence Pateman's conclusion so far as Locke's discussion of husbands' authority is concerned: "None of this disturbs Locke's picture of the state of nature as a condition 'wherein all the Power and Jurisdiction is reciprocal, . . . without Subordination or Subjection.' . . . The natural subjection of women, which entails their exclusion from the category of 'individual,' is irrelevant to Locke's investigation."[40] In other words, consistency is saved for Locke (according to Pateman) by inferring that when he says all men are equal, he *does* after all mean "men" in the narrow gendered sense. I have a lot of respect for Carole Pateman's work, and I am tempted to concede at least the following: if consistency is to be attributed at all costs to Locke's theory in the *Second Treatise*, then we must conclude that "women are excluded from the status of 'individual' in the natural condition . . . the attributes of individuals are sexually differentiated; only men naturally have the characteristics of free and equal beings."[41] That will be the price of insisting that the claims about equality have to be reconciled somehow with the claims about superiority: the only way to reconcile them is to read "Men" in "all Men by Nature are equal" (*Two Treatises*, 2.54) as referring only to males.

And if we go this far, we need not go very much further to infer that John Locke did not believe married women could own property or participate (as property-holders) in politics. Locke insists that no one truly has property in anything which another can rightfully take from her, when he pleases, against her consent (*Two Treatises*, 2.138). It seems to follow then from the claim that a husband's decisions about family property take precedence over his wife's, that wives cannot really be property-holders at all.[42] Moreover if there is any question about whether the family property is to be brought under the auspices of civil society in the social contract for its better protection etc., again it would seem to follow that the husband's will should rightfully prevail so that married woman are not normally to be understood as parties to the social contract in their own right. And so the whole fabric of apparent gender-equality unravels. Locke may have tried to give the impression of arguing against patriarchy, and he may even have pulled the wool over the eyes of a few gullible twentieth-century liberals. But it was all a trick, and feminist commentators are not fooled. They know that this is really a chauvinist wolf in egalitarian clothing.[43]

But in fact the position is still not entirely consistent, if we read Locke in the way that Pateman invites us to read him. On her interpretation, there are a number of unfortunate relics of Locke's commitment to equality that stand out inconveniently from his overall sexism.

First, Locke actually *does* talk about married women having their own property. In his discussion of just war toward the end of the *Second Treatise*, he insists that even a justly conquered husband does not forfeit his wife's estate: "For as to the Wife's share, whether her own Labour or compact gave her a Title to it, 'tis plain, Her Husband could not forfeit what was hers" (2.183).[44] Here, as elsewhere the ownership of property by women is used as the basis of an important political argument. In the *First Treatise*, too, Locke will not allow Filmer to evade the force of his insistence that God gave the world to Adam and Eve, not to Adam alone, on the basis of Eve's subordination:

> The Grant being to them, *i.e.* spoke to *Eve* also, as many Interpreters think with reason, that these words were not spoken till *Adam* had his Wife, must not she thereby be Lady, as well as he Lord of the World? If it be said that *Eve* was subjected to *Adam*, it seems she was not so subjected to him, as to hinder her *Dominion* over the Creatures, or *Property* in them: for shall we say that God ever made a joint Grant to two, and one only was to have the benefit of it? (*Two Treatises*, 1.29)

And this is followed by the great passage I quoted earlier (*Two Treatises*, 1.30), to the effect that the word "*Man*" must cover Eve as well—not just as a matter of semantics, but because she too bears the image of God, an intellectual nature, which does not belong to the male sex only.

Second, Locke says several times that women's status in marriage is determined by a contract to which the woman is a full and equal partner: "Conjugal society is made by a voluntary Compact between man and Woman" (*Two Treatises*, 2.78). Even the comment about the husband having the final say in the marriage, which is the source of our trouble here, is presented only as a weak and defeasible default condition for the contract, something that the parties may bargain around or something that may permissibly be displaced by a positive law stipulation of equality (2.82).

Third, once the children are provided for (2.80), Locke is at pains to emphasize that women have a right to separate from their husbands, if they like, and resume a life as independent members of the community (2.81–82). This, too, was a heterodox position in Locke's time, and as Melissa Butler notes, for several centuries afterward.

Put these positions together—women can own property in their own right; marriage is contractual; and marriage can be ended unilaterally by a woman, if her children are provided for—and the conclusion is inescapable: women are regarded in the *Second Treatise* as ordinary functioning persons, entitled to promote and protect their rights (including their property rights) through ordinary contractual arrangements. And if this is so, it is hard to see how Locke's extension of contractarianism into the political sphere could fail to apply to them also. The only way that land owned by a single woman can be brought under the jurisdiction of a polity is by the consent of the owner. And so far as married women are concerned, the only way in which they can be subjected to political authority is by their own consent. Locke seems to display no interest in the position that the husband consents on behalf of his wife; all his effort in this part of the *Second Treatise* involves the denial that conjugal power has anything in common with, and indeed anything much to do with, political power (*Two Treatises*, 2.83). The only relation to political power that Locke mentions is that the natural default principle of conjugal power may actually be abrogated by positive political arrangements.

I am not saying that Locke believed in women's suffrage (nor am I denying this). His position on the suffrage was that its distribution was a matter of choice or convention among the founding members of a society. The people, when they set up a government, may organize its legislature—and if it is an elective legislature, they may organize the basis of the franchise—any way they please (*Two Treatises*, 2.132). But it is implausible to suppose that Locke regarded women as being necessarily excluded from "the people" who constitute a government. Quite apart from the points we have already noted about women as property-owners and women as contractors, we need to bear in mind Locke's recognition of women as political actors. Women, he says, may be monarchs—he could hardly deny it, in light of English history—and he says that their political power is unaffected by the fact of their marriage (*Two Treatises*, 1.47).[45] When he talks of queens, he makes none of the disparaging remarks he makes about other controversial cases—for example, fools and infants wearing the crown in actually existing monarchies (1.123). But he does make fun of the position—which he thinks Filmer would have no choice but to adopt—that Elizabeth I was subject to the authority of her nearest male relative, as he makes fun also of the idea that in England Mary Tudor was subject to the authority of *her* husband, Philip of Spain (1.47).

Of course there were people in the seventeenth century who argued that women could not be among the fundamental constitutors of government. But they usually said so in quite forthright terms. Carole Pateman offers no explanation of why Locke did not follow Samuel Pufendorf and his own friend James Tyrrell in making the exclusion of women explicit. Pufendorf said that "states have certainly been formed by men, not women" and this is why the right of the father prevails.[46] Locke said nothing of the sort. But why would he be less forthcoming than Pufendorf if this (as Pateman suggests) was the main point of his argument? James Tyrrell said that "women are commonly unfit for civil business."[47] Again, why would Locke be less forthcoming on this than his friend?[48]

We know Locke was prepared to acknowledge that almost all states have been patriarchal in their actual historical origins. He talks about "how easy it was in the first Ages of the World, . . . for the *Father of the Family* to become the Prince of it" (*Two Treatises*, 2.74). And he says that it was important that people chose someone they naturally loved and trusted as their primeval ruler, for "without such nursing fathers[49] tender and careful of the public weal, all Governments would have sunk under the Weakness and Infirmities of their Infancy" (*Two Treatises*, 2.110). Yet Locke is adamant about inferring *nothing* from this about the appropriate shape or personnel for modern politics, except that it is sometimes a good idea to give political authority to people you trust. So far as fathers, husbands, males generally being appropriate occupants of political office, the conclusion is insistent: "An Argument from what has been, to what should of right be, has no great force" (*Two Treatises*, 2.103). This is quite at variance with the style of argument of those in the seventeenth century who we *know* held the position that Pateman is attributing to Locke.

Finally we may ask: why is Locke at such pains to insist that the Fifth Commandment is a commandment equally to love and respect one's mother as well as one's father, if he held the basically patriarchal view that Pateman attributes to him?[50] In this, as Melissa Butler notes, "Locke broke with one of patriarchy's strongest traditions."[51] His insistence on including mothers as well as fathers is strident and repetitive: it goes on for more than six pages in the *First Treatise*.[52] The Fifth Commandment establishes equality between the parents, says Locke; and he cites a dozen other biblical verses that join "father" and "mother" in the same way.[53] "Nay, the Scripture makes the Authority of *Father and Mother* . . . so equal, that in some places it neglects even the Priority of Order, which is thought due to the Father, and the *Mother* is put first, as Lev. 19. 3" (*Two Treatises*, 1.61). He rejects out of hand Filmer's suggestion that the man as "the nobler and the principal agent in generation" of children is entitled to the greater benefit of the Fifth Commandment.[54] If anyone has priority, it is the woman:

> For no body can deny but that the Woman hath an equal share, if not the greater, as nourishing a Child a long time in her own Body out of her own Substance. There it is fashion'd, and from her it receives the Materials and Principles of its Constitution; And it is so hard to imagine the rational Soul should presently Inhabit the yet unformed Embrio, as soon as the Father has done his part in the Act of Generation, that if it must be supposed to derive anything from the Parents, it must certainly owe most to the Mother. (*Two Treatises*, 1.55)

True, Locke occasionally slips back into describing parental authority as "paternal" authority (*Two Treatises*, 2.170). And since he is arguing against any patriarchialist inference from the rights of a father over his child, he often argues explicitly on that ground (2.69). But as Mary Shanley has pointed out, whenever the issue of mothers' rights was raised, Locke insisted that paternal power should be termed *parental*: "For whatever obligation Nature and the right of Generation lays on Children, it must certainly bind them equal to both the concurrent Causes of it" (2.52).[55]

Of course none of this actually contradicts the Lockean claim that we are finding problematic—namely, that men and women are unequal on the basis of their own abilities, quite apart from their relation to their children. But still: Locke's emphasis on equal rights for mothers and his dependence on such passages to knock away one of the major platforms of Filmer's patriarchalism does sit rather ill with Carole Pateman's view that Locke himself was a consistent patriarchialist and proud of it.

An Untidy Conclusion

I have no tidy resolution to offer. Locke's position on the natural subjection of wives *is* an embarrassment for his general theory of equality. And there is not, as Carole Pateman thinks there is, an alternative consistent position—Lockean patriarchalism—into which the claims about the subjection of women fit comfortably. What we are left with is a mess. Bible and nature are cited for the proposition that women are men's inferiors; and Bible and nature are cited for the proposition that women and men are one another's equals, endowed intellectually—both of them—with sense, will, and understanding in the image of God. The combination of the two positions leaves us unclear about how wholeheartedly Locke was prepared to follow through on his convictions about equality in this fraught and contested terrain. They confirm the hunch with which I began, that what we have here is a philosopher struggling *not altogether successfully* to free his own thought as well as the thought of his contemporaries from the idea that something as striking as the difference between the sexes must count in itself as a refutation of basic equality.

A little earlier I referred to Locke's notes to his *Paraphrase* of Paul's First Epistle to the Corinthians, and I want to end with one more reference to that posthumous work. I said earlier that those notes contain some of Locke's choicer phrases about the subjection of women. But Locke also made some interesting remarks about the specific argument of 1 Corinthians 11: 3–13 about women covering their heads when they pray or prophesy.[56] He refuses to view the passage—he calls it "this about women"—as straightforward. It seems, he says, "as difficult a passage as most in St Pauls Epistles."[57] In his long note he is at pains to interpret Paul's strictures about women covering their heads when they pray or prophesy as referring not to their ordinary participation in a congregation—for he can't imagine that there would be any issue about that—but to the extraordinary "performing of some particular publick action by some one person," a particular woman moved by the Holy Spirit, while the rest of the assembly remained silent.[58] And he says that although St. Paul was not countenancing the possibility of women taking it upon themselves to be regular "teachers and instructers of the congregation"[59]—"This would have had too great an air of standing upon even ground with men"[60]—still that background subordination "hinderd not but that by the supernatural gifts of the spirit he might make use of the weaker sex to any extraordinary function when ever he thought fit, as well as he did of men."[61]

There is a story that when John Locke himself attended a service led by a woman preacher in 1696, he wrote afterward to the preacher, Rebecca Collier, congratulating her on her sermon and observing that "women, indeed, had the honour first to publish the resurrection of the

Lord of Love," and why should they not minister again in modern times to "the resurrection of the Spirit of Love?"[62] The question remains unanswered, and it has been suggested that the attribution of this letter to Locke is spurious.[63] Be that as it may, it is perhaps not altogether surprising—and this may be as good a point as any on which to end an inconclusive essay—to find that among the early readers of Locke's *Paraphrase and Notes on the Epistles of St Paul*, there was one Josiah Martin who read the passages I have just quoted, "and transcrib'd them into my *Common-Place-Book*, thinking they might be of some Service, to vindicate the Doctrine of Friends [i.e. Quakers] concerning Women's *Preaching in the Church*."[64] Martin was impressed by Locke's gloss, and he challenged other readers and "all unprejudiced Persons" to consider "whether the Notes above-cited were not intended to evince and demonstrate, That Women as well as Men had and were to have the Gifts of Prayer and Prophecy, . . . and whenever Women were moved or inspired by the Holy Ghost, they had the same Liberty to speak in the Congregation as the Men."[65] For his part, Martin was convinced that this was what "Judicious *Locke*" meant, and that his sentiments were occasioned by an incident some years earlier—"That *John Locke* being at a Meeting, where a certain North-Country Woman was, who had been travelling on Truth's Account, was so affected with her Testimony, as to say afterwards in Words to this Effect *That something Divine and Extraordinary affected the Preaching of that Woman*"[66]—which seems to comport with the tenor of the letter Locke allegedly wrote to Rebecca Collier.

I accept that there is nothing probative in any of this. It is perfectly possible to say that women may be preachers—even inspired and extraordinary preachers—and still believe they are naturally subordinate to men. As I said, I don't think we can attribute a consistent position to Locke. Still, the impression he left on Josiah Martin is worth remembering, not last because it serves as a useful reminder that the things that strike *us* as evidence that Locke shared his contemporaries' views on the subjection of women did not always or necessarily strike his contemporaries that way.

Notes

1. John Locke says that this quotation is from Robert Filmer's *Observations on Hobbes*, at p. 253, but I have not been able to confirm that reference. See John Locke, *Two Treatises of Government*, ed. Peter Laslett (Cambridge: Cambridge University Press, 1988), 1.104.

2. Thomas Hobbes, *Leviathan*, ed. Richard Tuck (Cambridge: Cambridge University Press, 1988), 107.

3. There is an excellent account in John Dunn, *The Political Thought of John Locke: An Historical Account of the Argument of the "Two Treatises of Government"* (Cambridge: Cambridge University Press, 1969), 96–104.

4. For a general study of Locke's egalitarianism, see Jeremy Waldron, *God, Locke, and Equality: Christian Foundations in John Locke's Political Thought* (Cambridge: Cambridge University Press, 2002). This chapter is an adaptation of chapter 2 of that book.

5. See, e.g., Ronald Dworkin, *Taking Rights Seriously* (London: Duckworth, 1977), 227.

6. Robert Filmer, *Patriarcha and Other Writings*, ed. Johann P. Sommerville (Cambridge: Cambridge University Press, 1991), 15.

7. For example, see Lorenne Clark's verdict in "Women and Locke: Who Owns the Apples in the Garden of Eden?" in *The Sexism of Social and Political Theory: Women and Reproduction from Plato to Nietzsche*, ed. Lorenne Clark and Lynda Lange (Toronto: University of Toronto Press, 1979), 35: "I conclude, therefore, that Locke's theory does display unequivocally sexist assumptions."

8. "But perhaps 'twill be said, *Eve* was not made till afterward: Grant it so, What advantage will our A. get by it?" *Two Treatises*, 1.30.

9. Filmer, "Observations on Mr Hobbes' Leviathan," cited but not discussed by Locke at *Two Treatises*, 1.14. Note, however, the intriguing pun in the final line of the following extract from Locke's 1662 "Verses on Queen Catherine," in John Locke, *Political Essays*, ed. Mark Goldie (Cambridge: Cambridge University Press, 1997), 210:

> When the first man without a rivall stood
> Possest of all, and all like him was good:
> Heaven thought that All imperfect, till beside
> 'T had made another self, and given a Bride:
> Empire, and Innocence were there, but yet
> 'Twas Eve made Man, and Paradise compleat.

10. Nor is this the only place Locke considers the linguistic characteristics of general words like "man" and rejects a purely masculine interpretation. We might mention also the passage in John Locke, *An Essay Concerning Human Understanding*, ed. P. H. Nidditch (Oxford: Clarendon Press, 1971), 3.3.7, where Locke talks about the way children learn the meaning of that word—generalizing from nurse, and mother and father, and from any "complex idea they had of Peter and James, Mary and Jane."

> There is nothing more evident, than that the *Ideas* of the Persons Children converse with . . . are, like the Persons themselves, only particular. The *Ideas* of the Nurse and the Mother are well framed in their Minds; and, like Pictures of them there, represent only those Individuals. The Names they first gave to them are confined to these Individuals; and the Names of *Nurse* and *Mamma*, the Child uses, determine themselves to those Persons. Afterwards, when time and a larger Acquaintance have made them observe, that there are a great many other Things in the World, that in some common agreements of Shape, and several other Qualities, resemble their Father and Mother, and those Persons they have been used to, they frame an *Idea*, which they find those many Particulars do partake in; and to that they give, with others, the name *Man*, for example. And *thus they come to have a general Name*, and a general *Idea*. Wherein they make nothing new; but only leave out of the complex *Idea* they had of *Peter* and *James*, *Mary* and *Jane*, that which is peculiar to each, and retain only what is common to them all.

There is surely no discernable masculinist bias in this account of the way the meaning of "man" is formed out of the ideas of Peter, James, Mary, Jane, etc.

11. For a vivid account, see John Locke, "Homo Ante et Post Lapsum," in *Locke: Political Essays*, 321. For an account of their punishment, which, like most contemporary Christian accounts, mentions only Adam's transgression, see John Locke, *The Reasonableness of Christianity, as Delivered in the Scriptures* (Bristol: Thoemmes Press, 1997), 4–9.

12. This is noticed in Melissa Butler's fine essay, "The Early Liberal Roots of Feminism: John Locke and the Attack on Patriarchy," *American Political Science Review* 72 (1978): 142–43. (I have drawn on Butler's essay at a number of points.) For Locke's broader discussion of the relation between providence, divine appointment, and accident in these matters, see *Two Treatises*, 1.16.

13. See W. M. Spellman, *John Locke and the Problem of Depravity* (Oxford: Clarendon Press, 1988), 104ff.

14. John Locke, *A Paraphrase and Notes on the Epistles of St. Paul*, ed. Arthur W. Wainwright, 2 vols. (Oxford: Clarendon Press, 1987), 2:524.

15. Locke, *Reasonableness of Christianity*, 6.

16. Ibid., 7. This point is also important in Locke's argument about conquest, in *Two Treatises*, 2.179 and 182 ("The Father, by his miscarriages and violence, can forfeit but his own Life, but involves not his Children in his guilt or destruction").

17. There is a comment in the *First Treatise* about the words of Genesis 3:16 being directed to Eve and "in her, as their representative to all other Women" (*Two Treatises*, 1.47), but it seems to be *arguendo* (the passage being prefaced "if we will take them as they were directed . . ."). For Locke's theory of representation in regard to the Fall, see Ian Harris, "The Politics of Christianity," in *Locke's Philosophy: Content and Context*, ed. G.A.J. Rogers (Oxford: Clarendon Press, 1994).

18. See Filmer, "Anarchy of a Limited or Mixed Monarchy," in Filmer, *Patriarcha and Other Writings*, 145: "Eve was subject to Adam before he sinned; the angels, who are of a pure nature, are subject to God—which confutes their saying who, in disgrace of civil government or power say it was brought in by sin." (I fear that Butler, "Early Liberal Roots of Feminism," 138, misreads this as suggesting that the difference between man and woman is comparable to that between God and angel.)

19. Filmer, "Anarchy," in *Patriarcha and Other Writings*, 145: "Government as to coactive power was after sin, because coaction supposeth some disorder, which was not in the state of innocencey: but as for directive power, the condition of human nature requires it, since civil society cannot be imagined without power of government. for although as long as men continued in the state of innocency they might not need the direction of Adam in those things which were necessarily and morally to be done, yet things indifferent—that depended merely on their free will—might be directed by the power of Adam's command."

20. Cf. *Two Treatises*, 2.4: "We must consider, what State all Men are naturally in, and that is, *a State of perfect Freedom* to order their Actions, and dispose of their Possessions and Persons, as they think fit, within the bounds of the Law of Nature, without asking leave, or depending upon the will of any other Man."

21. 1 Corinthians 7:4: "The wife hath not power of her own body, but the husband: and likewise also the husband hath not power of his own body, but the wife."

22. Locke, *Paraphrase and Notes on the Epistles*, 1:199–200.

23. Cf. Hobbes, *Leviathan*, 97: "Covenants entred into by fear, in the condition of meer Nature, are obligatory." Hobbes of course did not concede that male strength inevitably prevailed: "There is not always that difference of strength or prudence between the man and the woman as that the right can be determined without War" (139).

24. In *Two Treatises*, 1.47, Locke says that Genesis 3:16—"thy desire shall be to thy husband, and he shall rule over thee"—can be read as a prediction rather than a prescription: "God, in this Text, gives not, that I see, any authority to Adam over Eve, or to Men over their Wives, but only fortels what should be the Womans Lot."

25. See, for example, the discussion of conquest and slavery at *Two Treatises*, 2.179.

26. John Locke, A *Letter Concerning Toleration*, ed. James Tully (Indianapolis: Hackett Publishing, 1983), 49.

27. A. John Simmons, *The Lockean Theory of Rights* (Princeton: Princeton University Press, 1992), 174.

28. Jeremy Waldron, *The Dignity of Legislation* (Cambridge: Cambridge University Press, 1999), 136ff.

29. He never makes any such claim about the magistrate or about legislative representatives in the *Second Treatise*. In *A Letter Concerning Toleration*, 36, Locke is at pains to deny that magistracy is best understood in terms of superior ability: "Princes, indeed, are born superior unto other men in power, but in nature equal. Neither the right nor the art of ruling does necessarily carry along with it the certain knowledge of other things."

30. See Locke's discussion in *Two Treatises*, 2.75 and 105 of adult children's reasons for choosing their fathers as rulers in primeval political society—"He was fittest to be trusted; Paternal affection secured their Property and Interest under his Care; . . . If therefore they must have one to rule them, . . . who so likely to be the Man as he that was their common Father; unless Negligence, Cruelty, or any other defect of Mind or Body made him unfit for it? But when either the Father died, and left his next Heir, for want of Age, Wisdom, Courage, or any other Qualities, less fit for Rule; or where several Families met, and consented to continue together; There, 'tis not to be doubted, but they used their natural freedom, to set up him, whom they judged the ablest, and most likely, to Rule well over them." See also Jeremy Waldron, "John Locke: Social Contract versus Political Anthropology," *Review of Politic* 51 (1989): 3–28.

31. Lorenne Clark is rightly insistent on this point: "Locke was quite prepared to challenge the deepest principles of English land law." See Clark, "Women and Locke," 33.

32. John Locke, "Essays on the Law of Nature," in *Locke: Political Essays*, 113, and "Virtue B," in ibid., 288.

33. Early in Locke, *Essay Concerning Human Understanding*, 1.3.32, there is a suggestion that "*Doctrines*, that have been derived from no better original, than the Superstition of a Nurse, or the Authority of an old Woman; may, by length of time, and consent of Neighbours, grow up to the dignity of *Principles in Religion or Morality*." Later Locke offers this observation about the idea of goblins and sprites: "Let but a foolish Maid inculcate these often on the Mind of a Child, and raise them there together, possibly he shall never be able to separate them again so long as he lives, but darkness shall ever afterwards bring with it those frightful *Ideas*" (2.33.10). See also the references in William Walker, "Locke Minding Women: Literary History, Gender, and the Essay," *Eighteenth-Century Studies* 23, no. 3 (spring 1990): 250–52.

34. Locke, *Paraphrase and Notes on the Epistles*, 1:222. One always has to be careful with Locke's *Paraphrase and Notes on the Epistles* that one is citing Locke and not St. Paul (in Locke's reconstruction of his teachings). My citations are to the *footnotes* in this posthumously published work, for it is there that Locke seems to comment in his own voice. These footnotes amount to substantial commentaries: for example, the footnote from which I have taken the phrases quoted in the text runs for three pages.

35. Butler, "Early Liberal Roots of Feminism," 143.

36. And Locke continues: "But this reaching but to the things of their common Interest and Property, leaves the Wife in the full and free possession of what by Contract is her peculiar Right, and gives the Husband no more power over her Life than she has over his. The *Power of the Husband* being so far from that of an absolute Monarch, that the *Wife* has in many cases a liberty to *separate* from him; where natural Right, or their Contract allows it; whether that Contract be made by themselves in the state of Nature, or by the Customs or Laws of the Country they live in; and the Children upon Such Separation fall to the Father or Mother's Lot, as such Contract does determine" (*Two Treatises*, 2.82).

37. Cf. Carole Pateman, *The Sexual Contract* (Stanford: Stanford University Press, 1988), 52: "The battle is not over the legitimacy of a husband's conjugal right, but over what to call it."

38. Mary Astell, "Reflections Upon Marriage," in *Mary Astell: Political Writings*, ed. Patricia Springborg (Cambridge: Cambridge University Press, 1996), 17–18. See also Patricia Springborg, "Mary Astell (1666–1731), Critic of Locke," *American Political Science Review* 89 (1995): 628.

39. This, by the way, was exactly Mary Astell's critique of Locke in *Reflections Upon Marriage*, 17: "If Absolute Sovereignty be not necessary in a State, how comes it to be so in a Family? or if in a Family, why not in a State; since no Reason can be alleg'd for the one that will not hold more strongly for the other."

40. Pateman, *Sexual Contract*, 53.

41. Ibid., 52.

42. Cf. Mary Beth Norton, *Founding Mothers and Fathers: Gendered Power and the Forming of American Society* (New York: Alfred A. Knopf, 1996), 290: "If property holders by definition could not be subject to the whims of another person, then no wife—no woman—could be the sort of property owner who could participate in the establishment of government."

43. Why Locke should have wanted to conduct this elaborate charade is another question. As I said at the beginning of this essay, he had no particular incentive of "political correctness" in this regard. I suspect that in the late seventeenth century, his costume of superficial respect for gender equality would cause him more trouble than the partriarchalism he was supposed to be trying to disguise. But we will let that pass, as we pursue the Pateman interpretation.

44. Mary Beth Norton mentions this passage in a footnote (Norton, *Founding Mothers*, 458 n. 19) but does not attempt to reconcile it with her own interpretation that "wives by definition owned no property" (290).

45. There is a complication here. It has to do with Locke's attitude to the joint monarchy of William and Mary. In the preface to the *Two Treatises*, Locke writes as though only the throne of "King William" deserved his support (Locke, *Two Treatises*, 137). Peter Laslett notes in his "introduction" to that work (53n) that supporters of the Glorious Revolution were initially divided on the question of joint sovereignty, and that the faction that Locke belonged to initially supported sovereignty for William only. But I see no warrant for Laslett's suggestion on page 174 that Locke would not have made the argument he made in *Two Treatises*, 1.47, after April 1689, when Mary Stuart was crowned joint sovereign with William. That event might have complicated his statement of the point, but it would not have detracted from the point itself (viz. that political authority should not be at the mercy of obstetrics). See also David Wootton, "John Locke and Richard Ashcraft's 'Revolutionary Politics,'" *Political Studies* 40 (1992): 92.

46. Samuel Pufendorf, *On the Duty of Man and Citizen According to Natural Law*, ed. James Tully (Cambridge: Cambridge University Press, 1991), 125.

47. James Tyrrell, *Patriarcha Non Monarcha* (London: Richard Janeway, 1681), 83. (This passage is actually cited by Pateman, *Sexual Contract*, 77.) Tyrrell also observed, that "there never was any Government where all the Promiscuous Rabble of Women and Children had Votes, as being not capable of it" (*Patriarcha Non Monarcha*, 83). See Butler, "Early Liberal Roots of Feminism," 139.

48. For the significance of Locke's silences compared with what his contemporaries and predecessors were writing, see Quentin Skinner, "Meaning and Understanding in the History of Ideas," in *Meaning and Context: Quentin Skinner and His Critics*, ed. James Tully (Princeton: Princeton University Press, 1988), 62.

49. This intriguing phrase is biblical in origin. See Isaiah 49:23: "And kings shall be thy nursing fathers, and their queens thy nursing mothers: they shall bow down to thee with their face toward the earth, and lick up the dust of thy feet; and thou shalt know that I am the Lord: for they shall not be ashamed that wait for me."

50. See *Two Treatises*, 1.6, 11, and 60–68. Locke says that if "honor thy father" is a basis for kingship, then the Law also "enjoyns Obedience to Queens" (*Two Treatises*, 1.11), and certainly by including the mother, it "destroys the Sovereignty of one Supream Monarch" (1.65).

51. Butler, "Early Liberal Roots of Feminism," 143.

52. Would it be unfair to apply the term "grudging" to Carole Pateman's concession that "Locke points out *more than once* that the Fifth Commandment does not refer only to the father of the family" (*Sexual Contract*, 52; my emphasis)? By my count the point is discussed not just more than once, but *explicitly and at length* in each of twenty different sections of the *Two Treatises*.

53. *Two Treatises*, 1.61. Indeed this is one of the rare occasions in the *First Treatise* when Locke cites the Gospel—"For God commanded, saying, Honour thy father and mother: and, He that curseth father or mother, let him die the death" (Matthew 15:4). See also *Two Treatises*, 1.66.

54. Filmer, *Observations on Mr. Hobbes*, 192, cited in *Two Treatises*, 1.55.

55. Mary Lyndon Shanley, "Marriage Contract and Social Contract in Seventeenth Century English Political Thought," *Western Political Quarterly* 32 (1979): 377.

56. Here is Locke's paraphrase of 1 Corinthians 3–10, in *Paraphrase and Notes on the Epistles*, 1:221–22:

> Christ is the head to which every man is subjected, and the man is the head to which every woman is subjected. . . . Every man that prayeth or prophesieth . . . in the church for the edifying exhorting and comforting of the congregation haveing his head covered dishonoureth Christ his head, by appearing in a garb not becomeing the authority and dominion which god through Christ has given him over all the things of this world, the covering of the head being a mark of subjection. But on the contrary a woman praying or prophesying in the church with her head uncovered dishonoureth the man who is her head by appearing in a garb that disowns her subjection to him. For to appear bareheaded in publick is all one as to have her hair cut off, which is the garb and dress of the other sex and not of a woman. . . . A man indeed ought not to be veyled because he is the image and representative of god in his dominion over the rest of the world, which is one part of the glory of god: But the woman who was made out of the man, made for him, and in subjection to him, is matter of glory to the man.

(This is from the paraphrase, not the notes, so—once again—we must remember this is not necessarily Locke's own view of the matter.)

57. Ibid., 1:220, note a.

58. Ibid., note c.

59. Ibid., 222, note x.

60. Ibid., note y.

61. Ibid., note z.

62. Locke to Rebecca Collier, November 21, 1696, reprinted in H. R. Fox Bourne, *The Life of John Locke* (New York: Harper, 1976), 453; cited in Butler, "Early Liberal Roots of Feminism," 150.

63. See the editorial comment in *The Correspondence of John Locke*, ed. E. S. DeBeer, vol. 5 (Oxford: Clarendon Press, 1980), 718.

64. Josiah Martin, *A Letter to the Author of Some Brief Observations on the Paraphrase and Notes of the Judicious John Locke, relating to the Womens Exercising their Spiritual Gifts in the Church* (London, 1716), 4.

65. Ibid., 9–10. Wainwright's "Bibliography" in volume 1 of his edition of Locke, *Paraphrase and Notes on the Epistles*, 96, indicates that Martin also published in the following year (1717) another book on the subject, with the pithy title: "A Vindication of Women's Preaching, as well from Holy Scripture on Antient Writings as from the Paraphrase and Notes of the Judicious John Locke."

66. Martin, *A Letter to the Author of Some Brief Observations*, 32.

9

"His Nuts for a Piece of Metal"

Fetishism in the Monetary Writings of John Locke

Carol Pech

Written within a historical context characterized by significant contestations over the meanings of currency and exchange, John Locke's monetary writings do not at first glance appear to lend themselves well to the more conventional protocols of feminist interpretation. As extended and detailed considerations of the coinage crisis of the 1690s, Locke's texts on currency only tangentially engage issues such as property, family, and

The title for this chapter is a quotation from John Locke's *Second Treatise*, section 46. This essay has benefited from the critical eyes of many, including Gil Harris, Kirstie McClure, Diane Rubenstein, Peter Stallybrass, and Linda Zerilli. I also especially thank Nancy Hirschmann for her patience and persistence.

consent that have frequently been the focus of feminist analyses of his other works. Yet when the perspective is shifted away from these points of concern to a closer consideration of how Locke articulates his views on money, gender provides a thematically significant force that allows for a reading of these works attuned to the details of both text and context. In an effort to begin to unpack the linguistic complexity that characterizes his texts on coinage, this reading examines how Locke constructs his monetary thought through a reliance on rhetorical attributes historically associated with the feminine—namely, a figurative language of fluidity and its attendant trope, metonymy. With such a focus, it is possible to trace out how a process of fetishism structures Locke's understanding of money across various texts. Locke's fetishistic fixation on money as silver is articulated through metonymic and fluid constructions that allow him to disavow the political and epistemological anxieties brought on by an increasingly abstract system of exchange. Thus a consideration of Locke's fetishism not only makes the intricacies of his texts more salient but also demonstrates the importance of modes of signification aligned with the feminine within particular historical contexts.

Money's Perversions

The use of the conceptual apparatus of the fetish in various accountings of the historical adventures of money has long been commonplace, especially in the wake of Karl Marx's identification of the "riddle of the money fetish . . . visible and dazzling to our eyes."[1] The real "magic of money" is that it serves as a "crystallization of the exchange-value of commodities" and hence becomes the overprivileged object of human fascination or, in other words, a fetish.[2] As a fetish, money takes on a "perverted appearance" which carries a non-imaginary "mystification that is characteristic of all social forms of labor."[3] The perversity and obsessive fascination Marx ascribed to the fetish became in turn the object of Freud's investigations. In his explication of fetishism, Freud argues that any given fetish serves to disavow the threat of castration as allegedly represented by the perception of a woman's phallic lack. Through the logic of fetishism, the fetishist does not simply deny a perceived fear but also recognizes its "reality"—however unwanted—through the process of displacement. By fixating on a particular object or quality, the fetishist finds a substitute for what appears to be lacking and thereby reaches a compromise "between the weight of the unwelcome perception and the force of his counter-wish."[4] As a result, the fetish "remains a token of triumph over the threat of castration and a protection against it" by successfully mediating the intense anxiety brought on by the perception of a profound danger, in whatever form.[5]

Recently, Jean-Joseph Goux's work has sought to bring together the analyses of both Freud and Marx to develop a more detailed examination of money's perverse association with the fetish. In so doing, Goux describes the history of money as one "marked by a progression toward abstraction and convention" during which "increasingly abstract signs are gradually substituted" for items with material value.[6] Within this movement toward a fully abstract concept of money, the fetish functions as a discrete stage where the overestimation of a privileged object (e.g., silver) serves to moderate the anxieties brought on by the rise of increasingly symbolic modes of signification. Put differently, according to Goux's adaptation of Lacan, money's fetish stage allows the subject to cling to some aspect of the material imaginary that is about to be lost with accession to the symbolic order.[7] Moreover, the point of hesitation marked by the fetish is decidedly gendered because it is located between what Goux construes as the masculine symbolic order and the feminine imagery. This ambivalence is only temporary, however, for the subject must recognize the abstracting elements of the symbolic order to attain subjectivity and thus the fetish is but a moment of token resistance to the loss that accession to the symbolic demands. Hence, for Goux, money's fetish stage as well as its connection to the imaginary vanishes with the presumably inevitable assertion of the forces of (paternal/masculine) symbolic signification over the (maternal/feminine) imaginary.

Although Goux's analysis is provocative, it lacks a consideration of those historical moments when understandings of money are particularly fraught and, more specifically, how fetishism and its gendered associations operate within texts written during such periods. Locke's monetary writings offer precisely this opportunity, for they vividly display the confusion and anxieties produced by the conceptual contentions over currency that occurred throughout the seventeenth century. In particular, an examination of the theoretical tensions within Locke's monetary thought benefits from a more nuanced focus on fetishism as constructed through the critical resources of a feminist reading. Such an approach is particularly prescient since early modern monetary discourse constituted a dense locus of associations among currency, language, and particular understandings of woman and the feminine. The connection between currency and language alone is familiar even to the late modern reader—for example, the notion of "coining" words is still quite common. Yet, even some of these connotations have faded in words such as "commerce," which are now largely confined to an economic meaning and have lost their early modern references to linguistic and intellectual exchange. A far more wide-ranging loss, however, has occurred in regard to money's early associations with gender and sexuality, which have virtually disappeared from modern view. Throughout the seventeenth century, words such as "clip," "counterfeit," and "coinage" itself were explicitly linked to women and concerns about sexuality, particularly promiscuity and illegitimacy.[8] Thus a feminist reading attentive to such differing details of historical context is especially able to demonstrate how the intricacies of Locke's texts interact to produce an intriguing form of monetary fetishism.

To bring this process of fetishism to the fore requires particular attention to those rhetorical features historically aligned with the feminine, evident in Locke's texts through the movements of metonymy as well as the fluid figurative language that he relies on to characterize the workings of a troubled monetary system.[9] Locke's articulation of his anxieties about currency through a language of fluidity gains theoretical significance when viewed in light of fluidity's gendered connotations within the particular historical context of early modern England. The frequent ascription of fluidity to femininity during this period derived in part from Aristotelian medical frameworks and especially Galenic humoralism, which portrayed women's bodies as far moister and colder than those of men.[10] Articulated not only within nascent scientific writings but also across a variety of other popular texts, "the cultural association of women and liquids was so deeply inscribed that it required little empirical support."[11] Moreover, the perceived leakiness of women's bodies first noted in medical texts acquired a normative cast since corporeal fluidity was often understood as excessive and as such "either disturbing or shameful."[12] As a consequence, the ascription of fluidity to femininity served "not only to insinuate womanly unreliability but also to define the female body even when it is chaste . . . as a crucial problematic in the social formations of capitalism."[13] The disturbance attributed to fluidity was not solely confined to the female body, but also extended to early modern discussions concerning the problems of rhetoric in which women were linked "with uncontrollable and even indecent garrulity" as well as with the "transportability of certain tropes."[14] Initially located in the materiality of women's bodies, fluidity thus became a defining characteristic of both the feminine and conventional representations of woman across a number of cultural registers.

The particular rhetorical difficulties posed by the fluidity ascribed to woman gain greater resonance when considered in light of Luce Irigaray's work. As Irigaray asserts, "historically the properties of fluids have been abandoned to the feminine" because the structure of language itself maintains "a *complicity of long standing between rationality and a mechanics of solids alone.*"[15] The preferred relation between rationality and solids, as well as the province of masculine privilege it sustains, threatens to be undone through the recognition or articulation of feminine fluidity. Such liquid features are therefore minimized or idealized "so as to keep it/them from jamming the works of the theoretical machine."[16] As a result of this occlusion, conceptualizing the implications of the historic privileging of solid over fluids is made quite difficult by a "*historical lag in elaborating a 'theory' of fluids.*"[17] Yet not only is fluidity itself elided, its subsumption by a masculine solidity generates a specific rhetorical effect evident in the "privilege granted to metaphor (a quasi solid) over metonymy (which is much more closely allied to fluids)."[18] The rhetorical antinomy poses its own challenge to pursuing alternative critical approaches, for as Roman Jakobson suggests, metonymy "easily defies interpretation" and consequently "nothing comparable to the rich literature on metaphor can be cited for the theory of metonymy."[19] Hence for Irigaray, the task is to develop different reading practices that do not simply reinscribe "a historical 'inattention' to fluids," but instead give voice to alternative or historically obscured modes of signification.[20]

Irigaray's linguistic critique provides an avenue through which to consider how Locke's reliance on a fluid figurative language and the privileging of a certain trope produces a decidedly gendered monetary discourse. When paired with an attunement to the complexities of context, such an approach allows for a reading of Locke's texts that seeks to account for not only differing levels of signification but also the historical circumstances that helped shape them. Yet to read for the fluid and metonymic language that characterizes Locke's fetishism is not to uncritically conflate historically enmeshed notions of femininity with feminist concerns. To collapse such distinctions is problematic, for as Teresa de Lauretis notes, the "subject of feminism" is best understood as "not only distinct from Woman with the capital letter, the *representation* of an essence in-herent in all women . . . but also distinct from women, the real, historical beings and social subjects who are defined by the technology of gender."[21] Rather, the subject of feminism is a "theoretical construct (a way of con-ceptualizing, of understanding, of accounting for certain *processes*, not women)."[22] Integral to such an approach are those practices of reading that either "refuse the question [of woman] as formulated" by historically dominant discourses that constitute such processes, or perhaps even bet-ter "answer deviously (though in its words), even to quote (but against the grain)."[23]

Answering deviously in this case entails analyzing how the fluidity associated with historically specific understandings of the feminine works to rhetorically figure a compelling form of fetishism within Locke's mone-tary writings. Employed as both trope and description, those features of signification aligned with femininity enable Locke to fetishize silver in ways that permit the acknowledgment of the increasingly symbolic char-acter of money while simultaneously disavowing its more radical conse-quences. This approach to Locke's texts concerning currency, however, does more than draw attention to the importance of fluid figurative lan-guage in developing a different reading of these relatively neglected works. Rather, by taking up de Lauretis's suggestion and reading Locke's works both with and against the grain, a feminist reading illuminates the diverse modes of signification elided by the arguably exclusive historical perspectives that inhere in scholarly approaches to a period frequently regarded as the founding site of distinctly modern political and economic vocabularies.[24] Through this kind of feminist reading, the myriad con-cerns apparent in Locke's texts—semiotic, epistemological, political—acquire a distinct theoretical salience which demonstrates that the monetary crisis of the 1690s involved much more than the particular fate of some shabby silver coins.

A Context of Crisis

At the close of the seventeenth century, England's monetary system was in a shambles of no small proportion. Plagued by the widespread practice of clipping (whereby coins were shaved of some of their precious metal) and out of sync with international money markets, by the mid-1690s

English currency was on the verge of collapse for the second time in less than seventy years. In many ways, this was hardly surprising, since throughout the century England had experienced a number of wrenching economic shifts as "new networks of buyers and sellers replaced the isolated economies of local consumption."[25] Increasing international trade and a fluctuating currency utterly transformed both domestic and international markets such that previously familiar aspects of exchange were completely transformed. Responding to these massive changes involved not only learning the new tricks of the trade but also developing fresh concepts that would allow for these newly emerging but still enigmatic processes to be understood. Money was particularly problematic, not only because of continuing problems with currency per se (e.g., clipping). In addition, "the idea of a commerce in money was loaded with implications subversive to the concept of the world as containing an order of real things. A commerce in money suggested fluidity instead of fixed points."[26] Throughout the seventeenth century, former conceptualizations of the market and in particular monetary relations were increasingly replaced by entirely different—and hotly debated—symbolic representations unleashed through new market forces.

The last and arguably most critical debate of the seventeenth century concerning money surrounded the coinage crisis of the 1690s. Largely brought on by war with France and exacerbated by the attendant dilemmas of clipping and the illegal smuggling of precious metals, the ill state of the coin was debated in various texts ranging from government reports to broadside ballads. Despite the founding of the Bank of England in 1694, the deterioration of the currency by the mid-1690s was so great that the public had lost faith in the acceptability of the coin then in circulation. In his 1695 proposal for recoinage, then secretary to the treasury William Lowndes evoked the severity of the situation quite vividly. "In consequence of the vitiating, diminishing, and counterfeiting of the current monies, it is come to pass, that great contentions do daily arise amongst the king's subjects, in fairs, markets, shops, and other places throughout the kingdom, about the passing or refusing of the same, to the disturbance of the public peace."[27] Action of some sort was clearly needed in order to prevent a total collapse of English trade as well as public security. Discussions over recoinage proposals were particularly heated, in part because the coinage debates of the 1690s brought questions concerning the value and very definition of money to a prominence not seen since the currency crisis of the 1620s.[28] Given the difficulty involved "in finding a definition of money that would be adequate to the many new roles it played," this was no small or lightly taken task.[29]

Concerns regarding definition were central to the numerous proposals relating to the reminting of English coin, Locke's proposal being but one of the plans proffered.[30] The main position opposed to Locke's stance on recoinage was best articulated by Lowndes, who called for the taking in of old coins at face (or extrinsic) value and reminting these coins at the same face value but with a lower silver content. Lowndes and his proponents in effect favored a devaluation of the currency to bring it into line with the unofficial going rate of exchange rather than attempt to restore the official—and now inflated—standard. For Locke, however, such proposals played directly into the hands of the clippers. Since clipped coins had come to circulate with little fear of effective legal sanction, the real measure of coin for Locke (i.e., its true intrinsic value) had been lost.[31] To reestablish the true value of money required the reassertion of the official legal weight of coin, not a policy that accommodated the unofficial standard set by the clippers who had helped precipitate the coinage crisis in the first place. As a consequence, Locke's proposal called for the taking in of old coin at weight (i.e., according to its intrinsic value) rather than as Lowndes proposed at face value. To remint and return coin at weight would reassert the previous lawful standard for silver content rather than create a new—and degraded—official measure. Although Locke's plan would initially lessen the number of coins in circulation, it would at the same time reestablish the certainty of intrinsic value for English coin.

Locke's contemporaries met his unflinching insistence on the importance of maintaining the integrity of intrinsic value with a very mixed reception. Opponents blasted Locke for his assertions that money's value relied almost completely on its silver content and regarded his resistance to the increasingly symbolic character of coin as at best naïve. Nonetheless, Locke's stance on intrinsic value resonated with William III, and recoinage was carried out from 1696 to 1698. Although the recoinage did not follow Locke's technical recommendations for implementation, many held him responsible for its initially deleterious effects on English markets.[32] As mixed as the immediate technical impact of Locke's monetary writings was, the texts themselves subsequently encountered their own difficulties. With the notable exceptions of Marx and John Maynard Keynes, Locke's specific works on money have until fairly recently languished outside the purview of critical attention.[33] In part this is because they have only lately appeared in a critical edition that provides a smoother negotiation of their considerable textual and contextual complexities. Yet scholars have long noted the importance of money to Locke's political thought, although the focus has most frequently been the *Second Treatise* rather than his works solely devoted to monetary issues.

Locke's presentation of the invention of money in the *Second Treatise* certainly does offer some initial insight into the difficulties he addresses in the writings on coinage. In laying out the self-governing and self-limiting character of property in the state of nature, Locke seemingly winds down his account with the assurance that "every Man should have as much as he could make use of . . . without straitning any body" (36).[34] This picture is radically altered, however, almost as soon as these words are read. There would have been enough for all in the state of nature "had not the *Invention of Money*, and the tacit Agreement of Men to put a value on it, introduced (by Consent) larger possessions, and a Right to them" (36). The agreement "*that a little piece of yellow metal* . . . should be worth a great piece of Flesh" (37) allows individuals to exceed the bounds of use and accumulate property; for "if he would give his Nuts for a piece of Metal, . . . he invaded not the Right of others" and may "heap up as much of these durable things as he pleased" (37). Moreover, this "inequality of private possessions, men have made practicable out of the bounds of Societie, and without compact" (50), and thus neither money nor the benefits and inconveniences brought with it have its source in government. Although the invention of money in the state of nature serves as the basis for the formation of civil society and the establishment of civil law, it remains for Locke uneasily outside governmental purview.

The complexities of the narrative location of money in the *Second Treatise* are thus important to ascertaining the ambiguity that the concept of money itself inherently involves, but this does not address a principle point of Locke's fearful attention throughout his monetary writing— namely, clipping and accompanying dilemmas such as counterfeiting. Such concerns were hardly Locke's alone, since throughout the early modern period the integrity of any currency was understood in direct relation to the political entity issuing it. Clipping, counterfeiting, and other forms of monetary abuse had been regarded as acts of high treason in English statute since the fourteenth century.[35] The coinage crisis of the 1690s therefore raised profound concern about not only the stability of the currency but also the legitimacy of the English state. The anxieties generated by clipping, however, were not solely political, for as already alluded to, coinage and its ancillary terms carried a variety of associations, including those related to gender and sexuality. Clipping in particular was a concept with a number of connotations used "to signify the corruption of language (words as the coins of intellectual exchange, communication), embracing, kissing, fornicating, theft, cutting, and battles in war—and may operate on several levels of meaning simultaneously."[36] The uncertainty and indeed violence ascribed to clipping—whether in regard to semiotic, moral, or sexual concerns—was the source of much anxiety. Many of these disturbing associations lingered well into Locke's own time and worked in consort with political worries to create a particularly dense discourse concerning money as well as its influence in human affairs.[37]

Given the profound apprehensions caused by the act of clipping, fetishism serves as a useful way to begin to unpack the multiple layers of meaning and attendant anxieties that circulate throughout Locke's monetary writings. Although the clippers arguably present the threat of castration that Locke seeks to deny across a number of levels (monetary, epistemological, political), it is not enough to merely identify the source of what he seeks to disavow because fetishism consists of more than a simple (albeit intense) denial. According to Freud, the process of fetishism also involves a rebellion of "the portion of his narcissism which Nature has, as a precaution, attached to that particular organ" that the subject thereafter strives to protect against the threat of castration.[38] Locke's fetishism includes not only a denial of the clippers' influence in currency affairs but also an intense recognition of the value nature attaches to his organ—in this case, money as silver. Locke's obsessive assertion of the intrinsic value of money is not merely an overvaluation of the importance of silver that would indeed make it a reified fetish, a privileged object of his fascination à la Marx. Rather, Locke's insistence on intrinsic value exists within a process of fetishism where the integrity of the privileged object—money as silver—is maintained through associations with particular natural attributes. These connections are not simply asserted as givens but rather construed by Locke through a specific understanding of the operations of signification. A closer examination of Locke's semiotics brings the intricacies of his fetishism to the fore and in particular, those aspects of the feminine on which his ability to successfully articulate the natural value of money depends.

The Signification of Fluidity

In the *Essay Concerning Human Understanding*, Locke divides language up in a number of ways with one of the most critical distinctions drawn between substances and mixed modes whose differences are found in how each is generated. Ideas of substances are formed from information of the external world "conveyed in by the *Senses*," from which simple ideas are formed and given names.[39] This is not solely an operation of mindful creativity, for "Names of Substances being not put barely for our *Ideas*, but being made use of ultimately to represent Things" (3.11.24). Substance names are thus not understood as inventions but are *intended* to be strict representations of things in the world. Mixed modes, however, are products of the "Workmanship of the Mind" that are "made by a voluntary Collection of *Ideas* put together in the Mind" (3.5.4–5). These mixed modes are "made by it [the mind] with great liberty" creating ideas "before any one individual of that Species ever existed" (3.5.5, 7). Furthermore, mixed modes do not themselves refer "to the real Existence of Things, there is no supposition of any thing more signified by that Name, but that barely complex *Idea*, the Mind itself has formed" (3.5.14).

Locke's struggle to come to terms with how language works produces an understanding of representation that poses a dilemma when it comes to money, which is both a substance (i.e., silver) and a mixed mode (e.g., a creation consented to in the state of nature). Money cannot be regarded as only a substance because its creation is predicated upon its ability to represent something else besides its silver content (e.g., property). Yet to regard money as only a mixed mode—and thus subject to the every twist and turn of language—is to give room to the dangerous possibility of reducing the ability of currency to act as a constant standard of value to virtually nil. Given this backdrop, Locke's insistence on the necessity of maintaining the intrinsic value of the coin begins to look rather different. Constantine George Caffentzis argues that according to Locke's semantic schema, the proposals of Lowndes and his advocates were based on endorsing money as purely a mixed mode, thereby separating it from its other characteristics as a substance.[40] For Locke, this was unacceptable and dangerous because the only way the symbolic certainty of money could be guaranteed was to insist on maintaining the silver standard. Thus asserting the importance of intrinsic value was in part a response motivated by semantic concerns intricately linked to worries not only about money per se, but the stability of the political as well. As evident in the *Second Treatise*, money undergirds not only trade and exchange but also civil society itself. Should the representational certainty of money be called widely into question—as it then was in Locke's eyes—much more than a disruption of trade could be at stake.

Yet to fully appreciate the complexity of Locke's understanding of language and its profound consequences in regard to substances and in turn, coinage, the analysis needs to be pushed further to a consideration of the underlying difference between nominal and real essence. Nominal essence refers to a conceptual entity consisting of the various properties ascribed to a thing under a single name and without which that thing would no longer exist. "Between the Nominal essence and the Name, there is so *near* a *Connexion*, that the Name of any sort of Things cannot be attributed to any particular Being, but what has this *Essence*, whereby it ansers that abstract *Idea*, whereof that Name is the Sign" (3.3.16). Whereas for nominal essence the name *is* the thing, real essence refers to those properties believed to inhere in the thing itself. The real essences, however, remain largely unknowable because the mind's faculties are constrained by what is observable in the material world. For Locke it is a futile endeavor to "range Things into sorts, and dispose them into certain Classes, under Names, by their *real Essences*, that are so far from our discovery of comprehension" (3.6.9). Hence nominal essences are the knowable if somewhat arbitrary constructs of the understanding, whereas real essences ultimately refer to those aspects of nature that either are not or cannot be known by the human mind.

The differences between real and nominal essence do not pose any critical problems for mixed modes, since they are by definition collections of ideas placed in close relation with each other "without examining whether they exist so together in Nature" (2.22.2). As such, a mixed mode is "the Name which is, as it were the Knot" that ties ideas together and thus "in these the *real* and *nominal Essence* is the same" (3.5.10, 14). Though mixed modes are certainly arbitrary and hence liable to linguistic uncertainties, for Locke these difficulties can be overcome with sufficient attention to how language is used and reforming the ways in which it is abused. In sharp contrast to mixed modes, substances raise a very different set of concerns with more troublesome implications. Unlike mixed modes, substances "are supposed conformable to the reality of Things, and are *referred to Standards* made by Nature" (3.9.11). Yet because those aspects of substances that relate to real essence are fully knowable only to God, "*the Names of Natural Substances, signify* rarely, if ever, any thing but *barely nominal Essences* of those species" (3.4.3). As a result of their necessarily nominal character, "'tis evident they [substances] *are made by the Mind*, and not by Nature" (3.6.26). Here the trouble begins, for "though the nominal Essences of Substances, are all supposed to be cop-ied from Nature; yet they are all, or most of them, very imperfect" (3.6.30) as they are the constructions of various and disagreeing human minds. Although Locke maintains the separation between nominal and real essence for substances that is collapsed in reference to mixed modes, he also makes it clear that substances share with mixed modes some of the latter's more arbitrary features (3.4.17).

Locke's understanding of the uncertainties of substances brings into sharp relief the semiotic complexity of his repeated assertions that money must be intimately associated with silver. As much as the other parts of language Locke examines, substances are equally subject to the "Inconve-niencies" (3.10.32) of the word abuse and semiotic mismanagement that he struggles against throughout the *Essay* and elsewhere. Given the nec-essarily constructed nature of substances, Locke cannot simply weigh a substantial silver anchor to weather the brewing tempest posed by the symbolic vagaries of purely mixed mode money. Locke is unable to posit a rather reified substance to serve as a reliable fetish object since sub-stances are as much a construct of the mind as the source of the fear that fetishism itself is designed to protect against. Hence, Locke's fetish must not be understood as simply an overprivileged object but rather as a posi-tion constructed through a *process* of fetishism that wards off the symbolic threats posed by the clippers. In addition, the process that characterizes Locke's fetishism is ultimately made possible by those modes of significa-tion historically aligned with the feminine that he relies on to articulate a particular understanding of money. Specifically, it is within the intricate constitution of the dual character of money as artificial (a name like any other) *and* as natural (silver, a substance unlike any other) that the complexities of Locke's fetishism and its feminine semiotics come to the fore.

Early on in both of his major works on currency, Locke makes clear his insistence on a bivalent understanding of money. Repeating a key aspect of the narrative found in the *Second Treatise*, money's most artifi-cial attributes derive from consent, which places "an imaginary Value upon Gold and Silver by reason of their Durableness, Scarcity, and not being very liable to be Counterfeited" (SC, 233). The artificial character of money conferred by consent does not, however, lead to the conclusion that "this measure of Commerce, like all other measures, is Arbitrary" (FC, 412). Those who think so "will be of another mind, when they consider that Silver is a measure of a nature quite different from all other" (412). Although consent is necessary to make money the agreed instrument of trade, "the intrinsick Value of Silver and Gold used in Commerce is nothing but their *quantity*" (SC, 234). Common consent confers on money the role of an artificial general equivalent in regard to other commodities, but the very existence of money also relies on the presence of natural, precious metals. "For it not being the denomination but the *quantity* of Silver, that gives value to the coin" (310). Thus the use of money is agreed to through common consent but its intrinsic value is heavily dependent on natural substances—in Locke's historical context, primarily silver.[41]

Although Locke rejects the notion that other natural substances such as wheat may serve as a reliable mode of currency, he is at pains to show that money is in very crucial ways no different from those natural commodities for which it serves as a standard measure. "This I suppose is the true *Value of Money* when it passes from one to another in Buying and Selling; where it runs the same Changes of higher and lower, as any other Commodity doth" (SC, 249). In order to justify the legitimacy of charging interest, Locke carries this argument further in order to demonstrate how money "comes to be *of the same Nature with Land*" (249). Interest "is not only by the necessity of Affairs, and the Constitution of Humane Society, unavoidable to some Men, but also to receive Profit for the Loan of Money, is as equitable and lawful, as receiving Rent for Land" (251). Through a series of such metonymic associations, Locke establishes the existence of a "Natural and Current *Interest* of Money" that "does not follow the Standard of the Law, but the price of the Market" (253). This insistence on the existence of a "true and natural Value" (212) for money later complicates the quality of Locke's fetishism and poses significant problems for his understanding of the law.

Why, however, understand these initial associations of money with the natural as *necessarily* metonymic? Technically, there are any number of ways in which Locke could have constructed this relationship—or so it would seem. Yet at this point Locke's semiotics serve as an important touchstone, for he is quite particular about what sorts of figurative language ought to be avoided. In his rather infamous attack on rhetoric in chapter 10 of book 3 in the *Essay*, Locke evinces great concern with the taking of words for things, particularly in relation to already too uncertain substances. The sort of word abuse that plagues the understanding of substances is for Locke further exacerbated by the use of rhetoric that is an obstacle to the understanding and which serves as a "powerful instrument of Error and Deceit" (3.10.34). Later, Locke cautions against the use of two tropes in particular—metaphor and synecdoche. In pursuit of the truth, men are gravely misled when "their Phancies [are] struck with some lively metaphorical Representations" (4.17.4). Similarly, Locke identifies among the "Trifling Propositions" hindering the increase of knowledge the instance "*when a part of the complex Idea is predicated of the Name of the whole*" (4.8.4), and this is a definition of synecdoche. That Locke goes on to examine the problems posed by synecdoche through the example of a precious metal (i.e., gold) is significant to understanding his writings on money.

Locke's suspicions of metaphor and synecdoche alone, however, neither necessitate a turn to metonymy nor constitute an absolute repudiation of the use of figurative language. Rather, his reservations regarding particular tropes emphasize Locke's subtle understanding of the constructed nature of *all* language that makes signification, at best, a very tricky business.[42] Again, the concerns with substances inherent in Locke's understanding of money serve to stress the absolute importance of attending to the workings of different tropes. Since the natural substance of money (i.e., silver) consists of a real essence that is unknowable, the best one can do is observe "the Properties that flow from this Essence," and even so these are not "easily known, or enumerated" (2.32.24). In tropological terms, metaphor in particular does not lend itself well to figuring such fluidity, for it is based on an act of substitution, where one thing takes the place of the other. Through this standing-in of one thing for another, metaphor almost completely covers over what it replaces. For Locke, however, such replacement is unacceptable, for money *must* be dual in character with nothing left out or inaccurately substituted—especially those natural attributes that flow from money's essential substantial features. Moreover, the flow of natural attributes from money's substantial character is doubled by the fluidity of these features themselves. The only trope that allows for the establishment of relations between things based on contiguity as well as the fluidity of movement found in money's natural aspects is the trope that Irigaray argues is most strongly associated with the feminine—metonymy.

In particular, Locke's reliance on metonymy to establish money's specifically natural attributes comes to life in his characteristic use of vivid figurative language to describe its necessity to trade. Money is described as "running in the several Channels of Commerce" that "in its Circulation [drives] the several Wheels of Trade, whilst it keeps in that Channel (for some of it will unavoidably be dreined into standing pools)" (SC, 236–37, 233). Locke concerns himself not only with questions of how much money should flow but also with "the quickness of its Circulation" (235). In lamenting the role of brokers, Locke maintains that they hinder "the Trade of any Country, by making the circuit, which the Money goes, larger, and in that Circuit more stops, so that the Returns must necessarily be slower and scantier, to the prejudice of Trade" (241). Locke's dependence on metonymy allows him to figure money's fluid operations in ways not possible via metaphor and synecdoche, both of which introduce a certain semiotic stasis through either substitution or reduction, respectively. Thus the natural features and functions attributed to money are in no way quaint figures employed to explain how currency *really* functions, nor is fluidity merely part of a larger whole somehow separate from the rest. Rather, money's fluid properties are *contiguous* with its other, less substantial properties and of greater import for understanding currency than its arbitrary mixed mode features. Yet Locke's metonymic association of money with a feminine semiotics of fluidity is not without its difficulties, and these add further twists to his perverse focus on silver coin.

Fetishism and Its Vicissitudes

As Paul de Man suggests, tropes are rarely dependable or predictable assistants in the construction of arguments because "tropes are not just travellers, they tend to be smugglers and probably smugglers of stolen goods at that."[43] In Locke's case, although metonymy provides the ability to constitute a desired relationship between money and silver, it also associates currency with the kind of unruly fluidity that also was relied on during the early modern period to characterize the disorder (e.g., cultural, linguistic) frequently ascribed to woman. As Irigaray suggests in her critique of phallocentric language, "fluid—like that other, inside/outside of philosophical discourse—is, by nature, unstable. Unless it is subordinated to geometrism, or (?) idealized."[44] Yet bringing fluidity under control is no simple matter precisely because its feminine connotations link it with a nature that "is forever dodging his [man's] projects of representation, of reproduction. And his grasp."[45] Thus Locke's reliance on metonymy in his monetary writings does more than enable the appropriate significa-tion of money's connection to the natural substance of silver. Rather, as the trope best able to figure contiguity, metonymy brings with it all the contrariness of a feminine fluidity that is "continuous, compressible, di-latable, viscous, conductible, diffusable, . . . unending, potent and impo-tent owing to its resistance to the countable."[46] Because of its unpredictability and its capacity for resistance, fluidity poses its own chal-lenges to allegedly more stable (masculine) entities for—aligned with the feminine—it is "always in a relation of excess or lack vis-à-vis unity."[47]

This excess and lack associated with fluidity is troublesome, for al-though the fluid nature of money allows it to drive trade, it also con-stantly threatens to undo the very system of civil society that it is supposed to uphold. To start with, money may indeed become a standing pool through hoarding or, alternatively, the raising of interest may result in "stopping so much of the Current of Money, which turns the Wheels of Trade" (SC, 224) that commerce could dry up. In the worst case, money does not lie stagnant or dry up but rather runs amok as evidenced in Locke's fear of the clippers. "Clipping is the great Leak, which for some time past has contributed more to Sink us, than all Force of our Enemies could do. 'Tis like a Breach in the Sea-bank, which widens every moment till it be stop'd" (FC, 472). Yet there is no overly simple solu-tion, for in bemoaning the existence of clipped coin, Locke suggests that the monetary crises would not exist "if our Money and Trade were to Circulate only amongst our Selves, and we had no Commerce with the rest of the World" (469).[48] Such a closed system of circulation in which the meaning of money can be closely controlled, however, is no longer possible "in any country that hath Commerce with the rest of the World" (SC, 264–65). Furthermore, commerce is a necessity "naturally fit" (223) for England if it wishes to obtain the silver it needs to coin unclipped and freshly minted money. Locke's specific historical context thus operates in ways that impel him to recognize that his necessarily fluid construction of money *must* be allowed to circulate beyond previously acknowledged channels in order to keep the system it supports alive.

Yet Locke's recognition of the necessity of extended circulation intro-duces not only a rather unpredictable fluidity but also the critical and anxiety-provoking problem of the relation between need and desire—or in Locke's terms, fashion. The tensions between what Locke terms use and necessity on one hand and fashion and fancy on the other are brought about by the very widening of circulation that he recognizes as the inescapable reality of monetary affairs. In several passages, Locke condemns the whims of fashion for undermining the principles of use and necessity which he maintains ought to govern trade and exchange. Whereas "things of Necessity must still be had . . . things of Fashion will be had as long as Men have Money or Credit" (SC, 276), especially in regard to the desire for the "newest French cut and Stuff" (231). Whatever Locke's difficulties with fashion and fancy, however, he is also perfectly aware that the roles they play cannot be reversed and acknowledges that the "Vent of any Thing depends upon its Necessity or Usefulness, as Convenience, or Opinion guided by Phancy of fashion shall determine" (244). Put differently, what Locke's frustrations with fashion underscore are those tensions symptomatic of the transition from an enclosed market economy based solely on need and demand to an increasingly abstract system of exchange operating through desire. As money gains wider circulation and becomes increasingly conventional, it also becomes the avenue for desire that carries with it the differing demands of symbolic modes of signification.

Caught between a historical rock and a semiotic hard place, Locke thus turns to fetishism to maintain an understanding of money that is becoming increasingly tenuous because of currency's expanded circulation and the rise of those modes of signification most liable to semiotic subversion. By acknowledging both the power of desire and the arbitrary aspects of the nominal features of coin, Locke partially recognizes the increasingly symbolic character of money. Yet by fervently insisting on money's profound links to silver, Locke is able to disavow the ways in which symbolic modes of signification have begun to sever the connections between currency and natural substances. The maintenance of this link is crucial not only in regard to the integrity of English money but to the stability of the political as well. Any possibility that this key connection could be—or has been—cut produces a profound anxiety that becomes the focus of Locke's disavowal. In order to sustain a fetishistic position that accomplishes all of this, however, Locke must rely on metonymic constructs that are always on the move. Much as Irigaray's analysis suggests, Locke's privileging of metonymy not only introduces an uncontrollable fluidity into his own texts but also unwittingly opens up the avenue of desires which brings the very anxiety-provoking semiotic abstractions that the clippers manage to manipulate so well. Located within an ever shifting historical context, Locke's fetishism begins to appear as if it is caught in its own semiotic double bind.

The vicissitudes of Locke's fetishistic assertion of money's metonymic association with natural fluidity are particularly evident in regard to the difficulties surrounding the relation between currency and law. Throughout his monetary writings, Locke notes the presence of a number of tensions between money's natural attributes and law, beginning with the assertion that natural value is "that respective rate they find any where without the prescription of Law" (SC, 325). Although this scenario is not inherently problematic, difficulties with currency soon arise, since "he that wants Money, rather than lose his Voyage, or his Trade, will pay the *Natural Interest* for it" rather than obey the prescriptions of civil law—or rather, force lenders to do so (218–19). Locke demonstrates at length how previous attempts at statutory control of the price of money utterly failed and concludes "that the price of Things will not be regulated by Laws, though the endeavours after it will be sure to prejudice and inconvenience Trade, and put your affairs out of Order" (282). The "flux of money" thus undermines the efforts and reason of people to control fiscal matters with any degree of success (283). The tensions between money and coin are so great that although civil law is necessary to establish the legitimacy of the king's stamp in the minting of coin, "'tis not necessary that it [currency] should have a fixed value set on it by publick Authority" (427). Rather, Locke asserts that any change in the value of money will occur "not by the force of Statutes and Edicts; but by the natural Course of things" (286).

The difficulties civil law appears to have confronting the strength of money's natural qualities pose a danger that goes beyond what the monetary writings alone suggest. In the *Second Treatise,* the transition from the state of nature to civil society is marked by a crucial metaphoric operation, in which civil law is instituted in the place of natural law. Of the "many things wanting" in the state of nature, foremost is the lack of "an *establish'd,* settled, known *Law*" to serve as "the common measure to decide all Controversies" (124). Although the "*stated Rules*" of civil society offer a remedy to the uncertainties surrounding natural law, such "*promulgated standing Laws*" must still "be conformable to the Law of Nature, *i.e.* to the Will of God" (135–36). The relationship Locke establishes between the law of nature and civil law is thus fundamentally metaphoric and designed to cover all the vexing "inconveniencies" existing within the state of nature—presumably not the least of which is money itself. Yet as a metonymic construct, money's fluid associations seemingly escape the metaphoric efforts of civil law to control it, and thus Locke's fetishistic focus on silver begins to look rather peculiar. On their own, the clippers threaten the authority of civil law to guarantee the extrinsic value of money, and without such guarantees, not only is the legitimacy of civil law questioned but that of the state as well (FC, 454). Yet Locke's own insistence on money's metonymic associations with the natural substance of silver also appears to pose a fluid and significant challenge to the stability of civil law. Although such assertions are consistent with money's origin in the state of nature, this seems a rather sad if not unsuccessful case of fetishism, since it apparently provokes more distress than it alleviates.

Locke's unrelenting articulation of money's fluid qualities begins to make more sense, however, with a closer consideration of how the clippers represent the threat of castration his fetishism seeks to deny. What the clippers place at risk is not simply the integrity of silver coin but the privileged relation between natural law and civil law Locke posits in the *Second Treatise*. Although England's increasing participation in world trade and related historical circumstances might themselves be pulling natural and civil law apart, the clippers deliberately amplify this tension. By manipulating the abstracting forces associated with desire, the clippers cause more dissemination of meaning than the metaphoric relation between natural and civil law can withstand—and with grave results.

> *Clipping*, and clip'd Money, have besides this robbery of the Publick other great inconveniences: As the disordering of Trade, raising Foreign Exchange, and a general disturbance which every one feels thereby in his private Affairs.

> *Clipping* is so gainful, and so secret a Robbery, that penalties cannot restrain it, as we see by experience. (FC, 418)

From this perspective, Locke's hostility to those proposals for recoinage that appeared to give in to the abstracting force of the clippers acquires some added complexity. By submitting to the new "standard" set by the clippers, Locke's opponents in the coinage debates were also guilty of severing civil law from the realm of natural law and of at least tacitly endorsing the rule of fashion or desire.[49] In so doing, such plans were just as likely to lead to the derogation of civil law as the schemes of the clippers they were designed to prevent. For Locke, bringing the dangerous situation to an end without falling prey to an equally treacherous solution required nothing else but asserting the natural substance of silver as *the* source of value. Again and again, Locke states that nothing "can put a stop to *Clipping*, now it is grown so universal, and Men become so skilful in it, but making it unprofitable" (FC, 418). Doing so required no change in civil law but rather simply its reassertion by "making all light Money go only for its weight" (418).

Locke's privileging of silver is thus symptomatic of a fetishism that results not only from the widening split between money's natural and symbolic features but also from a rupture between natural law and civil law caused by desire and fashion. The metaphoric relation between natural law and civil law of Locke's imaginary as exemplified in the *Second Treatise* is slipping away in the face of the increasing abstraction brought about by money's expanded circulation. Increasingly separated from natural substances and natural law, civil law wanders in directions that prevent it from effectively prohibiting clipping, thereby endangering the stability of civil society. Yet as deleterious as the effects of the emerging symbolic may be, the necessities of acknowledging it are overwhelming, for without it England's much needed engagement in world trade would become impossible. In asserting the natural substance of silver as the source of value for money in its extended travels, however, Locke is able to disavow the role of symbolic signification as the sole source of semiotic privilege. According to Locke's schematic, only the natural substance of silver can provide the true value of money and therefore remains the source of how meaning in the "economic" and, in turn, the political world is generated. By fetishistically maintaining a connection between money and the natural substance of silver, Locke is able to disavow the dangerous drift of civil law and retain some of the initial identification with natural law that would otherwise be severed by the modes of symbolic signification introduced by currency's expanded movements.

The success of Locke's fetishism, however, is not found in a totalizing attempt to fully resolve the anxieties raised by the increasingly abstract character of money and law. Through his reliance on metonymy and feminine fluidity, Locke's texts ultimately display what is in effect a splitting of civil law. Such splitting is consistent with the process of fetishism itself, for as Freud suggests, the defenses deployed by the fetishist (and ultimately the psychotic) entail a splitting of the ego that allows the subject to simultaneously maintain two incompatible positions.[50] Locke accomplishes something very similar, for in disavowing the authority of civil law to establish the *content* of value of money, he is then able to affirm its role in establishing the representational *form* of value for currency. In some critical ways, Locke could care less about the extrinsic, nominal value of coin. The stamp of the mint serves to guarantee the intrinsic value of currency, and as long as this is assured, call the coin what you will, "for 'tis Silver and not Names that pay Debts and purchase Commodities" (SC, 312). Locke is willing to cede to civil law governance over the significatory value of money—however arbitrary—as long as natural intrinsic value remains intact. Indeed, for those so attached to names and only concerned with the relation of civil law to extrinsic value, Locke provides a suggestion of his own. "If any one thinks a Shilling or a Crown in name has its value for the *denomination*, and not for the *quantity of Silver* in it, let it be tried; and hereafter let a *Penny* be called a *Shilling*, or a *Shilling* be called a *Crown*" (310). Hence, Locke's concerns with the affairs of civil law in regard to money end where recognition of natural substances as the source of value begins.

The intricacies of Locke's fetishism thus appear to provide him with the ideal solution to a series of semiotic, epistemological, and ultimately political quandaries. Yet as Freud's model of fetishism demonstrates, however well any fetishistic split initially works "everything has to be paid for one way or another, and this success is achieved at the price of a rift in the ego which never heals but which increases as time goes on."[51] The high cost of fetishism's psychic rift finds resonance within Locke's historical context, since the very abstracting forces of symbolic signification that were subject of his unease and the object of the clippers' manipulation succeeded in gaining hold with the rapid rise of credit in the early eighteenth century. Although Locke's fetishism thus seems to fade rather quickly into its own historical horizon, the significance of his monetary writings extends beyond their immediate context. The intensely complicated character of these texts indicates the importance of tracing out how Locke pulls together a variety of threads in an effort to address the difficulties posed by money within a conceptually dissonant historical context. Though the sorts of abstraction associated with the symbolic were prominent enough to constitute profound threats to the integrity of English currency and the legitimacy of the political, they were not yet entrenched enough to dictate the manner in which Locke was to deal with such anxieties. Whatever the assessment of his monetary fetishism, what remains remarkable is that Locke successfully articulated a meaningful response to the coinage crisis through a reliance on modes of signification historically associated with the feminine. Through a consideration of the semiotic intricacies of Locke's fetishism within its historical context, what is often regarded as a pivotal period in the establishment of specifically modern economic and political vocabularies begins to look far more complicated than commonly understood.

Parting Words

To read Locke's monetary writings with an attention to the role of metonymy and its attendant fluidity is not to ignore other linguistic features, for to pursue such a myopic reading is "to run the risk of producing an increasingly aphasic *critical* discourse."[52] Rather, focusing on the particular semiotic constitution of Locke's fetishism challenges the sorts of interpretive aphasia—whether found in historiography or more conventional Locke scholarship—that occlude modes of signification associated with the feminine or woman from critical view. In creating the room necessary for such considerations, reading with an attention to metonymy and fluidity involves more than locating another historically elided textual site that may be construed as feminine. In contrast to pursuing a reading *for* the feminine that would perhaps posit woman as the limit case for a particular discursive formation, this feminist reading of Locke argues that those linguistic features aligned with historically specific notions of the feminine have their own salient semiotic effects within a particular historical context. Locke relies on fluidity and metonymy *not* to simply figure disruption or to construct a place of exile immune from the anxieties of the emerging symbolic order. Instead, Locke's fetishism successfully resists the epistemological and semiotic threats posed by the rise of increasingly abstract modes of signification whether represented in the form of the clippers or otherwise. As a consequence, Locke's articulation of a feminine fluidity enabled him to construct an alternative position within the coinage debates that produced its own meaningful effects political and otherwise.

That Locke's articulation of metonymy is made prominent via the process of fetishism may cause a certain unease. Given the common gloss that sociality itself is founded on the exchange of women as fetishized

objects, arguing that Locke's fetishism is made possible by qualities historically associated with the feminine may appear to be a rather uninterest-
ing retracing of all too familiar territory. Yet the semiotic processes
characteristic of Locke's fetishism succeed at least temporarily in resisting
the abstracting symbolic forces that allegedly facilitate the exchange of
women and obscure those processes of signification that may be ascribed
to the feminine. Therefore, a consideration of how the feminine is articulated within the perverse arena of fetishism serves to considerably complicate—rather than simply reinscribe—the domination of what may be
termed the "syntax of exchange."[53] Rather than assume that woman has
always already been turned "into coins that have an established value in
the marketplace," Locke's texts offer the opportunity to explore how
modes of feminine signification were salient and able to at least temporarily "suspend and melt down all systems of credit" within a particular
historical context.[54] Although it raises as many questions as it may answer, reading Locke's texts with an attention to fetishism and the feminine semiotics that enable it does shed a different light on the
tremendous stakes involved in giving one's nuts for a piece of metal.

Notes

1. Karl Marx, *Capital*, vol. 1, trans. Ben Fowkes (New York: Vintage Books, 1977), 187.

2. Ibid.; Karl Marx, *A Contribution to the Critique of Political Economy*, ed. Maurice Dobb (New York: International Publishers, 1970), 48.

3. Ibid., 49.

4. Sigmund Freud, "Fetishism," in *The Standard Edition of the Complete Psychological Works of Sigmund Freud*, vol. 21, ed. and trans. James Strachey (London: Hogarth Press, 1961), 154.

5. Ibid.

6. Jean-Joseph Goux, *Symbolic Economies: After Marx and Freud*, trans. Jennifer Curtiss Gage (Ithaca: Cornell University Press, 1990), 49.

7. Goux's argument construes the imaginary and the symbolic as discrete stages rather than as mutually imbricated orders of signification. In contrast, my use of these terms assumes that although the symbolic order exists as the "register of language, social exchange and radical intersubjectivity," the imaginary as the register of identification "continues to coexist with it." Jane Gallop, *Reading Lacan* (Ithaca: Cornell University Press, 1985), 59. For another assessment of the imaginary and the symbolic, see Tim Dean, *Beyond Sexuality* (Chicago: University of Chicago Press, 2000).

8. Reference works that further explicate these relations include Sandra K. Fischer, *Econolingua* (Newark: University of Delaware Press, 1985), and Gordon Williams, *A Dictionary of Sexual Language and Imagery in Shakespearean and Stuart Literature*, 3 vols. (London: Athlone Press, 1994).

9. Throughout this essay, metonymy and metaphor are used in ways broadly consonant with Lacan's adaptation of Roman Jakobson's work and especially Luce Irigaray's subsequent interpreta-

tions. Metaphor is therefore understood as the trope associated with condensation and substitution, while metonymy is linked with contiguity and displacement.

10. For the association of fluidity with women, see Ian Maclean, *The Renaissance Notion of Woman* (Cambridge: Cambridge University Press, 1980); and for some of its implications for specific notions of woman and femininity, see Karen Newman, *Fashioning Femininity and English Renaissance Drama* (Chicago: University of Chicago Press, 1991). On fluidity's gendered connotations, see also Anne Carson, *Eros the Bittersweet* (Normal, Ill.: Dalken Archive Press, 1998).

11. Gail Kern Paster, *The Body Embarrassed: Drama and the Disciplines of Shame in Early Modern England* (Ithaca: Cornell University Press, 1993), 44.

12. Ibid., 25.

13. Ibid.

14. Patricia Parker, *Literary Fat Ladies: Rhetoric, Gender, Property* (London: Methuen, 1987), 110. See also Juliet Fleming, "Dictionary English and the Female Tongue," in *Enclosure Acts: Sexuality, Property, and Culture in Early Modern England*, ed. Richard Burt and John Michael Archer (Ithaca: Cornell University Press, 1994).

15. Luce Irigaray, *This Sex Which Is Not One*, trans. Catherine Porter (Ithaca: Cornell University Press, 1985), 116, 107.

16. Ibid., 107.

17. Ibid., 106.

18. Ibid., 110.

19. Roman Jakobson and Morris Halle, *Fundamentals of Language* (The Hague: Mouton, 1956), 81.

20. Irigaray, *This Sex*, 110, 106–7.

21. Teresa de Lauretis, *Technologies of Gender: Essays on Theory, Film, and Fiction* (Bloomington: Indiana University Press, 1987), 9–10.

22. Ibid.; italics in the original.

23. Teresa de Lauretis, *Alice Doesn't: Feminism, Semiotics, Cinema* (Bloomington: Indiana University Press, 1984), 7.

24. The term "economic" is used here with caution. As William Reddy contends, "the division of modern social life into separate spheres—political, social, economic, religious—is riddled with confusion and paradox." William Reddy, *Money and Liberty in Modern Europe* (Cambridge: Cambridge University Press, 1987), 114. Unreflective adoption of such conventional terms and boundaries in reference to the early modern period often tends to obscure the very phenomena they are employed to illuminate. Words such as "economic" therefore appear infrequently and supplanted by other terms in hopes of conveying—rather than covering over—a sense of those conceptual ambiguities that are of significant theoretical interest.

25. Joyce Oldham Appleby, *Economic Thought and Ideology in Seventeenth-Century England* (Princeton: Princeton University Press, 1978), 3.

26. Ibid., 44.

27. William Lowndes, *A Report containing an Essay for the Amendment of the Silver Coins* (London, 1695), in *Seventeenth-Century Economic Documents*, ed. Joan Thirsk and J. D. Cooper (Oxford: Clarendon Press, 1972), 701.

28. The 1620s monetary crisis involved a perceived shortage of coin and a host of anxieties about global commerce, vividly expressed in several tracts that used figurative language not unlike that employed by Locke, albeit in a very different political context. An inventory of Locke's library shows he owned at least a few of these tracts, and I examined these links between Locke and the 1620s crisis in my dissertation. For compelling analyses of the 1620s tracts, see Patricia Fumerton, *Cultural Aesthetics: Renaissance Literature and the Practice of Social Ornament* (Chicago: University of Chicago Press, 1991), and Jonathan Gil Harris, *Sick Economies: Drama, Mercantilism, and Disease in Shakespeare's England* (Philadelphia: University of Pennsylvania Press, 2004).

29. Appleby, *Economic Thought*, 199.

30. Locke's two major texts on money are *Some Considerations of the Consequences of the Lowering of Interest, and Raising the Value of Money* (originally published in 1691) and *Further Considerations Concerning Raising the Value of Money* (1695). *Some Considerations* was an amended and expanded version of his earliest works on interest initially written between 1668 and 1674. Page references to these texts are from John Locke, *Locke on Money*, ed. Patrick Hyde Kelly (Oxford: Clarendon Press, 1991). These works will be cited in the text as SC and FC respectively.

31. As Patrick Kelly notes, "intrinsic value" refers to "the origin of money, the source of its exchange value, and the ratio at which money exchanges for other commodities" and could also "denote the bullion value of a coin as opposed to its denomination." Kelly, introduction to *Locke on Money*, 86. Although all of these connotations are present in Locke's texts, Kelly maintains that Locke ultimately endorsed the view that the "capacity to function as the general medium of exchange is the intrinsic value of money as such, not simply a quality of the metals gold and silver" (87). Yet as my reading will demonstrate, Locke's use of intrinsic value is more complex than Kelly suggests, in part because the ability of money to act as a medium of exchange is, for Locke, heavily dependent on the maintenance of a particular relationship between currency and silver.

32. For an examination of Locke's role in the recoinage as well as the difficulties that arose during and after its implementation, see John Keith Horsefield, *British Monetary Experiments, 1650–1710* (Cambridge: Harvard University Press, 1960).

33. Recent works that consider Locke's monetary thought include Constantine George Caffentzis, *Clipped Coins, Abused Words and Civil Government: John Locke's Philosophy of Money* (Brooklyn: Autonomedia, 1989); Kelly, introduction to *Locke on Money*; Kirstie M. McClure, *Judging Rights: Lockean Politics and the Limits of Consent* (Ithaca: Cornell University Press, 1996); and James Thompson, *Models of Value: Eighteenth-Century Political Economy and the Novel* (Durham: Duke University Press, 1996).

34. John Locke, *Two Treatises of Government*, ed. Peter Laslett (Cambridge: Cambridge University Press, 1988). Further references are all to the *Second Treatise* and will be cited in the text by the section number.

35. Declaration of Treasonous Offenses, 1352, *Statutes of the Realm*, 25 Edw. 3, St. 5, c.2.

36. Fischer, *Econolingua*, 56.

37. See *The Oxford English Dictionary*, 2nd ed., s.v. "clip."

38. Freud, "Fetishism," 153.

39. John Locke, *An Essay Concerning Human Understanding*, ed. Peter Nidditch (Oxford: Oxford University Press, 1975), bk. 2, chap. 23, sec. 1. Subsequent references will be cited in the text by book, chapter, and section. All italics are in the original.

40. Caffentzis, *Clipped Coins*.

41. Throughout most of the seventeenth century, the great majority of English currency consisted of both gold and silver coins with gold having a more limited domestic circulation than silver. Although gold coin served as the instrument for wholesale and international trade as well as for saving, silver coin was *the* tool of virtually all other exchanges. As Barry Supple suggests, for all intents and purposes silver *was* money. Barry Supple, *Commercial Crisis and Change in England, 1600–1642* (Cambridge: Cambridge University Press, 1959), 173. Thus throughout this essay, silver remains the focus of attention as it was for Locke. For further reference on the relationship between gold and silver coin, see C.G.A. Clay, *Economic Expansion and Social Change: England, 1500–1700*, vol. 1 (Cambridge: Cambridge University Press, 1984).

42. For a further examination of attitudes toward the use and abuse of figurative language in the Restoration period, see Richard W. Kroll, *The Material Word: Literature and Culture in the Restoration and Early Eighteenth Century* (Baltimore: The Johns Hopkins University Press, 1991). For an analysis of the role of rhetoric in the history of empiricism and Locke's role therein, see Jules David Law, *The Rhetoric of Empiricism: Language and Perception from Locke to I. A. Richards* (Ithaca: Cornell University Press, 1993).

43. Paul de Man, "The Epistemology of Metaphor," *Critical Inquiry* 5 (Autumn 1978): 19.

44. Irigaray, *This Sex*, 112.

45. Luce Irigaray, *Speculum of the Other Woman*, trans. Gillian C. Gill (Ithaca: Cornell University Press, 1985), 134.

46. Irigaray, *This Sex*, 111.

47. Ibid., 117.

48. Although Locke uses "commerce" to refer to trade and monetary exchange, the term itself carried other, more explicit linguistic and sexual connotations throughout the seventeenth century. The reading developed here attempts to keep such multiple meanings in play and thus differs sharply from the analysis offered by Joshua Foa Dienstag, *"Dancing in Chains": Narrative and Memory in Political Theory* (Stanford: Stanford University Press, 1997). See the Oxford English Dictionary, 2nd ed., s.v. "commerce."

49. For an extended consideration of the "law of fashion" at work in Locke's monetary writings, see Caffentzis, *Clipped Coins*, 150.

50. On the role of splitting in fetishism, see Sigmund Freud, "Splitting the Ego in the Process of Defense," in *The Standard Edition*, vol. 23 (London: Hogarth Press, 1964). On the process of fetishism, see also Emily Apter, *Feminizing the Fetish: Psychoanalysis and Narrative in Turn-of-the-Century France* (Ithaca: Cornell University Press, 1991).

51. Freud, "Splitting the Ego," 275–76.

52. Barbara Johnson, *A World of Difference* (Baltimore: The Johns Hopkins University Press, 1987), 164.

53. This phrase comes from Karen Newman's critique of feminist preoccupations with theories of exchange, "Directing Traffic: Subjects, Objects, and the Politics of Exchange," *differences* 2, no. 2 (1990): 44.

54. Irigaray, *Speculum*, 234.

10

"Philosophy's Gaudy Dress"

Rhetoric and Fantasy in the Lockean Social Contract

Linda M. G. Zerilli

I confess, in Discourses where we seek rather Pleasure and Delight, than Information and Improvement, such Ornaments as are borrowed from them, can scarce pass for Faults. But yet, if we would speak of Things as they are, we must allow that all the Art of Rhetorick, besides Order and Clearness, all the artificial and figurative application of Words Eloquence hath invented, are for nothing else but to insinuate wrong *Ideas*, move the Passions, and thereby mislead the Judgment; and so indeed are perfect cheat.

—Locke, *An Essay Concerning Human Understanding*

Among the many philosophers and political theorists who have railed against rhetoric, John Locke surely counts as one of its staunchest opponents. Locke famously casts rhetoric as "the Abuse of Words"[1] and rhetoricians as those "whose business is only the vain ostentation of Sounds" (*Essay*, 3.11.7). Regrettably, this "perverting the use of Words" (3.2.5)— "perversion" being one of Locke's own favorite words to describe the practice in question—"have their place in the common use of Languages,

Thanks to Bonnie Honig, Gregor Gnädig, Kirstie McClure, and James Tully for their help with earlier versions of this essay. Thanks to Crina Archer and Lida Maxwell for their help with preparation of the manuscript.

that have made them currant." To which Locke adds: "It looks like too much affectation wholly to lay them by: and Philosophy it self, though it likes not a gaudy dress, yet when it appears in publick, must have so much Complacency, as to be cloathed in the ordinary Fashion and Language of the Country, so far as it consist with Truth and Perspicuity" (2.21.20).

Is this not the familiar lament of the man of reason and advocate of plain speech, who cannot conceal his disdain for those who require serious rational ideas to be dressed up in pleasing rhetorical form? According to Ernesto Grassi, Locke expresses the view, widely held among Western philosophers, that "to resort to images and metaphors, to the full set of implements proper to rhetoric, merely serves to make it 'easier' to absorb rational truth."[2] Philosophy wears a "gaudy dress" because, sadly, men are passionate creatures in need of images.

Generations of readers have interpreted Locke's works as monuments to rational speech and to a subject that searches for knowledge of things as they really are. In this spirit, Charles Taylor claims that such a subject emerges as part of the Lockean project of self-understanding, the means by which reason can attain full certainty of itself. In Locke's view, says Taylor, "many things have been declared authoritatively true . . . which have no real title to the name. The rational, self-responsible subject can break with them, suspend his adhesion to them, and by submitting them to the test of their validity, remake or replace them."[3] We recognize here the inherited image of Locke as slayer of the "Idols of the Mind." Taking control of our symbolic production demands that we exclude every rhetorical element in our thinking and speech, for affect disturbs the clarity of rational thought. Man in search of things as they really are, ever vigilant over the incursion of unexamined belief into the chamber of the enlightened understanding—what could be more Lockean than that?

Familiar though it may be, this account of the Lockean project tends to neglect those aspects of Locke's thought that call into question the power of reason and rational language in the adjudication of political and philosophical debates. However that thought shall guide the following reflections, my concern here is not to contest the idea that Locke seeks rational foundations for these debates but rather to show that rational thinking and speaking is parasitic on the very rhetorical—passionate, affective—speech Locke barely tolerates in "discourses where we seek . . . Pleasure" and would like to exclude in discourses in which "we would speak of Things as they are," that is, where knowledge is at stake. The idea that we could speak of things as they are without employing rhetoric is based on a misleading conception of what it means to know that such and such is the case. As Grassi explains:

> To prove [apo-deiknumi] means to *show* something to be something, on the basis of something. . . . Apodictic, demonstrative speech is the kind of speech which establishes the definition of a phenomenon by tracing it back to ultimate principles, or *archai.* It is clear that the first *archai* of any proof and hence of knowledge cannot be proved themselves because they cannot be the object of apodictic, demonstrative, logical speech; otherwise they would not be first assertions. . . . But if the original assertions are not demonstrable, what is the character of the speech in which we express them? Obviously this type of speech cannot have a rational-theoretical character.[4]

Grassi's challenge to philosophers like Locke is simple but significant: he shows that the indicative or rhetorical speech that grounds philosophical or rational speech "provides the very framework within which the proof can come into existence at all." This indicative speech, he writes, "is immediately a 'showing'—and for this reason 'figurative' or 'imaginative' . . . It is metaphorical, i.e., it shows something which has a sense, and this means that to the figure, to that which is shown, the speech transfers [metapherein] a signification; in this way the speech which realizes this showing 'leads before the eyes' [phainesthai] a significance." The premise of rational speech "is and must be in its structure an imaginative language."[5] This conclusion radically alters the relationship of rational speech and rhetorical speech. "The term 'rhetoric' assumes a fundamentally new significance; rhetoric is not, nor can it be the art, the technique of an exterior persuasion; it is rather the speech which is the basis of rational thought."[6]

If Grassi is right, then philosophy does need something like its gaudy dress. More to the point of this chapter, the core concepts of Lockean political theory—not least the social contract—would have to be rethought as exhibiting a fundamentally rhetorical structure. The stakes here are significant: Locke is easily one of the greatest thinkers on the subject of human equality and the fundamentally consensual basis of political relations. The classic story of the social contract, which vividly expresses equality and consent as the only legitimate ground for relations of political rule, is commonly interpreted, to speak with Jeremy Waldron, as having a "rational choice structure." In Waldron's view, as we shall see, the classic tale packs tremendous "normative punch"—it shows that men could not possibly have consented to their subjection—but lacks historical credibility. Thus Locke is led to narrate, parallel to the classic tale, a "gradualist, anthropological account" of the shift from "inchoate patriarchal authority to formal political institutionalization."[7] This account, however, offers no critical perspective from which to judge the (patriarchal and monarchical) relations of authority that developed over time. Thus the classic tale, says Waldron, provides a "moral template" with which to judge those relations as illegitimate. But how, exactly, does the classic tale do that? If it is to offer a perspective from which to judge historical events, this tale must exhibit a structure of freedom that, historically speaking, did not exist and, further, persuade the subject to see itself, notwithstanding its actual subjection, as free. We may take that freedom more or less for granted, but there is no reason to assume that a seventeenth-century reader would have.

Rather than read the classic tale as a moral template based on rational principles, I want to read it as an imaginative device that can facilitate the identification of oneself as a free subject. Read in this way, the social contract can be thought of as a rhetorical figure of the newly thinkable. It is around this figure that it becomes possible to organize a new political world and to tell a story of the emergence of a "we" that is not already given (as Filmer's account of the origin of commonwealths would have it) but is founded in a free act. Although Locke was deeply concerned with curtailing the forces of custom and early education that forged strange forms of affect, he no more thought one could eradicate such forms than one could create language anew. Accordingly, the problem for Locke as a political thinker is not to eliminate the affective basis of political association but to bind affect to a form or figure (the social contract) that symbolizes human freedom. This figuration of the new can only be a rhetorical language.

The Grammar of Desire

Rhetoric takes hold of men's minds in early childhood, usually at the hands of a woman. Locke's famous argument against the existence of innate principles, as William Walker explains, maps the origin of notions of sacred truth onto the figure of the woman as gatekeeper of Idols.[8] Proposing to account for why men are willing to die rather than abandon what they take for truth, Locke writes:

> This, however strange it may seem, is that which every days Experience confirms; and will not, perhaps, appear so wonderful, if we consider the *ways*, and steps *by which* it is brought about; and how really it may come to pass, that *Doctrines*, that have been derived from no better original, than the Superstition of a Nurse, or the authority of an old Woman; may, by length of time, and consent of Neighbors, *grow up to the dignity of Principles* in Religion or Morality. (*Essay*, 1.3.22)

What makes these "Principles" so extraordinarily difficult to question, says Locke, is that they are antecedent to all memory and thus come to be wrapped in an aura of the sacred or the natural (*Essay*, 1.3.23). G.A.J. Rogers asserts that "the principle has been taught as if it were an undeniable truth, even though it really had no higher source 'than the Superstition of a Nurse, or the Authority of an Old Woman.'"[9] But just the opposite is the case: the principles men later come even to die for are not initially taught as truths (or for that matter, as principles which one could decide for or against). What concerns Locke is the subject's inscription into an "inherited background against which I distinguish between true and false," as Wittgenstein would later put it.[10] The inherited background is composed of (ungrounded) figures not (grounded) truths; it is the always already there, that which allows us to raise doubts but which we do not normally doubt. What passes for innate principles lies outside the scope of "reflexion," to use Locke's term, or the Mind's consciousness of its own activity. The woman's authority is likewise secured inasmuch as the adult mind cannot remember the moment when it was first impressed with a rhetorical figure, usually conveyed through a story, which now takes the form of a principle; the mind cannot recognize this moment as part of its own development and thus, writes Walker, as "an instance of female presence or power."[11]

The *Essay* is haunted by the woman as she comes to stand for the origin of error. On the one hand, it would seem that to expose the woman at the origin of error and Idol worship, as Lockean empiricism tried to do, is to deprive her of the power that is rooted in a radical forgetting. It would appear to be sufficient, within the empiricist frame, to identify her as part of the external world that has made an impression upon our senses, the great original of all our ideas. In other words, by exposing the origin of our follies in the empirical figure of the woman who first cared for us, Locke hopes to restore to the Mind a sense of its own power. To remember her is to regain control over our symbolic production.

Notwithstanding Locke's attempt to locate the cause of our errors in an external cause and subject it to reason, he remains incredulous in the face of the very thing he purports to explain: the source of self-blindness and the mind's fanatical attachment to its Idols. "Men worship the Idols that have been set up in their Minds; grow fond of the Notions that they have been long acquainted with there; and *stamp the character of Divinity, upon Absurdities and Errors*, become zealous Votaries to Bulls and Monkeys; and contend too, fight, and die in defence of their Opinions" (*Essay*, 1.3.26)—with such a description Locke opens rather than closes the question of the origins of self-blindness. One can hardly believe that the empirical discovery of the real figure of the superstitious nurse or mother, or for that matter any childhood authority, would convince anyone to divest himself of that sort of affect.

Indeed, notwithstanding the search for empirical origins, Locke himself remains fully perplexed by the "something that blinds their [men's] Understandings" (*Essay*, 2.33.18) and puts them in the service of unreasonableness. What Locke presents as the cause begins to look rather more like the site of a displacement of the complex problem of the subject's attachment to Idols and other such affective props. The difficulties that this sort of attachment create for the sort of subject that we associate with the name John Locke become clearer if we turn to the section that was added to book 2 of the fourth (1700) edition of the *Essay*: "Of the Association of Ideas." As Cathy Caruth observes, this section stands in a peculiar relation to the tradition it founded, namely, associationism as it was developed most prominently by David Hartley. "The use of association to name a principle of rational thought," says Caruth, "altered the meaning it had in Locke's work, in which it referred to a thought process subversive of normal reasoning and described as 'madness.' . . . In transferring the name to 'rational thought' processes, the eighteenth-century empiricists effectively eliminated the phenomenon that, in Locke, had raised serious questions about the principles established in the rest of the *Essay*."[12] Much of the secondary literature on Locke repeats this gesture either by neglecting Locke's account of "the association of ideas" or by treating it as that which the rational self is duty-bound to control.

What then is this "madness," and what is it doing in a work that appears to assert the ultimate rationality of the mind? We should note first that such madness is not a general condition that affects only some men and is opposed to sanity. It is rather, as Locke says, "a Weakness to which all Men are so liable" (*Essay*, 2.33.4). Indeed "this flaw has its Original in very sober and rational Minds" (2.33.3). Furthermore, the madness appears on the scene, not when a man "is under the power of an unruly Passion, but [rather] in the steady calm course of his Life" (2.33.4). It is a "disease of the mind" that each is quick to find in the other but blind to in himself (2.33.1).[13] An otherwise critical man can exhibit a stubborn "Unreasonableness," refusing to yield "to the Evidence of Reason, though laid before him as clear as Day-light" (2.33.2). One would think him "fitter for *Bedlam*, than Civil Conversation" (2.33.4). Locke describes how the association of ideas works its spell:

> Some of our *Ideas* have a natural Correspondence and Connexion one with another: It is the Office and Excellency of our Reason to trace these, and hold them together in that Union and Correspondence which is founded in their peculiar Beings. Besides this there is another Connexion of *Ideas* wholly owing to Chance or Custom; Ideas that in themselves are not at all of kin, come to be so united in Mens Minds, that 'tis very hard to separate them, they always keep company, and the one no sooner at any time comes into the Understanding but its Associate appears with it; and if they are more than two which are thus united, the whole gang always inseparable shew themselves together. (*Essay*, 2.33.5)

We witness here, writes Caruth, how "every rational connection of ideas threatens to be plagued by an importunate outsider who pushes his way in on thought and plants his obscene presence in the way of proper thinking; and this rapidly expands in the passage into a vision of the mad understanding as virtually stampeded by gangs of imposters."[14]

Locke is hardly sanguine about the nature and pervasiveness of this obscene presence. So profoundly does this unnatural kinship of Ideas "set us awry in our Actions, as well Moral as Natural, Passions, Reasonings, and Notions themselves," he writes, "that, perhaps, there is not any one thing that deserves more to be looked after" (*Essay*, 2.33.9). But the measures Locke recommends to prevent these unnatural associations from ever forming, especially in young people, pale in the face of the threat itself. One can exercise greater vigilance over a child's education at the hands of tutors; one can discipline nurses who fill their young charges with "Ideas of Goblins" and other such "nonsense." However, not only are associations formed at all stages of life, their very nature, as Locke himself recognizes, is so unique to each subject, so utterly idiosyncratic and unpredictable, that no amount of vigilance can possibly anticipate the wholly unexpected nature of association: "This strong Combination of *Ideas*, not ally'd by Nature, the Mind makes in it self either voluntarily or by chance, and hence it comes in different men to be very different, according to their different Inclinations, Educations, Interests, *etc*" (2.33.6).

Consider the idiosyncratic character of this example, the final one of the chapter, which Locke gives, "if only for the pleasant oddness of it."

> It is of a young Gentleman, who having learnt to Dance, and that to great Perfection, there happened to stand an old Trunk in the Room where he learnt. The *Idea* of this remarkable piece of Houshold-stuff, had so mixed it self with the turns and steps of all his Dances, that though in that Chamber he could Dance excellently well, yet it was only whilst that Trunk was there, nor could he perform well in any other place, unless that, or some such other Trunk had its due position in the Room. (*Essay*, 2.33.16)

Following the spirit of Locke's *Essay*, we might say that this Gentleman should really try to relinquish his trunk. Surely he can learn to dance without it, and as a rational subject, is he not even duty-bound within the Lockean framework to do so? Things are not so simple. There is good reason to believe that Locke's text, even as it attempts to contain the threat it names, both recognizes the complexity of the subject's investment in its props and exhibits an ambivalent fascination with this perverse economy of desire (the story is told for "the pleasant oddness of it"). In this strange economy, the very ability of the subject to enter the grammar of the dance depends on the presence of an object or prop that bears no rational connection to the dance as a structured performance. All we can say is that the subject needs his prop, his fetish: with it, he dances not like a madman, but a proper Gentleman; without it, he cannot enter the symbolic register of the social space, that is, the commonly recognized grammar of the dance itself. To put this same point somewhat differently, the Gentleman's madness (or fetishism) makes him not "fitter for Bedlam, then Civil Conversation," but is the very condition both of his participation in the common discourse of social life and his moment of resistance to playing by the rules.

Were the Gentleman a mere oddity, the madness Locke describes would not be such a scandal. It is a scandal, however, because the madness is universal yet unpredictable, common to all yet utterly idiosyncratic in the particular form it takes. One could say that every subject has its "trunk": an apparently meaningless psychic object that the subject drags from place to place and that has no logical or publicly recognizable place in the social grammar, but without which such grammar remains meaningless for the subject. Locke would attenuate the threat of association by establishing a causal relation between the presence of the trunk and the ability to dance. Does this mean that parents should guard against trunks when teaching their children to dance? If a trunk can take on such significance for a Gentleman, what is to keep another equally unremarkable object from assuming the same strange status in the subject's fantasy life? The answer is: nothing—therein lies the disruptive power of association for an education in reason, a power that no pedagogy based on causal explanation can defeat. Should we ask, what is inside the trunk? We might say, no thing, but what Locke calls "noise" or "the insignificant buzz of purely empty sounds" (*Conduct*, sec. 45). In the trunk is the stuff of rhetoric, the ineradicable passion or desire in language and the subject, precisely that part of signification and subjectivity that is inventive, imaginative. This noise both enables symbolic meaning—the common grammar of the dance—and keeps the subject from being fully inscribed in that grammar. Psychoanalysis would call it the space of fantasy, in which each subject organizes its pleasure.

Within the Lockean framework, the Gentleman's trunk, which remains invisible to him but is all too visible to everyone else, undercuts another sort of fantasy: the fantasy of a wholly rational subject—that is, when rational is understood as free of the influence of passion or affect. After all, others too may have a "trunk" that remains invisible to them. To acknowledge the madness in the other, as the author of the *Essay* has done, risks being implicated in its strange economy, an economy that calls into question the ultimate rationality of the mind. Perhaps this is why Locke—as if to establish the proper distance from this pleasingly perverse tale—quickly adds: "If this Story shall be suspected to be dressed up with comical Circumstances, a little beyond precise Nature; I answer for my self, that I had it some Years since from a very sober and worthy

Man, upon his own knowledge, as I report it; and I dare say, there are very few inquisitive Persons, who read this, who have not met with Accounts, if not examples of this Nature, that may parallel, or at least justify this" (*Essay*, 2.33.16). This attempt to control the madness, its tendency to leak, appeals to the reputation of an unnamed interlocutor, whose solidity and sobriety guarantee the empirical character of the story. To embellish, after all, would be to don the gaudy dress. It would also entangle one in the very web of fantasy that Locke's story claims merely to observe or record.

Were association limited to dancing and the like, it would not be of such momentous concern to Locke. But these "frisking Ideas," he tells us, have leaked into virtually every aspect of social life. They are at the origin of philosophical battles and theological wars. Here they are not productive but destructive of the social bond. Searching for the cause of "the Irreconcilable opposition between different Sects of Philosophy and Religion," Locke settles on this "wrong and unnatural Combinations of Ideas." Association becomes a way of explaining what Locke, in his voice as the man of reason, is at a loss to explain: that the followers of theses sects would "knowingly refuse Truth offer'd by plain Reason." Not even "interest" can "be thought to work whole Societies of Men to so universal a Perverseness, as that every one of them to a Man should knowingly maintain Falsehood," Locke remarks. "There must be something that blinds their Understandings, and makes them not see the falshood of what they embrace for real Truth" (*Essay*, 2.33.18). Association, he declares, "gives Sence to *Jargon*, Demonstration to Absurdities, and Consistency to Nonsense, and it is the foundation of the greatest, I had almost said, of all the Errors in the World" (2.33.18). Partner in this crime against reason and reasonableness is nothing less than another form of association that too threatens to unleash "frisking Ideas" that are both necessary to and subversive of the social bond: language itself.

The Grammar of Mutual Intelligibility

The "Association of Ideas" leads directly into book 3 of the *Essay*, which concerns language. This transition makes sense when we consider how words themselves work on the model of association. As Grassi explains, there is a fundamentally inventive and creative dimension to language considered in its rhetorical aspect, which is the primary aspect that concerns Locke when he speaks about "the abuse of words." What at once fascinates and worries Locke here is the rhetorically based faculty of *ingenium*: the human capacity, as Grassi writes, to "surpass what lies before us in our sensory awareness" by "catching sight of relationships, of *similitudines* among things."[15] Akin to the process of association described earlier, *ingenium* creates connections between things that have none. Just as there is nothing logical or necessary in the relationship between a trunk and a dance, neither is there anything logical or necessary in the connections we create through the use of rhetorical language. In contrast to rational language, which never discovers anything new but only what is already given in the premises, *ingenium* is the art of invention. Rhetorical language "provides that which deduction can never discover."[16]

Locke's stance toward the *ingenious* dimension of language is ambivalent. This ambivalence is partly related to his non-naturalistic view of signification, which argued for the difference between *res* and *verba*. Locke holds that language is: (1) not a nomenclature, (2) arbitrary, (3) more or less voluntaristic, and (4) private. Language is not a nomenclature because it refers not to things in the world but to ideas in the mind; arbitrary, because there is no necessary connection between an idea and its sign; voluntaristic, because it is the individual alone who chooses to make a particular sign stand for a particular idea; and private, because the sign he chooses stands for an idea in his own head and because the connection between sign and idea is invisible to others.

Locke affirms language as the social bond: it enables thought, communication, and sociality. "To make words serviceable to the end of Communication, it is necessary . . . that they excite, in the Hearer, exactly the same *Idea*, they stand for in the Mind of the Speaker. Without this, Men fill one another's Heads with noise and sounds; but convey not thereby their Thoughts, and lay not before one another their *Ideas*, which is the end of Discourse and Language," be it "civil" or "philosophical" (*Essay*, 3.9.6; 3.9.2). This assertion, repeated many times in the *Essay*, would appear to connect Locke with a whole tradition of seventeenth-century efforts (e.g., those of Ward, Petty, Boyle, and Dalgarno) to purge language, especially philosophical language, of its figurative properties and to bring it into accordance with the real existence of things. The project to create "noise-free channels of communication and to produce authoritative systems of meaning," as Robert Markely puts it, can be seen in John Wilkins's *Essay towards a Real Character and a Philosophical Lan-*

guage (1668), a work sponsored by the Royal Society.[17] Wilkins declared war on polysemy and metaphor. The word should exactly match the thing; things of the imagination, because they did not exist, should have no word.

In important respects, Locke shares with seventeenth-century linguistic reformers the belief that contests of meaning are more about uncertain uses of words than about real differences in ideas. He wonders "whether the greatest part of the Disputes in the World are not meerly Verbal, and about the Signification of Words; and whether if the terms they are made in, were defined, and reduced in their Signification (as they must be, where they signify any thing) to determined Collections of the simple *Ideas* they do or should stand for, those Disputes would not end of themselves, and immediately vanish" (*Essay*, 3.11.7). He states that "a Man should take *care to use no word without a [precise] signification*, no Name without an *Idea* for which he makes it stand" (3.11.8). He rails against the willful "abuse of words," which only compounds the natural imperfections of language. And in his own modest contribution to linguistic reform, Locke even proposes a "Dictionary" composed of "little Draughts and Prints" of things "which are known and distinguished by their outward shapes" (3.11.25).

But there are several features of Locke's argument that set it at odds with the obsessions of universal language schemers and linguistic reformers. Although Locke agrees that the flagrant abuse of words should be curtailed, his understanding of the nature of linguistic signs raises questions about the effort to eliminate uncertainty in our speaking practices. "It is easy to perceive, what imperfection there is in Language, and how the very nature of Words, makes it almost unavoidable, for many of them to be doubtful and uncertain in their significations" (*Essay*, 3.9.1), he writes. I take the phrase "almost unavoidable" to mean that human knowledge is imperfect; there can be no absolute certainty in a postlapsarian world. We should remedy the defects of language where we can (e.g., the willful abuse of words), but we are not to worship the Idol of human perfectibility. The fantasy of "infallibility" yields such things as popes and kings. It is this fantasy that underlies as well all the wrangling over texts that are the source of political and religious conflict. Locke's semiotics is at odds not only with Adamicists, who long for the perfection of language before the Fall, then, but also with those reformers who would construct language anew. Besides, comments Locke: "I am not so vain to think, that any one can pretend to attempt the perfect *Reforming the*

Languages of the world, no not so much as that of his own Country, without rendring himself ridiculous" (3.11.2).

There are other ways of rendering oneself ridiculous. Not unlike the Gentleman and his Trunk, the language reformers, too, have a fetish: they believe that words can be brought back into an unmediated relation to things. As Locke remarks, "It is a perverting the use of Words, and brings unavoidable Obscurity and Confusion into their Signification, whenever we make them stand for any thing, but those *Ideas* we have in our own Minds" (*Essay*, 3.2.5). The language reformers are attached to the illusion of a perfect correspondence between words and things; they recreate the problem of uncertainty in signification that they pretend to eliminate. What is more, says Locke, the fantasy of a perfectly transparent and common language exhibits not only an obvious conceit but an implicit authoritarianism. "To require that Men should use their words constantly in the same sense, and for none but determined and uniform *Ideas*, would be to think, that all Men should have the same Notions, and should talk of nothing but what they have clear and distinct *Ideas* of. Which is not to be expected by any one, who hath not vanity enough to imagine he can prevail with [or force] Men, to be very knowing, or very silent" (3.11.2). If the abuse of words incites wars of (biblical) interpretation, the dream of a perfect, common language stifles public debate.

Seeking to repair the ruins of Babel, language reformers deny more than the "perfectly arbitrary" relation between signs and ideas, reinstating "a [supposedly] natural connexion between them." They also deny, says Locke,

> that every Man has so inviolable a Liberty, to make Words stand for what *Ideas* he pleases, that no one hath the Power to make others have the same *Ideas* in their Minds, that he has, when they use the same Words, that he does. And therefore the great *Augustus* himself, in the Possession of that Power which ruled the World, acknowledged, he could not make a new Latin Word: which was as much as to say, that he could not arbitrarily appoint, what *Idea* any Sound should be the Sign of, in the Mouths and common Language of his Subjects. (*Essay*, 3.2.8)

At the center of Locke's political semiotics is this "inviolable Liberty" of every man to make words stand for ideas in his own mind. The difference between Adam's liberty to name as he pleased and ours, says Locke, is "that in Places, where Men in Society have already established a Language amongst them, the signification of Words are very warily and sparingly to be alter'd." Since the signification of most words is regulated by "common Use," he who exhibits "an affected misapplication of them cannot but be very ridiculous. He that hath new Notions, will, perhaps, venture sometimes on the coining new Terms to express them: But Men think it a Boldness, and 'tis uncertain, whether common Use will ever make them pass for currant" (*Essay*, 3.6.51). Locke has little patience with men who are so vain as to coin new words, but it is important for his political semiotics to insist upon our inheritance of Adam's linguistic liberty. This liberty, in tandem with the arbitrary character of the sign, supports Locke's critique of Filmer's political semiotics: no man could possibly define for all posterity the absolute meaning of a word. Language is not substance; the sign has no core that persists through time, as Adamicists like Filmer would have it.

The wish to make language a substance, give the sign a core, is not unique to Adamicists and universal language schemers: it also animates the double character of what Locke calls the "secret reference" that men give to their words. "*First, they suppose their Words to be Marks of the Ideas in the Minds of other Men, with whom they communicate*"; and "secondly . . . they *often suppose their Words to stand also for the reality of Things.*" The first error concerns the anxiety of communication, that is, the worry that men "talk in vain, and could not be understood"; the second error concerns the anxiety of objectivity, that is, the worry that men be thought to speak of "their own Imaginations . . . [rather than] of Things as really they are" (*Essay*, 3.2.4, 5). The twin anxieties of communicability and objectivity that motivate appeals to a secret reference, then, raise the question of the relation between the imaginary and the real. In Locke's account, the secret reference is entangled in the perverse logic of association. "*There comes by constant use, to be such a Connexion between certain Sounds, and the Ideas they stand for,*" says Locke, "that the Names heard, almost as readily excite certain *Ideas*, as if the Objects themselves, which are apt to produce them, did actually affect the senses" (3.2.6). Words have the force of empirical objects: they create sensations that give rise to Ideas (in the subject) whose connection to reality is in question. Like the Gentleman and his Trunk, the subject that insists upon the secret reference has lost the proper relation to what is real.

This tendency to confuse words with things, says Locke, has its origins in our very formation as speaking subjects:

> Because by familiar use from our Cradles, we come to learn certain articulate Sounds very perfectly, and have them readily on our Tongues, and always at hand in our Memories . . . it *often* happens that *Men*, even when they would apply themselves to an attentive Consideration, *do set their Thoughts more on Words than Things*. Nay, because Words are many of them learn'd, before the *Ideas* are known for which they stand: Therefore some, not only Children, but Men, speak several Words, no otherwise than Parrots do. (*Essay*, 3.2.7)

This infantile spectacle of parrot-speech recalls Locke's account of how children receive "borrowed Principles" into their minds, which they later come to adore and even die for as adults. The woman (nurse or mother) is not named here, but her figure hovers over the "Cradles" that are. The parrot-man, if I may be permitted this shorthand, is foremost childish: in a state of active passivity he not only mimics the words of the woman who cared for him but becomes hostage to linguistic fetishism: he attributes substance to the sign and takes words for things. Above all, he is not in control of his symbolic production. As subject, he is more spoken than speaking.

The words that we have "readily on our Tongues, and always at hand in our Memories" are more like sounds without any distinct signification: they do not correspond to a clear idea in the mind but are like a melody (or lullaby) that plays in the back of one's head. In the *Conduct of the Understanding*, Locke describes these archaic, infantile memories as "the chiming of some particular words or sentence in the memory."

> It is a sort of childishness, if I may say so, of the understanding, wherein, during the fit, it plays with and dandles some insignificant puppet to no end, nor with any design at all, and yet cannot easily be got off from it. Thus some trivial sentence, or scrap of poetry, will sometimes get into men's heads, and make such a chiming there, that there is no stilling of it; no peace to be obtained, nor attention to anything else, but this impertinent guest will take up the mind and possess the thoughts in spite of all endeavors to get rid of it. (*Conduct*, sec. 45)

Singling out the chiming as the most debilitating form of the "transferring of thoughts" that "clog" our understanding and impede our reason,

Locke observes that, like the (unnatural) association of ideas, this meaningless noise afflicts even the most reasonable men, "persons of very good parts" (*Conduct*, sec. 45). The chiming marks a point of impasse, a sort of affective tie that binds the subject to an "object" (e.g., "some trivial sentence or scrap of poetry" or "the insignificant buzz of purely empty sounds" [sec. 45]). It is the task of the understanding, in Locke's view, to cast out the "impertinent guest," to still the noise, "immediately disturb and check it, [and] introduce new and more serious considerations" (sec. 45). After all, says Locke, "Men know the value of their corporal liberty, and therefore suffer not willingly fetters and chains to be put upon them" (sec. 45). A man should be "fully master of his own thoughts" (ibid.); the understanding (or ego) must be master in its own house.

Locke reassures his readers that, if diligent, they can prevail over the aforementioned threats to rational thought, but his examples suggest a less optimistic outcome of our "struggle to preserve the freedom of our better part" (ibid.). At stake in the struggle to keep at bay any passion that "take[s] possession of our minds with a kind of authority" (*Conduct*, sec. 45) that ought to be reserved for the understanding is man as a free and rational subject, which appears to be the basis of Locke's argument against absolutism and his defense of consent as the basis for legitimate government. The struggle, then, concerns heteronomy or rule by another. Just as it cannot be supposed that we would willingly put our understanding under the power of the "impertinent guest" who prevents the proper exercise of our reason, Locke argues, neither can it be supposed that "a Rational Creature . . . when free . . . [would] put himself into Subjection to another, for his own harm."[18] But what if the association of ideas that appears to be this Rational Creature's undoing were the condition for entering the very grammar of Lockean consent?

The Rhetorical Basis of the Social Contract

"The rational choice framework of the social contract story," writes Jeremy Waldron, "provides a basis for Locke's claim that arbitrary or absolute government could not possibly have been legitimized by the consent of those subject to it."[19] The problem, he adds, is that this story, which "divides the history of each territorial society into two sharply distinguished eras," "is historically and sociologically implausible"—a point that was not lost on Locke.[20] "Perfectly aware of the strain that the contract story placed on the credulity of his contemporaries," Waldron observes, Locke offered another story:

> Since time immemorial, social groups have been under the authority of one man, usually a father-figure or patriarch. . . . [His] authority was scarcely distinguishable from the natural rule of a parent over his children. . . . As the natural economy developed and the use of money became widespread, the . . . role of conciliatory, adjudicative and punitive authority became gradually more institutionalized. . . . Because the development of government was gradual and indiscernible, men could easily be mystified about its nature and justification; and Locke charts with the development of political institutions a concomitant growth in political ideology culminating in the fantasy of the divine right of kings. The course of human political development, on this second story, has left men bewildered and mystified and it is now the task of true philosophy—the task Locke takes upon himself—to dispel some of that mystification.[21]

According to Waldron, this gradualist story of the social contract is radically different from the classic account. Although the developmental story is more plausible, it lacks the classic tale's "normative punch," that is, "the theory of rights, representation, separation of powers, justified resistance, and so on." Waldron would solve this problem by reconciling the two stories such that the classic tale becomes the "moral template" placed by the judging subject over the developmental narrative. We can concede that, say, the British monarchy was established through a series of quotidian consensual acts (e.g., sons transferring the authority reserved for the father to his eldest heir and, eventually, from him to a king), but still claim that monarchical government is antithetical to the interests of men as free and rational subjects.

Locke does argue that men, when they (mostly tacitly) consented to all the little steps that led up to monarchy, were duped. But in my view, the classic tale is less a moral template constituted by rational principles than a rhetorical device that would mobilize the tenacious process of association (i.e., seeing connections between otherwise unrelated things) in facilitating the identification of oneself as a free subject. The task for Locke was to transform the instituted society that had naturalized a connection between two unrelated ideas: the idea of a father and the idea of a king. Locke would show, contra Filmer, that if there is a natural connection, it is between the idea of political society and the idea of consent. A radical Whig, Locke does not invent the idea of the consensual basis of political society any more than he invents the figure of the social contract—both were part of the social language of seventeenth-century liberalism—but he brings the idea of consent and that of political society together in such a way that they now seem like the commonsense basis for any rational discourse on politics. In this spirit Locke declares: "Reason being plainly on our side, that Men are naturally free . . . [and] that the *Governments* of the World . . . were *made by the Consent of the People*" (*Second Treatise*, sec. 104). Locke's rhetorical brilliance lies not only in this rescripting of English common sense but also in casting an absolutist like Filmer as a madman of sorts who has made a very strange association of ideas: the idea of a father and that of a king.

Deeply perplexed by the depth of men's attachment to Idols, Locke, we recall, described the association of ideas as a thought process that was subversive of reasoning and thus of human beings as free subjects. In the developmental narrative, Locke appears to offer a plausible account of the origins of political society and the divine right of kings. But association, we have seen, calls into question empiricism's search for causes and origins. Although it is not named as such and the developmental account would seem to exclude it, association is important to Locke's attempt to show how free subjects could have consented to (what turned out to be) their own subjection (in the developmental story). Locke's central point, after all, is that there is no natural relation or connection between the idea of a king and that of a father. In Waldron's view, Locke needed a developmental account in order to explain how such a connection could arise. This account traces the origins of such an illegitimate connection back to a cause like the insensible transfer of authority of sons to fathers and then to kings, in the same way that the *Essay*, trying to explain men's idolization of "Bulls and Monkeys," searched for a cause in, among other things, the figure of the superstitious nurse. Locke's developmental narrative does try to provide an empirical explanation for the fantasy of the divine right of kings. But as with the *Essay*, his attempt to locate the cause of our errors in an external event and thereby subject it to reason is deeply unsatisfying: it fails to account for the sheer force with which the idea of political qua paternal authority has taken hold of men's minds. If there is an uneasy connection between the classic tale and the

developmental story, it is not so much because the classic tale is historically implausible, which is what Waldron asserts, but because Locke cannot quite square his claim about men's natural freedom with their
consent to their subjection.

The fantasy of the divine right of kings is not explainable, finally, by
means of a developmental narrative, with its emphasis on the empirical
causes and origins of subjection (and that is one important reason for its
rather diffuse and rambling character). Rather, this fantasy is a vivid
example of that strange "Connexion of Ideas wholly owning to Chance
or Custom," which is how Locke described the association of ideas in the
Essay, that is, the madness to which even the most reasonable man is
liable. These Ideas, we recall, "that in themselves are not at all of kin,
come to be so united in Men's Minds that 'tis very hard to separate them,
they always keep company." What the contingent association of ideas
produces is the illusion of necessity. That the Gentleman learned to
dance with a Trunk standing in the room is a contingent fact that takes
on the force of necessity: he cannot dance unless that Trunk (or one like
it) stands in the room. That men came to transfer authority from fathers
to kings is also a contingent fact that has the force of necessity: they
cannot imagine a king who does not derive his authority from paternal
power.

Central to the task of figuring human freedom anew is the question of
memory. Responding to Filmer's claim that there are no historical examples of free and equal men who consented to a government, Locke holds
that just because we have not heard much of the state of nature doesn't
mean that there was no such state. "For 'tis with Commonwealths as with
particular Persons, they are commonly ignorant of their own Births and
Infancies" (*Second Treatise,* sec. 101). Responding to Filmer, Locke mar-
shals various historical accounts of the consensual origin of political society (secs. 101–3). But Locke's effort to disrupt the association of ideas
that produced the father-king figure and to recall the free origins of commonwealths, a time when men were not subjected, does not depend on
gathering historical evidence. In itself, that evidence amounts to nothing. (Filmer did not ignore the evidence Locke provides, he interpreted
it differently.) The evidence is always read through the lens of the present, that is, through what is given. The problem of memory, Locke recognizes, is that the past tends to present itself to us in the guise of necessity.
Recognizing that the entire thrust of Filmer's argument is that "it could
not have been otherwise"—a father is a king, necessarily—Locke would

have us remember the contingency at the origin of political society. Locke does not have to—and indeed does not—"deny, that if we look back as far as History will direct us, towards the Original of Commonwealths, we shall generally find them under the Government and Administration of one Man" (sec. 380). He concedes this history not only because it is a more plausible account of political society, but because he has found a way to tell the same story differently, that is, as a series of events that were caused contingently, not necessarily.

Although alternative stories, exceptions to the rule, can disrupt Filmer's seamless tale of paternal power, Locke's attempt to signify the free origin of political society does not rely on a series of counterexamples: it develops not a "rational choice framework," as Waldron asserts, but a rhetorical figure, the compact, with which to organize those examples according to the principles of human freedom and consent as the basis of legitimate government. This rhetorical figure is more than a moral template: it is not simply placed over historical events, as Waldron claims, but is an imaginative device that can be used to illuminate the past and aid us in "remembering" our free origins. What is the nature of this memory? Surely memory cannot mean reaching the true origin of political society as an empirical event—not because, as Hume claimed, there is no evidence of this event itself (e.g., the parchment on which the contract is written), but because, even if there were such evidence, the meaning of the event depends on the rhetorical figure that we use to illuminate it. In a sense, then, Locke not only calls on his readers to remember, he also suggests that, if memory fails, invent—or better, that memory in its proper sense demands invention, imagination. The failure of political imagination in the face of associations formed in the social, historical, political, and psychic context of heteronomy may well be the real problem that the classic tale of the social contract was meant to solve.

The critical reflection such a task involves proceeds by way of what Grassi called *ingenium* or what Cornelius Castoriadis calls "the creation of *figures* (or of *models*) of the thinkable."[22] Such questioning of established truths cannot take place all at once, observes Castoriadis, nor can it "occur . . . within a void, but is always paired with the positing of new forms/figures of the thinkable."[23] Whatever doubts we may raise about an "established truth" like the divine right of kings, in other words, begins with a creative moment of figuration, not by revealing the ungrounded nature of belief. Locke does reveal the ungrounded—i.e., irrational—nature of belief in kings, but his ability to do so rests on rhetorical language, that is, on figures like the social contract that offer a new way of seeing, a different way of judging and organizing our experience. This new way of seeing is what gives life to the rational principles Locke would have us adopt. A political theory of freedom like Locke's may posit truths, but it cannot do without rhetoric, even if sometimes this means donning the gaudy dress.

Notes

1. John Locke, *An Essay Concerning Human Understanding*, ed. Peter H. Nidditch (Oxford: Oxford University Press, 1979), bk. 3, chap. 10. Hereafter cited in the text as *Essay* with book, chapter, and section numbers.

2. Ernesto Grassi, *Rhetoric as Philosophy: The Humanist Tradition* (Carbondale: Southern Illinois University Press, 1980), 26.

3. Charles Taylor, *Sources of the Self: The Making of the Modern Identity* (Cambridge: Harvard University Press, 1989), 174.

4. Grassi, *Rhetoric as Philosophy*, 19.

5. Ibid., 20.

6. Ibid.

7. Jeremy Waldron, "John Locke: Social Contract versus Political Anthropology," in *The Social Contract from Hobbes to Rawls*, ed. David Boucher and Paul Kelly (London: Routledge, 1994), 56. In his latest work, Waldron emphasizes the Christian bases of Locke's commitment to human equality. The emphasis on human reason and in particular the human capacity for abstraction, however, remains. Jeremy Waldron, *God, Locke, and Equality: Christian Foundations in John Locke's Political Thought* (Cambridge: Cambridge University Press, 2002).

8. William Walker, "Locke Minding Women: History, Gender, and the Essay," *Eighteenth-Century Studies* 23, no. 3 (spring 1990): 245–68.

9. G.A.J. Rogers, *Locke's Philosophy: Content and Context* (Cambridge: Oxford University Press, 1994), 17.

10. Ludwig Wittgenstein, *On Certainty*, trans. Denis Paul and G.E.M. Anscombe (New York: Harper, 1972), sec. 94.

11. Walker, "Locke Minding Women," 250.

12. Cathy Caruth, *Empirical Truths and Critical Fictions: Locke, Wordsworth, Kant, Freud* (Baltimore: The Johns Hopkins University Press, 1997), 1.

13. John Locke, *Of the Conduct of the Understanding*, ed. Thomas Fowler (Oxford: Oxford University Press, 1901), sec. 41. Hereafter cited in the text as *Conduct* with section numbers.

14. Caruth, *Empirical Truths*, 23.

15. Grassi, *Rhetoric as Philosophy*, 8.

16. Ibid., 97.

17. Robert Markley, *Fallen Languages: Crises of Representation in Newtonian England, 1660–1740* (Ithaca: Cornell University Press, 1993), 32.

18. John Locke, *The Second Treatise of Government*, in *Two Treatises of Government*, ed. Peter Laslett (Cambridge: Cambridge University Press, 1960), sec. 164. Hereafter cited in the text as *Second Treatise* with section number.

19. Waldron, "John Locke," 54.

20. Ibid., 52, 55.

21. Ibid., 52, 53.

22. Cornelius Castoriadis, *World in Fragments: Writings on Politics, Society, Psychoanalysis, and the Imagination*, trans. David Ames Curtis (Stanford: Stanford University Press, 1997), 269.

23. Ibid., 271.

Notes on Contributors

TERESA BRENNAN, at the time of her death in February 2003, was the Dorothy F. Schmidt Eminent Scholar in the Humanities at Florida Atlantic University, and director of the Program on Public Intellectuals. She was the author of *The Interpretation of the Flesh: Freud and Femininity* (Routledge, 1992), *History After Lacan* (Routledge, 1993), and *Exhausting Modernity: Grounds for a New Economy* (Routledge, 2000). Published posthumously were *Globalization and Its Terrors: Daily Life in the West* (Routledge, 2003) and *The Transmission of Affect* (Cornell, 2004).

MELISSA A. BUTLER is a professor of political science and the chair of the Social Science Division at Wabash College, one of the last single-sex colleges for men. She has published on Locke, Rousseau, and Wollstonecraft in political theory and also on American foreign policy.

TERRELL CARVER graduated from Columbia University in 1968 and obtained a D.Phil. from Oxford in 1974. He is currently professor of political theory at the University of Bristol, U.K., and has published extensively on philosophical and methodological topics. His latest books are *The Postmodern Marx* (Manchester, 1998), *Men in Political Theory* (Manchester, 2004), and the coedited *Palgrave Advances in Continental Political Thought* (Palgrave, 2005).

NANCY J. HIRSCHMANN is the R. Jean Brownlee Endowed Term Professor of Women's Studies and a professor of political science at the University of Pennsylvania. Her book *The Subject of Liberty: Toward a Feminist Theory of Freedom* (Princeton, 2003) won the Victoria Schuck Award from the American Political Science Association for the best book on women and politics. She is also the author of *Rethinking Obligation: A Feminist Method for Political Theory* (Cornell, 1992), *Gender, Class and Freedom in Modern Political Theory* (Princeton, forthcoming), and several edited volumes.

KIRSTIE M. McCLURE teaches political theory and the history of political literature at UCLA, where she is affiliated with the departments of Political Science and English. Her publications include various essays on feminist theory, toleration, narrative, judgment, and the politics of print culture, as well as *Judging Rights: Lockean Politics and the Limits of Consent* (Cornell, 1996).

CAROLE PATEMAN is a professor of political science at UCLA. She is a Fellow of the American Academy of Arts and Sciences. Her publications include *Participation and Democratic Theory* (Cambridge, 1975) and *The Sexual Contract* (Stanford, 1988), for which she was awarded the 2005 Lippincott prize by the American Political Science Association. Her most recent publications are on the 1996 welfare reforms, on the idea of a basic income for all citizens, and with Charles Mills, *Contract and Domination* (Polity 2007).

CAROLE PECH received her doctorate in political theory from The Johns Hopkins University and is currently assistant director for the Health Sciences Institutional Review Boards Office at the School of Medicine and Public Health at the University of Wisconsin, Madison.

GORDON SCHOCHET teaches political philosophy and the history of political thought at Rutgers University. His publications include *Patriarchalism in Political Thought: The Authoritarian Family and Political Speculation and Attitudes Especially in Seventeenth-Century England* (Blackwell, 1975; reissued with the unfortunately modified title *The Authoritarian Family and Political Attitudes in 17th Century England: Patriarchalism in Political Thought*, Transaction, 1988); *Rights in Contexts* (Kansas, forthcoming); *Reformation to Revolution: Political Thought in the Early-Modern Period* (Polity, forthcoming); *The Varieties of British Political Thought* (coeditor and contributor; Cambridge, 1993); *Proceedings of the Folger Center for the History of British Political Thought*, 6 vols. (6 vols., editor and contributor; Folger Institute, 1990–93); *Questions of Tradition* (coeditor and contributor; Toronto, 2004); and numerous articles. He is the founding editor of *Hebraic Political Studies* and a founder of the Center for the History of British Political Thought at the Folger Shakespeare Library and a member of its Steering Committee.

MARY LYNDON (MOLLY) SHANLEY is a professor of political science and holds the Margaret Stiles Halleck Chair at Vassar College. She is author of *Feminism, Marriage and the Law in Victorian England* (Princeton, 1989), *Making Babies, Making Families: What Matters Most in an Age of Reproductive Technologies, Surrogacy, Adoption, and Same-Sex and Unwed Parents* (Beacon Press, 2001), and *Just Marriage*, which was edited by Deborah Chasman and Joshua Cohen (Oxford, 2004). She is editor, with Carole Pateman, of *Feminist Interpretations and Political Theory* (Polity Press and Pennsylvania State, 1990), with Uma Narayan, of *Reconstructing Political Theory: Feminist Essays* (Polity Press and Pennsylvania State, 1997), and with Daniel I. O'Neill and Iris Marion Young, of *Illusion of Equality: Engaging with Carole Pateman* (Pennsylvania State, forthcoming). Her articles and reviews have appeared in a wide range of scholarly journals. Her current work is on feminist perspectives on family law and on social justice issues concerning human reproduction.

JEREMY WALDRON is a professor in the Law School at New York University. His publications include *The Right to Private Property* (Oxford, 1988), *Liberal Rights* (Cambridge, 1993), *The Dignity of Legislation* (Cambridge, 1999), *Law and Disagreement* (Oxford, 1999), *God, Locke and Equality* (Cambridge, 2002), and numerous articles in legal and political philosophy.

JOANNE WRIGHT is an assistant professor of political science at the University of New Brunswick, Canada. She is the author of *Origin Stories in Political Thought: Discourses on*

Gender, Power and Citizenship (Toronto, 2004) and "Reading the Private in Margaret Cavendish: Conversations in Political Thought," in *British Political Thought in History, Literature, and Theory*, edited by David Armitage (Cambridge, forthcoming). Her current research explores Margaret Cavendish on war.

LINDA M. G. ZERILLI is a professor of political science at Northwestern University. Her publications include *Signifying Woman: Culture and Chaos in Rousseau, Burke, and Mill* (Cornell, 1994) and *Feminism and the Abyss of Freedom* (Chicago, 2005).

For Further Reading

Arneil, Barbara. "Women as Wives, Servants and Slaves: Rethinking the Public/private Divide." *Canadian Journal of Political Science* 34 (2001): 9–54.

Ashcraft, Richard. *Revolutionary Politics and Locke's "Two Treatises of Government."* Princeton: Princeton University Press, 1986.

Boucher, Joanne. "Male Power and Contract Theory: Hobbes and Locke in Carole Pateman's *The Sexual Contract.*" *Canadian Journal of Political Science* 36 (2003): 23–38.

Breitenberg, Mark. *Anxious Masculinity in Early Modern England.* New York: Cambridge University Press, 1996.

Burnette, J. "An Investigation of the Female-Male Wage Gap During the Industrial Revolution in Britain." *Economic History Review* 50 (1997): 257–81.

Burt, Richard, and John Michael Archer, eds. *Enclosure Acts: Sexuality, Property, and Culture in Early Modern England.* Ithaca: Cornell University Press, 1994.

Chappell, Vere. *The Cambridge Companion to Locke.* New York: Cambridge University Press, 1994.

Clark, Lorenne. "Women and Locke: Who Owns the Apples in the Garden of Eden?" In *The Sexism of Social and Political Theory—Women and Reproduction from Plato to Nietzsche,* ed. L. Clark and L. Lange. Toronto: University of Toronto Press, 1979.

Coole, Diana. "Re-reading Political Theory from a Woman's Perspective." *Political Studies* 34 (1986): 129–48.

Cooper, David E. "Scottish Communitarianism, Lockean Individualism, and Women's Moral Development." In *Women's Rights and the Rights of Man,* ed. A. J. Arnaud and E. Kingdom. Aberdeen: Aberdeen University Press, 1990.

Eisenstein, Zillah R. *The Radical Future of Liberal Feminism.* New York: Longman, 1981.

Elshtain, Jean Bethke. *Public Man, Private Woman: Women in Social and Political Thought.* Princeton, N.J.: Princeton University Press, 1981.

Erickson, Amy Louise. *Women and Property in Early Modern England.* New York: Routledge, 1993.

Foster, David. "Taming the Father: John Locke's Critique of Patriarchal Fatherhood." *Review of Politics* 56 (1994): 641–70.

Grant, Ruth W. "John Locke on Women and the Family." In *Two Treatises of Government and A Letter Concerning Toleration,* ed. Ian Shapiro. New Haven: Yale University Press, 2003.

Hansen, B. "Zur Feministischen Kritik der Politischen Theorie von John Locke." *Österreichische Zeitschrift für Politikwissenschaft* 22 (1993): 477–86.

Kann, M. E. "John Locke and the Political Economy of Masculinity." *International Journal of Social Economics* 19 (1992): 95–110.

———. *On the Man Question: Gender and Civic Virtue in America*. Philadelphia: Temple University Press, 1991.

Kelly, Kristin A. "Private Family, Private Individual: John Locke's Distinction Between Paternal and Political Power." *Social Theory and Practice* 28 (2002): 361–80.

Kerber, Linda. "The Republican Mother: Women and the Enlightenment, an American Perspective." *American Quarterly* 28 (1976): 187–205.

Kramnick, Johnathan Brody. "Locke's Desire." *Yale Journal of Criticism* 12 (fall 1999): 189–208.

Lembcke, V. L. "A Consideration of Locke's Educational Theories with Respect to the Woman Question." *Locke Newsletter* 21 (1990): 141–64.

Macpherson, C. B. *The Political Theory of Possessive Individualism: Hobbes to Locke*. Oxford: Oxford University Press, 1962.

Makus, Ingrid. *Women, Politics, and Reproduction: The Liberal Legacy*. Toronto: University of Toronto Press, 1996.

McClure, K. M. *Judging Rights: Lockean Politics and the Limits of Consent*. Ithaca: Cornell University Press, 1996.

Mendelson, Sara, and Patricia Crawford. *Women in Early Modern England, 1550–1720*. Oxford: Clarendon Press, 1998.

Nicholson. Linda J. *Gender and History: The Limits of Social Theory in the Age of the Family*. New York: Columbia University Press, 1986.

Nyland, Chris. "John Locke and the Social Position of Women." *History of Political Economy* 25 (1993): 39–63.

O'Donnell, Sheryl. "My Idea in Your Mind: John Locke and Damaris Cudworth Masham." In *Mothering the Mind: Twelve Studies of Writers and Their Silent Partners*, ed. R. Perry and M. W. Brownley. New York: Homes and Meier, 1984.

Okin, Susan Moller. *Women in Western Political Thought*. Princeton: Princeton University Press, 1979.

———. "Women and the Making of the Sentimental Family." *Philosophy and Public Affairs* 11 (1982): 65–88.

Pateman, Carole. "Women and Consent." *Political Theory* 8 (1980): 149–68.

———. *The Sexual Contract*. Stanford: Stanford University Press, 1988.

Pfeffer, Jacqueline L. "The Family in John Locke's Political Thought." *Polity* 33 (2001): 593–618.

Ready, Kathryn J. "Damaris Cudworth Masham, Catharine Trotter Cockburn, and the Feminist Legacy of Locke's Theory of Personal Identity." *Eighteenth-century Studies* 35 (2001/2): 563–76.

Rogers, Katharine M. *Feminism in Eighteenth-century England*. Urbana: University of Illinois Press, 1982.

Sample, Ruth. "Locke on Political Authority and Conjugal Authority." *Locke Newsletter* 31 (2000): 115–46.

Schochet Gordon J. *Patriarchalism in Political Thought: The Authoritarian Family and Political Speculation and Attitudes Especially in Seventeenth-Century England*. Oxford: Blackwell; New York: Basic Books, 1975. A second edition, with a new introduction by the author, was published by Transaction Books of New Brunswick, N.J., in 1988 under the title *The Authoritarian Family and Political Attitudes in 17th-century England: Patriarchalism in Political Thought*.

———. "The Significant Sounds of Silence: The Absence of Women from the Political Thought of Sir Robert Filmer and John Locke (or, 'Why Can't a Woman Be More Like a Man')." In *Women Writers and the Early Modern British Political Tradition*, ed. H. L. Smith. Cambridge: Cambridge University Press, 1998.

Simons, Martin. "Why Can't a Man be More like a Woman? A Note on John Locke's Educational Thought." *Educational Theory* 40 (1990): 135–45.

Squadrito, Kathy. "Locke on the Equality of Sexes." *Journal of Social Philosophy* 10 (1979): 6–11.

Staves, Susan. *Married Women's Separate Property in England, 1660–1833*. Cambridge: Harvard University Press, 1990.

Walker, William. "Locke Minding Women: Literary History, Gender, and the *Essay*." *Eighteenth Century Studies* 23 (spring 1990): 245–63.

Walsh, Mary B. "Locke and Feminism on Private and Public Realms of Activities." *Review of Politics* 57 (1995): 251–77.

Ward, Lee. "The Natural Rights Family: Locke on Women, Nature, and the Problem of Patriarchy." In *Nature, Woman, and the Art of Politics*. Ed. Eduardo A. Velásquez. Lanham, Md.: Rowman & Littlefield, 2000.

Weil, Rachel. "The Family in the Exclusion Crisis: Locke versus Filmer Revisited." In *A Nation Transformed: England in the Restoration*, ed. Alan Houston and Steve Pincus. Cambridge: Cambridge University Press, 2001.

Wright, Nancy E., Margaret W. Ferguson, and A. R. Buck. *Women, Property, and the Letters of the Law in Early Modern England*. Toronto: University of Toronto Press, 2004.

Zack, Naomi. *Bachelors of Science: Seventeenth-Century Identity, Then and Now*. Philadelphia: Temple University Press, 1996.

The following website is also a good resource for further reading suggestions: http://www .libraries.psu.edu/tas/locke/index.html#toc.

Index